POPULAR PROTEST AND
POLITICAL CULTURE IN
MODERN CHINA

POLITICS IN ASIA AND THE PACIFIC
Interdisciplinary Perspectives

Haruhiro Fukui
Series Editor

Popular Protest and Political Culture in Modern China: Learning from 1989, edited by Jeffrey N. Wasserstrom and Elizabeth J. Perry

Southeast Asia in the New International Era, Clark D. Neher

FORTHCOMING

Emerging Ocean Regimes in the "New Pacific," Biliana Cicin-Sain, Robert Knecht, and William Nester

China and Tiananmen, Lowell Dittmer

Japan's Land Policy and Its Global Impact, Shigeko N. Fukai

Mass Politics in the PRC: State and Society in Contemporary China, Alan P.L. Liu

POPULAR PROTEST AND POLITICAL CULTURE IN MODERN CHINA

Learning from 1989

EDITED BY

Jeffrey N. Wasserstrom
INDIANA UNIVERSITY

Elizabeth J. Perry
UNIVERSITY OF CALIFORNIA–BERKELEY

Westview Press
BOULDER • SAN FRANCISCO • OXFORD

Politics in Asia and the Pacific: Interdisciplinary Perspectives

Copyright © 1992 by Westview Press, Inc.

Published in 1992 in the United States of America by Westview Press, Inc., 5500 Central Avenue, Boulder, Colorado 80301, and in the United Kingdom by Westview Press, 36 Lonsdale Road, Summertown, Oxford OX2 7EW

Library of Congress Cataloging-in-Publication Data
Popular protest and political culture in modern China : learning from
    1989 / edited by Jeffrey N. Wasserstrom and Elizabeth J. Perry.
        p.   cm. — (Politics in Asia and the Pacific)
    Includes index.
    ISBN 0-8133-8032-4 — ISBN 0-8133-8031-6 (pbk.)
    1. China—History—Tiananmen Square Incident. 1989.   2. Political
culture—China.   I. Wasserstrom, Jeffrey N.   II. Perry, Elizabeth
J.   III. Series.
DS779.32.P67   1991
951.05′8—dc20   91-27191
                                                                        CIP

Printed and bound in the United States of America

The paper used in this publication meets the requirements
of the American National Standard for Permanence of Paper
for Printed Library Materials Z39.48-1984.

10   9   8   7   6   5   4   3   2   1

*This volume is dedicated to the unsung heroes
and forgotten martyrs of 1989—the farmers, teachers, workers,
entrepreneurs, policemen, smugglers, officials, and soldiers
who risked their careers and personal safety
to help students and other protesters escape arrest,
and the city dwellers of all classes
who died in the streets of Chengdu
and other places far from Tiananmen Square.*

CONTENTS

ACKNOWLEDGMENTS

The editors express appreciation to Anne E. Bock for expert assistance in preparing the manuscript for electronic typesetting and improving some of the prose. We also thank Susan McEachern of Westview Press for her encouragement and patience. Jeffrey Wasserstrom is grateful to the National Academy of Education for the Spencer Postdoctoral Fellowship that afforded him the time to complete this project. Elizabeth Perry thanks the Henry M. Jackson School at the University of Washington for research support.

Jeffrey N. Wasserstrom
Elizabeth J. Perry

INTRODUCTION: CHINESE POLITICAL CULTURE REVISITED

Elizabeth J. Perry

Since its inception following World War II, the field of contemporary Chinese studies has been confronted by a series of extraordinary events. The first generation of specialists, schooled in a sinological tradition that stressed China's unique cultural continuity, was immediately challenged by what seemed—at least on the face of it—a major rupture with the past: the Communist Revolution of 1949. Not surprisingly, efforts to explain this momentous aberration defined the initial contours of the field. Although scholarly opinion on the nature of the revolution was deeply divided, the debate centered on the extent to which the ideology and practice of Chinese communism could be said to reflect indigenous cultural influences, as opposed to a wholesale importation of the Soviet model.[1]

Once they had recovered from the initial shock of "losing" China, many analysts chose to take comfort in their sinology, emphasizing a peculiar political tradition intelligible only to the classically trained specialist. As C. P. Fitzgerald summarized this position, "The Chinese conceptions which underlie the theory of government are unique; unlike any others, and evolved in China. The roots are deep and nourished in a soil alien to the West; the flower is therefore also strange, and hard to recognize."[2] Superficial revolutionary changes were believed to belie a deeper continuity: "The Chinese Communists, embracing a world authoritarian doctrine in place of one local to China, have enlarged the arena in which old Chinese ideas can once more be put into practice, in more modern guise, expanded to the new scale, but fundamentally the same ideas which inspired the builders of the Han Empire and the restorers of the T'ang."[3]

Although never fully resolved (as academic arguments seldom are), the controversy surrounding the origins of Chinese communism abated as the storm of revolutionary struggle was overtaken by the calm of regime consolidation. A second generation of specialists set about the sober task of documenting the development of Chinese communism, which seemed increasingly to resemble its Soviet precursor in many respects.[4] Whether wedded to a totalitarian model or to a more pluralist perspective, this new generation of China scholars—now often trained as social scientists rather than as historians—identified numerous similarities to Soviet and East European counterparts.[5]

Just as the comparative communism perspective was gaining popularity, however, along came the Great Proletarian Cultural Revolution. Faced once more with the challenge of explaining the unexpected, those in the China field again were caught up in controversy. The dramatic break with Soviet-style communism exemplified in Mao's Cultural Revolution aroused renewed interest, and disagreement, over the continuing importance of indigenous political traditions. However, unlike the earlier debate on the revolution—the parties to which had emerged out of the discipline of classical sinology—the new round of controversy was led instead by scholars whose training and self-identity derived from the burgeoning field of political science. Drawing on recent trends in their discipline, many of these political scientists viewed the Cultural Revolution as a problem in "political development." Having accepted central precepts of the modernization paradigm, they stressed the role of "political culture"[6] in fashioning China's unorthodox and uncertain developmental path.

Modernization theorists emphasized the close relationship of political culture to "political socialization" (i.e., "the process whereby political values and attitudes are inculcated") and "secularization" (i.e., "the process whereby men become increasingly rational, analytical, and empirical in their political action").[7] In the case of China, distinctive patterns of childrearing and schooling (or "socialization") were blamed for the seeming irrationalities (or lack of "secularization") characteristic of Red Guard excesses during the Cultural Revolution. By this account, the Cultural Revolution constituted a crisis in political development whose origins could be traced back to peculiarities of Chinese culture—particularly as embodied in conflictual authority relations.[8]

Although strongly influenced by prevailing trends in political science, advocates of a political culture approach within the China field also departed methodologically from mainstream currents in their discipline. Most analysts of political culture, dovetailing their studies with the behavioral revolution then sweeping the U.S. social sciences, pursued their projects through statistical interpretations of large-scale attitude surveys.[9] By contrast, students of Chinese political culture—denied access to field research in mainland China—resorted to a much less rigorous brand of methodology. Personal impressions (presented as psychocultural analysis) were combined with small-scale surveys of unrepresentative samples in Taiwan and Hong Kong, as well as schematic references to philosophical texts and historical events, so as to cobble together a portrait of Chinese political culture that proved unconvincing to many in the sinological and social science camps alike.[10] As a result, the concept of political culture developed a rather unsavory reputation among China specialists. And as fascination with attitude surveys waned within the political science profession at large, the study of political culture was largely abandoned by other wings of the discipline as well.

The simultaneous fading both of the Chinese Cultural Revolution and of the disciplinary interest in political culture drew scholars of contemporary China back to more prosaic styles of comparative analysis. Elite policymaking—whether approached in terms of factionalism, bureaucratic politics, or ideology—dominated the field.[11] And those who deigned to search below the commanding heights of the political system for the activities of ordinary peasants and workers generally did so from a "structuralist" rather than a "culturalist" point of view.[12] Moreover, as post-Mao China embarked upon a reform program that resembled ongoing experiments in Eastern Europe and the Soviet Union, comparisons with other Communist systems regained currency.[13]

The Challenge of 1989

Today students of contemporary China are again confronted by a crisis in understanding prompted by a popular protest that defied the best predictions of specialists in the field. The unrest of 1989, during which protesters in Beijing and other major cities throughout China took to the streets to demand an end to official corruption and a guarantee of greater political freedom, shook the very foundations of Communist Party rule. Thanks to the capabilities of modern communications technologies, these same events also sent shock waves around the world. The occupation of Tiananmen Square, the confrontation between a lone protester and a row of government tanks, the erection of a "goddess of democracy" statue, and the June Fourth Massacre in which soldiers of the People's Liberation Army (PLA) turned their weapons upon unarmed citizens—images such as these appeared immediately on television newscasts across the globe, alternately inspiring and horrifying audiences and changing forever the way they thought about China.

The events of 1989 have had an equally profound impact upon those who study China for a living. Once again, the academic world has been forced to question many of its most basic premises about contemporary Chinese society and politics. The present volume is an attempt to take stock of some of the reconsiderations to which the 1989 movement has given rise. As was the case with the Communist Revolution of 1949 and the Cultural Revolution of 1966–1969, the uprising of 1989 has generated more controversy than consensus. Thus, the chapters that follow will not present a unitary interpretation. Rather, they introduce some of the ways in which leading scholars from different disciplines, with different areas of expertise and different methodologies, have started to place the recent events into perspective. Each chapter is meant to offer insights into distinctive features of the 1989 movement as well as to stimulate new thinking about contemporary China in general. Taken as a whole, they suggest some of the directions in which recent developments have already begun to alter the analysis of Chinese popular protest.

Despite the diversity of these contributions, they share a fascination with political culture, although the authors tend to shy away from that particular term, tainted as it is with unpleasant memories of past usage. As they did in the debates that followed earlier crises in the unfolding of the Chinese Revolution, scholars are again looking to indigenous precedents to answer why the outcome in Beijing differed so radically from that in Budapest, Bucharest, or Berlin. In so doing, they join a "culture craze" (*wenhua re*) that has also swept Chinese academic circles in recent years.[14]

The New Political Culture

Is this culturalist trend nothing more than a temporary (and perhaps misguided) phase, soon to be replaced by a more sober return to elitist and structuralist modes of analysis? As adherents of the neoculturalist perspective, we let our defense rest upon the belief that this approach differs significantly from many previous efforts to explain Chinese protest in cultural terms and offers a more credible, and thus longer-lived, means of interpreting political change.

Whereas earlier cultural initiatives were promoted variously by historians steeped in sinology or by political scientists seeking to link up with the latest disciplinary fad, the current turn to culture has attracted historians and social scientists alike. Happily, recent years have seen a blurring of the sharp division between history and the social sciences that emerged with the second generation of contemporary China specialists. Gone are the days when the year 1949 demarcated a strict disciplinary boundary that was to be trespassed only at some risk to one's professional standing.[15] Constructive interaction between history and the social sciences has moderated the eccentricities of antiquarianism, on the one hand, and paradigm faddism, on the other, to which each of these branches of learning—if left to its own devices—was often prone.

Another advantage today's scholars enjoy is the greater maturity and sophistication of both historical and contemporary studies. Thanks to a generous infusion of new talent into the China field, we have all learned a good deal about the *complexities* of Chinese society and politics—past and present. Our picture of "traditional" culture is a more refined one (with greater appreciation of temporal and regional variation) than was available to preceding generations.[16] And our understanding of the current scene has also been much advanced by the access to fieldwork and other previously unobtainable sources that have enlivened the past decade of research.[17]

One result of this new accumulation of knowledge is an aversion to static or monochromic portraits of Chinese culture. Differences in time period, social status, and geographical location were, we now realize, characterized by important distinctions in belief and behavior. As a consequence, the challenge to the student of contemporary Chinese popular protest is to discover which of a multitude of available cultural repertoires is being drawn upon. Moreover, recognition of the fluidity and flexibility of cultural practice alerts the analyst to the possibility of innovation and originality. Rather than seeing Chinese politics as forever condemned to a treadmill of repetitive patterns, we look instead for creative deviation and breakthrough. Such transformations in political culture, one hastens to add, are not necessarily in the direction of greater "secularization." One finds little evidence, in China or elsewhere, of a process whereby "traditional" orientations inexorably give way to more "rational" modes of thinking.[18] The dichotomous mentality underlying modernization theory, it turns out, is a poor guide to the complexities of political change in the real world.

But whether one is more impressed with continuity or with transformation (a matter on which the contributors to this volume differ among themselves), political culture is seen as an arena of *conflict* as well as consensus—rooted in, yet not reducible to, the social context.[19] Thus, in place of socialization (which was credited in modernization theory with creating value consensus),[20] neoculturalist approaches emphasize the importance of symbolism, language, and ritual. Such "discourses," if one may employ that overworked term, are viewed as loci of confrontation and contestation among social actors. Accordingly, the connection between political culture and social context is seen as intimate, indeed inseparable. As Lynn Hunt, a pioneer in the analysis of the political culture of the French Revolution, has written:

> Revolutionary political culture cannot be deduced from social structures, social conflicts, or the social identity of revolutionaries. Political practices were not simply the expression of "underlying" economic and social interests. . . . This is not to say, however, that the Revolution was only intellectual or that politics had primacy over society rather than vice versa. The revolution in politics was an explosive interaction between ideas and reality, between intention and circumstance, between collective practices and social context. If revolutionary politics cannot be deduced from the social identity of the revolutionaries, then neither can it be divorced from it: the Revolution was made by people, and some people were more attracted than others to the politics of revolution. A better metaphor for the relationship between society and politics [than the metaphor of levels] is the knot or the Mobius strip, because the two sides were inextricably intertwined, with no "above" and "below."[21]

By providing "equal time" for cultural practice and social structure, refusing to elevate either to the level of "independent variable," the neoculturalist perspective strives for a comprehensive understanding of political change. It is this feature of the approach, we submit, that will rescue it from the short-lived fates suffered by previous culturalist efforts.

A political culture approach predicts neither that China will remain forever unchanged nor that China is headed down the road of convergence (either with the liberal West or with other formerly Communist societies in Eastern

Europe). It does claim, however, that change must draw heavily on established cultural repertoires. To make sense of popular protest will therefore require serious attention to the language, symbolism, and ritual of both resistance and repression.[22] And these, in turn, can be deciphered only in historical context—as meanings established over generations of political practice. Of course no society is immune from outside influence; patterns of change in China are inevitably shaped by (and themselves shape) developments elsewhere. Yet the interpretation of foreign models will proceed in Chinese terms—variegated and variable as we now know these to be.

The chapters that follow examine the relationship between the events of 1989 and changing Chinese repertoires of resistance and repression. Preliminary as this excursion into neoculturalist analysis is, we hope that it will stimulate more sophisticated such endeavors in future. Recent reexaminations of the French Revolution demonstrate just how fruitful the approach can be.[23] In stressing the diversity of the cultural material from which both revolutionaries and authorities fashion their beliefs and behaviors, we aim toward a more refined understanding of the links to tradition than was evident in scholarship on the Communist Revolution and the Cultural Revolution.

The Protest of 1989 and Chinese Political Culture

The multiplicity of political legacies that confronted both reformers and protesters in 1989 is the subject of Ernest Young's contribution to this volume. As Young points out, contemporary Chinese are heirs to several very different anciens régimes: the imperial reign of the Qing dynasty (1644–1911), the chaotic warlord interregnum (1911–1927), the Nationalist rule of the Kuomintang (1927–1949), and communism under Chairman Mao (1949–1976). The often contradictory nature of these various traditions has resulted in an identity crisis for Deng Xiaoping's post-Mao reforms; confusion has surrounded the whole question of which aspects of the past are to be altered. Although anxious to demonstrate a transformative break with the conservative Qing, for example, reformers have been equally concerned to avoid the radical excesses of Maoism. Such dilemmas have led to a bewildering political discourse on the part of authorities and dissenters alike. Thanks to "the multitude of ghosts that China's modern history has conjured up," reformers turn into repressors and democrats into elitists. Young asserts that we are dealing in 1989 "not only with the persistence of an attitude or with the consequences of an at best slowly changing Chinese political culture, but also with a cumulative effect. Every generation's repetition of the rationale for postponing democracy produces a changing meaning as well."

This theme of change within repetition is further pursued by Joseph Esherick and Jeffrey Wasserstrom, who view the events of 1989 as "an exercise in political theater." Student protesters, even when improvising, worked from familiar "scripts" of state rituals and protest repertoires—some of which dated back for millennia and others of which were of relatively recent vintage. The centrality of ritual in imperial China was joined by new forms of popular protest at the turn of this century to render political theater a dominant mode of political expression. Efforts by the Communist state to tame this behavior into ritualized mass campaigns were not entirely successful, as both the Cultural Revolution and the protests of 1989 make clear. Yet, according to Esherick and Wasserstrom, Chinese street theater is politically limited. Unlike Eastern Europe, where democratic institutions played a critical role in translating street theater into programs for political change, in China a weak civil society has undermined the development of pluralist politics.

The importance of ritual in the construction of Chinese cultural identity is reinforced in James Watson's chapter. Watson emphasizes that at least prior to 1949 one became Chinese by *acting* Chinese, that is, by properly carrying out prescribed rituals. Not orthodoxy (or correct belief) but orthopraxy (or correct behavior) lay at the heart of what it meant to be Chinese. In both imperial and contemporary times, the state has made concerted efforts to control the definition of national cultural identity. Yet Watson argues that Communist China has seen a bifurcation between rural and urban culture, with the latter becoming more open to international influences. The state's attempt to reclaim control in the massacre of June 4 stands as "a disastrously violent reminder that the Chinese past is still very much alive in the present."

John Israel further explores "tensions between rulers who fall back upon patterns of traditional political culture and students who look to the outside world for new formulations." Placing the contemporary student movement in historical perspective (with particular attention to the precedents of the May Fourth Movement and the Cultural Revolution), Israel emphasizes the importance of social context in shaping patterns of protest. The backgrounds of the students, the structure of advancement open to them, and especially the capacity of the state are identified as critical determinants of student unrest.

Drawing on the historical background supplied by Israel, Vera Schwarcz elaborates on the comparison with earlier student movements. Superficial similarities between the events of 1989 and the May Fourth Movement of 1919, she argues, obscure a more disturbing parallel with the Cultural Revolution. Although quick to commemorate their link to May Fourth, many Chinese intellectuals overlooked the more painful lesson of the Cultural Revolution: Student idealism could be abused in the context of crowd politics. Like the Red Guards of the 1960s, students in 1989 were, according to Schwarcz, "swallowed by . . . the language of political revolution." Exhilarated with the heady taste of protest, they failed "to take notice of the heavy burden of the past that hung over the sea of red flags in Tiananmen Square."

Timothy Cheek further pursues the restraints on contemporary intellectuals, noting that most Chinese intellectuals have yet to make the transition from "priests" serving the interests of the state to independent professionals. Operating under a "social contract" that affords opportunities for public service and scholarship in exchange for obedience to the state, many intellectuals still cleave to their "old mandarin function." Cheek suggests that the events of 1989 may have worked to accelerate "the movement from priest-rentiers serving the cosmic state (Confucian or Leninist) to professionals salaried in a bourgeois society." But he concludes that this process is as yet not far advanced, a situation that helps to explain why China's popular protests did not result in the dramatic regime changes witnessed in Eastern Europe.

In my chapter I also stress the extent to which student protesters were fettered by tradition. In their subservient style of remonstrance, their search for political patrons, and above all their elitist moralism, students evidenced patterns of belief and behavior befitting the heirs of Confucianism. Picking up on the theatrical metaphor of Esherick and Wasserstrom, I emphasize the limited cast of characters included in the 1989 performance. Students reserved for themselves the starring roles, relegating workers, peasants, and entrepreneurs to the sidelines. The explanation for this undemocratic style is, I suggest, structural: Institutionalized links between students and state officials continued to limit alliances of intellectuals with other social groups.

The inegalitarian inclinations of student protesters is further explored in Lee Feigon's discussion of gender. Despite the prominence of Chai Ling and some other women leaders, males dominated the upper echelons of the 1989 protest movement. Moreover, neither men nor women showed a serious commitment to overcoming gender-based inequality. According to Feigon, women were prone to accept a state-defined image of femininity that accentuated their differences with men and to confine themselves to less public roles. Even the goddess of democracy, although ostensibly a challenge to state authority, "demonstrated the hollowness of this conception of feminine strength . . . and . . . highlighted the dependence of the student movement on the Chinese government." On the question of gender, as on the issues of democracy and economic reform, students were strongly influenced by state authority and logic.

State ideological authority is also the focus of Ann Anagnost's study of village compacts. Anagnost highlights the continuing importance of the Party's efforts to mold the thinking of the masses in the post-Mao period. It was this serious concern with ideology, she suggests, that prevented the Party from opening itself to dissent in 1989. Village compacts, although in theory intended to promote grassroots democracy, have actually served to reinforce state authority in the countryside. Despite close parallels with the use of village compacts in earlier periods, Anagnost emphasizes, the meaning of this institution has changed. In contrast to the sources of legitimacy of imperial regimes, in contemporary China "the Party's authority rests on its presumption to speak as the voice of the people."

Although Party-state dominance may be secure in the countryside, Stephen MacKinnon finds a different scenario in the urban sector. Noting that "it is hard to overestimate the effect in political terms of U.S. media penetration of Chinese cities," he stresses the importance of the press—both U.S. and Chinese—in promoting political change. MacKinnon draws parallels between journalism in the 1980s and in the 1930s–1940s (on the eve of revolution). He sees journalists in both periods as committed "to a higher kind of loyalty: to truth outside the state." Despite the effectiveness of Communist Party controls today, MacKinnon looks forward to "the leading contribution of both media to the creation of a civil society in China" by the end of the century.

According to Daniel Chirot, it was just such a process that ultimately brought down the Communist states of Eastern Europe. Important as economic problems were to this outcome, "utter moral rot" was the essential cause of the collapse. Once the utopian ideology of the Party had been discredited, charges of immorality fueled the public alienation. Central to this development was the growth of a civil society, where intellectuals and other urbanites wrote and talked about alternatives to the corrupt rule of the Party-state. Looking ahead, Chirot predicts that "more than ever, the fundamental causes of revolutionary instability will be moral. The urban middle and professional classes, the intellectuals and those to whom they most directly appeal, will set the tone of political change."

The relative weakness of Chinese urbanites has led many Western analysts of China to despair of the likelihood of fundamental political transformation in the near future. As Wasserstrom observes in his afterword to this volume, Western interpretations have tended to present the events of 1989 as tragedy— a noble quest doomed to failure. Controversy has surrounded the question of who the protagonists were (the students or Deng Xiaoping and Zhao Ziyang) and why they failed (whether because of circumstances beyond their control or because of their own shortcomings). Chinese accounts, by contrast, have often portrayed the uprising of 1989 as romance—a conflict between good and evil that results in the exaltation of the hero. Here again there have been disagreements over the identity of the protagonists (with Hu Yaobang, student martyrs, or PLA soldiers variously assuming this role in different versions) and over the meaning of their struggle. For his own part, Wasserstrom favors a tragic narrative that sees the uprising of 1989 "as related to but also significantly different from earlier PRC struggles." He concludes that "to leave open the possibility that the events of 1989 may have fundamentally altered Chinese political arrangements, and perhaps even Chinese political culture itself, is to suggest that those who died on June 4 may not have sacrificed their lives in vain."

Conclusion

The year 1989 will undoubtedly go down as a watershed in modern world history. Fittingly, the bicentennial of the French Revolution was marked by protests across the globe raising many of the same demands that we associate with the storming of the Bastille. In Eastern Europe these protests brought stunning political change, whereas in China the uprising was brutally suppressed. Yet the French precedent cautions against too early or too easy an assessment of the ultimate results. Now, two hundred years after the fact, scholarly reappraisals of the French Revolution are revealing a far more complicated—if no less consequential—event than was previously recognized.

Central to this reconsideration is an appreciation of the significance of political culture.[24] Liberating as the revolution was, it was also limited by the rhetoric and rituals of the past.

Comparisons with France thus offer both inspiration and admonition to the student of contemporary China. We must be alert to the heavy hand of history—including its unattractive as well as its appealing features—while remaining alive to the possibility of real change. Cultural traditions provide raw materials for political action, but not in any formulaic fashion. As the French historian Keith Baker puts it, "Political culture is a historical creation, subject to constant elaboration and development through the activities of the individuals and groups whose purposes it defines. As it sustains and gives meaning to political activity, so is it itself shaped and transformed in the course of that activity."[25]

That Chinese political culture gives shape to recognizable but flexible patterns of protest can be seen by comparison with Taiwan, another Chinese society recently rocked by popular unrest. In March 1990 a massive, week-long student sit-in occupied the Chiang Kaishek Memorial grounds in the center of Taipei. The demands (for dissolution of the national assembly and direct elections of the president) were different, but the style of protest was remarkably reminiscent of the previous year's student movement on the mainland. The Taiwan protesters donned the same white headbands, broadcast the same rock music, and undertook a similarly dramatic hunger strike. One Taipei student captured the special attention of the media precisely because of her striking resemblance to Chai Ling, the activist of Tiananmen fame. Yet there were important departures as well. In place of the U.S.-inspired goddess of democracy that loomed over Tiananmen Square, the Taiwan students erected a huge papier-mâché lily, a native plant symbolic of both purity and independence. And although Taipei protesters imitated the Beijing exemplar in establishing a picket line to separate themselves from ordinary citizens, they actually welcomed members of the labor movement, the farmers' movement, the women's movement, and environmental and homeless advocates inside the cordon.[26] Thanks to the socioeconomic changes of recent years, the distinctions between urban intellectuals and other social groups had become much less pronounced in Taiwan than was the situation on the opposite side of the straits.

The importance of innovation within tradition forms the central theme of this volume. The authors present popular protest as anchored in, yet not immobilized by, long-standing cultural practice. In analyzing the sources of change, moreover, we acknowledge the inextricable and interactive connections among society, economy, polity, and culture. Although this new political culture approach is still in its infancy in the contemporary China field,[27] its application to the study of political change elsewhere in the world is well established. Our hope is that the further development of this perspective among China scholars may improve our understanding of Chinese popular protest so that future uprisings will find us better prepared than was the case in 1949, 1969, or 1989.

Notes

1. Contributions to this early debate included John King Fairbank, *The United States and China* (Cambridge: Harvard University Press, 1948); Karl A. Wittfogel, "The Influence of Leninism-Stalinism on China," *Annals*, vol. 277 (September 1951), pp. 22–34; Wittfogel, *Oriental Despotism* (New Haven: Yale University Press, 1957); Wittfogel, "The Legend of 'Maoism,'" *China Quarterly*, no. 1 (January-March 1960), pp. 72–86, and no. 2 (April-June 1960), pp. 16–31; Benjamin Schwartz, "The Legend of the 'Legend of Maoism,'" *China Quarterly*, no. 2 (April-June 1960), pp. 35–42; and Joseph R. Levenson, *Confucian China and Its Modern Fate*, 3 vols. (Berkeley: University of California Press, 1958–1965).

2. C. P. Fitzgerald, *The Birth of Communist China* (Harmondsworth: Penguin, 1964), p. 20.

3. Ibid., p. 42.

4. Examples of the comparative communism approach are found in Donald W. Treadgold, ed., *Soviet and Chinese Communism: Similarities and Differences* (Seattle: University of Washington Press, 1967); and Chalmers Johnson, ed., *Change in Communist Systems* (Stanford: Stanford University Press, 1970). See also Thomas P. Bernstein, "Leadership and Mass Mobilisation in the Soviet and Chinese Collectivisation Campaigns of 1929–1930 and 1955–1956: A Comparison," *China Quarterly*, no. 31 (July-September 1967), pp. 1–42.

5. For recent critiques of both the totalitarian and pluralist perspectives, see Vivienne Shue, *The Reach of the State: Sketches of the Chinese Body Politic* (Stanford: Stanford University Press, 1988), ch. 1; and Andrew G. Walder, *Communist Neo-Traditionalism: Work and Authority in Chinese Industry* (Berkeley: University of California Press, 1986), chapter 1.

6. The standard definition of political culture as "attitudes, beliefs, values and skills which are current in an entire population, as well as those special propensities and patterns which may be found within separate parts of that population" appears in Gabriel A. Almond and G. Bingham Powell, Jr., *Comparative Politics: A Developmental Approach* (Boston: Little, Brown, 1966), p. 23.

7. Ibid.

8. The main statements of this position were Lucian W. Pye, *The Spirit of Chinese Politics* (Cambridge: MIT Press, 1968); and Richard Solomon, *Mao's Revolution and Chinese Political Culture* (Berkeley: University of California Press, 1971). More recently, Pye's *Dynamics of Chinese Politics* (Cambridge: Oelgeschlager, Gunn and Hain, 1981) and *The Mandarin and the Cadre* (Ann Arbor: University of Michigan Center for Chinese Studies, 1988) present updated versions of this line of analysis. Quite different approaches, from the perspective of psychohistory and sinology, respectively, were those of Robert J. Lifton, *Revolutionary Immortality: Mao Tse-tung and the Chinese Cultural Revolution* (New York: Vintage, 1968), and Thomas A. Metzger, *Escape from Predicament: Neo-Confucianism and China's Evolving Political Culture* (New York: Columbia University Press, 1977).

9. The standard was set by Gabriel A. Almond and Sidney Verba's comparative study of the United States, Great Britain, Germany, Italy, and Mexico: *The Civic Culture: Political Attitudes and Democracy in Five Nations* (Boston: Little, Brown, 1965).

10. For a critique from the sinological point of view, see Frederick W. Mote's review of Solomon, *Mao's Revolution*, in the *Journal of Asian Studies*, 32, 1 (November 1972); for a social science critique, see Richard Kagan and Norma Diamond, "Father, Son, and Holy Ghost: Pye, Solomon, and the 'Spirit of Chinese Politics,'" *Bulletin of Concerned*

Asian Scholars, 5, 1 (July 1973), pp. 62–68. Another critical review is John Gittings, "Bringing Up the Red Guards," New York Review of Books, December 16, 1971, pp. 13–17. A helpful overview of the debate can be found in Lowell Dittmer, "The Study of Chinese Political Culture," in Amy Wilson et al., Methodological Issues in Chinese Studies (New York: Praeger, 1983), pp. 51–68.

11. On factions, see Andrew J. Nathan, "A Factional Model of Chinese Politics," China Quarterly, no. 53 (January-March 1973), pp. 34–66; and the critique by Tang Tsou, "Prolegomenon to the Study of Informal Groups in CCP Politics," China Quarterly, no. 65 (January-March 1976), pp. 98–113. Also William L. Parish, "Factions in Chinese Military Politics," China Quarterly, no. 56 (October-December 1973), pp. 667–699. On bureaucratic politics, see David M. Lampton, The Politics of Medicine in China: The Policy Process, 1949–1977 (Boulder: Westview, 1977); and Kenneth Lieberthal and Michel Oksenberg, Policy Making in China: Leaders, Structures, and Processes (Princeton: Princeton University Press, 1988). On ideology, see Dorothy Solinger, ed., Three Visions of Chinese Socialism (Boulder: Westview, 1984); and Harry Harding, Organizing China: The Problem of Bureaucracy, 1949–1976 (Stanford: Stanford University Press, 1981).

12. William L. Parish and Martin King Whyte, Village and Family in Contemporary China (Chicago: University of Chicago Press, 1978); and Martin King Whyte and William L. Parish, Urban Life in Contemporary China (Chicago: University of Chicago Press, 1984); Walder, Communist Neo-Traditionalism; Jean Oi, State and Peasant in Contemporary China: The Political Economy of Village Government (Berkeley: University of California Press, 1989); John P. Burns, Political Participation in Rural China (Berkeley: University of California Press, 1988); David Zweig, Agrarian Radicalism in China (Cambridge: Harvard University Press, 1989). Notable exceptions to the structuralist mainstream are Richard Madsen, Morality and Politics in a Chinese Village (Berkeley: University of California Press, 1984); Perry Link, Richard Madsen, and Paul Pickowicz, eds., Unofficial China: Popular Culture and Thought in the People's Republic (Boulder: Westview, 1989); and Helen F. Siu, "Recycling Tradition: Culture, History, and Political Economy in the Chrysanthemum Festivals of South China," Comparative Studies in Society and History, 32, 4 (October 1990), pp. 765–795.

13. Elizabeth J. Perry and Christine Wong, eds., The Political Economy of Reform in Post-Mao China (Cambridge: Harvard University Press, 1985); Victor Nee and David Stark, Remaking the Economic Institutions of Socialism: China and Eastern Europe (Stanford: Stanford University Press, 1989).

14. The television documentary "He Shang" (River elegy) was one influential manifestation of this trend. (For further discussion, see Chapter 3 by James Watson.) See also Xiao Gongqin, Rujia sixiang de kunjing (The dilemma of Confucian culture) (Chengdu: Sichuan People's Press, 1986).

15. Important examples of recent works that defy the traditional dividing line are political scientist David Strand's Rickshaw Beijing (Berkeley: University of California Press, 1989) and historian Philip C.C. Huang's The Peasant Family and Rural Development in the Yangzi Delta, 1350–1988 (Stanford: Stanford University Press, 1990).

16. Paul A. Cohen, Discovering History in China: American Historical Writings on the Recent Chinese Past (New York: Columbia University Press, 1984), discusses these developments. See also David Johnson, Andrew J. Nathan, and Evelyn S. Rawski, eds., Popular Culture in Late Imperial China (Berkeley: University of California Press, 1985).

17. For an overview of the contemporary field, see Michel Oksenberg, "The Literature on Post-1949 China: An Interpretive Essay," in John King Fairbank and Roderick MacFarquhar, eds., The Cambridge History of China, vol. 13, pt. 1, (Cambridge: Cambridge University Press, 1985).

18. In *Comparative Politics*, pp. 24–25, Almond and Powell describe cultural secularization as "the process whereby traditional orientations give way to more dynamic decision-making processes involving the gathering of information, the evaluation of information, the laying out of alternative courses of action, the selection of a course of action from among these possible courses, and the means whereby one tests whether or not a given course of action is producing the consequences which were intended." One need look only as far as the Islamic revolution in Iran or the fierce ethnic conflicts now raging across much of Eastern Europe to grasp the obvious point that political change may not lead to cultural secularization.

19. This point is made in Lynn Hunt, "Political Culture and the French Revolution," *States and Social Structures Newsletter*, no. 11 (Fall 1989), p. 2. See also Lynn Hunt, ed., *The New Cultural History* (Berkeley: University of California Press, 1989).

20. This view was of course heavily influenced by the work of sociologist Talcott Parsons. For a critique of Parsons, see esp. Alvin Gouldner, *The Coming Crisis of Western Sociology* (New York: Basic Books, 1970).

21. Lynn Hunt, *Politics, Culture and Class in the French Revolution* (Berkeley: University of California Press, 1984), pp. 12–13.

22. Whereas the "new social history" has tended to stress the popular resistance side of the equation, studies by political scientists and anthropologists have often focused on the state's use of symbolic power to maintain legitimacy. See, for example, Murray Edelman, *The Symbolic Use of Politics* (Urbana: University of Illinois Press, 1964); Clifford Geertz, *Negara: The Theatre-State in Nineteenth-Century Bali* (Princeton: Princeton University Press, 1980); Raymond Cohen, *Theatre of Power* (New York: Longman, 1987); and David I. Kertzer, *Ritual, Politics, and Power* (New Haven: Yale University Press, 1988).

23. See esp. Keith Michael Baker, ed., *The Political Culture of the Old Regime* (Oxford: Pergamon, 1987); Colin Lucas, ed., *The Political Culture of the French Revolution* (Oxford: Pergamon, 1988); and François Furet and Mona Ozouf, eds., *The Transformation of Political Culture, 1789–1848* (Oxford: Pergamon, 1989).

24. See the works cited in note 23 above.

25. Baker, "Introduction," p. xii.

26. He Jinshan, Guan Hongzhi, Zhang Lijia, and Guo Chengqi, *Taibei xueyun* (The Taipei student movement) (Taipei: China Times Press, 1990), pp. 18, 32, 46, 94–95.

27. For an example of an insightful new work in this vein, see Peter Zarrow, *Anarchism and Chinese Political Culture* (New York: Columbia University Press, 1990).

1

IMAGINING THE ANCIEN RÉGIME IN THE DENG ERA

Ernest P. Young

Revolutionaries hasten to break eggs in order to make fresh omelets, we are told, whereas reformers favor less strenuous recipes for change, by which the ingredients are more gently and gradually introduced. The distinction strongly colors our ideas of political or social reform. It is with such vocabulary that we have marked the great turn taken by China after the death of Mao Zedong: from continuing the revolution to reformist modernization. Although both Mao and Deng Xiaoping have aspired to change China profoundly, under Deng the methods would minimize violence and hew to a practical gradualism, in contrast to the headlong ruthlessness of Mao's transformational mobilizations. One of the jarring aspects, then, of the brutal suppression of the Chinese protests of 1989 is the incongruity between the reformist character of Deng Xiaoping's regime since 1978 and its most unreformist attack on people who at least potentially were among reform's most enthusiastic constituents. In other words, why was the very embodiment of China's opening up, both to the outside and with respect to domestic economic and social organization, acting in a way that was so pernicious for the long-run success and development of those reforms? Why was the key player in the retreat from radicalism acting so recklessly? How could such a reformer be such a repressor?

The simplest explanation may be the best. One can argue that Deng's first priority had always been power and the perpetuation of the system that seemed to grant that power. He was willing to reform so far, but no further, and he always stopped when the reforms began to threaten the autocracy. According to this argument, Deng has always been a pragmatist who would use ideological claims to gain support for his programs but never let ideology get in the way of a practical concern with maintaining existing power relations. This kind of argument carries a good deal of weight because spring 1989 was not, after all, the first time since Deng's ascendancy that a liberal oppositional voice had been silenced.

Despite its attractions and a degree of fundamental validity, this explanation is problematic in two ways. First, it is so general that it applies to the behavior of political leaderships in many times and places. Second, it underestimates the continuing importance of ideological concerns within the Chinese Communist Party (CCP), an issue confronted more directly and treated in more detail in the chapter by Ann Anagnost. The search for finer explanations must, therefore, go on. One useful way to particularize an analysis of June 4, 1989, is to locate the Deng era within China's broader modern experience.

I follow here the lead of Paul Cohen. He has argued that Deng Xiaoping's modernization program can be understood as the continuation of "a kind of mainstream Chinese reformism" that reaches back in the modern era to the Self-Strengtheners of the late nineteenth century.[1] Cohen wishes to persuade us that the regimes of the Empress Dowager Cixi (for the years 1898–1900), of President Yuan Shikai, and of President Chiang Kaishek in the Nanjing era were reformist in many of the same ways that Deng's has been. Deng's version of modernization, he says, has shared more, though certainly not everything, with those unlikely predecessors than with the socially transformational or politically redistributive impulses of the Taiping rebels (1850–1864), the 1898 reform movement, the 1911 revolution, or the PRC in the early 1950s (not to mention the Maoist era of the Great Leap Forward and the Cultural Revolution). The bent of his argument is not to affirm Deng's reformist credentials, about which there would be little disagreement. Rather, he tries to establish and define the reformist character of the programs of Cixi, Yuan Shikai, and Chiang Kaishek, so that placing Deng in their line of succession becomes plausible.

Having shown how autocrats of earlier decades shared the reformism of Deng, Cohen then turns around and notes how Deng shares their authoritarianism: "The fact is, Deng's reforms are guided by a very potent ideology— we may call it an ideology of 'authoritarian modernization'—and it is precisely this ideology that Deng shares with his non-Communist predecessors."[2] Although he recognizes the vast differences in international and domestic circumstances between pre-1949 China and that of the 1980s, Cohen was moved by his analysis to a degree of skepticism about the future of reform under Deng. In a 1988 publication, he argued the need for "institutionalized arrangements for genuine power sharing" and saw no sign that Deng and colleagues were "prepared to countenance such a far-reaching move."[3] These remarks were underscored by events the following year.

Defining Deng's Ancien Régime

I should like to try a related but somewhat different approach to the relevance of China's history to Deng's reforms and to his decision to repress the protests of 1989. I hope it is an approach that illuminates not only Deng's behavior but also to some degree the character of the protest movement. The starting point is the question of the identity of the ancien régime.

We are accustomed to revolutions having an ancien régime. In fact, we cannot conceive of a revolution without one: If it were missing, a revolution would have to invent one. Indeed, anciens régimes to a considerable extent *are* invented as part of the revolutionary process. The historical image of the ancien régime is part of the ideology of the revolution and defines, by contrasts and opposites, the revolutionary program. Our favoring the French term over ordinary English signals the abstractness of the idea.

The French Revolution has provided us with the term, which was first invested with its modern meaning during the last decades of the eighteenth century. William Doyle, author of a short monograph devoted to the role of the concept in the revolution, stresses its originality, noting that "there had been no anciens régimes under the Ancien Régime."[4] Diego Venturino, who has written a chapter on the topic for a recent multivolume work on the political culture of the French Revolution, echoes this point in the very title he gives his piece: "La naissance de l'Ancien Régime" (The birth of the Ancien Régime).[5] Doyle and Venturino also stress the term's broad reference to all aspects of the old order (political, social, spiritual), and its dynamic, defining relationship to the revolution. Above all, they argue, it was an ideological construct, albeit a flexible one. Crystallizing out of the theme of reforming old abuses, the notion of an ancien régime came to refer to the past as a whole. It summoned up a vision of the past (privileged, feudal, chaotic, despotic, and so on) in the form of a legitimating antithesis to the revolutionary present. The ancien régime bequeathed manners and customs (*moeurs*) whose persistence explained delays and difficulties in realizing revolutionary purposes. Ultimately, Venturino writes, "the 'ancien régime' became a personage; an actor with personal character, a will, a role to fill; the negative pole in all events of the moment; in other words, the enemy."[6]

Probably less from imitation than from parallel impulses, modern revolutionaries everywhere, including those in China, have fashioned their own, appropriate "ancien régime." Revolutionaries characteristically construct an image of a rather static and unattractive society, ascribe it to their predecessor regime, and commit themselves to changing it. That the image in each case is invented does not mean that the picture of the former regime is simply or wholly false. It generally borrows heavily from experience. Yet it is not limited to experience and is crucially shaped by dreams and aspirations, as well as the need to justify.

Major reform programs, like revolutions, also have anciens régimes. An intrinsic part of a reform program is a conception of the entity that requires correcting and against which the reform movement defines itself. At least so it is in the contemporary Chinese case. Perhaps the Deng regime, as a reform movement arising within a far-from-extinct revolutionary tradition, is unusually alert to the problem of defining its ancien régime.

When we look at texts coming out of Deng's China for clues as to conceptions of the appropriate ancien régime, we seem to find a rather complicated answer. The candidates for what has been the relevant ancien régime for the Deng Xiaoping era are disturbingly numerous and various. They include the Maoist era, the Nanjing government under the Kuomintang (KMT), the warlord phenomenon, and the Qing. The last term opens out into broader conceptions of Confucian society and feudalism. The Maoist era and the Qing are particularly formidable historical images in the reformist imagination.

So in Deng's China the identification or definition of the ancien régime has involved the selection from among several eras, each with its own image. The meanings of the reform programs of the different layers of anciens régimes have been quite various, causing reformers some confusion about exactly what they were supposed to be reforming. As a result, the reform impetus has had, I would argue, a severe identity crisis. Inside this identity problem may lie clues to the repression of 1989.

Although the problem became more acute in Deng's era, it was not brand new. The problem's reflection—or its other face—can be seen in the CCP leadership's uncertainty regarding China's position in some schedule of historical change, a variability that goes well back into the Maoist era. The early redefinitions of China's status could be explained in terms of forward movement: from "New Democracy" in the 1940s and early 1950s (completing the tasks left unfinished by the bourgeoisie and extirpating feudalism) to building socialism in the middle of the 1950s. Suddenly in the late 1950s China was not only working on a very advanced version of socialism but was edging into communism, with all that such a transition implied about what needed to be reformed. This vision was soon abandoned, and in the 1960s the Chinese were warned by their supreme leader that the country was slipping backward toward capitalism—which involved yet another conception about the appropriate objects (and methods) of reform.

By the mid-1980s, a different leadership discovered that China was only in the preliminary stage of socialism. The notion drew sarcastic comment during the 1989 protests: "What was denounced as capitalistic yesterday could well be regarded as socialist today. Socialism, after several decades, has not yet entered its advanced stage; on the contrary, it has reverted to its elementary stage."[7] As the conception of reform again shifted after June 1989, the CCP has moved away from the idea of locating China's current development at so modest a stage.[8]

Each of these shifts, back and forth along some line of developmental progress, has implied a different choice of a relevant ancien régime. Perhaps one should say, especially with regard to the Deng era, that there is an attempt to have at hand several possibilities at once and to weave them into a single picture. The result is rent with contradictions. Let us explore the main elements of the Deng-era portrayal.

The top layer of anciens régimes has been the almost two decades of Mao Zedong's transformational regime—the Great Leap Forward, the Cultural Revolution, and all their works. It was the most important politically in the initial phase of the Deng reform era. In the Dengist view, by trying to transform China at breakneck speed into a socially and spiritually socialist, even communist, order, Mao had brought only ruin and chaos to the country. By no means incidentally, he had also inflicted great injury to its political and intellectual elite. The ideological purposes in the portrayal of this ancien régime were evident in the flattening out of the Maoist era, for example, in the notion of a ten-year Cultural Revolution ("the ten dark years"), homogenizing the considerable variability of policy in the last ten years of Mao's life.[9]

In this dimension—the undoing of the ancien régime of Mao Zedong—the Deng reforms had a markedly conservative coloring. That is, a major component of the reform program was dismantling institutions and programs intended to be socially transformative and putting in their place arrangements meant to restore some status quo ante (whatever their actual effects). There was a vigorous discrediting of the radical rhetoric of the Maoist era and a more modest effort to reduce the size of Mao himself.

Although Dengists have criticized the Maoist period for its lack of procedural regularity—administrative and legal—its lack of liberal political institutions is precisely an area that has *not* received much attention from Deng's regime. A sustained effort to correct China's lack of democratic institutions would have placed the Deng reform era in a relationship of relative radicalism with respect to Mao's politics, but we have not seen more than glimpses of such moves, and those short-lived. (It has been this neglect, of course, that has spawned a liberal opposition.)

In short, the Mao era has been a crucial ancien régime—the primary rationale for the Deng ascendancy. Nevertheless, there has not been a complete negation of it, as the continued use of the phrase "Mao Zedong Thought" to refer to the ideology of the CCP attests. Since June 1989, furthermore, there has been increased resort to Mao's sanctifying spirit to prop up a regime in trouble.

The politics of Deng's regime has evoked other anciens régimes as well. Brief mention may be made of the next two layers. Despite the political need to soft-pedal criticisms that might impede a deal with Taiwan, the notion that the PRC is based on a rectification of the failings of the KMT has remained relevant to political discourse. The protesters of 1989 readily picked up on the idea in order to highlight the corruption of the Deng administration. The same official malfeasance that had discredited the Nanjing government was now, astonishingly, a feature of the Communist Party.[10] On this point, Deng had to agree, for who would dispute the proposition that any respectable Chinese government had to represent the negation of this picture of the Nationalist ancien régime? One sign of just how potent criticisms of KMT-like misconduct are in contemporary China became clear during the months that followed the crackdown of June 1989. In this period, the Deng regime made few public attempts to redress most of the grievances the students had articulated, but it did launch a new drive against official corruption.

Deng and his hard-line supporters have also emphasized another feature of the Nanjing government since June 4: the KMT's alleged subordination to foreign power. In his much-quoted June 9, 1989, remarks to military commanders in Beijing explaining the necessity of the crackdown on "counterrevolutionary" forces, Deng warned against China's becoming "a bourgeois republic subordinated to the West" (*xifang fuyonghua de zichan jieji gongheguo*).[11] This was for Deng a stick to be used against the protesters. In various ways, as these examples show, the ancien régime of Chiang Kaishek remained a part of the definition of Deng's reform goals. Chen Xitong's June 30, 1989, "Report to the National People's Congress," perhaps the single most important comprehensive defense of the government's actions, provided numerous illustrations of this point. Not only does the report provide details concerning the alleged efforts Western forces made to "bring China under the rule of international monopoly capital" in 1989, it also argues that remnant supporters of the KMT and agents from Taiwan played a role in instigating the protests.[12]

The image of the warlord era as the pinnacle of twentieth-century disorder in China has also lived on as a standard for guiding policy. A reform program must check extreme decentralization or the creation of baronies. And it must retain the subordination of military to civilian authority. It was part of the charge against Mao that he had risked these dangers. As with every leader since the 1920s, Deng's responsibilities include repressing any sign of resurgent warlordism.

The most insistent, compelling alternative to the Maoist ancien régime for defining Dengist politics has been the Qing and the society associated with it. The Qing as a specific period and political phenomenon is actually too limited for what is involved in the portrayal of this ancien régime. "Feudal society" is the catchphrase, and the concept is as elastic as "traditional society" in Western parlance. In this usage, "feudal" is a pejorative masquerading as an analytic term, but one that evokes an array of linked characteristics drawn from particular conceptions of Chinese history. Among its notable features are a despotic monarchy, a creaky but oppressive bureaucratic administration, an exploitative landlord class, a stagnant economy, and a trod-upon peasantry, restive but culturally benighted. From a twentieth-century, Marxist-influenced perspective, "feudal" has carried with it the judgment of "backward."

The Chinese term that we translate as "feudal" (*fengjian*) did not fully acquire the pejorative meaning just described until a couple of decades into the twentieth century. However, the idea of a backward society inherited from China's long imperial experience was already being articulated by the end of the nineteenth century and quickly became general among the educated classes. Early twentieth-century Westernizing reform programs were constructed around some version of this idea, which served as the necessary ancien régime for reform or revolution. The political dimension of the old order was the first object of change. Social features were soon being added to the picture.

The first point about this ancien régime of the Qing, of "feudal society," that I wish to stress in its relation to understanding the Deng era is its contrast with the ancien régime of Maoism. With respect to feudalism, the Deng regime has conceived of itself not as rescuing China from the reckless schemes of change associated with Mao but as transforming by modernization a backward and inhibiting part of China's ancient inheritance. We see here a tension between gradualism and transformationalism that has marked the Deng era.

A second notable point about Deng's relation to this much older ancien régime is that he ascribes to it great continuing influence. Not only did his revolutionary and reformist predecessors fail to extirpate it, they were fatally undermined or contaminated by the ancien régime, so that their modernizing efforts foundered or were misdirected. Remarkably, Mao Zedong is no exception. Apparently Deng's own reforms are quite far from the desired goal of overcoming the power of feudal remnants in contemporary China. "Feudal society" is a truly old ancien régime, but it seems to be still a formidable one.

In this view of China's situation, how does one explain the persistence of feudal society after numerous reform regimes, revolutionary movements, and campaigns for social transformation? There has been no single answer, of course, but the key seems to lie in the Chinese peasantry. Karl Marx had laid down the theory in *The Eighteenth Brumaire of Louis Bonaparte*, which has enjoyed a revival in China. The argument is that the social circumstances of peasant life are conducive to ignorance and superstition—a backwardness that retards social progress for everyone. Peasant society is consequently fertile ground for both political despotism and mindless radicalism.

In this view, Mao's style of rule and his radical politics were a product of China's feudal backwardness. The argument was alluded to in the CCP's formal reinterpretation of its history in 1981.[13] It has been made explicit by a number of commentators, including Mao's chief Chinese biographer, Li Rui, who attributes Mao's autocracy and his policies in the Great Leap and the Cultural Revolution to his "neglecting the grim task of rooting out pernicious feudal influences," which have their ground in "a closed-door small-scale peasant economy and the system of feudalism, patriarchialism and despotism."[14] Apparently destroying the landlord class was not enough. Li Rui traces Mao's radicalism to "an ocean of peasant small-scale producers."[15] Mao's greatest contribution, then—in fashioning a rural strategy for coming to power—becomes at the same time the reason for the greatest errors of his rule. Immersion in the peasantry had imbued the Party with feudalism.

To this picture we might add that all this was made concrete in the numerous cadres of rural background who, by joining the Red Army during the revolution, eventually acquired power over urban populations. The urban folk saw themselves as more advanced culturally. Clashes between urbanites and their new peasant overlords were common. Hence personal experience gave concrete support to the theoretical point about damage from the feudal virus and about the peasantry as its most persistent carrier.[16]

Anciens Régimes and
the Roots of Dissent and Repression

What is the relevance of all this to what happened in China in spring 1989? Deng was defending his regime against many layers of problems—or so he would certainly see it. All those anciens régimes, with their unresolved issues, meant challenges on many fronts. The demonstrators, in this view, were unwitting Maoists, whom the authorities felt justified in describing as new Red Guards determined to take China into another Cultural Revolution, a line of argument Esherick and Wasserstrom discuss and critique in Chapter 2.[17] At the same time the frequent invocation of the danger of civil war drew its resonances not only from the Cultural Revolution but also from the warlord period. I have already mentioned the concern that the more radical Westernization ("bourgeois liberalization") allegedly espoused by the protesters would render China a "bourgeois republic subordinated to the West." The reference to the Nationalist regime is apparent.

The bedrock argument against liberalization of politics, or power-sharing, has remained China's backwardness—the persistence of "feudal society" in the late twentieth century. As a *People's Daily* writer said in July 1989:

> Our country's socialism . . . is still economically and culturally rather backward; history has bequeathed us very little democratic tradition; the influence of feudal thought is very profound; and many people have only a dim consciousness of democracy and legality; this sort of basic national condition has determined that the construction of a socialist democratic politics can only be a gradual process of step-by-step accumulation.[18]

His conclusion, citing Deng Xiaoping: Elections that included the whole population would produce chaos and civil war. One might paraphrase by saying that the 1989 protest movement had to be resisted because the Qing was not yet all gone.

Would it be going too far to say that Deng and his fellow gerontocrats felt embattled in part because of the confusing but reinforcing multiplicity of threats that the protests seemed to pose? Of course all these points were serving rhetorical needs and immediate purposes. Nonetheless, one still has to account for the rhetorical choices being made, and these kinds of choices provide clues to important thought processes.

In any case, this view of the world was certainly confusing, as became clear during the initial attempts the regime's defenders made to mount a persuasive propaganda campaign that would explain what had happened. How was it that in some people's minds "bourgeois liberalization" had supplanted the "four cardinal principles" (in brief, socialist ideology and party rule)? According to an early apologist named Lu Zhichao, in its keenness to refute leftism (that is, in reforming the Maoist ancien régime), the Chinese government overdid it and aroused doubts about socialism itself. Further, in the regime's drive to expand the economy (that is, overcoming the backwardness inherited from "feudal society"), it created and even rewarded interests contradictory to socialism. By opening China up to extensive contact with the outside world, Deng encouraged the comparison of China with advanced countries, so that the forty-year history of the PRC came to be seen by some as a total failure. The administration needed instead to spread awareness of the Chinese past (back to the Qing and other anciens régimes) and an accompanying sense of historical progress.[19]

Subsequent apologists for the regime have tried to clarify the issues. As Wasserstrom details in the Afterword, the authorities have sponsored a variety of collections of essays and documents that try to justify and explain the repression of 1989. In these works, authors set out to explain such things as what exactly the term *bourgeois liberalization* means, how precisely the West planned to turn China into a dependent state, and so forth. Nonetheless, these books do not resolve the questions that Lu's article raises. The reader is still left wanting to ask the Dengist ideologues which ancien régime creates the real problem and how exactly so many kinds of vestiges of the past have remained alive. They say that Maoism was a product of contamination from the old "feudal society" and thus impeded progress away from feudalism. Yet they also hold that Mao was criticized too much, so that people underestimated the progress that China has actually made from feudalism. When explaining why China should not liberalize politically, they say that the population is not ready. China is too backward for democracy, which would only bring breakdown. When explaining why liberal ideas have spread and produced a movement, they say that China's great strides under socialism—including with Mao—have not been sufficiently credited.

Protesters and the Anciens Régimes

The students and intellectuals involved in the 1989 protests, though they arrived at some different conclusions, shared in this discourse. Their beliefs regarding certain things—for example, the speed with which China should work to reform its political system—were undeniably quite different from those of the authorities they challenged. Nonetheless, the protesters shared many of the same assumptions and often invoked the same kinds of symbols as those whose power they sought to undermine. Feigon's exploration of gender (Chapter 8) and Perry's discussion of social elitism within the move-ment (Chapter 7) illustrate this point. So too does a closer look at the way protesters conceived of the anciens régimes that stood in the way of true revolutionary change. Like the Deng regime, dissenting students and intellec-tuals saw China plagued by multiple vestiges of the past, and (as with the authorities) their rhetorical stances may be interpreted in light of this vision of overlapping anciens régimes.

Just as Deng's side castigated the protesters for exposing China to the dangers of revived Maoism, the protesters accused Deng of "errors of a gravity no less than [those committed in] the 'Cultural Revolution.' "[20] In their "May 16th Declaration" in support of the protests, a group of leading dissident intellectuals also invoked the specter of the "ten bad years" and warned the authorities that to suppress the demonstrations would be to repeat one of the mistakes of the infamous Gang of Four.[21] Two months later, Yan Jiaqi, a leading dissident who had emerged from within Deng's reform movement and one of the signers of the declaration, called the crackdown of early June "far more cruel than the Cultural Revolution."[22] Despite the displays of Mao icons by some marchers—the meanings of which Esherick and Wasserstrom treat in the next chapter—protesters' references to the Maoist legacy usually had the same negative overtones as did the Dengist interpretation.

Although one cannot attribute to the protesters anything close to a unitary view, the prominence of the idea of a continuing influence from "feudal society" also stands out. The ancien régime of the Qing, in other words, was highly visible in the protesters' pronouncements, both rhetorically and analytically. Deng Xiaoping was likened to the Empress Dowager Cixi, "directing government from behind a screen."[23] The image of a monarchical Deng regime occurred frequently, one observer noting that "it has been 76 years since the demise of the Qing government. But China still has an emperor without a crown on his head. He is an old and muddleheaded dictator."[24] One finds the same assertions about the CCP's having been imbued with peasant feudalism, as an explanation not just of Maoism but also of Deng's autocracy.[25] The whole issue of China's achievements was stated most poignantly in a Beijing University poster of early May: "A century has gone by since the Reform Movement of 1898, and it seems we are still stuck at the starting line, trying to change our old ways and make our country strong."[26]

Surprisingly, the similarities between the Dengist analysis and that of the protesters concerning the continuing relevance of the Qing extend to an uncertainty about how to evaluate China's progress out of feudal society and the consequences for democracy. Early in the movement, one poster compared the government's excuse for not implementing democracy—that is, the people's backwardness—with Chiang Kaishek's rationale for political tutelage. Was it possible that the PRC had not improved on the Nanjing regime? Or, as the question was phrased on another poster, "How can it be that forty years of Communist rule have produced a citizenship that is not even fit for a democratic society?" We have observed the contortions of Deng apologists in dealing with this point. In this case, the poster-writer makes his or her own U-turn and accepts the idea that most Chinese could not properly adjust to democracy. The prescription is that only city folk, intellectuals, and Communist Party members should enjoy democratic privileges for the moment.[27] The young student leader Wuer Kaixi made a parallel point after the June events: that in an evolution toward democracy, peasants would not play a decisive role.[28]

I sense throughout the movement's wall posters, manifestos, and statements a searching on the part of the protesters for the relevant ancien régime. Was China's problem residual Maoism in the Deng order? Or in some curious way (implied by the Mao placards and in references to the relative purity and commitment of Mao and his era) was it not enough Maoism?[29] Was it the persistence or revival of a KMT legacy of official corruption? Was it a continuing feudalism in the Party? Or was the issue that defined the ancien régime for the protesters really the Deng reforms themselves (the matters of inflation and vice would be elements of analysis here)?[30] When students compared their protests to the May Fourth Movement of 1919 (an event Israel and Schwarcz treat in detail in Chapter 4 and Chapter 5, respectively), was their main point that the "feudal" modes of thought against which intellectuals of seventy years before had railed were still alive and well in the PRC? Was it that CCP officials were modern-day equivalents of the repressive warlords who had ruled China in 1919?[31] There is no reason that there should be a clear choice among these possibilities. Because both the warlord and Nanjing regimes had suppressed popular movements in their day, for example, there is no reason why the authors of the May 16th Declaration cited above should not have reminded their audience that the actions of these former rulers as well as those of the Gang of Four had been "recorded in China's history as pages of shame."[32] Nonetheless, further attempts to figure out how much emphasis protesters put on the unresolved problems left over from particular anciens régimes would be useful, as they could provide us with clues about the direction and possible future courses of the movement.

Democratic Impulses and Authoritarian Solutions: An Enduring Theme

In his studies of the idea of democracy in twentieth-century China, Andrew Nathan has tied the preference for authoritarian solutions to the perception of China as backward.[33] Successive generations of reformers and revolutionaries have drawn back at the edge of political democracy, as they calculated the risk of social disorder in any precipitate institutionalization of popular control of government. Liang Qichao, an early advocate of parliamentary government for China, became convinced in the first years of the century that the Chinese were not ready and must be prepared during an era of "enlightened despotism."[34] Even the optimistic Sun Yatsen endorsed a program of stages by which representative government would be introduced after a successful revolution—the early, predemocratic portions of which turned out to be almost indefinitely extendable, in the actual practice of KMT rule. In the 1980s, from Zhao Ziyang's circle emerged the notion of the "new authoritarianism" so reminiscent of Liang Qichao's conception.[35] The repetition of schemes to postpone democracy have been accompanied by repetition of the concerns about the unreadiness of the population. The image of the Chinese people as a sheet of loose sand—unable on their own responsibility to form a coherent citizenry—was shared by Yuan Shikai, Sun Yatsen, and Deng Xiaoping. Each believed that China would not easily entertain democratic politics.

Mao Zedong was among those who often dissented from the common view of the political backwardness of the Chinese majority. "The masses are more progressive than we are."[36] The implications that he drew for politics, however, were hardly liberal. Then intellectuals of the 1980s closed the circle by attributing Mao's illiberalism to the backwardness of the peasantry.[37]

My argument is broadly congruent with Nathan's analysis. My focus on the multiplicity of anciens régimes would lead me to add that by 1989 one is dealing not only with the persistence of an attitude or with the consequences of an at best slowly changing Chinese political culture but also with a cumulative effect. Every generation's repetition of the rationale for postponing democracy produces a changing meaning as well. Each round of authoritarianism produces a new image of what the consequences of backwardness are, of what the problems are for any reformer who would break fully out of China's "feudal" inheritance.

Could the reformer Deng Xiaoping be also the cruel tyrant of June 4, 1989, because of the multitude of ghosts that China's modern history has conjured up? Deng was faced with the uncompleted tasks of each previous reform and revolutionary movement. Their failures were examples of paths that should not be taken. And yet the protests were seen as pushing the regime to repeat old errors. As a challenge to Deng's authority, the movement was cast as an agent, no matter how unwitting, of revived Maoism, the foreign dependency of the KMT, the chaos of warlordism. It wished, in Deng's view, to force a precipitate jump into democracy, which threatened to release the large "feudal" residuum in the Chinese population. Faced with too confusing an array of anciens régimes, Deng ferociously defended the status quo. But there cannot be reform without forward motion. "Authoritarian modernization," what Paul Cohen describes as China's reformist mainstream, is in crisis.

Notes

1. Paul Cohen, "The Post-Mao Reforms in Historical Perspective," *Journal of Asian Studies*, 47, 3 (1988), pp. 518–540, esp. 533.

2. Ibid., p. 535.

3. Ibid., pp. 536–537.

4. William Doyle, *The Ancien Regime* (New York: Humanities Press, 1986); and "Presentation," in Colin Lucas, ed., *The French Revolution and the Creation of Modern Political Culture*, vol. 2, *The Political Culture of the French Revolution* (New York: Pergamon, 1988), pp. 3–9, quote taken from p. 6.

5. Diego Venturino, "La naissance de l'Ancien Régime," in Lucas, *Political Culture of the French Revolution*, pp. 11–40.

6. Venturino, "La naissance," pp. 18, 26–27.

7. Han Minzhu, ed., *Cries for Democracy* (Princeton: Princeton University Press, 1990), p. 153.

8. For example, a post-June 4 *People's Daily* article contained the following statements: "The building of socialism in China has taken no more than 40 years" and "China has been victoriously advancing along the socialist course for 40 years." Lu Zhichao, "Lun sixiang jiben yuanze yu zichan jieji ziyouhua" (On the opposition between the four cardinal principles and bourgeois liberalization), *Renmin ribao* (People's daily), November 1, 1989, pp. 1 and 8. The late 1989 formula held that China was fully socialist, not just at a preliminary stage. Only the level of prosperity was still elementary, and even that was not so low either.

9. The theme of marked changes in policy and power balances among the leadership in these years appears in Lowell Dittmer, "Mao Zedong and the Dilemma of Revolutionary Gerontocracy," in Angus McIntyre, ed., *Aging and Political Leadership* (Albany:

SUNY Press, 1988), pp. 151–180; and Frederick C. Teiwes, "Mao and His Lieutenants," *Australian Journal of Chinese Affairs*, vol. 19-20 (1988), pp. 1–80.

10. Han, *Cries*, p. 164.

11. The original version of this famous June 9 speech has been reprinted, in complete or excerpted form, to serve as the first document or preface for many official texts dealing with 1989. See, for example, Sichuan ribao bianchuan bu (Sichuan News Editorial Department), eds., *Xuechao, dongluan, baoluan* (Student storm, turmoil, revolt) (Chengdu: Sichuan People's Press, 1989), pp. 1–6; and Zhonggong Zhongyang Xuanchuanbu (CCP Central Propaganda Department), eds., *Jianyue yonghu dangzhongyang juece pingxi fangeming baoluan* (Firmly support the central government's decision to put down the counterrevolutionary upheaval) (Beijing: People's Press, 1989), pp. 1–2. An English-language version appeared in *Beijing Review*, July 10–16, 1989, pp. 18–21; this is reprinted with some explanatory notes, in Cheng Chu-yuan, *Behind the Tiananmen Massacre* (Boulder: Westview, 1990), pp. 226–230.

12. A translation of the full text of Chen's "Report" appears in Yi Mu and Mark Thompson, *Crisis at Tiananmen* (San Francisco: China Books, 1989), pp. 194–233, see esp. pp. 195 and 223.

13. Helmut Martin, *Cult and Canon: The Origins and Development of State Maoism* (Armonk, N.Y.: M. E. Sharpe, 1982), pp. 205–207.

14. Li Rui, "Study of Mao Zedong Thought Examined," *Renmin ribao*, March 28, 1988, p. 5.

15. Ibid.

16. One student wall poster charged that 75 percent of Party members had no more than an elementary school education; Han, *Cries*, p. 43. Apparently the poster-writer felt no need to explain why this fact was a criticism of the Party. Fox Butterfield conveys this outlook by describing an urbanite's resentment at the power over his career of a cadre of rural background; see his *China: Alive in the Bitter Sea* (New York: Times Books, 1982), pp. 286–287.

17. Along with the sources Esherick and Wasserstrom cite, see the comments attributed to Li Peng and Deng Xiaoping in Mu Wang, "The Actual Facts About the Power Struggle Within the Highest Leadership Stratum of Zhongnanhai," *Jing bao*, June 12, 1989, translated in Foreign Broadcast Information Service: China (hereafter, FBIS-CHI), 89-110, pp. 22–32; and Chen Fangen, "Deng Xiaoping's Instructions on Beijing Incident," *Guang jiao jing*, April 16, 1990, translated in FBIS-CHI-90-076, pp. 7–9.

18. Zhang Lin, "What Kind of Democracy Do We Need?" *Renmin ribao*, July 21, 1989, p. 6.

19. Lu, "On Conflict Between the Four Cardinal Principles and Bourgeois Liberalism," pp. 18–24.

20. Han, *Cries*, pp. 53 and 352.

21. The declaration is translated in Yi and Thompson, *Crisis*, pp. 163–166.

22. Wuer Kaixi and Yan Jiaqi, "Deng Will Have Thousands of People Killed," *Der Spiegel*, July 10, 1989, translated in FBIS-CHI-89-131, pp. 25–28.

23. Han, *Cries*, pp. 141–142.

24. Yan Jiaqi et al., "May 17th Declaration," *Ming bao*, May 18, 1989, translated in FBIS-CHI-89-095, pp. 47–48, and Yi and Thompson, *Crisis*, pp. 166–167.

25. Han, *Cries*, pp. 136 and 285.

26. Ibid., p. 170.

27. Ibid., pp. 33–35.

28. Wuer Kaixi and Yan Jiaqi, "Deng," p. 27.

29. See Michael Weisskopf, "Nostalgia for Mao Signals Discontent Among Chinese," *Washington Post*, July 22, 1989, p. A14, and the discussion in Chapter 2 of this book.

30. An important discussion of the role of the reforms as a contributing factor to the protests is Huang Yasheng, "The Origins of the Pro-Democracy Movement: A Tale of Two Reforms," *Fletcher Forum of World Affairs*, 14, 1 (1990), pp. 30–39.

31. Student attempts to present themselves as inheritors of the May Fourth legacy are discussed at length in Wasserstrom's Afterword.

32. Yi and Thompson, *Crisis*, p. 164.

33. Andrew Nathan, *Chinese Democracy* (Berkeley: University of California Press, 1985); and Nathan, *China's Crisis: Dilemmas of Reform and the Prospects for Democracy* (New York: Columbia University Press, 1990).

34. Nathan, like others writing about Liang Qichao, makes much of Liang's critical evaluation in 1903 of the cultural and political level of overseas Chinese, even in the free environment afforded them in the United States, and of Liang's inference that Chinese generally needed authoritarian rule. See, for example, *Chinese Democracy*, p. 60. Kenneth Scott Wong argues in a recent unpublished paper, "Liang Qichao and the Chinese of America: A Re-evaluation of His 1903 Travels in the New World," that there were a variety of inconsistencies, errors, and omissions in Liang's discussion of Chinese in the United States. Wong raises the question whether Liang fashioned his remarks on overseas Chinese to suit an argument that had its origins in other concerns.

35. For a critical discussion of this concept and its prominence in 1989, see Anita Chan and Jonathan Unger, "China After Tiananmen: It's a Whole New Class Struggle," *Nation*, January 22, 1990, pp. 79–81.

36. When citing this remark, which sums up a major theme in Mao's thinking, Nathan states that this side to Mao "spawned the democratic challenge" of the late 1970s. But he goes on to say that other and more profound sides to Mao—and to the Chinese tradition—fed into the suppression of that movement. *Chinese Democracy*, pp. 74 and 101.

37. Nathan puts it this way: "The consensus [among writers in all fields in the 1980s] has been that the cultural revolution was made possible by the peasant mentality of utopianism, egalitarianism, and authoritarianism shared by both Mao and the Chinese people." *China's Crisis*, p. 125. Similarly, in a study of Party analyses in the first years of the Deng era regarding the origins of Mao's personal dictatorship, Lawrence Sullivan finds a key element in these official explanations to be "the population's cultural and ideological backwardness"—including superstitious beliefs and a "peasant mentality." "The Analysis of 'Despotism' in the CCP, 1978–1982," *Asian Survey*, 27, 7 (1987), pp. 800–821.

2

ACTING OUT DEMOCRACY:
POLITICAL THEATER
IN MODERN CHINA

Joseph W. Esherick and Jeffrey N. Wasserstrom

For two and a half months in spring 1989, China's student actors dominated the world stage of modern telecommunications. Their massive demonstrations, the hunger strike during Mikhail Gorbachev's visit, and the dramatic appearance of the statue of the goddess of democracy captured the attention of an audience that spanned the globe. When we began work on this essay early in 1990, the movement and its bloody suppression had already produced an enormous body of literature—from eyewitness accounts by journalists and special issues of scholarly journals to pictorial histories and documentary collections—tracing the development of China's crisis. This flood of material,

This piece first appeared in the *Journal of Asian Studies*, 49, 4 (1990), pp. 835–865; it is reprinted here with the permission of the Association for Asian Studies. As befits an essay that continually crosses disciplinary lines between history and anthropology, this chapter is based upon firsthand observation as well as written and pictorial sources. Joseph Esherick was in Xian, Jinan, and northern Shaanxi in spring 1989, and Jeffrey Wasserstrom was in Shanghai during the protests of December 1986. Where no additional citation is given, information on these times and places comes from personal observation or discussion with participants.

The authors would like to thank the following people for sharing thoughts, criticisms, recollections, and unpublished papers: Jeffrey Cody, Dru Gladney, James Hevia, David Jordan, Barry Naughton, Michel Oksenberg, Elizabeth Perry, Frank Pieke, Henry Rosemont, Jr., Clark Sorenson, Frederic Wakeman, Jr., and two anonymous readers. Audiences at the University of Washington, the University of California, San Diego, and the University of Oregon provided helpful comments on an earlier version of this chapter. Grants from the Committee on Scholarly Communication with the PRC and Fulbright-Hayes supported the authors' research in China; grants from the University of Kentucky and the National Academy of Education made the writing and revising of this chapter possible.

which now includes important analytical works and textbook chapters as well, has continued during the past twelve months, but the problem that originally inspired us to write this essay remains.[1] As valuable as much of the available scholarship is—and some of it (including the other chapters in this volume) is valuable indeed—we still lack a convincing general framework that places the Chinese events within the context of China's modern political evolution and also provides a way to compare China's experience to that of Eastern Europe. Such an interpretation should help us understand why massive public demonstrations spurred the evolution toward democratic governance in Eastern Europe (a process Daniel Chirot traces in Chapter 11), but led only to the massacre of June 3–4 and the present era of political repression in China.

None of the most frequently mentioned characterizations of the movement seems truly adequate. For example, in the Chinese leadership's attempts to link the protesters with one or another of the anciens régimes, as Ernest Young delineates in the previous chapter, it has portrayed both the 1989 movement and its predecessor of 1986–1987 as manifestations of "bourgeois liberalism" or as acts of *luan* (chaos) reminiscent of the Red Guards in the Cultural Revolution or as some combination of the two. But if the 1989 protests were the result of "bourgeois" contamination, why was the most prominent anthem of the demonstrators *The Internationale,* and why did some students and workers carry pictures of early leaders of the CCP?

Official characterizations of recent protests as acts of *luan* are also unsatisfying to say the least. Protesters unquestionably committed disorderly acts in both 1986 and 1989. Nonetheless, most foreign observers were impressed by the discipline and orderliness of the students.[2] The prominence of march monitors, the security forces that maintained order in Tiananmen Square, the student "arrest" of youths for defacing a portrait of Mao—these activities hardly suggest an atmosphere of *luan.*

Depictions of the protesters of the late 1980s as contemporary Red Guards or remnant supporters of the Gang of Four are even more seriously flawed, as discussions by Young (Chapter 1) and Israel (Chapter 4) illustrate. There were certainly continuities between the 1960s and the 1980s in terms of protest tactics and symbols (e.g., the insistence upon free passage to Beijing, the pasting up of posters, the use of portraits of Mao in marches). This is hardly surprising because some of the young teachers who advised the students of 1986 and 1989 were former Red Guards, as were several leading dissident figures such as Su Xiaokang (whose work and influence Watson discusses briefly at the close of Chapter 3). Nevertheless, the complete lack of anti-Western rhetoric or devotional loyalty to any living CCP leader by the students of the late 1980s makes analogies with the Red Guards extremely tenuous, as do the generally negative references to the Cultural Revolution in protesters' posters.[3] Even some of the tactical and symbolic continuities between the late 1960s and the late 1980s noted above are more ambiguous than they at first appear. The Mao portraits carried by demonstrators in 1989 are a case in point. They may have reminded some onlookers of the Red Guards, but various kinds of evidence suggest that the main Mao being honored in 1989 was not the demigod of the Cultural Revolution but the selfless hero of the pre-1949 years and the early days of the PRC. This was certainly the implication of comments heard on the streets, which favorably contrasted Mao's behavior toward his own children during the 1950s with the nepotistic tendencies of contemporary leaders.[4] Because some of the protesters of 1989 carried posters of Zhou Enlai (who is revered in part for his opposition to the Gang of Four) whereas others carried posters that showed Mao flanked by his erstwhile second in command, Liu Shaoqi (who became the chief target of Red Guard fury), portrayals of the recent demonstrations as a revival of Cultural Revolution extremism seem still more unconvincing.[5]

The analyses offered by Western social scientists, foreign journalists, and Chinese dissidents, though considerably more persuasive than the official CCP line, are also problematic. Many, especially the professional Peking-ologists of political science, stress the role that power struggles between Li Peng and Zhao Ziyang played in shaping the 1989 events.[6] There is no doubt that internal divisions paralyzed the party leadership in April and May, preventing an effective response to the demonstrators. But at the start of the movement, one of the protesters' most common abusive rhymes in Beijing and Tianjin was "Ziyang, Ziyang, xinge buliang" (Zhao Ziyang, Zhao Ziyang, you are not a good man) and as late as May 19 (long after the Voice of America and BBC broadcasts had been focusing on the Li-Zhao conflict) the protesters' posters and slogans in Xian still had two central targets: Deng Xiaoping and Zhao Ziyang. Corruption in Zhao's immediate family made him so unpopular that it is impossible to see him successfully manipulating the movement for his own ends. Indeed, like Hu Yaobang before him, Zhao Ziyang became a hero only after (and to a large degree because) he was ousted from power by the alliance of hard-liners and party elders around Deng.

The Western press and Chinese dissidents abroad usually characterize the events of China's spring as a "democracy movement." There is no question that *minzhu* was frequently invoked in the protesters' banners and slogans, but it would be hasty to associate *minzhu* (literally, rule of the people) with any conventional Western notion of democracy. Consider, for example, Wuer Kaixi's words in the televised dialogue with Li Peng on May 18. Early in the meeting, Wuer Kaixi explained what it would take to get students to leave Tiananmen Square: "If one fasting classmate refuses to leave the square, the other thousands of fasting students on the square will not leave." He was explicit about the principle behind this decision: "On the square, it is not a matter of the minority obeying the majority, but of 99.9 per cent obeying 0.1 per cent."[7] This may have been good politics—and Wuer Kaixi certainly made powerful theater—but it was not democracy.

The hunger-striking students in Tiananmen Square had adopted a position designed to preserve their unity and enhance their leverage with the government. But in elevating the principle of unity above that of majority rule, they were acting within the tradition of popular rule (*minzhu*) thinking in modern China. When Sun Yatsen assumed the presidency of the Republic of China in January 1912, his message to the revolutionary paper *Minlibao* was a simple slogan (in English): "'Unity' is our watchword"[8]—not "democracy" or "republicanism," but "unity." Closer to the present, the dissident magazine *Enlightenment* wrote in 1979 of the miraculous effects that the "fire" of democracy would have on the Chinese people:

> The fire will enable people completely to shake off brutality and hatred, and there will be no quarrel among them. They will share the same views and principles and have identical ideals. In lofty and harmonious unity they will produce, live, think, pioneer, and explore together. With these dynamic forces they will enrich their social life and cultivate their big earth.[9]

Although Western democratic notions are normally linked to pluralism and the free competition of divergent ideas, *minzhu* in China is here linked to a vision in which people will "share the same views" and have "identical ideals." It is thus difficult to analyze the events of China's 1989 spring as a "democratic movement" in the pluralist sense of the term.[10]

Nor do the words and deeds of the protesters of 1986–1987 or 1989 fit easily with more radical Western ideas of direct or participatory democracy. In many cases the students seem to have read the *min* in *minzhu* in a limited sense to refer not to the populace at large but mainly or exclusively to the educated elite of which they are part. This elitist reading of *minzhu* was clear in the wall posters that appeared in Shanghai in December 1986, many of which took their lead from the speeches Fang Lizhi gave at the city's Tongji University earlier that year. The main theme of these posters, as in many of Fang's lectures and writings, was not that the CCP should be more responsive to the ideas of China's masses but rather that it should allow the intelligentsia a greater voice in national affairs.[11] This elitist strain carried over into student tactics in 1986: At one point, when Shanghai workers came out to support their protesting "younger brothers," the students told them to go home.

The situation in 1989 was somewhat different, for at times students actively sought (and received) the support of groups not connected to the intelligentsia. Nonetheless, as Chapters 7 and 8 stress, some educated youths and older intellectuals continued to see democratic reforms in elitist, inegalitarian terms. For example, two foreign observers found Fujian students deeply disturbed by the suggestion that general elections would have to include the participation of the peasantry.[12] Other reports highlight student distrust of the *laobaixing*, or untutored masses (a distrust symbolized by the groups of students who roped themselves off from bystanders during some marches); the intelligentsia's lack of concern for the needs of workers and peasants; and the appeal that ideas associated with the "new authoritarianism" had within protest circles in 1989.[13] Western critics and Chinese dissidents alike have also taken leaders of the movement to task for behaving in nondemocratic and elitist ways, both at the time of the occupation of Tiananmen Square and during the formation of new protest leagues in exile.[14]

The preceding comments do not mean that there was nothing "democratic" about the movement. Clearly, there was a great deal about the protests—the calls for freedom of speech, the demands for popular input into the way China is governed—that Westerners associate with the term "democracy." We do not wish to imply that Chinese are somehow incapable of understanding or acting upon Western concepts of democracy. Nor do we wish to imply that a Chinese movement must meet a stringent set of contemporary Western standards to earn the accolade "democracy movement." After all, as Donald Price has observed, we consider many Western states to have been "democratic" long before they reached the stage of universal suffrage.[15] The point we do wish to stress is simply that, given the various contours of meaning the term *minzhu* had in 1989, labeling the protests a "democracy movement" does not take us very far in our efforts to make sense of them. In some cases, in fact, it obfuscates more than it clarifies.

China's Spring as Political Theater

It would seem that a more productive way to understand the events of April–June 1989 is to view them as an exercise in political theater. Scholars as diverse as E. P. Thompson and Clifford Geertz, working on political systems as dissimilar as eighteenth-century England and nineteenth-century Bali, have demonstrated the value of interpreting politics in theatrical terms, that is, as symbol-laden performances whose efficacy lies largely in their power to move specific audiences.[16] This approach would seem ideally suited for analysis of the Chinese protests of 1989. As essentially nonviolent demonstrations that posed no direct physical or economic threat to China's rulers, the protests derived their power almost exclusively from their potency as performances that could symbolically undermine the regime's legitimacy and move members of larger and economically more vital classes to action.

A number of the more insightful analysts of the Chinese protests of 1989 have already highlighted the importance of symbolism and role-playing. Frank Pieke has analyzed the "ritualized" quality of protest actions in one essay and has highlighted the significance of audience participation in the Chinese marches in another piece. Perry Link has compared the petitioning at Tiananmen Square to "morally charged Beijing opera." In a related vein, Dru Gladney and Lucian Pye have interpreted the symbolic implications of a variety of student actions and texts, and David Strand has used theatrical metaphors to capture the mood and explain the impact of student demonstrations in Beijing since 1919.[17] Our goal is to expand upon these themes and to place the events of 1989 in a larger historical and theoretical context. In particular, it seems important to examine the relationship between political theater and ritual—a more tightly prescribed form of cultural performance that was so vital to the governance of imperial China.

What, then, was the political theater of 1989? First, it was street theater: untitled, improvisational, with constantly changing casts. Though fluid in form, it nevertheless followed what Charles Tilly calls a historically established "repertoire" of collective action.[18] This means that even when they improvised, protesters worked from familiar "scripts" that gave them a shared sense of how to behave during a given action, when and where to march, how to express their demands, and so forth. Some of these scripts originated in the distant past, emerging out of traditions of remonstrance and petition stretching back for millennia. More were derived (consciously or unconsciously) from the steady stream of student-led mass movements that have taken place since 1919 (discussed in more detail in Chapter 4). Thus, for example, in 1989 when youths carrying banners emblazoned with the names of their alma maters paraded from school to school and called on students at other institutions to join their fight to *jiuguo* (save the nation), they were following closely in the footsteps of participants of the May Fourth Movement and other protesters of the Republican era (1911–1949).[19]

State rituals and official ceremonies supplied other potential scripts. The April 22 funeral march in memory of Hu Yaobang was a classic example of students usurping a state ritual, improvising upon an official script to make it serve subversive ends.[20] Chinese funerals (especially those of wealthy or politically important figures) have always been key moments for public ritual.[21] As newspaper accounts of early twentieth-century funeral processions show, these ceremonies were an important opportunity for elite families to display their status, with musicians and hired mourners joining family and friends, carefully ordered by age, gender, and social status, in a symbolic representation of the proper social order.[22] In the People's Republic, memorial services for important political leaders are a critical political moment, and the composition of funeral committees is carefully scrutinized for clues to changing political alignments.[23] Here is a political ritual with all the liminality that Victor Turner's conception requires: transitional between two preferably stable political states and thus highly dangerous.[24]

The particular danger in the case of political funerals arises from the possibility that unauthorized people will usurp the ritual and rewrite the script into political theater of their own. The most famous previous example of this was in fact not quite a funeral but the Qingming remembrance that followed soon after the death of Zhou Enlai in 1976. It produced the first "Tiananmen incident," in which thousands of Beijing residents used the opportunity to pay their respects to Zhou and in the process level a wide variety of direct and indirect attacks on the Gang of Four.[25] Critical to the nature of such ceremonies is that the authorities cannot prohibit them: They are politically required rituals of respect for revolutionary heroes. But when students usurp the ritual, they can turn it into political theater. Thus the funeral march becomes a demonstration. Though they march behind memorial wreaths to the deceased and carry their official school banners, they also chant slogans and hoist signs with their own political messages.

Marches of this sort inevitably lead to the central square of the city. That square normally faces the seat of government authority, which is also likely to be the venue for an official memorial service. At this point, the demonstration becomes a petition movement. The most dramatic was the petition of 1989 presented by three students kneeling on the steps of the Great Hall of the People. The symbolism of this petition was important, for it demanded an explanation of the background to Hu Yaobang's resignation as general secretary of the Party in 1987. This demand focused attention on the fact that the party leaders who were orchestrating the official ceremonies inside the Great Hall were precisely the same men who had removed Hu Yaobang from power. Thus, the street theater unmasked the hypocrisy of the official ritual and revealed the students on the streets to be the true heirs to the legacy of Hu Yaobang. In the end, the officially required ritual becomes the mechanism for attacking the authorities.[26]

Once the public stage has been captured, the street actors are all the more free to write their own script. In Beijing they proved extraordinarily creative, successfully upstaging two more state rituals: On the seventieth anniversary of the May Fourth Movement, the party's formal commemorations paled before the students' protest marches; and later that month the welcoming rally students held for Gorbachev—complete with signs bearing slogans in Russian and Chinese—stole the thunder from the official ceremonies of the summit. One reason for the success of these protests, and for the relative weakness of the official rituals they mocked, came from their respective settings. Throughout much of May, students were in full control of Beijing's symbolic center, Tiananmen Square. The government was forced to hold its gatherings in less public and less powerful venues—the Great Hall of the People on May 4, the airport to welcome Gorbachev.

The group hunger strike launched in Beijing in mid-May, which was replicated in several other cities within days, was another stroke of creative genius. As Watson notes in Chapter 3, although dissident officials in imperial times sometimes refused food to show their displeasure with a ruler and protesters of the Republican era and Cultural Revolution period occasionally used hunger strikes as a tactic, this kind of group fast was not a central element of the Chinese student protest repertoire until the influential one performed in Hunan in 1980. Its use in 1989, by students who compared their strike to those of dissidents in other nations, showed how internationalized models for dissent had become.[27]

The placement of the statue of the goddess of democracy in Tiananmen Square—directly between two sacred symbols of the Communist regime, a giant portrait of Mao and the Monument to the People's Heroes—was another powerful piece of theater. Though Western journalists often treated this twenty-eight-foot icon as a simple copy of the Statue of Liberty and the Chinese government insisted that this was so, the goddess was in reality a more complex symbol combining Western and Chinese motifs, some employed reverently, some ironically. Some features of the goddess did resemble the Statue of Liberty (an exact replica of which was carried through Shanghai in mid-May), but others called to mind traditional boddhisattva and even socialist-realist sculptures of revolutionary heroes found in Tiananmen Square. It was also reminiscent of the giant white statues of Mao that were carried through the square during National Day parades of the 1960s. A potent pastiche of imported and native symbolism, the goddess statue appeared on the square just as the movement was flagging, bringing new crowds of supporters and onlookers to the area.[28]

Street theater of this sort is also dangerous, however, because it is impossible to control the cast. As noted above, students tried at times to keep the *laobaixing* at arm's length, but this was not always possible, and in many cases organizers anxious to swell the number of protesters encouraged bystanders from all walks of life to join the crowd. Inevitably, this attracted members of the floating population of youths who had been in and out of trouble with the state apparatus. Mistreated by police or public security men in the past, many bore grudges they were anxious to settle. It appears that these young men were responsible for some of the violence that broke out as early as April 22 in Xian and Changsha and on June 3 in Beijing.

Once we recognize the movement as an instance of political theater, it becomes tempting to rate the performances. One of the best acts was put on by Wuer Kaixi in the dialogue with Li Peng. The costuming was important: He appeared in his hospital pajamas. He upstaged the premier by interrupting him at the very start. Later in the session, he dramatically pulled out a tube inserted through his nose (for oxygen?) in order to make a point. Especially for young people in the nationwide television audience, it was an extraordinarily powerful performance.

For older viewers, however, perhaps the most riveting act was performed by the Chinese Central Television (CCTV) news announcer Xue Fei as he read the official martial law announcement on May 20. Again, costuming was important: He wore all black, the suit rumored to have been borrowed for the occasion. And he read the announcement from beginning to end without ever lifting his eyes from the page, in a perfect imitation of the tone reserved for funeral eulogies. Xue Fei's performance was a scene witnessed, understood, and remembered by virtually every television viewer in the country.

In any performance, the audience is critical. In street theater, audience participation becomes part of the drama, and this was certainly true in Beijing and other cities in 1989.[29] First, citizens lined the parade route to applaud the student demonstrators. Then, there were banners announcing support and stands set up to provide food and drink. By the end, the nonstudent crowds had been fully drawn into the act, as the citizens of Beijing came out in force to block the army's entrance after the declaration of martial law.

Television provided a powerful new dimension to the movement's audience appeal. Most obviously, with the world press gathered for the Gorbachev visit, the demonstrators gained a global audience. That audience certainly helped dissuade the leadership from an early use of force against their critics. But the domestic television audience was at least as important. Through television, by mid-May Chinese across the country could directly witness the scale of the massive demonstrations in Beijing, and that knowledge emboldened the young people who launched their own protest marches in cities all across China. Furthermore, the Beijing demonstrators were keenly aware of the power of this new medium, as they showed through their demand for a live broadcast of their dialogue with the government. As a political mode, theater is only as powerful as the audience that it can move; and this theater certainly inspired and energized hundreds of millions of people in China and across the world.

As ritual and theater, the actions of the demonstrators naturally call forth certain responses from the authorities, and the efficacy of official performance is substantially dependent on how well they play these roles.[30] The party leadership's failure to acknowledge in any way the petition of the students kneeling on the steps of the Great Hall was a major violation of ritual, and it significantly increased public anger against official arrogance.[31] This is important because ritually correct responses to earlier student petitions—such as those submitted in 1918 (the year before the May Fourth Movement) and 1931 (when Japan invaded Manchuria) by youths angered at the way Chinese authorities were handling relations with Japan—had helped to defuse potentially volatile situations.[32]

The refusal to acknowledge the student petition in April was but the first of a series of unskillful official performances. When Li Peng was forced to join the televised dialogue with the student leaders, for example, he was clearly unsuited for his role and very uncomfortable in it—and predictably he played it very badly. Later, the visit of Li, Zhao Ziyang, and other party leaders to the hospitalized hunger strikers was another ritually required act of compassion, this one performed somewhat more adroitly. The loyalist rallies the Party organized in the suburbs of Beijing during the week before the massacre were remarkable, but far less effective, acts of official theater: Participants told Western journalists that officials had instructed them to take part, and televised coverage of the events showed a mixture of bored, unhappy, and embarrassed faces.[33] Even the tanks of June 4 can be seen as a kind of theater. One does not choose tanks for their efficacy in crowd control—this was a performance designed to show irresistible power.

For official theater, however, nothing was more important than the ritual *biaotai* that followed the movement's suppression. These public statements of one's position (and here the only permissible position was one in favor of the regime) began with provincial leaders, regional military commands, and functional ministries of the national government. Broadcast on the national news and reported in the press, they announced the speed with which the constituent parts of the state apparatus fell in behind the new central Party leadership. These *biaotai* of Party and military elites were followed by similar performances in schools, factories, research institutes, and administrative bodies across the nation as virtually every urban citizen was required to account for his or her actions since April and publicly announce solidarity with the new hard-line policies. Such rituals were a special form of performance (*biaoyan*). The participants were clearly *acting*—most were not sincere— and everyone knew it. They recited memorized scripts, with key phrases lifted from articles and editorials in the *People's Daily*. Because few believed the words they were uttering, most of the *biaotai* were bad theater. But the regime's unremittent insistence on their performance testifies to the importance of such theater in the Chinese political system.

It should be noted that politically sensitive members of the Chinese public recognize the practices described above as a form of theater. In their view, politics is a performance, and public political acts are often interpreted in that way. Thus, for example, a typical reaction to Li Peng's speech announcing martial law was to evaluate it as a performance, and the reviews were uniformly bad: Words were mispronounced, the tone was too shrill, and so on. As one Beijing intellectual put it: "He should have been wearing a patch of white above his nose"—the standard makeup of the buffoon in Beijing opera. Protesters at times presented Li as the clown or villain in propaganda presentations based on traditional theatrical forms. One Beijing street performance (transmitted to a large crowd by way of an improvised sound system), for instance, combined comic cross talk with operatic motifs to portray the attempts of a courtesan (representing Li Peng) to flatter, appease, and thereby gain the protection of an old man (representing Deng Xiaoping). The symbolism of the piece was clear to the crowd, who showed its appreciation for this mockery of China's two top leaders by laughing uproariously.[34]

Metaphors from the world of the theater are so much a part of the language of politics in modern China (as elsewhere) that protesters and observers continually adopted theatrical turns of speech. When protesters attacked Li Peng and Deng Xiaoping, the slogans they used included "Li Peng xiatai!" (Li Peng, get off the stage!) and "Xiaoping, Xiaoping, kuaixie xiatai" (Deng Xiaoping, Deng Xiaoping, hurry up and get off the stage).[35] Whenever previously little known actors play a major political role, there is discussion of who their *houtai* (backstage managers) might be. And after the Tiananmen incident, there was significant debate as to whether or not it should be termed a "tragedy."[36] But the sense in which the Chinese people see all this as performance was most powerfully suggested by a wise old peasant from northern Shaanxi who, when asked the difference between Mao Zedong and Deng Xiaoping, simply laughed and said, "They were just singing opposing operas [*chang duitai xi*]!"

Ritual and Theater

Our discussion to this point has used two terms to describe public political performances: "ritual" and "political theater." These terms, as we define them here, refer to two distinctive genres of action, though the line demarking the two is not always clear, as many acts include both ritualistic and theatrical elements.[37] Before exploring the gray area where the forms overlap, we must distinguish the two ideal types, because the differing degrees to which a polity depends upon and leaves legitimate space for one or the other genre of activity have profound implications for the nature of politics in that system. Thus, the ritual-infused politics of imperial China was qualitatively different from China's twentieth-century politics, with its distinctive political theater.

There are almost as many definitions of ritual as there are anthropologists. Defined most loosely, the term refers to virtually any "rule-governed" or "communicative" activity, in which case everything from strictly ordered coronations to highly improvisational demonstrations would qualify as political rituals.[38] We will use the term in a narrower sense here. Borrowing heavily from Clifford Geertz's work, we will define rituals as "traditionally prescribed cultural performances that serve as models *of* and models *for* what people believe."[39]

Such a definition conforms well with the Confucian sense of *li*, a term frequently translated as "ritual," the meaning of which Watson discusses in some detail and with considerable insight in his chapter on cultural identity. *Li* serves to support and reinforce the existing status quo, bringing order to a community, reaffirming the distinctions between and bonds connecting its individual members, and generally giving people a shared sense of how to behave correctly in a wide range of circumstances. Taking our lead from Confucius and his followers, we will highlight this system-maintenance function of ritual, a function also stressed by Emile Durkheim and his followers.[40]

We must also, however, take account of recent critics of the functionalist approach to rituals, which in the words of one writer treats the acts simply as "a sort of all-purpose social glue."[41] Again building upon the work of Geertz, we will highlight the symbolic nature of rituals as acts with hidden meanings that need to be decoded.[42] And following Victor Turner, we will stress the processual and dynamic nature of rituals.[43] According to Turner, though rituals serve to confirm existing hierarchical relations, these relationships are frequently suspended or temporarily overturned during the ritual *process*. This creates a volatile and potentially dangerous situation: There is always the chance that (as with Hu Yaobang's funeral) people will capitalize upon the instability or liminality of the process and subvert it to other ends.

To put Turner's point another way, there is always the chance that people will turn a ritual performance into an act of political theater. Central to the notion of ritual, in our sense of the word, is the idea that only careful adherence to a traditionally prescribed format will ensure the efficacy of the performance.[44] With any significant departure from a traditional script, any break with what Watson calls "orthopraxy," a ritual ceases to be ritual. Ritual thus gives relatively limited play to the creative powers of scriptwriters or actors, and as soon as participants break away from traditional structures, their actions become theatrical. Theater, by nature, is more liberated from the rigid constraints of tradition and provides autonomous space for the creativity of playwrights, directors, and actors. This gives theater a critical power never possessed by ritual: It can expose the follies of tradition (or the follies of abandoning tradition), mock social elites, or reveal the pain and suffering of everyday life.[45]

Although he is talking about *aesthetic* theater (the formal dramas of the stage), Turner makes additional distinctions between theater and ritual that are relevant to our more metaphorical use of the term.[46] One such distinction, particularly important in the Chinese context, has to do with role-playing and the audience. Role-playing is central to all ritual, and Chinese ritual is particularly concerned to fix each individual in his or her proper social role. Participation is by invitation only, each participant assigned a specified role. Rituals separate people into superior and inferior, elder and younger, male and female. In short, according to the *Li Ji* (Classic of ritual), "without [rituals] there would be no means of distinguishing the positions of ruler and subject, superior and inferior, old and young."[47] But paired with this role for ritual was another role that Confucians gave to music: Music unites. Thus the *Li Ji* notes that the *li* "make for difference and distinction," but "music makes for common union."[48] It does so because it creates an undifferentiated audience, and that is what theater does as well. As one leading dramatic theorist writes: "Theater comes into existence when a separation occurs between audience and performers."[49] The homogeneity of the audience should not be over-stressed because different members of the audience may identify with different characters or respond to different themes. But in general the relatively undif-ferentiated audience in theater (as opposed to the carefully stratified *partici-pants* in ritual) enjoy a shared experience and may be drawn toward a common identity. At the very least, the audience, in its anonymity, is freed to interpret the drama and identify with particular roles as it wishes. This is quite different from ritual, which, by involving all the "audience" forces each participant into a prescribed role, and a particular place in the sociopolitical structure.

Theater, then, is a cultural performance before a mass audience. *Political theater* is theater that expresses beliefs about the proper distribution and disposition of power (defined broadly, or in what Anagnost characterizes in Chapter 9 as a "Foucauldian" sense) and other scarce resources. Unlike political rituals, which in our limited definition always perform a hegemonic function of confirming power relations, political theater often challenges or subverts the authority (or in E. P. Thompson's phrase "twists the tail") of ruling elites.[50]

Although political theater can be (and often is) counterhegemonic, it is by no means always so. Groups within the ruling elite can use political theater to defend their position against attacks from below or to maximize their power vis-à-vis other elite groups. The rowdy London street parades by eighteenth-century supporters of the new Hanoverian regime, which were staged to offset Jacobin mockeries of George I; the gatherings held by U.S. political parties or civic groups to show support for presidential candidates or honor national holidays; and the patriotic mass rally German students organized for Otto Bismarck in 1895 to mark the Iron Chancellor's eightieth birthday—these are but a few examples of acts of political theater that uphold rather than challenge the hegemony of ruling institutions or elites.[51]

Having distinguished ritual from theater, we must now note what the two forms have in common. Perhaps the most fundamental similarity between them is that both ritual and theater are performed for social effect. Language and symbols are used not primarily to convey truths but to produce effects—on the participants or the audience or the gods. This is "pragmatic speech," whose function is to *move*, not to inform. One sees this most clearly in linguistics, in what J. L. Austin has called the "performative utterances" of ritual. In a marriage ceremony, the "I do" is not a report on one's mental act of acceptance; the words *in themselves* complete the act.[52] As such, it is not meaningful to debate the truth value of such utterances: All that counts is that uttering the words had the prescribed effect of completing the marriage ceremony. Similarly, in the Chinese ritual discourse, it would be quite inappropriate to take literally the polite refusal of a gift or the confession of unworthiness when offered a position.[53] These polite phrases are not spoken to express one's true intentions or feelings, and a literal reading of the words uttered in such cases would cause a complete misinterpretation of the ritual. It is the *symbolic effect* of the words, in the context of the total verbal and nonverbal *performance*, that really counts: The words and actions convey a posture of humility, of thanks, and of respect for the other party in the social transaction.[54]

These simple points are important for interpreting events in China, for we will understand the protesters' actions better if we focus on their symbolic meanings and intended effects than if we scrutinize their words in search of some coherent political program. The slogans, big-character posters, pamphlets, open letters, and speeches of the protesters were replete with emotive statements of commitment and dissent. They were proclamations of personal positions, moral statements of resolve. They announced the role a participant was committed to play in the emerging political drama; they rarely put forward an analysis of the failings of the Chinese political system, much less a concrete program for political change. But this was natural, for theirs was a performance designed to impress and move an audience, not an essay or lecture designed to inform.

To say this is certainly not to suggest that the movement was *merely* playacting. In the post-Reagan era, there are grave risks in writing of politics as performance. One can easily be misunderstood as suggesting that it is all fakery: artificial props, carefully staged events, all medium and no substantive message. That is not our intent. Our point is rather that it makes a good deal more sense to analyze performed actions and utterances not for their truth value but for their symbolic meaning. For example, on April 21 and again on April 27, many students at Beijing universities wrote out last testaments (*yiyan* or *yishu*). They proclaimed their willingness to die for democracy, freedom, their homeland; they said good-bye to their parents and begged their forgiveness and understanding.[55] It makes little sense to ask whether these students really knew what "freedom" and "democracy" meant, and still less sense to ask whether they were truly prepared to die for their beliefs. These last testaments were powerful public statements of great symbolic meaning. They revealed a fundamental alienation from the regime and a willingness to make great (perhaps even the ultimate) sacrifice for an alternative political future.

Ritual and theater have more in common than their involving symbolic action. There is also a great deal of borrowing of scripts between ritual and theatrical performances, in part because the roots of the two cultural forms are so closely intertwined. Most aesthetic theater grew originally out of ritual performance: Greek tragedy from the dithyramb sung around the alter of Dionysus, medieval European passion plays from the Catholic mass, acrobatics and magic acts from shamanistic practices.[56] The earliest forms of Chinese drama likewise had their roots in sacrificial rites.[57] The bond between Chinese opera and ritual performance is evident in everything from the use of Mulian plays in conjunction with funeral rites to the traditions of staging theatrical performances to entertain the gods.[58]

Political theater also borrows heavily from ritual scripts, though often inverting the meaning of these scripts. In sixteenth-century France, religious rioters frequently mocked their opponents' most sacred rites in acts of political theater: Protestant paraders would force a priest to burn his vestments; Catholics would parody Protestant prayers by transposing the words "devil" and "God."[59] Twentieth-century U.S. antiwar demonstrators have similarly found a variety of ways of turning ritual occasions into theatrical ones (by holding marches on holidays designed to honor the military) and ritual objects (flags, draft cards, army fatigues) into theatrical props.[60]

The transmission of texts between ritual and political theater is by no means always unidirectional: Some ritual performances have their roots in what Turner calls "social dramas."[61] This is not surprising, as one function of rituals is to heal wounds between groups by symbolically reenacting instances of social conflicts (ranging from wars and feuds to shouting matches and bitterly contested elections) and then concluding with a symbolic reintegration of the community.[62] Thus some rituals simultaneously commemorate and deradicalize subversive acts of political theater. Recent work on the French Revolution by scholars such as Mona Ozouf suggests that the Jacobins and others were interested in creating new festivals precisely in order to "represent radical aspirations, while at the same time curbing them."[63] As Lynn Hunt argues, French festivals of the decade after 1789, combining symbolic reenactments of attacks on the ancien régime with ritualized pledges of loyalty to the new order, both "recognized" and "partially defused" the revolutionary potential of the populace.[64]

The mutual borrowing of scripts between political theater and ritual gives the relationship between the forms what one theorist calls a "braided" quality: The two strands continually overlap and reemerge, alternately taking precedence over each other.[65] One of the best illustrations of how this kind of relationship works has direct relevance for understanding the events of 1989: the transformations of the May Fourth Movement from ritual to theater and back. When students took to the streets in 1919 to protest imperialist threats from abroad and warlord corruption at home, they established the classic script for student political theater. Subsequently, both the Kuomintang and the CCP have tried to use the political theater of the May Fourth Movement as the basis for new rituals of conciliation. Though the two parties have commemorated May Fourth differently, both have sought to turn the May Fourth anniversary into a safe revolutionary festival.[66] The script begins with a replay of the conflict of 1919, usually through speeches describing and praising the actions of former student protesters. The ritual then moves into a healing phase, in which official speakers emphasize that there is no longer a division between the interests of the nation's rulers and its youth because the present regime is carrying on in the May Fourth tradition. These speakers claim that the duty of contemporary students is to prove their patriotism by working hard to help the party build a new China rather than by protesting, and the members of the audience (often students) show their acceptance of this interpretation by clapping, shouting loyalist slogans, and singing loyalist songs.

These official attempts to "recognize" and "defuse" the revolutionary potential of students in this fashion have never been wholly successful, as educated youths have repeatedly managed to transform May Fourth rituals back into May Fourth theater. They have done this by emphasizing the reenactment aspect of the official ritual yet denying the reconciliatory phase. In 1947 under the Kuomintang, for example, some Shanghai students chose to engage in anti-KMT propaganda work rather than attend official commemoration activities. But the most dramatic case of subversion occurred in 1989, when Beijing students upstaged the Communist Party's festival to literally retrace the steps of their predecessors of seventy years before. What made this piece of street theater so subversive was its implication (clearly spelled out in banners and slogans) that the ideals of the May Fourth Movement (which the CCP claimed to represent) remained unfulfilled and needed to be fought for on the streets. (For more discussion of the May Fourth commemorations of 1989, see Chapter 5.)

Despite these symbolic links between ritual and theater, it remains important to distinguish between the two and to note when one or the other predominates within a specific political system. It is particularly important for our purposes because the impact of street theater is in part determined by the degree to which political theater is seen as having a legitimate connection to governance. To illustrate this point, we must briefly review the roles of ritual and theater in Chinese politics, past and present.

Political Ritual in Imperial China

Few cultures have given ritual as crucial a role in governance as did China. Confucius argued that "If [a ruler] could for one day 'himself submit to ritual,' everyone under Heaven would respond to his goodness."[67] As Confucianism emerged as a distinct school of thought in ancient China, this notion of rule by ritual became central to its teaching. As various scholars have noted, the administrative weakness of the imperial state, the comparatively small size of its formal bureaucracy, combined with the Confucian disdain for rule by regulations and coercive punishments to make ritual indispensable for the maintenance of social order.[68] Confucian ritual was primarily a secular ritual, but for Confucius, as Herbert Fingarette has put it, the secular was sacred.[69] Elaborate ceremonies governed all social relationships and guaranteed that the human society would operate in harmony with the cosmic order. A central concern of political philosophers was defining, categorizing, and describing the correct practice of the li associated with relationships among heaven, the emperor, officials, and members of the populace at large.

Imperial ritual, the highest genre of li, was overwhelmingly confined to the palace and the special temples for imperial sacrifices near the capital.

Within the walls of the Forbidden City, the rituals were extraordinarily elaborate (one thinks of the opening scene of the movie *The Last Emperor*). The places, costumes, gestures, and words of the participants were all carefully choreographed to display the ordered hierarchy of the court and bureaucracy and the emperor's unique role connecting human society to the greater cosmos. But high walls and imperial guards excluded the general public from any participation, and the carefully prescribed roles of the participants excluded all possibility for political theater.[70]

The most notable exceptions to the patterns of imperial confinement were the hunts and southern tours of the Kangxi and Qianlong emperors of the Qing. The emperors were greeted by vast crowds as forerunners assembled all officials, as well as local gentry and commoners, to kneel and greet the imperial arrival and departure. But the emperor traveled in an enclosed sedan chair or barge, before which the people were to prostrate themselves, so that even on tour, the pattern of imperial seclusion was not entirely abandoned. The Kangxi emperor occasionally used his tours and hunts to meet ordinary peasants and inquire of their crops and especially of any oppression by local officials. But the extraordinary nature of these contacts is suggested in a Jesuit account, according to which the peasants "were all eager to see his Majesty, who instead of concealing himself gave everyone the liberty of coming near him." Such Jesuit sources are important because the official record is silent on contacts of this sort between the emperor and the people—which itself suggests the ritually problematic nature of such contact.[71]

Official ritual tended to imitate the imperial. Officials were, to paraphrase Alexander Woodside, "spiritual micro-monarchs."[72] They replicated the imperial sacrifice to the Altar of the Soil and Grain and led worship at the Confucian temple. Day-to-day ritual was largely confined to the tribunal or to the private ritual of visits with local notables or other bureaucrats. Officials on tour were proceeded by criers and banners ordering silence and reverence, and, again, the public bowed before them. The arrival and departure of officials did at least provide the ritual (at these liminal moments) of a procession, and these rituals could provide opportunities for the public to express their regret over the departure of a popular official (or opposition to the arrival of an unpopular one).[73] But in general *participatory* political rituals, of the sort that are most easily transformed into political theater, were absent from the official vision of how politics should operate. Instead, there were rigidly stratified hierarchic forms in which the ritual leader (emperor, official, or kin-group patriarch) confronted a mute audience that in many cases (because prostrate) never even saw the ceremonial head.[74]

The contrast to European royal and civic ritual is striking. From the fourteenth century, the royal entry to a city was one of the most important forms of ritual procession. But on entering a city, the monarch would be met (confronted?) by the city's armed militia, handed the keys to the city (an act of fealty, but also a gesture to a guest), and welcomed with street pageants symbolically portraying the virtues the citizenry expected of its ruler.[75] In some German cities jealous of their civic autonomy, the burghers' welcome of their prince or bishop could turn into an armed show of force in which townspeople confronted their sovereign as a rival.[76] But everywhere these ceremonies provided an opportunity for the corporate bodies of urban life (universities, guilds, parliaments or senates, clergy, militia, lawyers, merchants, and tradespeople) to organize and openly announce their place in the public order. As a consequence, even monarchical rituals "tended to describe the essence of national kingship in such a way as to exalt civic virtues and encourage the preservation of urban liberties."[77] All the more was this true of civic rituals on such feast days as Corpus Christi, when the autonomous strength of the corporate groups that made up European civil society was regularly given ritual legitimacy and public display.[78]

One notable feature of Chinese political rituals is the general absence of public speaking. There were, of course, the *xiangyue*, the public lectures on the Sacred Edict. But all accounts agree that this form quickly atrophied in the Qing and never caught on in Chinese culture.[79] China lacked the rhetorical tradition of Greek and Roman forums or of many nonliterate societies. Confucius was suspicious of men with "clever words" (who he believed were seldom men of "humanity"), and Confucian bureaucrats clearly preferred the authority of the written word.[80] Orthodox religious ritual provided no rhetorical models: China had no congregational religion with regular weekly sermons. Consequently, in the very limited civil society of guilds (*huiguan*) that grew up in late imperial China, there were neither the ecclesiastic nor the Roman republican models for public meetings and speeches that one sees in merchants' and artisans' guilds in Europe.

In short, rhetoric and expressions of public opinion—even expressions that supported rather than challenged the status quo—had little place in official Chinese politics. This can be seen by the distinction China's classical philosophers drew between rule by *li* (ritual, traditional practices, correct actions that are carried out spontaneously, almost instinctively, simply because they are "right," not because they are proved to be so) and rule by *fa* (laws and statutes that are obeyed to gain reward or avoid punishment). Neither the idealistic Confucians who considered governance by *li* the only moral form of rule nor the pessimists who argued that the only stable political systems were those that relied heavily upon governance by *fa* devoted much attention to strategies that do not fall into either of these categories.[81] The possibility of using persuasion, organized displays of popular opinion, rhetoric, and other theatrical methods that are neither *li* nor *fa* to maintain control is seldom addressed by either Confucians or Legalists, though a concern with rhetoric is central to classical Western political philosophy.[82] Even the simple act of gathering together to discuss political issues was frequently seen as subversive and thus an act to be controlled by *fa*, as the repeated edicts limiting the activities of academies issued during the Ming dynasty illustrate.[83]

The one legitimate political activity that provided an opening for political theater was the right to petition officials for the redress of grievances. In ancient China a "complaint drum" (*dengwen gu*) was supposedly placed before a ruler's palace to summon attendants to hear a grievance. The drum continued in use in imperial times, and the Qing placed it just southwest of Tiananmen. Nonetheless, the Qing code was interpreted in such a way as to discourage strongly such direct appeals to Beijing, and most petitions were presented to local authorities.[84] Naturally, the right to petition led frequently to a political theater of mass demonstrations, which might develop into riots or even rebellions.[85] A late nineteenth-century account of such a petition movement evokes images of modern protest repertoires:

> I once saw a procession of country people visit the yamens of the city mandarins. . . . Shops were shut and perfect stillness reigned as twenty thousand strong, they wended their way through the streets, with banners flying, each at the head of a company and each inscribed with the name of the temple where the company held its meetings. "What is the meaning of this demonstration?" I inquired. "We are going to reduce taxes," was the laconic answer.[86]

Such mass petition movements were surely unusual, but the script was well enough known to be replicated when necessary. Furthermore, a significant feature of the Chinese case was the replication of the bureaucratic hierarchy in the world of the gods. Consequently, gods were petitioned—and far more frequently than officials. Thus religious ritual could serve, in Emily Ahern's words, as a "learning game," teaching ordinary Chinese "how to analyze (and so manipulate) the political system that governed them."[87]

Petitions provided one small avenue of public access into the otherwise closed realm of legitimate politics in imperial China. But the state dealt harshly with any attempt to use petitions for more than personal grievances. They were not to be an excuse for public debate on matters of policy. As Confucius said, "He who holds no rank in a state does not discuss its politics."[88] Even as China began the slow process of reform in the wake of the Opium War, movement toward a public politics outside the state was exceptionally slow. When Lin Zexu, in disgrace after the outbreak of the Opium War, revealed in a letter to a friend his support for the acquisition of ships and guns, he closed by urging, "I only beg that you keep [these ideas] confidential. By all means, please do not tell other persons."[89] Even the famous reform essays of Feng Guifen, written around 1860, were not published until they were brought to the attention of the emperor in 1898.[90] But after the Sino-Japanese War of 1894–1895, and especially in the course of the twentieth century, Chinese politics changed fundamentally, and central to that change was the emergence of a new space for, and new kinds of, political theater.

Political Theater in Twentieth-Century China

In the final years of the Qing dynasty, the New Policies introduced a series of reforms that ushered in a new era of Chinese politics. First, there were the new schools, which brought together a politically engaged student class in urban centers across China. Soon these students were organizing protests against foreign-financed railways, boycotts of U.S. goods because of U.S. restrictions on Chinese immigration, and broad movements for political reform. They wrote big-character posters, spoke from street corners, and staged mass demonstrations (sometimes including costumed characters) to dramatize their concerns.[91] Some of these demonstrations built upon classic ritual forms—as in a 1906 funeral procession by Changsha students to bury the ashes of two revolutionaries who had committed suicide.[92] As Mary Rankin and William Rowe have shown, an increasingly assertive civil society grew out of earlier networks of gentry activists, local managers, merchant guilds, and charitable organizations. Chambers of commerce and educational associations aggressively sought to set agendas for local political affairs. As constitutional reforms began in 1909–1910, China had its first experience with electoral politics. Provincial assemblies elected in 1909 immediately provided the basis for political parties, as like-minded individuals grouped together in a variety of reformist associations. But reformers also relied upon analogies to establish political forms to press their views—most notably the series of petitions presented to the court in favor of a rapid transition to full constitutional government. The new local, provincial, and national assemblies became forums for speech-making. Political rhetoric began to be an important part of the political process. Radical Chinese students in Japan founded the Society for the Practice of Oratory (Yanshuo Lianxi Hui), and some dissidents (like Wang Jingwei) established their political reputations as eloquent public speakers.[93]

Chambers of commerce and the provincial assemblies were two of the most prominent institutions of this new civil society. It is significant that all of the provincial assemblies and many of the chambers of commerce were located in new, specially constructed buildings. The architecture of these structures symbolized the break with the past. Chinese styles of walled compounds and enclosed courtyards were generally eschewed. Instead, the chambers and assemblies were located in large, Western-style buildings of brick or stone, opening directly onto the streets and including spacious auditoriums (*huitang*) for a modern politics of meetings. The new schools also built auditoriums, especially in the Republican period, and the function of the new architecture was explicitly acknowledged. One commentator on the auditorium at Qinghua University in Beijing noted that because the art of public speaking was so undeveloped in China, the school's new auditorium "may well be regarded as the Forum Romanum where budding Ciceros will deliver their orations."[94] Sports stadiums attached to missionary schools, another imported form of architecture, also provided venues for the new politics.[95]

This politics of public meetings, speeches, and demonstrations was so new in China that its forms and models had to be borrowed from other types of performances. Foreign models were one natural source of inspiration for these public activities, especially as so many speakers and protesters had either studied abroad or been trained in missionary schools in China (where preachers' sermons provided regular reminders of the power of oratory). A *North China Herald* account of a 1903 protest meeting held to condemn Russian imperialism notes that at the beginning of the meeting "a set of rules, translated from the English [*Robert's Rules of Order*?], for the governance of public speakers and meetings were . . . read, printed copies of which were also distributed to the audience."[96] Two years later, in an article on the anti-U.S. boycott of 1905, the same Shanghai newspaper noted that the United States should at least be heartened that the movement was being carried out in a "characteristically American manner," complete with public assemblies and the election of delegates to representative bodies.[97] Many of the most ardent protesters in 1905 had been trained by U.S. missionaries, and these missionaries' conferences and assemblies may well have served as influential "object lessons" in governance for radical Chinese youths. It is no mere coincidence that one of the most effective public speakers at boycott meetings in Shanghai was Ma Xiangpo, an educator and former priest who had studied under those most skillful of Western rhetoricians: the Jesuits.[98]

Besides foreign models for oratory and rallies, activists in the new politics also borrowed metaphors and techniques from Chinese theater. When the first public organizing went on in the late nineteenth and early twentieth centuries, before the new architecture was in place, the most common meeting places were guild halls (*huiguan*) and temples, which were equipped with stages for operatic performances. There politicians mounted platforms (*tai*) to address the audience. Meetings began with a *kaimushi*, a curtain-raising. Speechmaking was a kind of performance (*yanjiang* or *yanshuo*).

Given the influence of imported political models and theatrical venues and metaphors, it should come as no surprise that both operas and *xinju* (new theater) plays—dramatic performances that mixed elements of Chinese and Western dramatic genres—became "important vehicles of propaganda" for revolutionaries.[99] Shanghai's Chunliu She (Spring Willow Society) performed *xinju* works with names such as "Blood of Patriotism" that "advocated revolution and satirized and laid bare the corruption of the ruling government."[100] The founder of this troupe, Wang Zhongsheng, was executed for his activities in 1911—a sign that the Manchus were well aware of the potential persuasive power of theatrics—earning him a reputation as a revolutionary martyr to the Republican cause.[101]

The new republic inaugurated in 1912 brought forth a political theater appropriate to China's new democratic forms. We see this in magazines and photo albums about this period.[102] Politicians array themselves at railway stations or in front of meeting halls for ceremonial portraits. Naturally, they mount stages to deliver speeches. They parade into cities in open limousines, with flag-waving crowds lining the streets. Now, for the first time, political leaders are brought face to face with the people: Gone is the bowing and the taboo on visual contact. The people see, hear, evaluate, and react to the politicians of the early republic. The purpose, of course, is to make the new politics public and *open*. Indeed this new politics is symbolized in the term for holding a meeting: *kaihui*, or to open an assembly.

The Kuomintang's experiments with patriotic mass mobilization were the most conscious efforts to use political theater to foster political commitment and legitimacy for the new regime. Their most dramatic efforts would begin with an incident that threatened China's national sovereignty. KMT leaders at the national and local levels would sponsor mass rallies against the aggressor, usually Japan. Yellow trade unions, pro-KMT youth groups, and other loyalist organizations would mobilize people to attend these rallies, at which official speakers would praise the Kuomintang as the nation's leading patriotic and revolutionary force, and the crowd would be encouraged to mix cries of "Long live the republic" and "Long live the Nationalist party" with slogans criticizing the foreign foe. Later, local party branches or government bureaus might arrange for petitioners or carefully screened representatives of "legitimate" groups to travel to Nanjing to present their views to top KMT figures, or urge civic groups to launch patriotic fundraising drives.[103]

Whatever the specific techniques the KMT used, the intent was the same: to mobilize popular outrage to reinforce rather than subvert the status quo. Sometimes, as during the New Life Movement, this mobilization merged with attempts to foster Chiang Kaishek's personality cult. Even when not directly associated with cultic practices, however, KMT mass mobilization drives always relied heavily on ritual forms—bows to party and national flags, recitations of Sun Yatsen's last will at the start of meetings, orchestrated visits to the National Father's tomb by petitioners who visited the capital.

Most of these drives left a great deal of room for spontaneous political theater. As such, they might have served as the basis for a new form of politics, in which mass expressions of popular opinion, albeit carefully stage-managed, would play a role in determining and legitimizing public policy. But these new forms of public performance never seemed to catch on in China. The foreign rhetorical models were alien, and the analogy to theater linked politics to an occupation viewed as morally suspect in China.[104]

Political theater encountered two concrete problems. First, China's rulers never developed a mechanism to connect this new open politics of speeches and meetings to the "real" politics of governing. As studies by Andrew Nathan and Lloyd Eastman have shown, the governance of China remained a matter of factional alliances and patronage networks, of personal connections and secret deals.[105] Electoral politics, the most common Western form for connecting political theater to the business of governing, never appealed to the Chinese. Liang Qichao observed it in the United States and found it fraught with fraud, ignorance, and corruption.[106] When Yuan Shikai disbanded the elective assemblies in 1914, there was minimal protest from the disenfranchised citizenry.[107] In the years after 1927, the Kuomintang sporadically tried to reimplement electoral politics. But campaigns at the local level were so corrupt that they convinced neither foreign observers nor the Chinese electorate that the casting of votes had any real impact on governance. If these campaigns and elections qualified as theater at all, they represented burlesque or farce rather than serious political drama.[108]

Second, experiments at mass mobilization were consistently undermined by the tendency of patriotic popular movements to get out of hand and end up as attacks on those in power. Thus the Nationalist era witnessed periodic swings between official encouragement of and violent repression of popular mobilization, the complex dynamics of which are explicated in recent works by Christian Henriot and Wang Ke-wen.[109] The first major swing took place in spring 1928, when party leaders first supported then suppressed popular expressions of outrage over the Jinan incident in which the forces of Chiang Kaishek had been temporarily blocked by Japanese troops; one of the last important swings came in spring 1946, when party leaders encouraged urbanites to attend rallies against "Soviet imperialism" in February, then, as the United States replaced the USSR as the target of popular patriotic indignation, quickly began to argue that all mass gatherings were subversive acts.[110]

When officials failed to shape the mass movements into controlled performances, they turned to a set of repressive tactics that observers of last year will find all too familiar. The regime would declare all collective gatherings illegal, close newspapers (except for foreign ones protected by extraterritoriality) that printed favorable accounts of popular protests, arrest activists, and, if necessary, use violence against those who continued to take to the streets. This kind of repression reflected a continuation of the traditional dichotomy of *li* (ritual) and *fa* (law or coercive control) alluded to above. Though imperial emperors and officials called forms of collective action that threatened the hegemony of their rule "heterodox" whereas the KMT branded such behavior "counterrevolutionary," both regimes saw force as the only response left when they lost control of ritual or "ritualized" political theater.

The Kuomintang's failure to make either elections or mass mobilization an integral part of governance meant that the open politics of political theater became increasingly associated with protest. The traditional forms for mass petitions provided protest movements with a well-established Chinese repertoire that was lacking for hegemonic political theater. The events of May 4, 1919, established the Republican model for petition-based mass action: Students from the leading universities marched to the central square, Tiananmen, and attempted to present their petitions. Further demonstrations followed in Beijing in the early 1920s, but the May Thirtieth Movement was the next episode of truly national significance. These were, in the words of Mao Zedong, the years in which "the Chinese proletariat and the Chinese Communist Party mounted the political stage."[111] A new wave of activism followed the Japanese invasion of Manchuria, culminating in the December Ninth Movement of 1935.

These dates—May 4, May 30, December 9 (each of which is discussed in more detail in Chapter 4)—were all watersheds in the history of Republican China. They form the markers for conventional periodization, the topics of classroom lectures. They also became anniversaries calling forth celebratory rituals modeled on the original events. Most importantly, they defined the repertoires for a new political street theater. Students always played a leading role, marching from their campuses behind banners proclaiming their school affiliations. They shouted slogans, waved flags, cheered onlookers, petitioned the authorities, and clashed with police. On their campuses they wrote big-character posters; outside they set up platforms to speak to the citizenry. Although the authorities criticized them for neglecting their studies, suppressed their illegal marches, and condemned their disruption of law and order, the press broadcast news of their activities throughout the country and the power of theater was undeniable. From the December Ninth Movement of 1935, and increasingly in the late 1940s, the Communists recognized the power of this theater and its capacity to delegitimize KMT rule, and they worked quietly behind the scenes to encourage further demonstrations.

After 1949 the Communist Party sought to ritualize this theater: to incorporate and domesticate its repertoires into campaigns. The Party was well aware of the danger of uncontrolled political theater: Many of its key leaders had risen to prominence through their roles in student and worker demonstrations. They understood the power of independent student unions, which were called, under the Kuomintang as in 1989, *xuesheng zizhihui* (student self-government societies).[112] Accordingly, the Communists banned all autonomous associations. But they did not wish to abandon the theater—only to monopolize the capacity to organize it, to succeed here (as elsewhere) where the KMT had failed. Thus it became one of the important functions of work units and the party-sponsored mass organizations (of youth, women, workers, peasants, etc.) to mobilize constituencies for mass demonstrations.

The result was the "campaign style" of Maoist politics—a style that prevailed until the late 1970s.[113] In the ritualized demonstrations that accompanied every major campaign, or that marked important dates on the revolutionary calendar, people would march forth behind their unit's or mass organization's banners, with lots of red flags, drums, and cymbals, and head for the central square. In the nation's capital, national minorities would join in native costume while the party leaders looked down from the elevated platform of Tiananmen itself. The same ritual would be repeated in cities across the country, with local leaders in their own elevated reviewing stands.

During the Cultural Revolution, Mao loosened the controls on these political rituals, and the students quickly devised their own innovative repertoires of street theater. "Ghosts and monsters" were paraded through the streets in dunce caps; offending teachers and cadres were put on stage with arms bound behind their backs in the airplane position; books were burned, art destroyed. But Cultural Revolution street theater quickly degenerated into something too disorderly even for Mao, as rival Red Guard gangs fought physical battles in schools, factories, and streets.

By the late 1960s, this revived theater had to be suppressed, and by 1980 the party revised the constitution to prohibit all big-character posters, leaflets, and demonstrations. In fact, under Deng Xiaoping, the party tried to abandon both the campaign ritual of the pre–Cultural Revolution period and the political theater of the "ten years of chaos" and rule purely by administrative routine. But the Tiananmen demonstrations in honor of Zhou Enlai and against the Gang of Four in 1976, the Democracy Wall Movement of 1978–1979, the Hunan protests of 1980, the student demonstrations in Beijing in 1985 and in Shanghai and other cities in 1986 and 1987, and finally China's spring of 1989 demonstrated that political theater cannot be totally suppressed. Some public rituals are always necessary, and in those events, there is always the danger that students or other actors will usurp the stage and turn the official ritual into their own political theater.[114]

Interpreting the Political Theater

As performance, the truth-value of the words and actions in this political theater is not terribly important. But that does not imply that this theater is meaningless—only that we have to pay more attention to its symbolism than to the literal meaning of its utterances. Let us consider the symbolism of 1989. The first function of political theater is quite simply to be heard. The point of the street demonstration is to gain attention. Initially, the audience is a dual one: the general population (both urban residents who witness the demonstration directly and those who can be reached through the medium of television) and the authorities. But it is the authorities who are the real audience; the value of the people is largely instrumental. The more support the demonstrators can gain from the citizenry—the larger the applauding crowds lining the demonstration route, the more concrete contributions of food and drink, the more symbolic aid in the form of banners or citizens' support groups, the greater the monetary contributions from citizens and small business—the more leverage the demonstrators will gain with the authorities.

That the authorities are the real audience is demonstrated by the petition format. But this petition is also important in that it acknowledges the fundamental legitimacy of the government to which one appeals for redress. Later, the petition is replaced by the appeal for a dialogue. Again, this is fundamentally a demand to be heard. But underlying this demand—even more clearly in dialogue than in petition—is a claim to entrance into the polity.[115] Groups previously excluded from the political process seek through demonstration, petition, and dialogue to be taken seriously by the authorities as participants in the political decisionmaking process. Even some of the violence of the demonstrations, the rock throwing and arson, can be interpreted as efforts to gain attention, to be heard—efforts by those less skillful with and less trusting of words than intellectuals and university students.

The *public* nature of political theater is its second most important characteristic. Street theater invites all citizens to join. Once Tiananmen Square was occupied, the students often debated strategy and made decisions in public, there for all to see. They demanded a live broadcast of their dialogue with the government leaders. Symbolically, such theater stands in direct contrast to the secrecy of the Party-state. Significantly, the model for all such demonstrations in China, the May Fourth demonstration of 1919, protested against the secret diplomacy that had preceded the Versailles conference. Street theater invariably symbolizes a call to open up the political process, and the very secrecy (and lack of accountability) of the Party-state in China naturally calls forth this sort of dialectical opposite.

Finally, student strikes and, even more dramatically, the hunger strike, present images of selflessness—a key value in contemporary China, with models from Norman Bethune to Lei Feng. These acts were extraordinarily effective. The most common praise of the student movement was that their motives were entirely patriotic, for love of country (*aiguo*). They sought nothing for themselves—unlike, some said, workers who might strike for higher pay. These students asked nothing, accepted not even food, and wished no more than the good of the nation. Their acts of self-denial stood in obvious contrast to the self-serving and corrupt leadership they attacked. No privilege of the Party leadership was more visible than the enormous banquets they consumed at public expense. Now here were students refusing to eat anything at all.[116]

Finally, the last testaments that the students wrote out, plus the hunger strike and related gestures, located the students within a rich tradition of political martyrs. These activities, as Dru Gladney and others have noted, linked the students to Qu Yuan, the loyal minister of the third century B.C. who showed his willingness to "die for the affairs of the nation" by committing suicide after his ruler refused to heed his advice.[117] Such actions also recalled earlier generations of student martyrs, from Chen Dong (a Song dynasty protester who was executed for his criticisms of government corruption and who served as a model for some May Fourth activists) to Yao Hongye and Chen Tianhua (two frustrated Hunanese activists who committed suicide in 1906), and the hundreds of youthful demonstrators killed by foreign and native authorities during the Republican era. When students at Tiananmen Square swore collective oaths to sacrifice their lives—the last and most prophetic of which was taken on June 3—they were enacting a scene from the May Fourth Movement. Similarly, when Chai Ling bit her finger and wrote out a protest slogan with her own blood, she stepped into a role that student protesters of 1915 and 1919 had played.[118] With all this theater, the students appealed to a tradition of principled dissent and revolutionary action that the Party itself had legitimized and mythologized in the attempt to claim such theater as its own.

If we are to understand the enormous appeal of the student demonstrations in Beijing and across China, we must begin by appreciating these symbolic meanings of their protest. The slogans—attacking the corruption of official profiteers (*guandao*), calling for a freer press, mocking China's highest leaders, advocating a never-defined "freedom" and "democracy"—were certainly important. But they gained their power because the very repertoire of the movement symbolized a demand for a voice in government, for a more open political process, and for an end to leadership by a self-serving elite.

A Comparative Perspective

As Chirot argues in more detail in Chapter 11, the 1989 demonstrations in China were clearly part of a larger, worldwide crisis of state socialist systems.

In Eastern Europe the Communist Party has been toppled from power in one country after another. In the Soviet Union the Party is in the process of renouncing its monopoly on power, and various ethnic groups—led by Lithuania, but including all the Baltic states and the peoples of the Caucasus region—have been moving steadily toward some form of greater autonomy from Moscow. Increasingly, China (along with North Korea, Vietnam, and Cuba) is looking like the last refuge of socialism. As a current Chinese joke has it—playing on the official cant that "Only socialism can save China"— now "Only China can save socialism."

In each of the European transitions, street demonstrations have played a critical role. This was, of course, most obvious in the dramatic events of East Germany and Czechoslovakia. There, an utterly peaceful political transformation—a "velvet revolution," to use the Czech phrase—was brought about by unarmed civilians protesting in the streets. Because exactly the same sort of political theater brought forth troops and tanks and unprecedented bloodshed in China, it is necessary to try to explain the contrasting result.

Part of the answer clearly lies in factors quite beyond the scope of this essay. The Communist Party of China (and the parties of Vietnam, Cuba, and, to a lesser degree, Korea) made its own revolution. Each of these countries thus differs from the state socialist regimes of Eastern Europe, which were to one degree or another brought into being and propped up by the Soviet Red Army. Consequently, when Gorbachev made it clear that the Brezhnev Doctrine was dead and the Soviet Union would no longer come to the rescue of unpopular East European regimes, those regimes fell very quickly.

In addition, China and the remaining state socialist regimes are all poor Third World countries. They have large, impoverished, and still poorly educated rural populations. At least in China, there is unquestionably substantial peasant discontent over a variety of issues—the payment for grain requisitions in IOUs instead of money, the government's failure to deliver promised supplies of chemical fertilizer. But in general peasants displayed little sympathy for the demands of the student demonstrators. Only the attack on corruption struck a responsive chord. And when the crackdown came, rural residents tended to believe the government contention that the peasant soldiers of the People's Liberation Army would not fire on unarmed civilians unless there was a genuine threat to law and order. In short, China's large peasant population remained largely preoccupied with its own immediate material interests, and it viewed these interests as dependent on continued political stability. Consequently, China's peasantry provided a reservoir of support for the hard-liners in Beijing that was missing in any East European regime.[119]

More germane to our discussion, however, is the role played by the institutions of civil society in Eastern Europe—a role that Chirot alludes to as well in his chapter. These long-neglected institutions proved to have sufficient life to structure the opposition movement and sustain it until victory. The most obvious example is the Catholic church in Poland. As a gathering place and refuge for dissidents in the Solidarity movement, the Catholic opposition was fundamental to the breakthrough in Poland—which was, after all, the first domino to fall. It clearly did not hurt to have a Polish pope during Solidarity's long years of travail. Hungary was the next country to make serious moves in the direction of pluralism, and here the old democratic parties played a crucial role. In Czechoslovakia, the dissident groups among the intellectuals were clearly better organized than anyone previously believed. In East Germany, the Evangelical (Lutheran) church helped to shelter dissident intellectuals and a small independent peace movement. Bulgaria witnessed a nascent environmental movement, which played a critical role. In Lithuania, there was again the Catholic church, plus the role of national movements and linguistic solidarity.[120]

Virtually all of the institutions of civil society in Europe are imbued, to one degree or another, with aspects of democratic culture. We sometimes forget, as we focus on the hierarchic structures and stately rituals of the Catholic church, that the pope is elected and councils of bishops and other more local institutions have often operated on democratic principles. On a more mundane level, artisan guilds would, on their feast days, constitute themselves as a "republic" to manage their affairs and discipline their members.[121] When, therefore, civil society has been allowed to prosper, it has brought with it, in the West, a discourse and a culture already shaped by electoral forms and at least a minimal tolerance of dissent.

In Eastern Europe, such institutions of civil society played the absolutely critical role of translating the symbolic meaning of street theater into systematic programs for political change. When the Party-states of Eastern Europe were forced to sit down to negotiate with the street protesters, there were people with organizational experience and programmatic ideas who could negotiate the delicate transition to democracy. The glamour-seeking media has hardly focused on this process, sometimes leaving the impression that dramatic demonstrations led to government collapse and then a natural evolution to electoral forms. But that is hardly a plausible scenario, and when the full story is told we will surely find a critical role of civil society in presiding over that perilous political process.

It is not enough, however, to focus on institutions alone. The small and vulnerable groups of dissident intellectuals and workers in Eastern Europe could certainly not match the organizational might of the Party-state in these countries. But if there is one lesson that the rapid collapse of Communist parties in Eastern Europe and Russia has taught us, it is that social scientists have misled us into accepting an excessively reified notion of what "institutions" are. We have been led to think of the Party-state almost as a physical structure, of unshakable size and weight and power. Now we are in a position to recall that such "structures" are, in fact, made up of *people* who are bound together by certain rules and habits, interests and aspirations, rituals and shared identities. The people who make up these institutions are not mindless parts of a party "machine," acting always and unfailingly in the interest of that machine. (Gorbachev and his supporters in the Soviet Union obviously cannot be understood if we identify them only as leaders and servants of the Communist Party machine.)

Once we escape an excessively institutional approach to politics in state socialist systems, we are in a better position to appreciate the impact of the culture of civil society, or (to use Pierre Bourdieu's useful term) the habitus that reemerged from the collective memory to give life to the East European movements of dissent. One participant/observer of the Polish experience has noted "the explosion of national memory . . . the massive turnout for anniversary celebrations" that followed the first Solidarity struggles of 1980–1981.[122] In small rituals and mass celebrations, the habitus of democratic governance was revived from a culture rich in civic rituals and the theater of popular rule.

As we noted above, China's imperial state allowed minimal development of civil society. The late Qing and the Republican era witnessed a brief flowering of civil society, but its roots were not deep. In addition, as David Strand has shown, this new civil society found it difficult to escape the old politics of personal networks, and the leaders of the new civic institutions tended to look for patrons within the state.[123] The habitus of autonomous associations was still weakly developed. In addition, civil society in China never provided an adequate foundation for pluralist politics. To a large degree, it revealed this weakness in its rhetoric. Mary Rankin has observed that the Chinese press (both a component and a mouthpiece of China's nascent civil society) tended to speak of the "people" as an undifferentiated whole— usually standing against an opposing symbolic category, "officials," that is, the state.[124] Thus when Chinese began to speak of "rule by the people" (*minzhu*), the "people" were an undifferentiated whole. The separate "republics" of civil society were not sufficiently legitimized to bring, with the idea of democracy, the pluralism bred in the corporate roots of European civil society.

Under the PRC, the budding sprouts of republican civil society were cut off altogether. The rhetoric of the undifferentiated people was usurped by the state to establish a "people's democratic dictatorship." Dissidents were safely excluded as "enemies of the people." Pluralism existed neither in the organization of society nor in the rhetoric of politics. Both the Party-state and its opponents appealed to the virtue of "unity." But only the party existed as a functioning political organization. The tragic result of this combination of circumstances is that the Chinese Communist Party can justly claim that there is no political force outside the Party capable of ruling China. Many of the hunger-strikers conceded this point in May 1989, and they were probably reflecting the consensus of most of the protesters. In the wake of the June Fourth Massacre, the party's claim to legitimacy rests on little more than this fact: There is no alternative to the CCP. The *reason* there is no alternative is simple enough: The Party will not permit one to exist. To preserve their fragile legitimacy, the Party leaders must rigorously suppress any hint of pluralism: no autonomous student or workers' unions, no publications that might provide an alternative voice, no civil society. Then they can present the Chinese people with a bleak choice: either continued Communist rule or chaos.

Without a civil society, only street theater remains as a mode of political expression. No Chinese regime has ever been able to suppress it altogether.

The smooth functioning of Chinese politics requires public rituals to celebrate the ideals of the revolution and the Party-state that emerged from it. In time, students will again find an opportunity to usurp those rituals to perform their own political theater. Then the question will again arise: Can they (and the state) find a mechanism to connect this theater to the complex task of governing more than a billion Chinese?

Postscript

During the months since this essay first appeared in the November 1990 issue of the *Journal of Asian Studies* (JAS), we have received a number of instructive comments from fellow historians and specialists in disciplines (anthropology, philosophy, literature) other than our own. In addition to the criticisms and queries in these informal communications, scholarly contributions such as the chapters by Ann Anagnost and Elizabeth Perry in this volume have extended or challenged certain points we made. All of this has led us to look back at some parts of our original essay with a critical eye, though, upon reflection, we remain committed to our central argument. As a result we have decided to make only minor changes in preparing this essay for this volume. Nonetheless, it seemed worthwhile to address briefly three of the most important issues that our colleagues have raised.

1. *Definitions of li and ritual.* Both before and after the piece appeared in JAS, a number of people (including Henry Rosemont, Jr., and Frank Pieke) raised objections to our definitions of these concepts, arguing that we left too little room for the kind of innovation that often takes place during the performance of ritual acts and the way in which codes of *li* change over time as a result of such creative departures from received scripts. These critics have a valid point. However, we continue to see an important (though admittedly slippery) distinction between political theater and cultural performances that put a much higher premium upon faithful replication of a series of actions in a traditional fashion. To avoid confusion, we would be happy to find words other than *ritual* and *theater* to distinguish these two types of performance, but we have yet to discover more suitable terminology.

2. *The unimportance of public speaking and public ritual in imperial China.* Several colleagues have suggested that we may have overstated the seclusionary and nonoratorical nature of pre–twentieth-century politics. Most particularly, some (including Mary Rankin and Ann Anagnost, who addresses the issue in an extended note to her chapter) have raised questions about our claims regarding the lack of public speaking traditions. We have little doubt that, at least compared to the European case, political oratory was relatively unimportant in China prior to the twentieth century and that, above the most local level, public speaking played a decidedly minor part in formal politics. Nonetheless, some scholars have observed that the political content of story-telling performances suggests that the contrasts may not be as stark as we have drawn them. Others have noted that public speaking skills were often

seen as a prerequisite for village leadership, though we would observe that the "ability to talk" (*huishuo*) is as likely to refer to interpersonal mediating and brokering skills as to a capacity for oratory. It is clear that China specialists need to study public speaking more closely. We also need a much better sense of how state rituals at the imperial, provincial, and local levels operated in practice. Were they always as "private" as they were supposed to be in theory? Work in progress by James Hevia, Angela Zito, and others promises to speak to this issue.

3. Civil society, East and West. Finally, comments on our JAS article and recent work on related topics (including various contributions to this volume) suggest that the reemergence or stifling of civil society traditions in differing political environments will continue to be a topic of considerable interest within the China field (and Eastern European studies) for some time to come. Most of what we have heard on this issue has reaffirmed our conviction in our original arguments. Nonetheless, there are certainly avenues that deserve more detailed exploration. Michael Duke, for example, has (in personal correspondence) brought up the question of the different degrees of ruthlessness shown by Eastern European Communist parties and the CCP when dealing with political dissidents. He notes that people like Vaclav Havel and Lech Walesa were able to emerge from prison alive and sane and were apparently treated quite differently from Chinese dissidents like Wei Jingsheng. Duke suggests a distinctive Eastern European habitus in such matters that does not exist in contemporary China. To begin to address such issues, we need first to get a much more nuanced picture of both Chinese and Eastern European civil society traditions. Fortunately, important steps in this direction are already being made by people like Daniel Chirot (whose contribution to this volume addresses the Eastern European case) and David Strand (whose valuable discussion of Beijing's "public sphere" appeared as we were preparing our JAS piece to go to press).[125]

Notes

1. Jonathan Mirsky's "The Empire Strikes Back," *New York Review of Books*, February 1, 1989, discusses early English-language works by journalists and sinologists; Tony Saich and Nancy Hearst, "Bibliographic Note," in Tony Saich, ed., *Perspectives on the Chinese People's Movement* (Armonk, N.Y.: M. E. Sharpe, 1990), pp. 190–196, provides an extremely useful overview of these and somewhat later English-language works, as well as of books in other Western languages and Chinese. Of extant English-language works, Human Rights in China, ed., *Children of the Dragon* (New York: Macmillan, 1990) provides perhaps the best single-volume introduction to the movement, combining as it does accounts by foreign eyewitnesses (including Orville Schell and Perry Link), background essays by leading sinologists (such as Jonathan Spence), an impressive collection of photographs, and translations of some key Chinese-language speeches, interviews, and documents.

2. Keith Forster, "Impressions of the Popular Protest in Hangzhou, April/June 1989," and Josephine Fox, "The Movement for Democracy and Its Consequences in Tianjin," *Australian Journal of Chinese Affairs*, 23 (1990), pp. 97–120 and 133–144; Frank

Niming [pseud.], "Learning How to Protest," in Saich, *Chinese People's Movement*, pp. 82–104.

3. Although official references to the Red Guard legacy had some effect in alienating support for the students in 1986, such Cultural Revolution imagery was much less effective in 1989, in part because the students confronted the argument head on. They demanded that the leadership apologize for labeling the movement a form of *dongluan* (turmoil)—a term that has become a code word for the Cultural Revolution.

4. For example, a report in the *San Franciso Chronicle*, May 19, 1989, p. A24, quotes a worker from Hubei saying: "At least Mao was honest. . . . He even sent his son to the Korean War. Nowadays, the leaders send their sons to America."

5. For an interesting comparison of the uses Red Guards and the protesters of 1989 made of Mao portraits, see *Washington Post*, May 24, 1989, p. 1. For additional discussion of the similarities and differences between the Red Guards and the protesters of 1989, see Jeffrey N. Wasserstrom, *Student Protests in Twentieth-Century China: The View from Shanghai* (Stanford: Stanford University Press, forthcoming), epilogue, and the chapters by Israel, Schwarcz, and Young in this volume.

6. See, for example, Lowell Dittmer, "China in 1989: The Crisis of Incomplete Reform," *Asian Survey*, 30, 1 (1990), pp. 25–41; and Gerrit W. Gong, "Tiananmen: Causes and Consequences," *Washington Quarterly*, 13, 1 (1990), pp. 79–95.

7. *Renmin ribao* (People's daily), May 19, 1990, p. 1; Zhaoqing, Gejing, and Suyuan, *Xueran de fancai* (Bloody scenes) (Hong Kong: Haiyan, 1989), p. 204. Interestingly, the U.S.-government–operated Foreign Broadcast Information Service: China (hereafter, FBIS-CHI) reversed the meaning of this passage in its translation. See FBIS-CHI-89-096 (May 19, 1989), p. 15. Perhaps FBIS was uncomfortable with this explicit rejection of majority rule.

8. *Sun Zhongshan xiansheng huace* (Dr. Sun Yatsen: A photo album) (Beijing and Hong Kong, 1986), plate 199.

9. *Enlightenment*, no. 2, cited in Andrew Nathan, *Chinese Democracy*, (Berkeley: University of California Press, 1985), p. 6.

10. Although *Chinese Democracy* is replete with useful examples of this sort, Nathan seems blind to this issue and concludes with a quite unsupported discussion of "the West's—and the Chinese democrats'—identification of democracy with pluralism" (p. 227).

11. Here we follow the argument Richard C. Kraus presents in "The Lament of Astrophysicist Fang Lizhi," in Arif Dirlik and Maurice Meisner, eds., *Marxism and the Chinese Experience* (Armonk, N.Y.: M. E. Sharpe, 1989). For an alternative view of Fang's version of democracy, see Chapter 6 of this volume.

12. Mary S. Erbaugh and Richard C. Kraus, "The 1989 Democracy Movement in Fujian and Its Consequences," *Australian Journal of Chinese Affairs*, 23 (1990), pp. 145–160, esp. p. 153.

13. See, for example, Forster, "Hangzhou," p. 98; Niming, "Learning"; Henry Rosemont, Jr., "China: The Mourning After," *Z Magazine* (March 1990), pp. 85–96; Anita Chan and Jonathan Unger, "China After Tiananmen: It's a Whole New Class Struggle," *Nation*, January 22, 1990, pp. 79–81.

14. Note this May 1989 exchange between a youth, barred from boarding a bus where Wuer Kaixi was resting, and a student security guard. "'What kind of democracy is this?'" [the youth] fumed. 'What kind of freedom? You are just like the country's leaders.' Responded the guard: 'You are right. But you are harming our unity. Don't say such things.'" *Newsweek*, May 29, 1989, p. 21. One of the earliest (and still one of the best) discussions of this sort of behavior at Tiananmen Square is Sarah Lubman, "The Myth of Tiananmen Square: The Students Talked Democracy But They Didn't

Practice It," *Washington Post*, July 30, 1989. Criticisms of the new exile leagues appear in Yuen Ying Chan and Peter Kwong, "Trashing the Hopes of Tiananmen," *Nation*, April 23, 1990, pp. 545, 560–564; and Chan and Unger, "China After Tiananmen," pp. 79–81.

15. Comments at a roundtable at the 1989 national meetings of the American Historical Association.

16. Thompson, "Patrician Society, Plebeian Culture," *Journal of Social History*, 7, 4 (1978), pp. 382–405, and "Eighteenth-Century English Society: Class Struggle Without Class?" *Social History*, 3, 2 (1978), pp. 71–133; Clifford Geertz, *Negara: The Theatre-State in Nineteenth-Century Bali* (Princeton: Princeton University Press, 1980).

17. Frank Pieke, "Observations During the People's Movement in Beijing, Spring 1989" (paper presented at the International Institute of Social History, Amsterdam, July 7, 1989), and "A Ritualized Rebellion: Beijing, Spring 1989" (unpublished conference paper, 1990); Dru Gladney, "Bodily Positions and Social Dispositions: Sexuality, Nationality and Tiananmen" (paper presented at the Institute for Advanced Study, Princeton, April 26, 1990); Lucian Pye, "Tiananmen and Chinese Political Culture: The Escalation of Confrontation from Moralizing to Revenge," *Asian Survey*, 30, 4 (1990), pp. 331–347; and David Strand, "Protest in Beijing: Civil Society and Public Sphere in China," *Problems of Communism*, 34, 3 (1990), pp. 1–19. All unpublished papers cited with authors' permission; Link's comments on Beijing opera are cited in Strand, "Protest in Beijing."

18. Charles Tilly, *From Mobilization to Revolution* (Reading, Mass.: Addison-Wesley, 1978).

19. Strand, "Protest in Beijing"; Jeffrey Wasserstrom, "Student Protest in the Chinese Tradition," in Saich, *Chinese People's Movement*.

20. This phenomenon of protesters transforming an authorized procedure into radical street theater is by no means unique to China, as Charles Tilly's discussion of rural unrest in *The Contentious French* (Cambridge: Harvard University Press, 1986), esp. pp. 116–117, illustrates.

21. Pye, "Tiananmen and Chinese Political Culture."

22. *North China Herald*, November 19, 1902, pp. 1076–1077; November 24, 1917, pp. 467–468.

23. For a more detailed discussion of the importance of funerals in Chinese political, social, and cultural life, and references to relevant works on the topic, see James Watson's contribution to this volume.

24. Turner, *The Ritual Process: Structure and Anti-Structure* (Ithaca: Cornell University Press, 1969), esp. ch. 3: "Liminality and Communitas."

25. Yan Jiaqi and Gao Gao, *"Wenhua dageming" Shinianshi* (A ten-year history of the "Cultural Revolution") (Tianjin: Tianjin renmin chubanshe, 1986), pp. 586–640.

26. This pattern is hardly unique to China. Compare this account of a key demonstration by tens of thousands of youths on November 17, 1989, in Prague. It was one of the major events leading to the fall of the Communist government in Czechoslovakia. "The memorial for Jan Opletal, the student killed by the Nazis, was sponsored by the official student organization but was transformed into a demonstration for freedom, political change and the dismissal of the Communist Party leader, Milos Jakes." (*New York Times* [national ed.], November 18, 1989.) Needless to say, Czechoslovakia—where the theaters were transformed into the headquarters of the democratic opposition, and a playwright, Vaclav Havel, was elected president—is an excellent place to look for examples of political theater.

27. For student comments on hunger strikes in other parts of the world, see Yi Mu and Mark V. Thompson, *Crisis at Tiananmen* (San Francisco: China Books, 1989), p. 172; and *Newsweek*, May 29, 1989, p. 21.

28. For general discussions of the goddess of democracy statue's construction and symbolism and photographs of the statue, see Han Minzhu, ed., *Cries for Democracy* (Princeton: Princeton University Press, 1990), pp. 342–348; Human Rights in China, *Children*, pp. 116–122; Yi and Thompson, *Crisis*, p. 372; and Chapter 8 in this volume. Dru Gladney notes the parallels between the goddess and Cultural Revolution Mao icons in his "Bodily Positions and Social Dispositions"; for photographs of such statues being carried through Tiananmen Square, see *Beijing Review*, October 3, 1969, p. 7, and *China Reconstructs* (December 1986), p. 3; and for a photograph of Shanghai students carrying a replica of the Statue of Liberty, see the *New York Times Magazine*, June 4, 1989, p. 28.

29. Insightful firsthand accounts of audience reaction to and participation in Beijing events is provided in Pieke, "Observations," and Niming, "Learning."

30. Suggestions from Barry Naughton were very helpful in inspiring and formulating these ideas.

31. Among the students, there was significant criticism of the servile posture of the kneeling petitioners. But it appears that by adopting this traditional ritual, the petitioners gained substantial sympathy and support among the general populace. See Lianhebao editorial department, ed., *Tiananmen yijiubajiu* (Tiananmen 1989) (Taipei: Lianjing chuban shiye gongsi, 1989), pp. 60–61; Han, *Cries*, pp. 63–64.

32. *North China Herald*, June 8, 1918, pp. 571–572; *Minguo ribao*, June 1 and 2, 1918; John Israel, *Student Nationalism in China, 1927–1937* (Stanford: Stanford University Press, 1966), pp. 60–61 and passim.

33. "Dueling Demonstrations in Beijing," *San Francisco Chronicle*, June 1, 1989, pp. A21–A25.

34. We are grateful to Henry Rosemont, Jr., who witnessed this performance, for describing it to us.

35. Wu Mouren et al., *Bajiu Zhongguo minyun jishi* (Annals of the 1989 Chinese democracy movement) (New York: privately published, 1989), pp. 262 and 267.

36. Michel Oksenberg provoked our thinking on this point. It became clear during Nixon's visit to China in November 1989 that Chinese and Western connotations of the term *tragedy* are quite different. Western notions derived from Greek drama link tragedy to unalterable fate or to some "tragic flaw" of the person who suffers the tragic fate. Thus, from a Western perspective, calling the events of June 3–4 a "tragedy" tends to objectify them and even to remove responsibility for the bloodshed from the hands of the Chinese leadership. In this sense, use of the term *tragedy* was an attempt to soften the implications of the term *massacre*; it is perhaps significant that years earlier, Nixon had no difficulty terming the student deaths at Kent State a "tragedy." But the Chinese word is closer to our sense for *melodrama* and implies a clear villain—which the Chinese leadership correctly understood to be themselves. For an example of an official denial that June 4 was a tragedy, see *New York Times*, September 27, 1989, p. 8; for Nixon's comment on Kent State ("when dissent turns to violence it invites tragedy"), see Kirkpatrick Sale, *SDS* (New York: Random House, 1973), p. 638; and for further discussion of the differences between English and Chinese understandings of *tragedy*, see the Afterword to this volume.

37. Here and in later sections, we draw heavily upon the discussion in Richard Schechner, "From Ritual to Theater and Back," in Richard Schechner and Mady Schuman, eds., *Ritual, Play, and Performance* (New York: Seabury Press, 1976), pp.196–222.

38. Stephen Lukes, "Political Ritual and Social Integration," *Sociology*, 9, 2 (1975), pp. 289–305, criticizes overly broad definitions of the term, but Lukes's own more limited definition still encompasses most forms of popular protests as well as ceremon-

ials that serve to uphold the status quo. In an earlier work, one of us has followed Lukes's lead and analyzed Chinese student demonstrations as "political rituals"; see Jeffrey Wasserstrom, "Taking It to the Streets: Shanghai Students and Political Protest, 1919–1949" (Ph.D. dissertation, University of California, Berkeley, 1989).

39. See in particular, Clifford Geertz, "Religion as a Cultural System," in his *Interpretation of Cultures* (New York: Basic Books, 1973), pp. 87–125.

40. See Emile Durkheim, *The Elementary Forms of the Religious Life*, trans. J. W. Swain (London: Allen and Unwin, 1915); for citations to and a highly critical review of other Durkheimian studies of ritual, see Lukes, "Political Ritual."

41. Robin Horton, cited in Victor Turner, *From Ritual to Theater* (New York: Performing Arts Journal Press, 1982), p. 82.

42. For Geertz's approach, see the various essays in *The Interpretation of Cultures* and his "Blurred Genres: The Refiguration of Social Thought," *American Scholar* (Spring 1980), pp. 172–176.

43. Turner's classic statement on the topic was *The Ritual Process: Structure and Anti-Structure* (Ithaca: Cornell University Press, 1969); see also his "Social Dramas and Ritual Metaphors," in Schechner and Schuman, *Ritual, Play, and Performance*, 97–122.

44. If, for example, a priest were just to pour wine into a chalice, dump wafers into a bowl, and pass them around without the proper words and gestures, transsubstantiation would not occur and the communicants would not partake in the body and blood of Christ. Schechner uses the believed efficaciousness of rituals as the main criteria for differentiating them from theatrical performances in his essay "From Ritual to Theater and Back."

45. Jean-Christophe Agnew, *Worlds Apart: The Market and the Theater in Anglo-American Thought* (Cambridge: Cambridge University Press, 1986), pp. 103–112.

46. Turner, *From Ritual to Theater*, esp. pp. 52–55. Geertz is less helpful in this regard. Although he writes at length about the "theater state" of Bali, his language (e.g., in *Negara*, p. 102, he writes of "the ritual extravagances of the theater state") both fails to distinguish between ritual and theater and tends to treat theater as a mass ritual to which all responded with a uniform belief.

47. *Li Ji* (Classic of ritual), ch. 1, verses 27, 63, in Fung You-lan, *A History of Chinese Philosophy*, vol. 1, trans. Derk Bodde (Princeton: Princeton University Press, 1952), p. 339.

48. Ibid., Chapter 1, 28, 97–99, p. 343.

49. Schechner, "From Ritual to Theater and Back," p. 211.

50. In both "Patrician Society, Plebeian Culture," and "Eighteenth-Century English Society," Thompson analyzes "countertheater" of "threat and sedition" through which England's common people challenged the gentry's "theater of hegemony." Although these insightful articles forcefully illustrate the subversive potential of theater, we have avoided Thompson's "theater/countertheater" terminology because "theater of hegemony" blurs the important distinction between regularly repeated "rituals" (such as coronations) and other kinds of improvised, theatrical shows of force or majesty that support the status quo.

51. Nicholas Rogers, "Popular Protest in Early Hanoverian England," *Past and Present*, 79 (1978), pp. 70–100; Susan G. Davis, *Parades and Power: Street Theatre in Nineteenth Century Philadelphia* (Philadelphia: Temple University Press, 1975); Konrad Jarausch, *Students, Society, and Politics in Imperial Germany* (Princeton: Princeton University Press, 1982), pp. 3–6.

52. J. L. Austin, "Performative Utterances," in Austin, *Philosophical Papers* (London: Oxford University Press, 1962), pp. 220–239.

53. The proper forms of these rituals were precisely delineated in the ancient text, the "Ceremonies and Rituals." For a translation, see John Steele, *The I-li* (London, 1917).

54. In divination rituals that mimic these social transactions, an undesirable result may come from choosing the wrong polite words. Therefore, according to one informant, "You keep throwing the blocks until a yes comes up, each time slightly changing what you say. That is because you might have made a mistake in giving your address, or you might not have been polite . . . enough in speaking to the god." Emily M. Ahern, *Chinese Ritual and Politics* (Cambridge: Cambridge University Press, 1981), p. 32.

55. Lianhebao, *Tiananmen yijiubajiu*, pp. 69–71; Han, *Cries*, pp. 126–127; Pye, "Tiananmen and Chinese Political Culture," p. 341.

56. Jacques Burdick, *Theater* (New York: Newsweek Books, 1974): pp. 7–41; E. T. Kirby, "The Shamanistic Origins of Popular Entertainments," in Schechner and Schuman, *Ritual, Play, and Performance*, pp. 139–149.

57. Colin MacKerras, *The Chinese Theatre in Modern Times* (Amherst: University of Massachusetts Press, 1975), p. 13.

58. For relevant citations concerning funeral rites, see Watson's chapter; for other kinds of dramas performed for the gods, see Joseph Esherick, *The Origins of the Boxer Uprising* (Berkeley: University of California Press, 1987), pp. 63–64 and passim.

59. Natalie Davis, "The Rites of Violence," in *Society and Culture in Early Modern France* (Stanford: Stanford University Press, 1975), pp. 152–188. Other chapters in this book, such as "The Reasons of Misrule," also provide insights into the relationship between rituals and political theater.

60. For relevant citations, see Wasserstrom, *Student Protests*, ch. 10; see also Lukes, "Political Ritual," pp. 294 and 299.

61. "Social Dramas and Ritual Metaphors," in Schechner and Schuman, *Ritual, Play, and Performance*, pp. 97–122.

62. Some sample rituals that reenact violent struggles can be found in Schechner, "From Ritual to Theater and Back," pp. 196–202. The final moments of U.S. electoral campaigns, after the voting ends, often take on a ritual character: First groups converge at the headquarters of rival candidates, where they revel and make their final symbolic attacks upon the character of the opponent; then, to conclude the ritual, the losing candidate calls the winner to politely concede to and congratulate his or her former adversary.

63. Lynn Hunt, *Politics, Culture, and Class in the French Revolution* (Berkeley: University of California Press, 1984), p. 99; see also Mona Ozouf, *Festivals and the French Revolution* (Cambridge: Harvard University Press, 1988).

64. Hunt, *Politics, Culture, and Class*, p. 60.

65. Schechner, "From Ritual to Theater and Back," p. 211.

66. For a provocative discussion of these uses of May 4, see Vera Schwarcz, *The Chinese Enlightenment* (Berkeley: University of California Press, 1986), pp. 240–282; this topic is dealt with at length in Jeffrey N. Wasserstrom, "Revolutionary Anniversaries in Guomindang and Communist China" (paper presented at the Pacific Coast regional Association for Asian Studies meetings, Stanford, June 1990).

67. Confucius, *Lunyu*, 12:1, in Arthur Waley, trans., *The Analects of Confucius* (New York: Vintage, no date), p. 162.

68. Susan Naquin and Evelyn Rawski, *Chinese Society in the Eighteenth Century* (New Haven: Yale University Press, 1987), p. 88 and passim; Charles Hucker, *The Traditional Chinese State in Ming Times* (Tucson: University of Arizona Press, 1961), pp. 67–68; various contributions to Kwang-Ching Liu, ed., *Orthodoxy in Late Imperial China* (Berkeley: University of California Press, 1990); and Angelo Zito, "Grand Sacrifice as

Text-Performance: Writing and Ritual in Eighteenth-Century China" (Ph.D. dissertation, University of Chicago, 1989).

69. Herbert Fingarette, *Confucius: The Secular as Sacred* (New York: Harper and Row, 1972).

70. For more details on imperial rituals, see Zito, "Grand Sacrifice as Text-Performance"; Naquin and Rawski, *Chinese Society*; and Gugong bowuguan yuan (Palace Museum), eds., *Zijincheng dihou shenghuo* (Lives of the emperors and empresses in the Forbidden City) (Beijing: China Travel and Tourism Press, 1983), pp. 108–111.

71. The quote is from Jean Baptiste Du Halde, *The General History of China*, trans. Richard Brooks (London: J. Watts, 1736), p. 349; for a general treatment of the tours and comments on the official record, see Jonathan D. Spence, *Ts'ao Yin and the K'ang-hsi Emperor, Bondservant and Master* (New Haven: Yale University Press, 1966), pp. 125–136.

72. Alexander Woodside, "Emperors and the Chinese Political System" (paper presented at the Four Anniversaries China Conference, Annapolis, September 10–15, 1989).

73. Kung-chuan Hsiao, *Rural China: Imperial Control in the Nineteenth Century* (Seattle: University of Washington Press, 1967), pp. 449–450.

74. Especially when compared to Chinese theater audiences, the silence of ritual "audiences" is notable. In this regard, the "profound silence" that Jesuit observers recorded in the vast crowds greeting the Kangxi emperor suggests that imperial tours were closer to rituals than theatrical performances; Spence, *Ts'ao Yin*, p. 136.

75. Roy Strong, *Art and Power: Renaissance Festivals, 1450–1650* (Berkeley: University of California Press, 1984), pp. 7–11.

76. Thomas A. Brady, Jr., "Rites of Autonomy, Rites of Dependence: South German Civic Culture in the Age of Renaissance and Reformation," in Steven Ozment, ed., *Religion and Culture in the Renaissance and Reformation* (Kirksville, Mo.: Sixteenth-Century Journal Publishers, 1989).

77. Lawrence M. Bryant, *The King and the City in the Parisian Royal Entry Ceremony* (Geneva: Librairie Droz, 1986), p. 22.

78. David M. Bergeron, *English Civic Pageantry, 1558–1642* (Columbia: University of South Carolina Press, 1971); Edward Muir, *Civic Ritual in Renaissance Venice* (Princeton: Princeton University Press, 1981).

79. Hsiao, *Rural China*, pp. 194–201; Victor Mair "Language and Ideology in the Written Popularizations of the *Sacred Edicts*," in David Johnson, Andrew Nathan, and Evelyn Rawski, *Popular Culture in Late Imperial China* (Berkeley: University of California Press, 1985), pp. 325–359.

80. In Waley, *Analects*, 1:3; Wing-Tsit Chan, *A Sourcebook of Chinese Philosophy* (Princeton: Princeton University Press, 1963), p. 20.

81. For an important recent discussion of the contrasting meanings of *li* and *fa*, which inter alia shows the extent to which these two terms dominate classical Chinese conceptions of politics, see Benjamin Schwartz. *The World of Thought in Ancient China* (Cambridge: Harvard University Press, 1985), pp. 102–104, 321–349, and passim. As Schwartz notes (pp. 102–104), even idealistic Confucians such as Confucius himself accepted that their vision of rule by *li* alone was utopian, and that in reality punishments and force would have to play some role.

82. An interesting discussion of this topic by a nonsinologist that draws attention to contrasts between the Chinese and Greek traditions is J.G.A. Pocock, "Ritual, Language, Power," in *Politics, Language and Time: Essays on Political Thought and History* (Chicago: University of Chicago Press, 1989), pp. 42–79. We are grateful to Daniel Gargola for drawing our attention to this piece.

83. John Meskill, "Academies and Politics in the Ming Dynasty," in Charles Hucker, ed., *Chinese Government in Ming Times* (New York: Columbia University Press, 1969), pp. 149–174.

84. Derk Bodde and Clarence Morris, *Law in Imperial China* (Philadelphia: University of Pennsylvania Press, 1973), pp. 464–466.

85. For some relevant examples, see Elizabeth J. Perry, "Tax Revolt in Late Qing China," *Late Imperial China*, 6, 1 (1985), pp. 83–112; Tsing Yuan, "Urban Riots and Disturbances," in Jonathan Spence and John Wills, eds., *From Ming to Ch'ing* (New Haven: Yale University Press, 1979); and Lin Yu-tang, *A History of the Press and Public Opinion in China* (1936; reprint, New York: Greenwood, 1968).

86. William Martin, *A Cycle of Cathay* (New York: F. H. Revell, 1900), pp. 91–92, cited in Hsiao, *Rural China*, p. 434.

87. Ahern, *Chinese Ritual and Politics*, p. 92.

88. *Lunyu*, 8:14, in Waley, *Analects*, p. 135.

89. Cited in Ssu-Yu Teng and John K. Fairbank, eds., *China's Response to the West: A Documentary Survey, 1839–1923* (Cambridge: Harvard University Press, 1979), p. 28.

90. Ibid., p. 50.

91. Edward J. M. Rhoads, *China's Republican Revolution: The Case of Kwang-tung, 1895–1913* (Cambridge: Harvard University Press, 1975), pp. 86 and 95–96.

92. Joseph W. Esherick, *Reforms and Revolution in China: The 1911 Revolution in Hunan and Hubei* (Berkeley: University of California Press, 1977), p. 56; see also Rhoads, *China's Republican Revolution*, p. 88.

93. Mary Rankin, *Elite Activism and Political Transformation in China: Zhejiang Province, 1865–1911* (Stanford: Stanford University Press, 1986); William Rowe, *Hankow: Community and Conflict* (Stanford: Stanford University Press, 1989). Rankin mentions the oratory society in "The Emergence of Women at the End of the Ch'ing: The Case of Chiu Jin," in Margery Wolf and Roxann Witke, eds., *Women in Chinese Society* (Stanford: Stanford University Press, 1975), p. 51.

94. Chao Hsueh-hai, "Tsing Hua New Buildings," *Tsing Hua Journal*, 3, 7 (June 1918), p. 38. We are grateful to Jeffrey Cody for bringing this quote to our attention.

95. "The First Stadium in Shanghai," in Zhou Yuehua, ed., *Anecdotes of Old Shanghai* (Shanghai: Shanghai Cultural Publishing House, 1985), pp. 154–156, describes various political gatherings held at the St. John's sports field. Complaints about the lack of appropriate public gathering places can be found in various early twentieth-century newspaper reports; see, for example, Cai Yuanpei's comments in *North China Herald*, May 7, 1903, p. 885.

96. *North China Herald*, May 7, 1903, p. 885.

97. Ibid., August 11, 1905, p. 322.

98. Ruth Hayhoe, "Towards the Forging of a Chinese University Ethos: Zhendan and Fudan, 1903–1919," *China Quarterly*, no. 94 (June 1983), pp. 323–341; and British Foreign Office records 228/2155.

99. MacKerras, *Chinese Theatre*, p. 48.

100. Zhou, *Anecdotes*, p. 32.

101. MacKerras, *Chinese Theatre*, p. 49.

102. See, for example, *Sun Zhongshan xiansheng huace*; and *Guomin geming huace* (An illustrated history of the national revolution) (Taipei, 1965).

103. For more details on KMT-sponsored mass movements (and citations to the relevant literature on the topic, some of which is discussed below as well), see Wasserstrom, *Student Protests*, ch. 6, 7, and 9.

104. MacKerras, *Chinese Theatre*, pp. 78–79 and 95–96.

105. Andrew Nathan, *Peking Politics, 1918–1923: Factionalism and the Failure of Constitutionalism* (Berkeley: University of California Press, 1976); Lloyd Eastman, *The Abortive Revolution: China Under Nationalist Rule, 1927–1937* (Cambridge: Harvard University Press, 1974).

106. Chang Hao, *Liang Ch'i-ch'ao and Intellectual Transition in China* (Cambridge: Harvard University Press, 1971), p. 239.

107. Ernest P. Young, *Liberalism and Dictatorship in Early Republican China: The Politics of the Yuan Shih-K'ai Presidency* (Ann Arbor: University of Michigan Press, 1976), pp. 148–155.

108. Various pieces in the March and April 1946 issues of *China Weekly Review*, which describe Shanghai's first "free" elections and include admissions by KMT officials concerning some improprieties, illustrate this point. See particularly "Democratic Elections," March 16, pp. 48–49; "Scandal in Yunnan: Bribery Quite Common in 'Elections' Paper Declares," April 27, pp. 184–185; and "Officials Held on Ballot Box Stuffing Charge," May 11, p. 235.

109. Christian Henriot, "Le Gouvernement Municipal de Shanghai, 1927–1937," (doctoral dissertation, Sorbonne, 1983); Wang Ke-wen, "The Kuomintang in Transition" (Ph.D. dissertation, Stanford University, 1985). See also John Israel, *Student Nationalism in China, 1927–1937* (Stanford: Stanford University Press, 1966); and Patrick Cavendish, "The 'New China' of the Kuomintang," in Jack Gray, ed., *Modern China's Search for a Political Form* (London: Oxford University Press, 1969).

110. For details, see Wasserstrom, *Student Protests*, ch. 9.

111. Mao Zedong, "Xin minzhu zhuyi lun" (On new democracy), in *Mao Zedong xuanji* (Collected works of Mao Zedong), vol. 2 (Beijing: People's Publishing House, 1952), p. 690.

112. Israel, *Student Nationalism*, p. 24.

113. Charles P. Cell, *Revolution at Work: Mobilization Campaigns in China* (New York: Academic Press, 1977).

114. Along with examples given earlier, the student protests of 1985 and those of 1986–1987 began on anniversary dates—September 18 and December 9—set aside for official commemorations.

115. This point owes much to Charles Tilly's studies of collective action, see esp. *From Mobilization to Revolution*.

116. The symbolic appeal of this selflessness helps to explain why, especially since June 4, criticisms of student movement leaders within the dissident community have focused on acts of extravagance and indulgence as well as undemocratic procedures. As Chan and Kwong note ("Trashing the Hopes of Tiananmen," p. 562), attacks on Wuer Kaixi and others have tended to stress allegations that they have squandered funds on "luxury hotel accommodations, banquets and other questionable expenses."

117. Gladney, "Bodily Positions and Social Dispositions."

118. For further information on and relevant citations for the various continuities between student protests, past and present, alluded to in this paragraph, see Wasserstrom, *Student Protests*, ch. 2, 3, and epilogue.

119. David Zweig, "Peasants and Politics," *World Policy Journal* (Fall 1989), pp. 633–645. Esherick's impressions from fieldwork in North Shaanxi in June and July 1989 generally support Zweig's analysis.

120. See Vladamir Tsimaneau, "Eastern Europe: The Story the Media Missed," *Bulletin of Atomic Scientists*, 46, 2 (1990), pp. 17–21; Pawel Machcewicz, "The Solidarity Revolution," *Polish Perspectives*, 32, 3 (1989), pp. 14–25; and, for further discussion and additional citations, Chapter 11 below.

121. Robert Darnton, *The Great Cat Massacre and Other Episodes in French Cultural History* (New York: Vintage, 1985), pp. 85–89.

122. Machcewicz, "The Solidarity Revolution," p. 19; Bourdieu defines his concept of habitus in *Outline of a Theory of Practice*, trans. Richard Nice (Cambridge: Cambridge University Press, 1977), pp. 72–87.

123. David Strand, *Rickshaw Beijing* (Berkeley: University of California Press, 1989), and "Protest in Beijing."

124. Rankin, *Elite Activism*, p. 166.

125. Strand, "Protest in Beijing."

3

THE RENEGOTIATION OF CHINESE CULTURAL IDENTITY IN THE POST-MAO ERA

James L. Watson

The Red Guards will sweep dirty old water from the earth. The Red Guards will destroy the old world and create a new world.
—1966 middle school slogan, Lo Fulang, *Morning Breeze: A True Story of China's Cultural Revolution*

Cultural accumulation and advance demand that we build first and destroy later—creating the new while not destroying the old. When we build a new building, it is not necessary to tear down an old one; so it is with our cultural legacy.
—Wang Meng, "The Principal Contradiction in Culture"

Prelude

This chapter was written while the drama of Tiananmen Square was being played out in full view of a world audience. The television images of Chinese students demonstrating in Beijing were so riveting they gave viewers the vicarious thrill of participating in a historic "event." The live broadcasts were multivariant in their symbolism—and irony. Twenty-two years earlier the same square had been the venue for another set of demonstrations represent-

---

This essay was originally prepared for the Four Anniversaries China Conference held in Annapolis, September 10–15, 1989. The original conference paper will be included in the proceedings of that conference to be published by the University of Michigan, Center for Chinese Studies. This amended version is published here with the permission of the University of Michigan.

ing an earlier generation of students who also hoped to change the nature of China's political system. The goals and public rhetoric of the two movements were radically different, but one important symbol remained constant: the enigmatic portrait of Mao Zedong looming over the square. When vandals attacked the portrait on May 23, students reacted with anger and expressed great concern that this act might be used as a pretext for troops to clear the square. Said one, "Mao was a good guy. There was no need to abuse him like that."[1]

Here, in the heat of a political movement, we witnessed the process by which history is reconstructed. For many Chinese, that same image of Mao conjures up unpleasant memories of the Cultural Revolution. During my first trip to China in the late 1970s, the chairman's portrait was everywhere. Today, except in Tiananmen Square, one is hard pressed to find depictions of Mao displayed in public. Two gigantic statues of him were removed from the campus of Beijing University only twelve months prior to the spring demonstrations.[2] The statues had become an embarrassment for a generation of teachers and administrators who had participated—some as persecutors, others as "bad class" victims—in the Cultural Revolution. On May 23, 1989, however, a new generation of students too young to remember the 1960s had appropriated the memory of Mao for their own purposes. He had been transformed into a symbol of selflessness and rectitude in an era characterized by corruption, alienation, and self-doubt.

The public sufferings of the hunger strikers (jueshizhe) created further powerful images that television made immediate and tangible. And this, of course, is precisely the point: Fasting is a political act that conveys an unmistakable message to the world at large. In fact, given their expectation that the state-controlled media in China would deny them access to the Chinese people, it seems likely that the Beijing students chose consciously to appeal to an international television audience. The news of young people courting death through fast could then be sent back to China literally over the heads of party authorities, by the Voice of America (VOA) and BBC. As it turned out, both Chinese print media and, to a limited extent, local television broadcast the news of the hunger strike.[3] But there can be little doubt that U.S. and other foreign networks' satellite broadcasts of the fasting, complete with howling sirens and fainting students, had much to do with the creation of an international media event—which, in turn, helped student leaders convert the small-scale demonstrations into China's most serious political crisis since the death of Mao and the subsequent arrest of the Gang of Four in 1976.[4]

By attempting to ignore the demonstrations, party authorities all but conceded the manipulation of the media to the students. After gaining the attention of the world's television audience through the drama of the fast, student leaders could concentrate on presenting their messages. Slogans were simplified (corruption in high places, intransigent leaders, the promise of democracy). Earlier complicating issues such as inflation, job placement, and student living conditions were dropped. It is obvious that the students were far more sophisticated in their ability to *use* the media than were their opponents, who remained behind closed doors, conducting politics in the time-tried but increasingly outdated mode that has characterized Communist parties since the early twentieth century. As a result, politics can never be the same in China.

The Pursuit of Chinese Cultural Identity in the Post-Mao Era

Few foreigners who lived or worked in China during the preceding five years could fail to have noticed the high level of alienation and despair that characterized intellectual life, particularly in the universities. This was partly a consequence of frozen salaries and rising inflation. With the entire society plunging headlong into the pursuit of personal affluence, intellectuals had to join the scramble for new sources of income (e.g., by marketing their foreign language and management skills) or stand aside and watch their standard of living fall below that of workers with minimal education. Financial problems were obviously important, but teachers, writers, and researchers were also deeply concerned about the evolution of Chinese culture in the post-Mao era. The self-sacrificing ethic of the early Communist movement (1949–1957) appealed to many intellectuals who participated in the construction of a new socialist culture. Having seen these dreams shattered during the late 1950s and 1960s, they had high hopes for the reforms instituted in the late 1970s. After ten years of reform, however, there was still no agreement on what kind of society China was to become. The Communist Party had lost credibility, and its leaders were incapable of enlisting mass support for a new vision of the future. Equally alarming to many intellectuals was the prospect that China had abandoned its past in an effort to join the modern world.

It is unclear whether ordinary Chinese workers and farmers shared the intellectuals' sense of despair about the future or the present. In my own research (1985, 1986, 1988) among rural peoples of Guangdong and Jiangsu, quite the opposite impression emerged, namely, that farmers were delighted with the economic reforms. In most of the areas I visited, living standards had doubled and tripled in the past five years; the responsibility system in agriculture was welcomed by everyone, save a few diehard cadres who obviously longed for the days when they controlled the destiny of local residents.[5] It is true, of course, that my field research was conducted in two of China's wealthiest areas (the Pearl River Delta and the Jiangnan region); the same sense of buoyancy may not have prevailed in the North China Plain. Myron Cohen's recent research suggests, however, that the reforms have also generated a new sense of optimism about the future in rural Hebei.[6]

Prior to the reforms, being sent to the countryside was equated with lifelong exile and poverty. Today, ironically, certain rural areas (e.g., Guangdong's Zhongshan and Xinhui counties) are attracting illegal migrants from northern cities; these itinerants do not speak Cantonese and work for wages that no self-respecting Guangdong farmer would even consider accepting. Some parts of rural China are therefore losing a stigmatized image.

What does this growing split between rural and urban mean for China's future? Martin Whyte has suggested that two cultural systems may be emerging, one in the cities and another in the countryside.[7] I am convinced that Whyte is correct. Before pursuing this argument, however, I need to say more about the nature of cultural identity in Chinese society.

In what sense is post-Mao Chinese culture "Chinese"? This essay examines the question from an anthropological perspective. *Culture* in this context is not a reflection (exclusively) of the arts, literature, and philosophy. Rather, the term *culture* as I employ it is intimately related to perceptions of appropriate lifestyle—which in turn is incorporated into a sense of personal identity. Culture is embedded in family patterns, religious beliefs, political attitudes, and in the rituals of everyday life. Furthermore, culture, like one's sense of identity, is constantly changing.

Contemporary definitions of culture have been adapted to fit the fluid, boundary-defying expectations of the postmodern world. Most U.S. anthropologists—including such influential figures as Clifford Geertz and Marshall Sahlins—now see culture as a set of symbolic representations and expectations that people must *construct* for themselves.[8] It is no longer perceived as a list of traits inherited passively from ancestors in preordained or immutable form, as earlier notions would lead us to expect.[9] Culture in today's world has to be negotiated, transacted, and achieved. This approach thus stresses the active participation of people who cooperate—some willingly, others not—to create an acceptable culture. State authorities are, of course, directly involved in this creative process, but in the end it is the acceptance and routinization of cultural forms by ordinary people that matters most.

Since 1949 the Chinese people have experienced two or three traumatic attempts to destroy key elements of their "traditional" (i.e., presocialist) culture. Closely associated with these movements have been state-sponsored campaigns to construct competing versions of a new socialist culture—the most notable being the Great Proletarian Cultural Revolution launched in 1966. An earlier and in some respects more far-reaching campaign to obliterate the old and fabricate the new occurred during the Great Leap Forward (1958–1960). China's presocialist culture was, and to a certain extent still is, a very difficult nut to crack.

Cultural Identity in Late Imperial and Republican-Era China

There can be little doubt that late imperial China, in comparison to other premodern, agrarian societies, exhibited a high degree of cultural integration. Serious divisions based on kinship, ethnicity, and regional loyalties did, of course, exist in China, but—unlike Europe or South Asia—the dominant historical theme is one of ever-increasing incorporation and co-optation. One need only read Eugen Weber's *Peasants into Frenchmen* to appreciate just how integrated China was during its late imperial era. Weber's account of the period immediately preceding World War I (1870–1914) makes it clear that the idea of "France" as a modern nation-state, with a shared culture and a corporate identity that tied all citizens together, did not exist until it was consciously created by Parisian social engineers for the purposes of national mobilization.[10] Benedict Anderson's speculations on the origins of modern nationalism are also relevant here: The Chinese at the turn of the twentieth century could not "imagine" the state as an integral part of their personal identity, but they had no difficulty identifying with the abstraction we call Chinese culture.[11]

In China the notion of a unified culture predated, and made possible, the fabrication of a modern Chinese state following the collapse of the imperial order in 1911. People of all stations in life—peasants, workers, landlords, merchants, officials—already related to China's grand tradition with its ancient history. For ordinary Chinese, this abstraction was concretized and represented in everyday discourse as the "civilized" (*meiwenhuade*) way of life; those who did not follow accepted norms were defined as "uncivilized" or "savage" (*yemande*). Notions of civility, conformity, and order are thus at the heart of what all Chinese accepted as the irreducible basis of their cultural identity. The point I wish to emphasize is that the vast majority of Chinese, irrespective of class background, life experience, or education, shared this vision of the acceptable way of life during the late imperial era (there were, of course, dissenters, such as the Taiping rebels and members of various Daoist sects). The notion of a shared culture began to unravel during the late nineteenth and early twentieth centuries, culminating in the May Fourth Movement (see Chapters 4 and 5), but it survived for most people until the political campaigns of the Communist era.

What were the main elements in this vision of a shared culture? Some have stressed the role of an ideographic (i.e., nonphonetic) script that cuts across speech communities, thereby allowing educated people from different regions to share a common literary/philosophical tradition.[12] Others have argued that it was the autocratic power of the Chinese state, projected through a complex bureaucracy, that held the society together.[13] Still others point to China's elaborate hierarchy of commercial centers and marketing communities as the key to cultural unity.[14] All of these explanations are, of course, correct. One cannot conceive of "China," or the abstraction we call Chinese culture, without a common script, a centralized state, and a complex hierarchy of central places.

My own approach to the problem of cultural identity stresses two interrelated features of everyday life: a shared oral tradition and the central role of ritual. During the late imperial era everyone—from the emperor in Beijing to the lowly duckherd in the Pearl River Delta—celebrated important life transitions with the same set of rites. They also shared essentially the same oral tradition, expressed in folktales, myths, and legends.

Shared Oral Traditions and Visions of History

David Johnson has argued that it was drama, or, more precisely, the stories and emotions communicated in popular opera, that helped forge a shared sense of "Chineseness" among all strata of people. As Johnson notes, the audiences of opera varied greatly, but the stories remained basically similar over time and space.[15] The essential feature of Chinese opera was that everyone was exposed to the performances at one time or another in their lives. The poor stood in the back or watched from the sides while local worthies occupied the more expensive seats in front. Future magistrates and ministers of state sat with their amahs learning about intrigue, honor, and duty. In the process, according to Johnson, all parties in this audience came to share certain key values and modes of emotional expression.[16]

Opera was only one of many performative media that served to communicate and inculcate shared values. Perhaps the most obvious were folktales and oral epics told to the young by elders or professional storytellers.[17] This feature of culture is the most difficult for non-Chinese to penetrate. Even after decades of experience in China and fluency in the language, foreigners cannot hope to master the enormous corpus of folklore that—until recently—most Chinese shared as a matter of course.[18]

The early phases of elementary education are also critical for generating and perpetuating a sense of cultural/national identity, particularly in respect to history. The sequence of dynasties; the names of emperors, sages, and villains; and the great myths of cultural longevity ("We have thousands of years of unbroken history") were all taught as part of the curriculum—formal and informal—in China during the late imperial and Republican eras.[19] This received, sanitized vision of history is still taught today in Taiwan and, to a limited extent, in Hong Kong but not—it would appear—in the People's Republic.

The Role of Ritual in the Construction of "Chineseness"

Another way to address the problem of cultural identity in China is to ask the question: What makes Chinese culture "Chinese"? What, in other words, are the basic elements of the cultural equation that allowed some residents of that vast country to call themselves "Chinese" (Han) and be accepted as such, whereas other peoples were labeled "barbarian" (*fan*, or, more politely, *shaoshu minzu*, minority peoples)? The set of cultural attributes that made a person Chinese appears to have little to do with a shared creed or set of prescribed religious beliefs. There was never a unified clergy in China charged with the responsibility of dispensing truth, as in Christendom. The closest parallel to the Western church hierarchy in China was the imperial bureaucracy, but Chinese officials were relatively few in number and were preoccupied with the practical aspects of governance, not religious beliefs.

In examining the processes of cultural construction, it is perhaps best to begin with the distinction between Han and non-Han. Chinese ordinarily present this as a straightforward dichotomy: One either is or is not Han. The key diagnostic feature here is whether a set of people are deemed to have *wen*, variously translated as civilization, learning, or elegance. Han Chinese by definition perceived themselves as civilized, whereas non-Han peoples (such as the Miao, Yao, and Zhuang) were categorized, by Han, as uncivilized.[20] In historical terms, however, the distinction between Han and non-Han was never so simple, particularly in the south.[21] Over the centuries whole populations, on the order of European states, have made the transformation from non-Han to Han.[22] More recently, in the wake of post-Mao reforms, certain groups that had been recognized as Han are seeking to reclaim—and, in the process, reconstruct—earlier non-Han identities.[23] These labels, therefore, are purely cultural and are not racial or biological in any obvious sense.

To be Chinese in this context meant that one played by the rules of the dominant culture and was judged to be a good performer by those who took it upon themselves to make such judgments—neighbors, local leaders, imperial officials. What, then, were the rules of the game? How did one become Chinese and maintain one's "Chineseness"? From the perspective of ordinary people, to be Chinese was to understand and accept the view that there was a correct way to live one's life. This was reflected most directly in the enactment of public rituals associated with the life cycle—namely, the rites of birth, marriage, death, and ancestorhood. Correct performance of these rites was one clear and unambiguous method of distinguishing the civilized from the uncivilized or, when considering marginal peoples, the cooked from the uncooked.[24] Put another way, practice rather than belief was what made one Chinese in the eyes of others.

As an example of the principles involved, one can cite the complex rituals surrounding death in China. Based on a survey of ethnographic evidence, I have elsewhere concluded that the basic form of funeral rites is (or was) similar throughout the empire.[25] There were, of course, interesting regional variations, but in general all Chinese—from the poorest farmer to the emperor himself—performed the same sequence of ritual acts at funerals.[26] This sequence of acts might be called the elementary structure of Chinese funerary ritual; the proper performance of the sequence distinguished civilized from uncivilized rites.

By emphasizing orthopraxy (correct practice) rather than orthodoxy (correct belief), I do not mean to imply that beliefs are somehow irrelevant to the construction of "Chineseness." This is obviously not the case. For instance, key elements of the funeral sequence were (and in some areas still are) supported by an underlying belief system that the majority of Chinese no doubt shared.[27] Important as these beliefs were, it was anxiety over the practice of the rites, in the correct sequence, that took precedence over discussions of meaning or symbolism in the everyday discourse of ordinary people. This does not mean, however, that there was no variation in performance. As long as the acts were accomplished in the approved sequence, there was room for infinite variety in ritual expression. Herein lies the genius of the (presocialist) Chinese approach to cultural construction: The system allowed for a high degree of variation within an overarching structure of unity.

The Chinese cultural system thus allowed for the free expression of what outsiders might perceive to be chaotic local diversity. The domain of ritual, in particular, gave great scope to regional and subethnic cultural displays. The system was so flexible that those who called themselves Chinese could have their cake and eat it too: They could participate in a unified culture yet at the same time celebrate their local or regional distinctiveness.

Imperial officials were, of course, intimately involved in the standardization of funerary ritual, but it would never have been possible to impose a uniform structure of rites on a society of such vast size and complexity. More subtle means were required. There is good evidence that imperial officials were engaged in the promotion of a standardized set of funeral and mourning customs throughout the empire; the same is true for marriage rites.[28] Accepted norms were enshrined in manuals available in even the smallest towns of the realm.[29] Given what we know about the distribution of power in late imperial China, it is probable that local elites subscribed to the accepted customs and encouraged a kind of ritual orthopraxy in the communities under their control: They led by example. Unacceptable practices were gradually suppressed or modified to conform to centralized models.[30]

This may have been the mechanism for the superimposition of a standard ritual structure, but we know little about the process of acceptance. Is the standardization we now perceive a consequence of government-sponsored social engineering carried out over many centuries, or is it the result of voluntary adoption by the general populace? Need we assume that these processes were mutually exclusive? Although it is obvious that there must have been strong incentives for people of all classes and regional backgrounds to cooperate in the cultural construction of a standardized set of rites, much more work needs to be done before we can answer these questions. What is clear, however, is that the preoccupation with ritual practice—rather than religious beliefs—made it possible for imperial authorities, local elites, and ordinary peasants to agree on the proper form for the conduct of key rituals.

Orthopraxy in Everyday Life

One can find the origins of what I take to be the unique (presocialist) Chinese approach to the construction of cultural identity as far back as the Confucian *Analects* and perhaps earlier. By many interpretations the central theme of Confucianism is harmony in thought and action; correct ideas follow from proper behavior.[31] In this sense orthopraxy is primary to, and takes precedence over, orthodoxy. At the core of Confucian notions of order is the principle of *li*, defined by Benjamin Schwartz as "all those 'objective' prescriptions of behavior, whether involving rite, ceremony, manners, or general deportment."[32] The Confucian approach to *li* is relevant to cultural construction:

Following correct form ensured that one was playing the game of culture by civilized rules and, in so doing, one reaffirmed one's "Chineseness."

It will come as no surprise to learn that the vision of Chinese culture presented in this essay derives from the highly personalized experience of having conducted ethnographic surveys and lived among Cantonese villagers for extended periods of time during the last decades. My cultural instructors in the villages of Hong Kong's New Territories and Guangdong's Pearl River Delta knew little of the formal teachings of Confucius or Zhuxi, but they knew a great deal about *li*, or *laih*, as it is pronounced in colloquial Cantonese. Villagers used the term in ordinary speech; one heard it dozens of times each day. To them it was not an abstract, philosophical concept but rather a mundane idea that had concrete associations. Constant references were made to funeral *li*, wedding *li*, and the *li* of ancestral rites; the term permeated their discourse on social activities. One of the worst remarks one could make about someone was that the person was "without *li*" (*mouh laih*, or *meiyou li*), meaning oblivious to proper behavior, impolite, and uncivilized.

In the Cantonese village context, *li* (*laih*) is best translated as "proper form," associated closely with correct performance. To perform a ritual properly, in the local view, was to follow its *li*. A funeral or a wedding had a recognized form (*li*) and deviations from that form caused great concern. Older people often stood on the sidelines of funerals, watching like hawks to make certain that proper form was followed. They did not hesitate to shout advice and dissent when they saw (what they perceived to be) departures from standard ritual practice. Cantonese funeral priests were choreographers of public ritual: They told people where to stand, how to sit, when to wail, what to eat, whom to greet, when to leave. If the ritual went awry or was not completed in the appointed time, disaster was certain to follow, not just for the bereaved but for the entire community.

Thus the villagers' concern for proper form (*li*) was not simply a matter of aesthetics or personal predilections. It was the glue that held the cosmos together. Without *li* there would be chaos (*luan*), another concept that had concrete associations for most ordinary Chinese. Among rural Cantonese, *luan* conjured up visions of banditry, famine, and that ultimate symbol of social breakdown—cannibalism. Villagers in the Pearl River Delta have a rich corpus of folklore focusing on (mythic) massacres carried out by imperial troops who intervened to reestablish order when local society collapsed.[33] The message is clear: Those who depart from accepted norms of ritual and action invite retribution of the most terrifying kind.

But this is not to say that Cantonese villagers were social automatons, rotely performing rituals over which they had no control and little understanding. Nor should they be seen as puppets dancing on strings of convention held by agents of the state. Stressing orthopraxy rather than orthodoxy had profound consequences for all social classes. It allowed China to attain a level of cultural integration that was never possible in other, large-scale agrarian societies.[34] The processes of cultural construction outlined in this essay involved the active participation of all Chinese—not just scholar-bureaucrats but farmers, artisans, merchants, and workers. There is evidence, for instance, that imperial officials were forced to accept, adapt, and co-opt mortuary customs that first emerged among the peasantry.[35] The standard Chinese funeral that one still sees in Taiwan, Hong Kong, and in rural areas of the PRC appears to be timeless but is in fact an amalgamation of ancient and modern rites.[36] Ordinary people, such as the ancestors of my Cantonese consultants, had as much to do with creating and promoting this amalgamation as anyone else in the realm, including the emperor himself.

Ritual Form and Cultural Identity in Socialist China

As those who have followed developments in post-1949 China well know, traditional rituals of the sort discussed above were rigorously attacked by Communist Party officials during the late 1950s and the late 1960s.[37] Funeral and burial rites were obvious targets of social engineering, especially in south China, where activists objected to the "feudal" implications of the ancestral cult. Ancestor worship was intimately related to the political activities of powerful lineages that owned great stretches of double-crop rice land in Guangdong and Fujian. The land was held as corporate property by the descendants of key ancestors; in some parts of Guangdong, over 50 percent of the best paddy was controlled by ancestral estates.[38] One of the first actions by land-reform cadres in the early 1950s was the confiscation and redistribution of rights to cultivate the corporately owned land that financed ancestral rites. They also introduced a cremation campaign that struck at the very heart of the ancestral cult: If the bones of key ancestors are not exhumed, preserved in ceramic pots, and reburied in horseshoe-shaped tombs, the exchange relationship between living and dead cannot take place.[39]

Besides attacking the foundation of traditional mortuary rites, Communist authorities attempted to introduce a new set of socialist rituals, based roughly on Soviet models.[40] Although field research on this problem has yet to be done, it would appear that these new rites have had most influence in the larger cities, among the professional classes. The state-sponsored modifications involve the promotion of cremation and the abolition of burial, replacing banquets and ostentatious mourning displays with frugal memorial services, and substituting eulogies extolling the deceased's contribution to the building of socialism for traditional religious observances. In the countryside, by contrast, there is considerable evidence that late imperial-style funerals and burials are still common and that, since approximately 1980, rural peoples have begun to invest heavily in mortuary rituals of all kinds. My own ethnographic surveys in Guangdong, Jiangsu, and Shandong in the mid-1980s certainly suggested that this was the case; scholars who have conducted similar kinds of research recently in other parts of the Chinese countryside have also found the same thing to be true in their areas.[41] Whyte has argued in a recent essay on funeral rites that there is a growing cultural gap between urban and rural lifestyles in post-Mao China, reflected most clearly in life-crisis rituals. He notes that urbanites, partly because of the exigencies of city living, have embraced state-sponsored models for funerals and burials. Rural people, by contrast, have been less willing to adopt socialist rites, especially those involving cremation and "thrifty" mourning customs. Although the study in question focuses on funeral rites, as Whyte's earlier work on marriage customs shows, his analysis could be applied equally well to other important life-cycle rituals.[42]

Does China's no longer having an agreed-upon set of rites (to mark birth, marriage, elderhood, death, ancestorhood, etc.) mean that it no longer has a unified culture? In the past, as I have argued, one of the central experiences of life that helped hold China together was that people of all social stations— rich and poor, rural and urban, official and common—performed life-crisis rituals according to the same basic form. The disappearance of a unified cultural tradition is something that concerns many Chinese, particularly of the older generation. The physical destruction of the "four olds" (old thought, old customs, old culture, and old morals) during the Cultural Revolution is paralleled by an erosion in knowledge about the past.[43]

The disappearance of folk knowledge appears to be most common among urban, educated people who were born after 1955 and hence were raised in the aftermath of the antisuperstition campaigns that characterized the 1950s and 1960s. This is the same cohort that considers traditional funeral rites to be "feudal" vestiges of the past. On numerous occasions in China I have been given tours of temples and religious shrines by young urbanites who know almost nothing about the history, symbolism, or social background of the institutions involved. While teaching anthropology at Sun Yatsen (Zhongshan) University in Guangzhou in 1985, I discovered that my students did not know even basic *chengyu* (popular sayings reflecting ancient wisdom) and that the majority had no conception of traditional Chinese symbolism in folk arts and crafts.

The Chinese countryside is quite another matter: Rural people of all ages may be (generally) less sophisticated in their knowledge of science, world affairs, and literature, but they are more attuned to presocialist popular culture than are urbanites. Folktales, religious symbolism, festivals and celebrations, taboos and proscriptions, calendrical observations, and other aspects of "traditional" folk knowledge are still considered relevant to the conduct of everyday life. This does not mean, of course, that rural people are unaffected by forty years of socialist cultural reconstruction. The contract farmer of the 1980s is very different from the tenant/smallholder peasant of the prerevolutionary era. It is a mistake to see the emergence of religious celebrations and ostentatious displays as a simple "revival" of presocialist cultural forms.

Socialism has transformed rural culture in complex and as yet little understood ways. For instance, the Chinese kinship system has been altered to suit socialist production patterns, first by the influences of collectivization and more recently by the requirements of contract farming (i.e., the responsibility system). As a consequence of these political changes the family—or, more precisely, the household—has been greatly strengthened as a meal-, budget-, and labor-sharing unit.[44] In certain regions the family may now be even more central to the livelihoods of rural people than it was during the prerevolutionary period, given the absence of alternative institutions that once served as the organizational framework for economic or social activities (e.g., voluntary associations, religious cults, irrigation societies, etc.).

Corporate lineages and clans do not appear to have reemerged as viable social institutions even in those parts of rural Guangdong where they dominated social life prior to the 1950s. Private worship of domestic (i.e., recently deceased) ancestors is evident everywhere in Guangdong, but corporate worship of more remote, lineage ancestors (at Ming and Qing era tombs) has not been tolerated in most counties. Local party officials have encouraged the renovation of selected ancestral halls as a means of attracting funds from émigrés and overseas Chinese, but collective worship in these halls is discouraged. Temples dedicated to important deities have also been rebuilt in the rural areas of Guangdong, Fujian, and Jiangsu. There are many reports of local people worshiping in these renovated tourist attractions, much to the embarrassment of party officials.[45]

An interesting problem for future research is the emergence of a new, socialist body of folklore, such as exists in the Soviet Union and Eastern Europe.[46] In arguing that Chinese urbanites no longer find traditional sayings, epics, songs, and symbols relevant to their lives, I certainly do not mean to imply that this sector of the society is devoid of folklore. As anyone who has lived or worked in urban China knows, there is a rich (and rapidly growing) tradition of stories, witticisms, ditties, and deliciously vicious metaphors that enliven the speech of ordinary people. Much of this emerging folklore takes the form of subtle (and not so subtle) commentary on the rigors of life under socialism. Nearly everyone in China's major cities, for example, can recite the following ditty, which parodies the official claim that socialism has allayed all fears of economic distress by giving everyone an "iron rice bowl" (unassailable job security):

Mao Zedong gave us the iron rice bowl.
Deng Xiaoping punched a hole in it.
Zhao Ziyang came along and smashed it.

The significance of such lore (some additional examples of which appear in Chapters 2 and 7) is difficult to determine at present. The thrust, however, seems to be an emerging tradition of political criticism that uses humor and metaphor as a means of saying the unsayable, much as jokes are used in the Soviet Union. Based on limited observations in China and interviews of PRC visitors in the United States, it appears that the new tradition of political folklore is most common among Chinese urbanites.

The Construction of New Cultural Identities in China

The bifurcation of culture into rural and urban forms as outlined in this chapter may be part of a general trend toward the renegotiation of "Chineseness" among people in the PRC. One wonders whether a new notion of collective identity, based on a new set of standardized rites and unifying symbols, will emerge from the old.

It is possible to interpret the Cultural Revolution as a state-sponsored movement in that direction, shifting from an emphasis on outward behavior and practice to a central concern with inner beliefs and purity of thought. The political campaigns of that era were designed to break the traditional mold, in a shift from form to content. "Redness," judged by inner conviction, was stressed above all else; Red Guards and other activists did not allow people to fall back on ritual form or standardized behavior. This new, revolutionary approach required public confession, conversion, and whole-hearted acceptance of Maoist doctrine. Richard Madsen calls this a system based on "rituals of struggle," constituting a departure from older notions of ritual as a means of maintaining community cohesion.[47]

No one knew how to act during the early years of the Cultural Revolution. Behavioral conventions and norms of public etiquette were not only challenged; those who adhered to the "old" forms were deemed to be ideologically deficient. By the 1970s, however, routinization began to set in, and people learned techniques of distancing, and thereby reritualizing, political activity.[48]

The results of the Maoist preoccupation with orthodoxy—disruption, disintegration, and anomie on a massive scale—are by now universally recognized. It would appear that the construction of a new cultural identity through the imposition of a centrally controlled ideology was an unmitigated disaster for China. This, at least, is one way to read recent history.

What dare one say about the post-Mao reform era? It would be a gross simplification of recent political developments to argue that the reforms of the late 1970s and 1980s constitute a total repudiation of Maoist doctrine, returning the society to a system based on performance rather than ideology (see Chapter 9 for further discussion). Nevertheless, some of the public rhetoric emanating from Beijing did seem to suggest as much. Deng Xiaoping himself set the tone of the reform era with his famous axiom: "It doesn't matter whether a cat is black or white, as long as it catches mice."

Rural people interpreted this and other pronouncements as a sign that the ideological heat was off and that performance (read production) would henceforth be rewarded, irrespective of class background or inner conviction. The much-heralded campaign to "Let a Few Lead the Many to Wealth" was also aimed primarily at rural people. In fact, it is safe to say that the post-Mao reforms have had the most economic impact in the countryside and that urbanites—save for a relatively small number of entrepreneurs and independent contractors—have been reduced to the role of disgruntled spectators. The resentment felt toward nouveau riche farmers has become a serious social problem in some regions, with urbanites freely commenting on the unfairness of economic policies. Meanwhile, the cultural gap between rural and urban may be growing wider each year. To be "Chinese" no longer implies that one shares the same sense of cultural identity. The key symbols that helped hold China together (shared rites, folkloric traditions, a common notion of proper lifestyle) no longer have the same meaning.

That university students relied so heavily upon what are essentially foreign (or international) symbols in their Tiananmen Square demonstrations (i.e., fasting, slogan-bearing headbands, V for victory signs, a version of the Statue of Liberty) is revealing and significant. These internationalist forms of political expression have been incorporated into the urbanite culture that is emerging in China's central cities. Thus, in terms of the symbolic reconstruction of a new sense of cultural identity, the activists in the square and their supporters probably have more in common with their Chinese compatriots in Hong Kong, Taipei, and New York than they do with their remote kin in the rural districts of Anhui and Guangdong.

Postscript

The Beijing massacre occurred after this conference paper had been completed. The crackdown, concentrated in China's major urban centers, undoubtedly worsened the sense of despair that had already begun to characterize Chinese intellectual life.[49] The massacre will inevitably have a profound effect on the current generation of educated youths and their attempts to reconstruct an acceptable notion of Chinese cultural identity. By mid-June 1989, PRC students and visiting scholars of my acquaintance were already asking themselves some deeply troubling questions: "What kind of people are ruling our country?" "How could this happen in the 1980s, with the whole world watching?" One twenty-one-year-old student from Beijing told me during the week following the massacre: "My friends and I have talked all night. We have concluded that this is not just a problem of one man or one party. The blame is more general. We think there is something fundamentally wrong with our society. Everything has to be changed, especially the mentality of the Chinese people. This will take at least fifty years, maybe a hundred years."

The echo of voices from the May Fourth era are all too obvious. Until the very day of the massacre, many Chinese intellectuals were engaged in a movement to reexamine the foundations of Chinese cultural identity. The television epic "He Shang" (River elegy, literally, "early death on the river") is perhaps the best-known product of this movement. It was shown on Chinese Central Television in June 1988 and sparked a major controversy. The series builds on the Yellow River as a symbol of Chinese culture and history; the yellow waters are tyrannical and unpredictable, both life-giving and life-destroying. The river never changes and yet is always changing. To many Chinese the message of the film was clear: Only by rejecting the past and rebuilding a new political culture could China hope to enter the modern world.

It is significant that the principal writer of "He Shang," Su Xiaokang, was included on the June 23 list of seven top intellectuals wanted by the state for "counterrevolutionary crimes." The authorities were sending a clear message by this act: Henceforth, the Communist Party intended to control the redefinition of Chinese cultural identity. This was too important a matter to be left to "unreliable" intellectuals and ordinary people. Thus, for the third time in forty years the Party propaganda apparatus appeared to be gearing up for yet another attempt to dominate the ongoing debate regarding the future of "Chineseness." In the meantime, those intellectuals and young people preoccupied with such questions had been given a disastrously violent reminder that the Chinese past is still very much alive in the present.

Notes

1. *New York Times*, May 24, 1989.

2. For a description of the demolition, see *Far Eastern Economic Review*, November 17, 1988.

3. See also the extraordinarily detailed and sympathetic account of the student movement in *Beijing Review*, May 29, 1989.

4. The question why Beijing students chose fasting, a form of political protest that is essentially foreign, is a fascinating and complex one. There are, of course, parallels in Chinese history. During the Ming-Qing transition, an exemplary official, Liu Zong-zhou (1578–1645), fasted for twenty days, killing himself to protest the rise of Manchu authority. The *Shiji* (Book of history) records two legendary heroes of the Zhou dynasty, Boyi and Shuqi, who starved to death in a protest against political injustice. In more modern times, there have been occasional group hunger strikes. For example, one accompanied a Shanghai labor dispute of the 1930s, the Red Guards staged group fasts during the Cultural Revolution, and in 1980 students and teachers in Hunan turned to a hunger strike during a forerunner to the campus-based protests of 1986–1989. The influence of these various precedents (and especially the events of 1980) should not be discounted. But prior to 1989, in contrast to nations such as Korea, where fasting has been an important technique for dissidents throughout the modern period (personal communication, Kim Kwang-ok), in China hunger strikes were not a central part of the protest repertoire. The visual images and verbal messages conveyed by students in the square seem to suggest that the cultural models for the Beijing actions were Gandhi's anti-imperialist fasts and the hunger strikes associated with the U.S. civil rights movement—both of which are often depicted in the Chinese media. For a description of a sample Cultural Revolution hunger strike, see Gao Yuan, *Born Red: A Chronicle of the Cultural Revolution* (Stanford: Stanford University Press, 1987), pp. 227–231; my comment on the Shanghai worker dispute is based on a personal communication from Elizabeth Perry; the 1980 Hunan fast is discussed in Yi Mu and Mark V. Thompson, *Crisis at Tiananmen* (San Francisco: China Books, 1989), pp. 43–44. I am grateful to K. C Chang, Hao Chang, and Paul Cohen for bringing historical precedents for the 1989 hunger strikes to my attention.

5. For background on and a good overview of the responsibility system, see Kathleen Hartford, "Socialist Agriculture is Dead; Long Live Socialist Agriculture! Organizational Transformations in Rural China," in Elizabeth J. Perry and Christine Wong, eds., *The Political Economy of Reform in Post-Mao China* (Cambridge: Harvard University Press, 1985).

6. Myron Cohen, "Family, Society, and the State in a North China Village" (paper presented at the 1987 annual meeting of the American Anthropological Association).

7. Martin Whyte, "Death Ritual in the People's Republic of China," in James L. Watson and Evelyn S. Rawski, eds., *Death Ritual in Late Imperial and Modern China* (Berkeley: University of California Press, 1988).

8. Important examples of works that emphasize the creative rather than passive aspects of culture include: Clifford Geertz, *Negara: The Theatre-State in Nineteenth-Century Bali* (Princeton: Princeton University Press, 1980); Marshall Sahlins, *Culture and Practical Reason* (Chicago: University of Chicago Press, 1976); and David M. Schneider, *American Kinship: A Cultural Account,* 2d ed. (Chicago: University of Chicago Press, 1980).

9. For further discussion, see Elvin Hatch, *Theories of Man and Culture* (New York: Columbia University Press, 1973), pp. 20–24.

10. Eugen Weber, *Peasants into Frenchmen: The Modernization of Rural France, 1870–1914* (Stanford: Stanford University Press, 1976).

11. Anderson, *Imagined Communities: Reflections on the Origin and Spread of Nationalism* (London: Verso, 1983).

12. See, for example, the argument in Ho Ping-ti, "The Chinese Civilization: A Search for the Roots of Its Longevity," *Journal of Asian Studies,* 35, 4 (1976), pp. 547–554. John DeFrancis, *The Chinese Language: Fact and Fantasy* (Honolulu: University of Hawaii Press, 1984), attacks this line of argumentation and the very notion that the Chinese script is ideographic and nonphonetic. His approach, however, is not generally accepted.

13. Karl Wittfogel, *Oriental Despotism: A Comparative Study of Total Power* (New Haven: Yale University Press, 1957).

14. G. William Skinner, "The Structure of Chinese History," *Journal of Asian Studies,* 44, 2 (1985), pp. 271–292.

15. Johnson, "Actions Speak Louder Than Words—The Cultural Significance of Opera in Late Imperial China" (paper presented at the 1987 conference of U.S.-Japanese historians, Occidental College and the Huntington Library). See also Barbara E. Ward, "Regional Operas and Their Audiences," in David Johnson, Andrew Nathan, and Evelyn Rawski, eds., *Popular Culture in Late Imperial China* (Berkeley: University of California Press, 1985).

16. Johnson takes the same kind of approach to literary audiences in "Communication, Class, and Consciousness in Late Imperial China," in Johnson et al., *Popular Culture.*

17. For background, see Vena Hrdlickova, "The Professional Training of Chinese Storytellers and the Storytellers' Guilds," *Archiv Orientlni,* 33 (1965), pp. 225–248; David Johnson, "The Wu Tzu-hsu *Pien-wen* and Its Sources" *Harvard Journal of Asiatic Studies,* 40 (1980), pp. 93–156 and 465–505.

18. Wolfram Eberhard, *A Dictionary of Chinese Symbols* (London: Routledge, 1986); Arthur H. Smith, *Proverbs and Common Sayings of the Chinese* (New York: Dover, 1914).

19. Evelyn S. Rawski stresses the unified curriculum during these eras in *Education and Popular Literacy in Ch'ing China* (Ann Arbor: University of Michigan Press, 1979) and her chapter on "Economic and Social Foundations of Late Imperial Culture," in Johnson et al., *Popular Culture.*

20. In recent decades, central authorities have discouraged the use of pejorative terms—that is, Chinese words whose sense corresponds roughly to the English *barbarian, uncivilized,* or *savage*—when speaking of non-Han. Nonetheless, one still hears these terms in Taiwan and in many parts of the People's Republic.

21. See, for example, the discussion of Han-Yao interactions in Guangdong in David Faure, "The Lineage as Cultural Invention: The Case of the Pearl River Delta," *Modern China,* 15, 1 (1989), pp. 4–36.

22. Wolfram Eberhard, *China's Minorities: Yesterday and Today* (Belmont, Calif.: Wadsworth, 1982); Harold J. Wiens, *Han Expansion in South China* (Hamden, Conn.: Shoestring Press, 1954).

23. David Y.H. Wu, "The Meaning of Minority Culture: The Example of the Bai in Yunnan, China," *Human Organization*, 49, 1 (Spring 1990), pp. 1–13.

24. The metaphor of cooking is frequently employed by ordinary Chinese when discussing non-Han communities, as Susan Naquin and Evelyn S. Rawski note in *Chinese Society in the Eighteenth Century* (New Haven: Yale University Press, 1987), pp. 127–128. The dichotomy between "cooked" and "uncooked" is still common in today's Taiwan, where it is used to designate the degree to which Taiwan's original inhabitants have been assimilated into Han culture.

25. James L. Watson, "The Structure of Chinese Funerary Rites: Elementary Forms, Ritual Sequence, and the Primacy of Performance," in Watson and Rawski, *Death Ritual*.

26. On the rites performed for the emperor, see Evelyn S. Rawski, "The Imperial Way of Death," in Watson and Rawski, *Death Ritual*.

27. For discussion, see Emily M. Ahern, *The Cult of the Dead in a Chinese Village* (Stanford: Stanford University Press, 1973), and Stuart E. Thompson, "Death, Food, and Fertility," in Watson and Rawski, *Death Ritual*.

28. The standardization of one or both of these two sets of lifestyle rituals is discussed in Eberhard, *Dictionary of Chinese Symbolism*; Evelyn Rawski, "A Historian's Approach to Death Ritual," in Watson and Rawski, *Death Ritual*; Susan Naquin, "Marriage in North China: The Role of Ritual" (paper presented at the 1988 Conference on Marriage and Inequality in Chinese Society, Asilomar, Calif.; and Susan Mann, "Grooming a Daughter for Marriage: Brides and Wives in the Mid-Ch'ing Period," in Rubie S. Watson and Patricia B. Ebrey, eds., *Marriage and Inequality in Chinese Society* (Berkeley: University of California Press, 1990).

29. James Hayes provides information on some of these handbooks in "The Popular Culture of Late Ch'ing and Early Twentieth Century China: Book Lists Prepared from Collecting in Hong Kong," *Journal of the Hong Kong Branch of the Royal Asiatic Society*, 20 (1980), pp. 168–183. Susan Naquin discusses handbooks relating to funerals in "Funerals in North China: Uniformity and Variation," in Watson and Rawski, *Death Ritual*. A useful discussion of the Neo-Confucian text that served as a model for many late imperial ritual handbooks is discussed in some detail in Patricia B. Ebrey, "Education Through Rituals in the Sung Dynasty," in John Chafee and William Theodore DeBary, eds., *Neoconfucian Education: The Formative Stage* (Berkeley: University of California Press, 1990).

30. James Watson, "Standardizing the Gods: The Promotion of T'ien-hou (Empress of Heaven) Along the South China Coast," in Johnson et al., *Popular Culture*; see also Naquin, "Funerals in North China," for the standardizing role of ritual specialists.

31. On Confucianism, see Herbert Fingarette, *Confucius: The Secular as Sacred* (New York: Harper and Row, 1972). For important discussions that carry similar themes back into the pre-Confucian era, see K. C. Chang, *Art, Myth, and Ritual: The Path to Political Authority in Ancient China* (Cambridge: Harvard University Press, 1983), pp. 101 and 108; and David N. Keightley, "Archaeology and Mentality: The Making of China," *Representations*, 18 (1987), pp. 91–128.

32. *The World of Thought in Ancient China* (Cambridge: Harvard University Press, 1985), p. 67.

33. James L. Watson, "Waking the Dragon: Visions of the Chinese Imperial State in Local Myth," *Journal of the Anthropological Society of Oxford* (1989).

34. The contrasts with India (South Asia) are particularly clear. Prior to the British raj, South Asia was not dominated by a centralized state system. In fact, as David Washbrook has argued, the very notion of "India" as a political-cultural entity did not emerge until relatively late in the colonial era. See his "Gandhi and the Creation of 'India'" (paper presented at the India-China Seminar, Fairbank Center for East Asian

Research, Harvard University, 1987) and also Bernard S. Cohn, "Representing Authority in Victorian India," in Eric J. Hobsbawm and Terrance Ranger, eds., *The Invention of Tradition* (Cambridge: Cambridge University Press, 1983). For further exploration of the contrasts between the Chinese and Indian cases, as well as references to important discussions of the role of ritual in defining South Asian cultural identity, see the footnotes to the version of this paper to be published in the *Proceedings of the Four Anniversaries Conference* (Ann Arbor: University of Michigan, Center for Chinese Studies, forthcoming).

35. Patricia B. Ebrey, "The Early Stages in the Development of Descent Group Organization," in Patricia B. Ebrey and James L. Watson, eds., *Kinship Organization in Late Imperial China* (Berkeley: University of California Press, 1986), esp. pp. 20–29.

36. Rawski, "A Historian's Approach."

37. See, for example, William L. Parrish and Martin K. Whyte, *Village and Family in Contemporary China* (Chicago: University of Chicago Press, 1978); Donald E. MacInnis, *Religious Policy and Practice in Communist China* (New York: Macmillan, 1972).

38. Rubie S. Watson, *Inequality Among Brothers: Class and Kinship in South China* (Cambridge: Cambridge University Press, 1985).

39. James L. Watson, "Of Flesh and Bones: The Management of Death Pollution in Cantonese Society," in Maurice Bloch and Jonathan Parry, eds., *Death and the Regeneration of Life* (Cambridge: Cambridge University Press, 1982).

40. Christel Lane, *The Rites of Rulers: Ritual in Industrial Society: The Soviet Case* (Cambridge: Cambridge University Press, 1981); Christopher A. Binns, "The Changing Face of Power: Revolution and Accommodation in the Development of the Soviet Ceremonial System," pt. 2, *Man*, new series 18, 4 (1980), pp. 170–187.

41. Myron Cohen and David Wu, personal communications. See also Parrish and Whyte, *Village and Family*, pp. 255–256; and William R. Jankowiak, "The Soul of Lao Yu," *Natural History*, 97, 12 (1988), pp. 4–11.

42. Whyte, "Death Ritual in the People's Republic of China." See also earlier works by the same author, such as "Rural Marriage Customs," *Problems of Communism*, 26 (1977), pp. 41–55; and "Revolutionary Social Change and Patrilocal Residence in China," *Ethnology*, 18, 3 (1979), pp. 211–227.

43. During the Cultural Revolution, Red Guards destroyed many historical monuments, including graves and tombs; see Anita Chan, Richard Madsen, and Jonathan Unger, *Chen Village: The Recent History of a Peasant Community in Mao's China* (Berkeley: University of California Press, 1984).

44. Myron Cohen, "Family, Society, and the State in a North China Village" (paper presented at the 1987 annual meetings of the American Anthropology Association); Louis Putterman, "The Restoration of the Peasant Household as a Farm Production Unit in China," in Perry and Wong, *Political Economy of Reform*.

45. Jerry Dennerline, personal communication.

46. In discussions at the Four Anniversaries Conference, Paul Pickowicz noted that this should really be described as "postsocialist" folklore.

47. Richard Madsen, *Morality and Power in a Chinese Village* (Berkeley: University of California Press, 1984), pp. 22–26.

48. Martin K. Whyte, *Small Groups and Political Rituals in China* (Berkeley: University of California Press, 1974); David Zweig, *Agrarian Radicalism in China, 1968–1981* (Cambridge: Harvard University Press, 1989).

49. On this problem, see Perry Link's interesting article in the *New York Review of Books*, June 29, 1989, pp. 38–41, written just prior to the military intervention.

4

REFLECTIONS ON "REFLECTIONS ON THE MODERN CHINESE STUDENT MOVEMENT"

John Israel

In winter 1968, when an earlier version of the following essay first appeared, China was reeling from the convulsions of the Red Guard Movement, and Mao, disenchanted with his Frankenstein monster, was sending millions of young rebels to the countryside. At that time the full dimensions of the Cultural Revolution were not yet clear, and my analysis of that event was highly speculative.

Research on Chinese student movements has developed apace over the past two decades, thanks in large part to the work of two of the other contributors to this volume. Vera Schwarcz's study of *The Chinese Enlightenment* has changed our views of various aspects of the May Fourth Movement of 1919 and the way participants in that event responded to subsequent rounds of demonstrations.[1] Jeffrey Wasserstrom's forthcoming volume on campus unrest in Shanghai, with its emphasis upon the symbolic, the structural, and the comparative, also marks a conceptual breakthrough in our understanding of student protest.[2] My "Reflections" (1968) should be read as an early attempt at synthetic analysis that may, incidentally, shed light upon recent events. I have let the original essay stand basically unchanged, although I have allowed the editors of this volume to cut two sections of it that had less relevance for

"Reflections on the Modern Chinese Student Movement" first appeared in *Daedalus*, 97, 1 (Winter 1968), in the issue entitled "Students and Politics." It is reprinted here with the permission of the American Academy of Arts and Sciences.

placing the events of 1989 into perspective. I have also tried to bring the piece up-to-date in an addendum.[3]

REFLECTIONS ON THE MODERN
CHINESE STUDENT MOVEMENT (1968)

The Students of the Song dynasty (960–1279) would scarcely recognize their modern descendants. The former were seasoned scholars whose erudition secured their place in society. Through mastery of the prescribed classics, they aspired to the highest rungs of officialdom. Even degree-holders who failed to gain governmental positions became members of the "gentry" elite, entitled to special privileges and charged with numerous social responsibilities. Intellectuals were also expected to criticize officials—even emperors—who failed to live up to the standards of the Confucian ethos. For two thousand years, the scholar-official elite served the Chinese state well.

By the time of the Opium War (1839–1842), however, the traditional scholar had become an anachronism. The classics failed to prepare China for the multifaceted challenge of the modern West. Beginning in the 1860s, the Qing dynasty sought reinvigoration through a series of reforms, but none was equal to the need. By the end of the nineteenth century, the combination of external pressure and internal decay had proved too much for the rulers of the sprawling empire. In 1911 the dynasty collapsed, and a republic was established. Republican aspirations were quickly crushed, however, under the despotism of Yuan Shikai. From 1916 to 1949, national reunification eluded warlord rulers, the Kuomintang government, and the Japanese. Throughout these years, reformers in various parts of the Chinese subcontinent followed in the footsteps of their Qing forebears. In retrospect, even their boldest efforts were but preludes to the measures of Mao Zedong.

Youth and Revolution: 1895–1949

The Chinese student movement was both conditioned by and a condition of this historical transformation. Bridging traditional and modern movements was the Memorial of the Examination Candidates at the close of the first Sino-Japanese War (1894–1895). More than 1,200 scholars, who assembled in Beijing for the triennial examinations, demanded a protracted war against Japan. In so doing, they played the historic role of heirs to their twelfth-century predecessors and forerunners of their twentieth-century successors. A truly modern student movement could, however, develop only with modern educational institutions. The first Western-style missionary college (St. John's) was founded in Shanghai in 1879, and the first modern public university (later to be called Beijing University, or "Beida") was officially established in Beijing in 1898. But a certain ambivalence clouded educational reform: How could modern colleges prepare candidates for the traditional examinations? The contradiction was resolved in 1905, when the desperate dynasty abolished the 1,300-year-old examination system.

Thereafter no careerist incentive remained for memorizing the classics, nor was there assurance that alternative courses of study would bring success. The modern student thus felt an unprecedented degree of insecurity. His personal dilemmas were compounded by a pervasive sense of national shame stemming from China's backwardness and helplessness vis-à-vis the imperialist powers. Many resolved these problems by going abroad for study, hoping to return with the prestige of a foreign degree and a technological or philosophical understanding of the modern world. The Manchu dynasty, in its declining years, encouraged students to follow this path, assuming they would come home both skillful and grateful. By September 1906, 15,000 Chinese were studying in Japan. From the government's point of view, the reform was a disaster; uprooted youths, free of Chinese controls and exposed to inflammatory ideas, provided an educated following for such radical reformers as Liang Qichao and rebels like Sun Yatsen. Students from all over China came together in Tokyo and returned to foment revolution. Recipients of government scholarships helped bring down the Manchus in 1911.

Deriving its energy from the unstable combination of China's historic grandeur and modern humiliation, the student movement developed an explosive potential. Its targets were oppression from abroad as well as inept government at home. It seemed increasingly obvious to young patriots that both would have to be eradicated if China were to become a strong modern state. The new education reinforced these sentiments. Reformers prescribed a stridently nationalistic course of study, conveyed to the younger generation through chauvinistic textbooks taught by patriotic teachers. Hence, the anti-imperialist theme of 1895 resounded with growing intensity in the twentieth century. In 1905, students joined merchants in an anti-U.S. boycott protesting discriminatory immigration policies. When Japan presented Yuan Shikai with the infamous 21 Demands in 1915, Chinese students in Japan returned home by the thousands to join demonstrations against this threat to their nation's sovereignty.

The 1915 movement was a prologue to the Beijing demonstration of May 4, 1919, which marked the emergence of students as a major force in national politics. The impetus for this historic demonstration was another manifestation of foreign imperialism, but its full significance can be understood only in the context of China's accelerating social and intellectual revolution. In the cities of China's eastern seaboard, where foreign-style institutions flourished under the protection of the unequal treaties, new social classes were emerging: bilingual merchants, financiers, and industrialists; an urban proletariat; a foreign-educated intelligentsia; and modern students. In the homes of the last, a "family revolution" ensued as the experience, teachings, and institutions of the older generation became increasingly irrelevant to the needs and aspirations of the young. Revolutionary ideas were nationally disseminated through a multitude of popular magazines, newspapers, and political societies. The effects of these changes were felt both in cosmopolitan Shanghai, hub of economic modernization and refuge for China's political and intellectual rebels, and in Beijing, which remained the nation's cultural capital.[4]

In this volatile climate, Beida emerged as the main center for cultural criticism and intellectual activism. From 1916 on, thanks to the efforts of a new chancellor, Cai Yuanpei, who promoted the startling idea that a university should be a forum for the free development of diverse views, students at the school were exposed to iconoclastic professors who taught them to question traditional values. The doctrines of these teachers, some of whom also recommended science and democracy as panaceas for China's ills, found a receptive audience, for Beida's students had ample reason to feel rebellious: Their personal futures were uncertain; the republican revolution had ended in chaos; the country was at the mercy of corrupt militarists and foreign aggressors; and their own parents persisted in preaching obsolete notions of virtue and filial piety. The halls of Beida resounded with a cacophony of names and isms: Dostoevsky and Kropotkin, Russell and Dewey, Shaw and Ibsen, Wilson and Lenin; democracy, equality, science, socialism, individualism, self-determination, nationalism, internationalism, and Bolshevism.

China's young rebels contrasted China's dreary present with a hopeful future. As war ended in 1918, they heard Woodrow Wilson promise equality to nations and dignity for mankind. They felt certain that the Versailles conference would recognize the claims of their country, which had sent 200,000 coolies to aid the allies on the Western front. Principles of justice demanded that China regain its sovereign rights to the province of Shandong (birthplace of Confucius), seized by Japan in 1915. But youthful hopes proved illusory. By the end of January 1919, reports reached Beijing that Great Britain, France, and Italy had signed secret treaties agreeing to support Japan's claims to Shandong. On the heels of these tidings came even more foreboding news. Outraged by these events, representatives of various student groups gathered at Beida and planned an orderly protest demonstration for May 4. The demonstration began peacefully but ended in violence when a group stormed the home of a pro-Japanese official, beat alleged traitors discovered within, ransacked the house, and set it afire. News of May 4 reached China's new social classes via modern communications. Students demonstrated in Tianjin, Shanghai, Nanjing, Wuhan, and other cities. Workers staged sympathy strikes. Merchants joined an anti-Japanese boycott. Professors demanded the release of arrested agitators. Local student groups proliferated, and on June 16, 1919, delegates gathered in Shanghai and formed the National Student Association (NSA).

The organization of a national body was a formidable accomplishment, for the unifying influence of a common written language and shared nationalistic sentiments were counterbalanced by powerful centrifugal forces: mutually incomprehensible dialects, regional loyalties, and the country's size. Considering these obstacles and in view of China's lack of experience with representative democracy, it is not surprising that the national body came to function in a highly elitist manner. City and provincial congresses were composed of delegates popularly elected at constituent schools, and these groups in turn sent delegates to meetings of the national union. The structure operated, however, in a Leninist fashion, more centralist than democratic. Even at the local level, professional and amateur agitators skilled in propaganda, oratory, and controlling mass meetings were generally able to dominate the majority of less interested and less adept schoolmates. The absence of democracy notwithstanding, by the mid-1920s the National Student Association had become one of the most influential voices of public opinion in China. It was less effective, however, as an organ of control, and even during nationwide movements, the nature and intensity of student political activity continued to vary according to local educational, political, geographical, and cultural conditions.

The May Fourth Movement was the turning point in China's cultural upheaval. Just as the revolution of 1911 had constituted a definitive break with efforts at monarchial reform, the New Thought of the late 1910s marked a radical departure from attempts at halfway modernization in the world of ideas. For the first time, eminent intellectuals advocated wholesale Westernization and total abandonment of China's Confucian heritage. The reaction of educated youth was highly favorable; henceforth, the more novel and shocking an idea, the more likely it was to win a receptive audience. The demonstration of May 4 also ushered in a decade of radical anti-imperialism: Vehement protests against the unequal treaties alarmed China's foreign community and an anti-Christian movement jolted missionary schools. Disenchanted with the fruitless promises of Wilsonian liberalism and wooed by Soviet envoys, alienated intellectuals and students formed the Chinese Communist Party. Among them was Mao Zedong, a twenty-seven-year-old former Beida library assistant who had received his political baptism as a high-school student leader.

Sun Yatsen, too, was carried along by the radical post–May Fourth tide. Frustrated by twenty years of political failure, he welcomed the counsel of Comintern agents; he agreed to accept Russian aid, revamp the KMT along Leninist lines, form a united front with the Chinese Communists, and establish the apparatus for mass mobilization, including a youth bureau. During the mid-1920s, students under both KMT and CCP leadership organized workers and peasants for political action. In Canton, the KMT's newly founded Whampoa Military Academy set out to mold an indoctrinated military elite under Commandant Chiang Kaishek. Students from all over China flocked to this mecca on the Pearl River.

As Chiang consolidated his forces, a series of atrocities by warlords and foreigners stimulated student nationalism and boosted the fortunes of the KMT-CCP alliance. An incident on May 30, 1925, was the most famous of these. As with the May 4 demonstration the immediate cause was an imperialist outrage: A Japanese foreman in a Japanese-owned Shanghai factory had shot and killed a Chinese worker. Protesting students in the foreign-controlled International Settlement had been jailed. When a crowd gathered in front of a police station to demand their release, a British officer impulsively ordered his men to fire. The slaughter of unarmed students by foreign police on Chinese soil evoked a nationwide storm of protest. Twenty-four days later, indignation reached a new peak when British and French machine gunners mowed down Whampoa cadets and other youthful paraders in Canton. On March 16, 1926, more anti-imperialist student demonstrators were massacred by troops of the Beijing warlord, Zhang Zuolin. When Chiang Kaishek launched the Northern Expedition on July 9, 1926, to rid the country of warlordism, China's educated elite responded with enthusiasm.

Beneath the façade of unity, both KMT and CCP maneuvered for the inevitable showdown. Chiang struck first. On April 12, 1927, he began the Party Purification Movement. This anti-Communist campaign, which began in Shanghai and spread throughout the country, resulted in the summary execution of many student radicals. The purge, rupturing as it did the bond between the KMT and a significant element of the younger generation, neutralized much of the enthusiasm that had been created by the success of the Northern Expedition and the establishment of a national government in Nanjing. A further blow to student activists was the ruling party's decision to discontinue mass movements. Student unions were to be replaced by apolitical self-governing associations, and youngsters were to stick to their books.

Youth lost enthusiasm for a government that wasted precious resources in fighting warlords and Communist remnants at the expense of social reforms, but they also recognized the Nanjing regime as China's only hope. Indeed, they might well have set their sights on bureaucratic, technocratic careers had not Japan invaded Manchuria in September 1931. The Chinese government's failure to resist prompted young war hawks to flock to Nanjing. For three months in fall 1931, thousands of student zealots descended upon the capital, often lying on railway tracks to halt traffic until free transportation was provided. Foreign Minister Wang Zhengting (a former YMCA student leader) was nearly beaten to death by a student mob on September 28. But the protest was relatively peaceful until December, when a radical minority from Beijing steered the movement in a revolutionary direction. Violent demonstrators manhandled KMT officials and wrecked the offices of the party newspaper, thereby forcing the government to adopt suppressive measures.

Once leftists had been jailed or driven underground, youthful nationalism was dampened by increasing political, social, and economic stability and by a hiatus in Japanese aggression. Official exhortations to "save the nation by study" were apparently making an impression. New moves by the invader, however, brought students once more to the streets in what came to be called the December Ninth Movement. In December 1935, the Japanese were demanding an "autonomous region" in north China, and Beijing students were alarmed by Chiang's ambivalent response: "We shall not forsake peace until there is no hope for peace; we shall not talk lightly of sacrifice until the last extremity." They feared they would become subjects of a north China version of the Japanese puppet state in Manchuria known as Manchukuo.

On December 9 and 16, large demonstrations, in which students from the U.S.-influenced Yanjing and Qinghua universities played the leading roles, provoked a nationwide response among students and intellectuals that was reminiscent of May 4. They also spawned the National Salvation Movement, which pushed Chiang toward a united front with the Communists and resistance to Japan. In May 1936, a new pro-Communist National Student Association was founded. The contrast between this and the troublesome but still loyal NSA, dissolved seven years earlier by the Ministry of Training, symbolizes the leftward trend among student activists during a decade of KMT rule.

The majority of the student generation of the 1930s committed themselves to no political party, offering their allegiance to whoever would lead the country against Japan. Because they realized that only Nanjing had the power to fill this role, they applauded Mao Zedong's call for a national united front but reserved their most enthusiastic support for Chiang Kaishek when he indicated willingness to lead the nation into war. Though thousands of idealistic youth joined the Communists in the hills of Shaanxi between 1936 and 1939, tens of thousands retreated to the Nationalists' refuge in the southwest.

To the casual observer, the period of the war against Japan (1937–1945) witnessed an unprecedented unity of Chinese youth under the leadership of Chiang. It is certainly true that during the early war years, as the government fought, students rallied to China's defense and risked their lives to aid the country's hard-pressed armies. It soon became apparent, however, that the war would be won elsewhere than in China. Morale deteriorated behind the lines as the government diverted men and supplies to blockade the Communists, while inflation and black marketeering sapped China's economic and psychological reserves. In the colleges of Chongqing, Chengdu, and Kunming, students pawned books and clothes to supplement meager government subsidies, prepared their lessons by kerosene lamps, suffered from malnutrition, and frequently contracted tuberculosis. Official policy dictated that these youths remain at their desks. Hoarded like the precious national resources they unquestionably were, the educated elite found no adequate outlet for their patriotic idealism. By late 1943, when students were finally encouraged to enlist in the army, cynicism had already begun to erode the foundations of academia.

The contrast with the Communist zones was striking. There students were trained and indoctrinated in special schools and sent to the countryside to mobilize the population for guerrilla warfare. The Communists emerged from the war with sufficient numbers of trained, dedicated young cadres to govern an area of a hundred million people. The nationalists had increased the number of students in institutions of higher learning from 41,609 in 1936, to 78,909 in 1945, and 155,036 in 1947. Aside from a loyal following in the Three People's Principles Youth Corps, however, these students were apathetic, if not hostile, toward the ruling party.

In the cities of east China that had been liberated from Japanese rule, the war's end reunited two groups—refugees returning from exile in the interior and residents who had collaborated, actively or passively, with the Japanese and their Chinese puppets. For both of these groups, the psychological effect of eight years of war had been disruptive.[5] The refugees nursed sentiments of self-pity and resentment. They viewed themselves as unsung heroes who had endured nearly a decade of unrequited suffering for the nation. Further sacrifice seemed unjust, especially as those who had remained behind seemed to have prospered by cooperating with the invader. Many of the former collaborators, for their part, felt a need to atone for the compromises they had made.

Sensitive youth from these two groups crowded onto postwar campuses and provided the material for a series of student rebellions that reached a crescendo in the anti-hunger, anti–civil-war movement of May 1947. In the emporium atmosphere of Shanghai and other cities, wartime restraints had given way to crass materialism. An inflationary economy hungry for consumer goods favored importers, speculators, and influential officials. But in the schools, shortages and inflation meant further sacrifices for teachers and students. To returning refugees, the ramshackle housing, substandard diets, shortages of books and laboratory equipment, and restraints on freedom that had been endured as necessary during the struggle against Japan now seemed not merely unnecessary but intolerable. Students who had spent the war years in occupied China were inclined to sympathize with the Communists on practical and psychological grounds. Many felt that they had no future under the Kuomintang, which discriminated in favor of youngsters who had shared the bitterness of wartime "exile." The CCP, in contrast, presented itself as a forward-looking organization dedicated to universal ideals of youth. By enlisting in this noble cause, they might expiate feelings of guilt over the past and open up new possibilities for the future.

Caught in a downward spiral typical of governments in the final stage of revolutionary overthrow, Chiang's regime vacillated between reform and force. Eleventh-hour moves to establish institutions of representative government failed to placate U.S. and domestic critics and did nothing to halt political polarization, stem the devastating inflation, or prevent civil war. In this milieu, the Communists channeled youthful frustrations into demonstrations against civil war, U.S. military misconduct, and Chinese police brutality. The government's response was "counterproductive"; bullyboys beat demonstrators, and gunmen assassinated opponents, yet official propagandists asserted that the highest priority of postwar reconstruction was the extermination of Communist rebels. Increasingly, the government became convinced that force was the answer in the cities as well as the rural areas. Police arrested thousands of students and intellectuals suspected of Communist sympathies and muzzled the left-wing press. Such action lent credence to Communist charges of fascism and won additional recruits for the widening ranks of Mao's supporters. As the People's Liberation Army swept southward, student reaction ranged from stoic acceptance to jubilation.

This historical survey must conclude on a cautionary note. Although Chinese students, individually and collectively, were important in their country's modern transformation and an essential ingredient in the victory of

Chinese communism, the student movement was not a sufficient cause for this victory. Mao's contribution to Communist practice was not his utilization of students (a universal phenomenon among Communist parties) but his use of peasants in a political-military context. Students contributed heavily to the CCP's leadership and were a source of harassment to the KMT, but mass movements of urban intellectuals remained ancillary to the struggle in the villages and on the battlefield.

Students and the Ruling Parties: KMT and CCP

Perennial student dissatisfaction with the status quo has created problems for both KMT and CCP rulers. By evaluating their divergent responses under varying conditions, one may consider whether the modernization process in China has made student rebellion inevitable.

The Kuomintang suffered from internal weaknesses as it entered the political-ideological arena. In retrospect, it seems clear that this ruling party, badly divided as it was, had slim hopes of satisfying China's college students. Filled with the high expectations common among youth in modernizing societies, these radicals were inevitably disappointed when mortal beings failed to solve unsolvable problems. In industrialized countries such as the United States and postwar Japan, young idealists may be expected to mature into integrated units of the "establishment." Yet this is impossible unless the established order offers well-defined rewards—social, economic, and psychological. Considering the series of convulsions that have shaken Chinese society since the mid-nineteenth century, it is not surprising that many of the young intelligentsia eventually were drawn into the Communist camp. Nor is it surprising that the temporary loosening of authoritarian controls in 1957 produced a student rebellion and that the staging of a massive revolutionary movement under official auspices was necessary to forestall another outburst a decade later.

But the CCP, for all its blunders, has controlled the student movement far more skillfully than its rival had. The Kuomintang's short-lived success with the younger generation ended when the Party came to power, and the abolition of extramural student organizations betrayed the KMT's lack of confidence in its own ability to compete with the Communists and other dissidents. Moreover, this negative policy failed to gain support from two key factions—the Chen brothers' Organization Clique or CC Clique and the Whampoa Clique in the military. During the early and mid-1930s, these groups competed, more or less clandestinely, with Communist organizers in the schools. After the outbreak of the second Sino-Japanese War, the party reversed its negative policy by establishing the Three People's Principles Youth Corps under Whampoa leadership. The corps' achievements, facilitated by wartime patriotism, were nullified after V-J Day. Under attack from jealous Party regulars, the corps was amalgamated with the Party in 1947.

In the post-1949 period, the Communists have been plagued by competition between civilian and military factions in their Party for control of the youth movement. After the failure of the Great Leap Forward, militant Maoists criticized the CCP and its adjunct, the Youth League, for their policies of retrenchment. These ideological purists, led by Lin Biao and his adherents in the People's Liberation Army, circumvented the league and organized the Red Guards in summer 1966. The Guards' countrywide crusade was made possible by the army's organizational and logistic support.

The generation gap, which perplexes Communist leaders today, is accentuated by a cult of youth that has provided opportunities and problems for adult politicians ever since the May Fourth Movement.[6] Students led both KMT and CCP through their formative years, but both the KMT (which had been in existence for more than two decades before 1927) and the CCP (which had operated for nearly three decades prior to 1949) inevitably lost touch with the younger generation. The KMT, as we have seen, responded negatively to the challenge. During the early 1950s, the CCP promoted student political action in a series of mass movements controlled by the Party and the Youth League. But from the mid-1950s to the mid-1960s, functions of mass organizations were appropriated by the Party-league apparatus, league leadership became the preserve of middle-aged men, and its membership grew older.

The Red Guard imbroglio of the Cultural Revolution reminds us that the CCP's relationship with the students has not been free of contradictions. Since the 1920s, the Party has realized the value of students in organizing workers, peasants, and intellectuals. By defining the class nature of students as wholly or partly petit bourgeois, the Party has been able to use them both as allies in united fronts and as scapegoats for the Party's failures. Communist ideologists have, however, found reliance upon such a privileged elite embarrassing to the Party of the proletariat. Thus, students have been expected to lose their sense of separate identity and to become one with the masses. Party ideologues repeatedly quote Mao Zedong's dictum: "The ultimate line of demarcation between the revolutionary intellectuals, on the one hand, and nonrevolutionary and counter-revolutionary intellectuals, on the other, lies in whether they are willing to, and actually do, become one with the masses of workers and peasants."[7]

Practical as well as ideological problems have compounded the Party's dilemma. By the Yan'an period, the CCP was no longer a clique of intellectuals but a rural-based, political-military movement. This made it difficult for the CCP to absorb the urban intellectual youths who streamed in from Beijing, Tianjin, and other cities. From the viewpoint of the Red Army veterans of the Jiangxi Soviet and the Long March, these recruits were bookish and undisciplined. Thought reform was the Maoist cure for such ailments. The wartime movement labeled *zhengfeng* (to correct unorthodox tendencies) was the first in a continuing series of attempts to remold students and intellectuals.[8]

Tensions underlying student-Party relations since the mid-1920s still exist. Students remain largely bourgeois in family origin, hence untrustworthy, though their skills are needed as much as ever. CCP leaders fear that half a century of revolution may be negated by residual habits of traditional careerism and modern professionalism among the young. The very structure of

Chinese education contains built-in contradictions. The Communists inherited a university system modeled on the West's, with a Western-trained faculty and designed to produce graduates dedicated to the disinterested pursuit of truth via "scientific" disciplines. With their newly acquired skills, these youths have sought to enter careers that would both further their own interests and modernize their homeland. The Communists regard such attitudes as unfortunate hangovers from China's feudal and semicolonial eras. The pursuit of individual self-interest is thought to be incompatible with the development of the state, and the disinterested quest for scientific truth is considered secondary to the development of a "correct" Maoist Weltanschauung. The attempt to reconcile the contradictory purposes of education is formulated in the slogan, "Both red and expert." Changes in emphasis between these two desiderata have produced a series of crises, most notably the Great Proletarian Cultural Revolution, with its offshoot, the Red Guards.

Red Guard membership initially was granted only to politically active students of proletarian origin. Youngsters with these qualifications had been accepted in institutions of middle and higher education during the Great Leap Forward, when it was more important to be red than expert. It was they who suffered when the pendulum swung back and academic performance became more important than ideological orthodoxy. Hence, in spring and summer 1966 they became enthusiastic recruits in campaigns to expel "bourgeois" chancellors, to revamp the system of entrance examinations, and to close the schools so that students could devote all their time to politics. These youth had but one hope for advancement in the highly competitive educational and economic systems—that political activism would replace academic achievement as the principal criterion of success. If the Communist leadership failed to satisfy their expectations, its quest for a generation of revolutionary successors would be doomed to failure. If it ceased to reward academic and technological achievement, however, its vision of a modern industrialized China would be shattered and the country forced to fall back on its overcrowded rural hinterland.

Thus the CCP, like the KMT, has been trapped by its own ideology, by its failure to satisfy the expectations of youth who have taken the Party's teachings too literally. The Nationalists lost their student following by not acting sufficiently nationalistic; the Communists are threatened by rebellious youth who demand that they practice communism.

The course of the Chinese student movement follows logically from China's history. The nation entered the twentieth century stumbling in the shadow of its past brilliance. Unlike Russia, where centralized despotism made anarchism attractive, China was weak, divided, and exploited. Hence, the goals of the student movement were state-oriented: internal unity, solidarity against foreign foes, national power through modernization, and national identity through social revolution. Nationalism was equally important in helping students retain their personal identity as Chinese even while they were discarding their traditional heritage in favor of foreign innovations.

The nationalism of the 1905–1911 movement was both racist and modern. Its assumption was that China would grow strong if the alien Manchus were dethroned and traditional governmental forms were replaced with republican institutions. Nationalism in the garb of anti-imperialism and anti-Christianity developed rapidly after the 21 Demands and reached its peak after the May Thirtieth incident. Like anti-Manchu nationalism, it blamed foreigners for China's woes, and this enhanced its appeal. Students supported the goal of the Northern Expedition—national unification via military conquest—but failed to appreciate Chiang's continued obsession with this program during the Japanese invasion of the 1930s. Civil war had less nationalistic appeal than anti-imperialistic war. Between 1937 and 1945, the KMT and CCP vied for popular support, each arguing that it embodied the principle of national solidarity against the Japanese.

After the war, the KMT contended that its struggle against Communist rebels carried on the task of national unification begun in the fight against the Manchus and continued in the Northern Expedition and the anti-Japanese crusade. But instead of a decadent dynasty, venal warlords, or imperialistic Japanese, the KMT faced a resurgent Communist movement. Mao, who had also established his patriotic credentials during eight years of resistance, offered a "new democratic" China as an alternative to the discredited government of the postwar Kuomintang. Convinced that the KMT was the main obstacle to internal harmony and that continued attempts to extirpate the Communists could lead only to interminable civil war, the students became Chiang's harshest critics during this crucial period.

Even though successive generations of Chinese students may be characterized as nationalistic, this does not imply an absence of change. Political circumstances altered the quality of that nationalism from decade to decade. The most influential force for change was the intrusion of partisan politics into every sphere of student activity: hence the enormous difference between the nonpartisan May Fourth Movement of 1919 and the highly politicized May Thirtieth Movement six years later, to say nothing of events in 1935 and 1947. This intrusion reached its logical conclusion after 1949, when the student movement became a tool of Party control. Partisan politics have similarly engulfed other areas of Chinese life—most notably in literature, where the social consciousness of the 1920s evolved into the revolutionary polemics of the 1930s, the patriotic homilies of the war years, and then state indoctrination after 1949. Student politics have also varied greatly in intensity. Movements have flourished in modern China when governments appeared weak and inept. Only those able to control the nation's territory, manage its educational system effectively, and carry out energetic programs in domestic and foreign policy have generally succeeded in avoiding massive student protests: hence the frequency of student disorder during the late Qing and warlord periods. The promise of unity and reform gave the Nanjing government relative immunity from 1928 to September 1931 and from 1932 to December 1935. The December Ninth Movement erupted in the least-controlled university (Yanjing) of an insecure area (north China), endangered by vacillation in foreign policy. National resistance to Japan and tight KMT control of southwest China's campuses dampened student protest during the war, but governmental weaknesses encouraged its reemergence in 1945.

There has been a tension in Chinese student thought between the desire for personal liberty and the quest for a strong state, but by and large liberty has been a secondary issue.[9] When the government has been strong, students have grumbled about suppression of civil liberties, but they have not rebelled. Only weak governments have had to answer for repressive policies. No rulers allowed greater academic freedom than the warlords, who were more concerned with fighting battles than with running schools, but none elicited more bitter student opposition. KMT thought control failed because it was conceptually and operationally deficient, not because students valued freedom of thought above all else. CCP means of coercion have been more oppressive and more effective. The Communists mastered techniques of internal social control; the Kuomintang always seemed to approach students from outside. Internal discipline, whether in a Beijing school or a Yan'an thought-reform center, was more acceptable than external control by school administrators or military police. In areas under Kuomintang control, pro-KMT students were easily detected, labeled "running dogs," and isolated. Pro-CCP students were admired as self-sacrificing idealists.

Aside from its technical proficiency, the CCP was fortunate to arrive on the scene just in time to collect the fruits of revolutionary harvest. A century of national humiliation and a succession of thwarted reforms had imparted an irresistible allure to radical solutions. In the politics and literature of the students, as of the nation at large, unsuccessful parents bequeathed a profounder radicalism to their children. The generation of monarchial reform symbolized by Kang Youwei (born 1858) was followed by one of republicanism epitomized by Sun Yatsen (born 1866) and finally by the communism of Mao Zedong (born 1893). In this context, the Neo-Confucianism of Chiang Kaishek (born 1888), modeled as it was upon the conservative reformer Zeng Guofan (born 1811), seemed strangely out of place.

The intellectual, psychological, and moral vacuum left by the breakdown of the universal Confucian order was too vast to be filled by the relativistic pragmatism of John Dewey and Hu Shi. A new and totalistic worldview was necessary—one that would explain China's failures without undermining national pride—hence the appeal evoked by a theory that blamed imperialists and reactionaries but exculpated the Chinese people. Leninism did this. It analyzed a perplexing and oppressive environment in simple terms and plotted a corrective course of action. In its united-front version (incorporated into Mao's New Democracy), Leninist doctrine reserved an important role for the petit bourgeois intellectuals. This was essential to an intellectual elite whose consciousness of its own political preeminence had survived the demise of Confucianism.

Mao offered China's students an attractive blend of the modern and the traditional, a combination by no means unique to Chinese communism. Superficially, Chinese communism appeared to be anything but modern. Under Mao's hegemony, life in the regions was technologically primitive compared with the urbanized sector under Chiang. In terms of social mobilization, however, Mao's efforts to bring the masses into politics were highly modern, even though they drew upon an indigenous tradition of peasant rebellions. Mao adapted a radically modern ideology to Chinese conditions by finding the source of absolute virtue in the downtrodden rural masses. In the Communist countryside, students found assurance that they could be both pure and progressive, radical reformers and 100 percent Chinese. On his side, Chiang's attempt to foster Confucian values in a foreignized urban environment seemed to combine the least appealing features of past and present.

Similarities between the Red Guard phenomenon and student movements of the past can be found only at a high level of historical abstraction. For example, frustrated careerism and betrayed idealism continued to unsettle China's youths. Students still viewed themselves as incorruptible social critics, and the purity of their protests was, as before, compromised by adult intrigue. One can isolate features of the Red Guards reminiscent of the traditional censorate, the Boxer uprising, and the post–May Fourth student movements, to say nothing of the Hitler Youth.[10]

The historian, however, is more impressed by the discontinuities. The most striking of these is the change in scale. In December 1931 the capital city of Nanjing was deluged with an unprecedented 16,600 demonstrators. In the late months of 1966, Beijing received 11 million. This is indicative of a second fundamental change: The present government is the first in modern Chinese history capable of disciplining and mobilizing students on all levels throughout the country. Even the Red Guards, a product of internal struggle, testify most eloquently to this development. Unlike pre-Communist student movements, they represent an induced rebellion of part of the system against the whole, not a more or less spontaneous attack by an extralegal revolutionary force. Finally, the nationalistic component of the Red Guards was relatively weaker than in pre-1949 student movements. To some extent, this is a tribute to the Communists' success in removing the two principal targets of student protest: internal disunity and foreign exploitation. But chaos, for which the Red Guards were partially responsible, shattered national unity and invited outside interference. Thus, there was no reason to suppose that adulation of the Maoist cult had permanently superseded the tradition of nationalistic student protest.[11]

ADDENDUM

Movements Since the Cultural Revolution

The Red Guard Movement was terminated, as it had been launched, by fiat issued by the Great Helmsman, Mao Zedong. To add to the irony, the People's Liberation Army, the same institution that had facilitated the Red Guards' creation, was charged with the task of bringing it to an end. Mao called the movement to a halt because it had veered out of control. Although the Red Guards had promoted his own power, humbled bureaucrats, and steeled a generation of "revolutionary successors," factional warfare had brought China to the verge of anarchy.

With Red Guards doing hard labor in communes, factories, and frontier settlements, the saga of modern China's student movements had seemingly played itself out. However, appearances were deceiving, partly because this generation of Chinese youth molded by the Cultural Revolution, who trickled—then flooded—back into the cities in the course of the 1970s, were cut from no ordinary cloth. Though their ideals had been shattered, they had been thoroughly politicized. Even while idolizing Mao Zedong, moreover, they had learned to think for themselves and to choose their own courses of action.

Certain parallels can be drawn between the generation of the 1960s, tempered in the caldron of the Cultural Revolution, and that of their parents, hardened by the rigors of the war with Japan. Both had been mobilized by a nationwide crusade championed by a supreme leader who entered the crisis with nearly universal support. Both suffered disillusionment with the leader but retained a capacity for political commitment. During the late 1940s, youthful idealism found outlet in protests against the corrupt, oppressive Kuomintang and, during the early 1950s, in mobilization under the leadership of the victorious Communists—suggesting that they had not repudiated ideological commitment per se but were prepared to transfer that commitment to a more effective Chinese government. Because the depth of belief in Mao was so much more intense than it had ever been for Chiang, the failure of the Cultural Revolution was followed by a real "crisis of faith." By the 1980s, young and early middle-aged Chinese had come to rely heavily on foreign models and images for change. When it became evident that no viable alternative to Communist rule existed, some fled abroad while others placed their hopes faute de mieux in a reformed and enlightened version of the existing political order.

Qualities of self-reliance, independence, and courage made the cohort of the late 1960s and early 1970s unique among post-Liberation students, whose aspirations were choked by the tight network of political and social institutions that defined their lives. Reemerging as a force to be reckoned with in the mid-1970s, this generation has continued to play an important role both in person and by dint of influence and example for the younger generation.

At the time of Zhou Enlai's death in January 1976, China's universities were barely recovering, having reopened as "revolutionary" institutions only in 1971. Their students had gained admission mostly through recommendations and good connections rather than through scholastic achievement, and their academic work was diluted with ideological indoctrination, political activities, and manual labor. By 1972, when they learned that Mao's trusted successor, Lin Biao, had betrayed the chairman, these young men and women were already disillusioned with revolutionary extremism. On April 5, 1976, together with tens of thousands of fellow Beijingers, they converged on

Tiananmen Square, using the pretext of public mourning for the late Premier Zhou as a cover for thinly veiled criticism of the ultraleftists.

Once the square had been cleared and demonstrators beaten and jailed, the triumphant Maoists seized the opportunity to blame the trouble on Zhou's protegé, Deng Xiaoping. Deng fled south to safety, but his period of "exile" was brief. By December 1978, following the death of Mao and the arrest of the Gang of Four, he became leader of a new governing coalition of rehabilitated cadres, most of whom could be considered modernizers and reformists.

Deng's reemergence was greeted with enthusiasm by intellectuals and students. To them he promised—as had Zhou Enlai in his speech of January 1956—better working conditions, more professional autonomy, and, most important, honor and respect for their contribution to the new society. From now on they would be judged by intellectual quality and professional achievement rather than class origin and political enthusiasm. No longer classified as "petit bourgeois," or worse, they were now to be honored as "brain workers." Just as Zhou's promise of professional autonomy had been followed by the Hundred Flowers Movement of 1956–1957, which encouraged "a hundred schools of thought to contend," so was Deng's promise followed by moves toward greater intellectual freedom. But in the 1980s as in the 1950s, the demands of students and intellectuals collided with the limits of CCP tolerance.[12]

The first clash occurred at the Democracy Wall, which blossomed in November 1978, just as Deng was preparing to make his move for power at the historic Third Plenum of the Eleventh Central Committee. Critical of Mao and his successor, Hua Guofeng, the Democracy Wall activists helped to create a favorable climate for Deng's reformist agenda. However, once their broader demands for liberalization were clear, Deng turned against them and closed the wall down.

The most prominent Democracy Wall leaders were young men and women in their late twenties and early thirties whose formal education had been interrupted or terminated by the Cultural Revolution—scarcely "students" in the usual sense of the word. However, as veterans of the Cultural Revolution, they carried with them the intrepid dedication to principle typical of their generation. A straight line thus links the Red Guards of the late 1960s, the April 5 protestors of 1976, and the Democracy Wall activists of 1978–1979.

Because the university entrance examinations of 1977 and 1978 had been opened to older students who had lost their chances for higher education because of the Cultural Revolution, it was not uncommon to find undergraduates in their early thirties during the Democracy Wall period. By the mid-1980s, however, the typical entering freshman was an eighteen-year-old who had developed political consciousness during the relatively stable post-Maoist era. Such a student had little experience in the "real world" but had gained access to the university as an academic overachiever who had passed a series of entrance exams beginning as early as kindergarten. These young men and women, it seemed, aspired to nothing more than graduate study abroad and a secure future in a government or private job. This scarcely seemed a generation likely to rush to the barricades.

Nobody could have predicted the crescendo of protest of the late 1980s. The overture was the Beijing anti-Japanese action of September 18, 1985; the leitmotif—democracy—was established in December 1986; the finale sounded with the roar of tanks and the rattle of automatic weapons in June 1989. The 1985 flurry of activity was, in fact, just that—a small-scale and short-lived protest against a resurgence of Japanese imperialism. The incident was stimulated, I might note, by the fortieth anniversary of the defeat of Japan and a wave of officially condoned articles reviving memories of Japanese atrocities— just as inadvertently preparing the ground for anti-Japanese protests as had the Kuomintang press in 1928 and 1931.

One of the striking features of the 1985 movement—and of the ones that followed—was the ambiguous attitude toward the Dengist reforms. Surely few students would have reversed the ideological and economic loosening up of the post-Mao years. And even fewer could condone the philistine materialism and rampant corruption that accompanied prosperity. The main target was not Japan but rather Chinese officials who used the Japanese connection to feather their own nests. By drawing attention to corruption in the area of foreign trade, however, the young students were giving ammunition to opponents of reform. Perhaps because most students had no desire to play into the hands of the old guard and because Party leaders managed the situation with some finesse, things soon quieted down.

The outburst of 1986–1987 was less easily contained. The immediate background was a wave of official liberalization more sweeping in scope than anything that had come before, including a celebration of the thirtieth anniversary of the Hundred Flowers Movement and talk of institutional reform in the political realm. Even the outspoken critic Fang Lizhi was allowed to express his ideas in the official press. Stimulated by these promising developments, students took to the streets with a demand for "democracy." The slogan was extremely inchoate, students made little effort to attract support from workers and other social groups, and resentment over inflation and corruption had not reached a boiling point. Hence, authorities were able to bring the movement to a halt by punishing a handful of high-level intellectuals, cashiering Party Chairman Hu Yaobang for sheltering dissidents, arresting a few workers, and intimidating student demonstrators. The timing of the movement, just before final examinations and the long Chinese New Year's vacation, also helped to calm things down.

However, suppression did nothing to solve the basic problem—the younger generation's disillusionment with the Party's leadership. With the removal of Hu and his replacement by the politically inadequate Zhao Ziyang, the vision of structural change initiated from the top receded into the distance. At the same time, social, economic, and intellectual forces let loose during the Dengist years continued to gather strength, helping to pave the way for the dramatic events of spring 1989.

The florescence of iconoclastic and democratic ideas that preceded the 1989 uprising finds its antecedent in the New Culture Movement that helped set the stage for the demonstration of May 4, 1919. This period of intense protest against the deficiencies of Chinese culture and the concomitant search for alternatives was highlighted by a widespread faith in science and democracy. But because there was scant hope that these ideals could be realized through involvement in the Byzantine warlord politics of the time, intellectuals tended to look beyond the existing system to a new order.

The relationship between the climate created by their ideas and the May Fourth Movement is problematic. The students agreed that China's traditions were rotten and that the politics of the warlord era were beneath contempt— but rather than confine their quest to the cultural realm, they created a politics of mass mobilization, turning the collective power of the people against the corrupt and traitorous warlord rulers.

The students' action took the New Culture Movement leaders by surprise. Some, such as Chen Duxiu, were swept into the vortex. Many others, however, stood aside or confined themselves to high-minded but ineffectual proclamations. Though there was general sympathy for the students' goals, there was doubt about whether taking to the streets was the answer to the profound problems on the New Culture agenda.

In 1989, student demands were more deeply rooted in the ideology of reformed Marxism and Western liberalism. Hence the links between the intellectual climate preceding the movement and the movement itself were stronger than they had been in 1919. The example of elders unafraid to challenge the status quo was undoubtedly an important conditioning force for students who marched and sat in from April 18 to June 4. Nonetheless, when the uprising began, Fang Lizhi and other leaders of the "salon" culture kept their distance from the demonstrators lest they give substance to accusations of incitement to riot such as had been used to discredit them in 1987. Their probity, however, did not prevent officials from finding a conspiratorial nexus linking the demonstrations to the salons.

Themes in Student Movements:
Continuities, Discontinuities

The interplay between older and college-aged intellectuals is but one characteristic feature of Chinese student movements that continued into the 1980s. Youthful discontent still draws from frustrations over intractable problems and inadequate or misdirected leadership; from tensions between rulers who fall back upon patterns of traditional political culture and students who look to the outside world for new formulations; and from the gulf between the high aspirations and exalted self-image of rising intellectual elites and the discouraging political and economic prospects that await them after graduation.

Protest movements since the Cultural Revolution inevitably bear the mark of that epochal event—and yet in many ways patterns of earlier movements remain in evidence. Students continue to apply pressure on officials to live up to their own values, in this case the promise of the Communist revolution—

a better life to the people and equality of opportunity if not absolute egalitarianism as an inseparable part of the socialist credo.

Though a majority of present-day students, like the traditional degree-holders, are drawn from politically and culturally favored groups, they must prove themselves through academic competition, and their self-image is that of an achievement-based elite—or at least an aspiring elite. Just as Confucian literati lambasted imperial in-laws, eunuchs, and favored officials whose positions rested upon status, money, connections, and inherited privilege, their modern descendants heap obloquy upon the heads of corrupt cadres, their families, and friends, who usurp hard-to-come-by opportunities for university admission, study abroad, and job placement. Wealth and power, as they see it, can exercise no legitimate claim over achievement and virtue. Protest against bureaucratic malfeasance also built upon themes popularized by Mao—especially during the Cultural Revolution, when the notion that China's literate minority had a duty to expose official misdeeds through big-character posters and other means received legitimacy and high-level sanction. Whatever aspects of Maoism may have been discredited, his attack on bureaucratic arrogance and privilege established deep roots.

Students carry on the legacy of traditional literati. Never did traditions assert themselves with greater force than during the incident of April 22, 1989, in which young petitioners knelt on the steps of the Great Hall of the People. Students-as-petitioners in the remonstrating mode was also evident in earlier movements. In 1989, however, the mode changed from supplications to demands, most dramatically with Wuer Kaixi's throwing down the gauntlet in the nationally televised May 18 meeting with Li Peng.

This self-conscious radicalization of a student movement in which students move from remonstrance to denunciation reiterated the 1931 pattern—in which hopeful *petitioners* were succeeded by angry *demonstrators*. Unfortunately, successful movements, such as those of December 9, 1935, and December 1, 1945, have moved not toward confrontation but toward reconciliation, under the influence of CCP united-front strategies. But the powerful and well-entrenched Communist dictatorship could not very well provide leadership for assaults on itself, leaving the students without disciplined and experienced organizational support.

We must bear in mind, of course, that Chinese students do not attack strong central governments except as a last resort. What laid the stage for the confrontation of the late 1980s was a level of inflation unequaled in post-1949 China, with a concomitant rise in the level and visibility of corruption and a growing disparity between the nouveaux riches and the impoverished intellectuals who were part of the hard-hit salaried class. The convergence of these phenomena was reminiscent of the 1940s, during the latter stages of the war and the civil war, when latent resentment against one-party rule became manifest during a period of rampant inflation and corruption. In fact, neither inflation nor corruption in the late 1980s equalled that of the 1940s, but that those old enough to remember the KMT era made the comparison suggests the depths to which the CCP regime had fallen in the eyes of the intellectuals.

Protests against unchecked autocracy were voiced during the late Manchu era, the Yuan Shikai reign, and the period of KMT rule, and "democracy" has been in vogue since the New Culture era. In the 1980s, abuses of power by high-level leaders and by bureaucrats gave particular force to the abstract concept of democratic rule. Indeed, if the ill-defined term *democracy* has any common meaning to its Chinese advocates, it is: Get the officials off our backs. It has less in common with contemporary U.S. notions of universal suffrage, free elections, and majority rule than with the eighteenth-century motto "Don't tread on me." But it draws even more deeply from the Chinese ideal of righteous, virtuous, responsible, and responsive government historically championed by good emperors and upright officials.

Taken in its broadest sense as an expression of resentment against overbearing officials, the democracy movement garnered widespread support among varied sectors of the population. In fact, because resentment was so diffuse, 1989 eclipsed earlier instances of popular support for embattled students—from merchants in the anti-U.S. boycott of 1905, the "new armies" prior to 1911, and a broad spectrum of urban, and even rural, groups during the May Fourth and subsequent periods. As he lay in his glass sarcophagus, bearing slight witness while Beijing's proletariat charged forth to support the students camped outside his marble mausoleum, Mao might have recalled his encomium of 1939: "How should we judge whether a youth is a revolutionary? How can we tell? There is only one criterion, namely, whether or not he is willing to integrate himself with the broad masses of workers and peasants and does so in practice." We shall never know whether or not a secret smile crossed Mao's waxen lips, for his tomb was closed to the public for the duration of the demonstrations.

At times students have carried the united-front tactic to its extreme by appealing to official henchmen—police and even soldiers. During the December Ninth Movement, they sent propagandists into the camps of Song Zheyuan's Twenty-ninth Army outside of Beiping and of Zhang Xueliang's revanchist-minded northeastern refugees stationed in Xi'an. On the windswept Beijing boulevards students upbraided their assailants with cries of "Chinese don't hit Chinese!" while the blunt edges of broadswords rained down upon their padded gowns. In 1989 there was a more positive appeal appropriate to the post-1949 era: "The people love the PLA; the PLA loves the people!"

Another hallmark of student movements during the new era is their scale. Some 3,000 had gathered at Tiananmen on May 4, 1919; fewer than a thousand may have marched on December 9, 1935; 7,000 or 8,000 on December 16. These numbers are infinitesimal compared to the million Red Guards who hailed Chairman Mao on August 18, 1966. But even more impressive than this million who came at the behest of their leader were the estimated million who marched in open contempt of government prohibitions on May 23, 1989.

Along with the increase in scale was a quickening in communications and a broadening arena of impact. In the early twentieth century, circular telegrams were the preferred means for spreading word to other cities. In 1935 Edgar and Helen Snow rallied the foreign press. In 1966, though the world knew little about the inner workings of the Cultural Revolution, the Red Guards were an inspiration to rebellious youth from Japan to Peru. By 1989 communications had become worldwide and instantaneous. Fax machines linked students to compatriots in North America, Great Britain, and Japan, and television networks carried images of their daring deeds to audiences throughout the world, creating a climate of public sympathy that governments could not ignore.

If the medium has undergone a dramatic change, the message is more familiar. Among the characters who reappeared in 1989 were those aged veterans of the New Culture era, "Mr. Science and Mr. Democracy" (see Chapter 5). Repeated demands for the implementation of these precepts shows both how appealing they continue to be—and how elusive. Many intellectuals had been attracted to the Chinese Communists because they had reason to believe that Marxism was both scientific and democratic. Now the call for science and democracy has been turned against the Communists, whose bureaucratic modus operandi is deemed unscientific and whose political behavior is judged undemocratic. Seventy years ago, of course, science and democracy were widely accepted goals but conspicuously absent from the slogans of May Fourth, which voiced more immediate political demands. In 1989, however, these talismanic words were emblazoned in huge characters on student banners—an expression of profound disillusionment with a regime they anathematized as "feudal"—the same term that earlier generations had applied to the warlords and Chiang Kaishek.

If one of the chief targets of pre-1949 movements—feudal rulers—remains alive and well (see Chapter 1), another—imperialist aggressors—has receded from view. The main reason is clear: The PRC government has enjoyed dramatic success in unifying the country, ousting invaders, and eliminating special privileges for foreigners on Chinese soil—except of course for privileges voluntarily conferred by the Chinese government. Since the end of the Korean War, foreign powers have been involved only obliquely, when domestic issues were projected abroad. Thus when the Red Guards attacked "revisionism" on the part of Nikita Khrushchev and his successors, their real concern was the alleged danger of similar forces within China.

During the 1989 uprising, the imperialist menace was used exclusively by the government, which accused students of being manipulated by outside forces, and it was the students who were compelled to reaffirm their patriotism. Xenophobic attacks on "bourgeois liberalism" were reminiscent of the use of "Bolshevism" as a scare tactic half a century earlier. It is ironic that Deng himself is not immune to infection by the germs of that ultimate bourgeois liberal, Hu Shi, for his remark that the color of the cat doesn't matter so long as it catches mice is little more than a restatement of Hu's "more talk of problems, less talk of isms." Deng's awareness of his vulnerability to charges of ideological softness is undoubtedly one reason why isms are reaffirmed even as their policy implications become problematic.

Students now dismiss Deng's Four Cardinal Principles (socialism, dictatorship, CCP rule, and Marxist-Leninist-Maoist thought) just as their precursors once mocked Chiang Kaishek's Confucian shibboleths (propriety, righteousness, probity, and conscience) during the New Life Movement. As was true of their Republican predecessors, however, the students themselves are by no means immune from ideological absolutes that are undefined and linked only vaguely to practical solutions—witness the almost talismanic invocation of "democracy."

By identifying dissent as dangerous and seditious, Chinese rulers justify the use of coercion and violence against their own citizens. In imperial China, protesting intellectuals frequently paid with their lives. In modern times, persistent critics from Song Jiaoren to Deng Yanda to Wen Yiduo were singled out for assassination. Broadswords and fire hoses were used on December 16, 1935, machine guns on March 18, 1926. For the wholesale slaughter of young dissidents, one could find a precedent in the Kuomintang's Party Purification Movement of 1927, but the targets then were not students as such but all elements affiliated with the Communist Party. The post-1949 sequel—the application of state terror against landlords and "counterrevolutionaries" during the early 1950s—was, likewise, an attempt to eliminate elements actually or potentially hostile to a new order.

One reason the CCP seldom had to resort to violence against students, as I confidently stated in my 1968 essay, was because the Party had "mastered techniques of internal social control." In contrast to the KMT, which stifled educated youth, it appeared that the Communists mobilized them. By the time these thoughts appeared in print, the PLA had been called in to crush recalcitrant Red Guard organizations, with casualties greatly exceeding those of June 4. Nonetheless, I continued to believe in the Communists' efficacy in organization and mobilization until I found myself in a Chinese student demonstration. It was September 18, 1985, and I was standing among the hundreds of Beida students pressed against a locked main gate. Suddenly a young man climbed onto a low wall, lifted a megaphone to his lips, and urged the crowd to forgo its planned march to Tiananmen Square in favor of an officially sponsored rally. A demonstrator turned and said to me, "He's supposed to be our 'student body president,' but he's really an official fink."

The CCP leaders, who came to power as successful patrons of student activism, now suppress organized protests and try to confine students to academic pursuits in the interests of nation building. Though it has taken them a bit longer than the KMT, which adopted these policies within a year of seizing power, the Communists have attained a similar posture. The present leadership's efforts to produce university graduates who are technologically skilled and politically docile evoke memories of policies followed by Chiang Kaishek's wartime minister of education, Chen Lifu. How Chiang would have loved the notion of teaching Beida's freshmen military discipline by sending them to boot camp in Shijiazhuang!

The Shijiazhuang ploy is the latest in a series of CCP efforts to humble proud intellectuals by "sending them down" to live among workers, peasants, and soldiers. Such discipline is considered necessary because, among other things, students continue to be drawn from politically and socially favored groups. Descendants of the imperial literati, of Westernized intellectuals, and of the old bourgeoisie continue to win disproportionate rewards in the academic rat race, where they are joined by sons and daughters of well-placed officials. The top ranks of academe, however, contain few representatives of the putative beneficiaries of the revolution, the workers and peasants.

Another more or less constant factor since the May Fourth period is geography. Now, as then, Beijing and Shanghai remain twin foci for student protests. However, China's higher educational map has become somewhat better balanced than it was in 1949, allowing students in provincial capitals to play important supporting roles. For example, remote Guiyang was a center for the Democracy Wall Movement; the University of Science and Technology in Hefei sparked the protests of 1986; and Chengdu was a scene of large-scale violence in 1989. Beida retains its symbolic importance as the pacesetter. Even though Beijing Normal University and People's University had shared the spotlight during the 1989 movement, only at Beida were entering students sent off for a year of military training.

The destruction of the 1989 movement, the diaspora of its leaders, and the radicalization of its intellectual and student supporters recall the fate of the reforms of 1898. The shift of focus from China to overseas students and exiled intellectuals gives us a sense of déja vu. It requires but a modest exercise of historical imagination to see dissidents such as Liu Binyan or Yan Jiaqi as the Liang Qichaos of their generation, vacillating between frustrated hopes for an enlightened authoritarianism and far-fetched dreams of democracy. It would, however, require a far greater mental leap to place the astrophysicist Fang Lizhi, much less student leaders such as Wuer Kaixi or Chai Ling, in the shoes of Sun Yatsen. Though an appreciation of the past informs our understanding of the contemporary scene, in short, it can scarcely tell us what will happen next. It does little, for example, to help us determine whether the 1989 uprising was a last hurrah or a new beginning.

A sense of history is crucial, however, for understanding how student protest has become a central and enduring feature of contemporary Chinese political culture. As the preceding pages and other chapters in this volume show, the students of 1989 need to be seen as part of several overlapping traditions of revolt, as successors to the remonstrating scholars of imperial times, the campus activists who spearheaded the mass movements that threatened the warlords and then the KMT, and the youthful iconoclasts of the first decades of the Republican era. In light of the enduring potency of each of these three traditions, the key question is not whether campus activism will continue to play a central role in Chinese politics in the years to come, for that seems certain. What is less certain is just how each of the three traditions described above, as well as the legacy of the Red Guards from which the activists of 1989 tried to distance themselves, will shape the words and deeds of the next set of student protesters. Although history may not tell us precisely what the future holds, in short, in this case at least it does tell us to watch for the reappearance of a variety of issues, tactics, and themes, all of which have long pedigrees but all of which have also been invested with different meanings by different generations of youths.

Notes

1. Vera Schwarcz, *The Chinese Enlightenment* (Berkeley: University of California Press, 1986).
2. Jeffrey N. Wasserstrom, *Student Protests in Twentieth-Century China: The View from Shanghai* (Stanford: Stanford University Press, forthcoming).
3. I wish to thank my colleague Mark Lupher for his critical reading of an earlier draft of the Addendum and his valuable suggestions for improvements.
4. Joseph Tao Chen draws a vivid comparison between Beijing and Shanghai in *The May Fourth Movement in Shanghai* (Leiden: Brill, 1971). These two cities, containing the majority of China's college students until 1937, have been the major vortexes of twentieth-century student politics.
5. For some of the observations in this paragraph and the following one, I am indebted to the insights of Lucian Pye, who served as an intelligence and Chinese-language officer in the U.S. Marines in Beijing and Tianjin from September 1945 to April 1946. Letter to the author, September 12, 1967.
6. The writings of Ba Jin (Pa Chin), portraying the breakdown of the traditional family, have been a mirror and a model for several generations of adolescent rebels. See Pa Chin, *The Family* (Beijing: Foreign Languages Press, 1958), and Olga Lang, *Pa Chin and His Writings: Chinese Youth Between the Two Revolutions* (Cambridge: Harvard University Press, 1957).
7. Mao Zedong, *Selected Works*, vol. 3 (New York: International Publishers, 1954), pp. 10–11.
8. For the Zhengfeng movement, see Boyd Compton, *Mao's China: Party Reform Documents, 1942–44* (Seattle: University of Washington Press, 1952). For a study of "remolding" from a psychoanalytic point of view, see Robert J. Lifton, *Thought Reform and the Psychology of Totalism* (New York: Norton, 1961), esp. pt. 3, "Thought Reform of Chinese Intellectuals."
9. See Chow Tse-tsung, "The Anti-Confucian Movement in Early Republican China," in Arthur W. Wright, ed., *The Confucian Persuasion* (Stanford: Stanford University Press, 1960), p. 309.
10. See John Israel, "The Red Guards in Historical Perspective," *China Quarterly*, no. 30 (April-June 1967), pp. 26–30.
11. I would like to thank the Committee on Contemporary China of the Social Science Research Council, whose grant made this research possible, and the East Asian Research Center at Harvard University, which provided facilities for my work.
12. The oscillation between tighter and looser controls over intellectuals has not been limited to the instances cited here but has been a recurrent pattern since 1949.

5

MEMORY AND COMMEMORATION: THE CHINESE SEARCH FOR A LIVABLE PAST

Vera Schwarcz

The great events, they are not our loudest but our stillest hours. Not around the inventors of new noises, but around the inventors of new values does the world revolve. It revolves inaudibly.

—Friedrich Nietzsche

China today is in danger of losing its past. Like a snail robbed of its shell, it has nothing to pull back into, little to carry forward with certainty. No homecoming to memory is allowed: The mass movement of 1989 did not happen. The government claims it was nothing but "counterrevolutionary turmoil" instigated by a handful of "hooligans." The authorities have honored the soldiers who died during the repression of June by calling them "revolutionary martyrs" (see the Afterword for more details), but the students and ordinary citizens killed in Beijing, Chengdu, and other cities may not be mourned publicly. On the first anniversary of the June Fourth Massacre, in fact, even to wear white (the traditional Chinese color of mourning) or black (its Western equivalent) was forbidden. Remembrance of the dead—which, as James Watson suggested in Chapter 3, has long been the anchor of personal, familial, and to a certain extent national identity in China—is crushed under the weight of officially mandated amnesia. To compensate for the stifling of personal memory, China has gone through a period of loud, official comme-

An earlier version of this essay appeared in the *Wilson Quarterly* (Fall 1989); it is reprinted here with that journal's permission.

morations and spectacles. First came the 1989 celebrations of the seventieth anniversary of the May Fourth Movement and the fortieth anniversary of the founding of the People's Republic on October 1, and then a year later came a new round of state rituals associated with the Asian Games, which were designed to convince the world that life had returned to normal in Beijing. In all of these ceremonies, the CCP tried to use or disguise the meaning of the past, never to encourage historical remembrance. . . . But can commemoration replace memory?

This question was not as stark nor as urgent during the celebrations, discussions, and demonstrations I witnessed in Beijing during April and May 1989. I had gone to China to attend two conferences dealing with the May Fourth Movement. One took place at the Sleeping Buddha Temple on the outskirts of Beijing from April 30 to May 3. The second took place in the downtown of the capital from May 5 to May 8 and was sponsored by the Chinese Academy of Social Sciences (CASS). In both settings Chinese scholars from the mainland, Hong Kong, Taiwan, Singapore, and the United States gathered to celebrate an earlier student-led movement for democracy. For a few days in early May, it seemed as if the present had overtaken the past. It seemed as if public commemoration of the event of 1919 could be expanded to accommodate the dreams of a new generation of Chinese intellectuals.

During the May Fourth Movement of 1919, students and teachers of Beijing University had taken to the streets to protest China's mistreatment at the Versailles peace conference. They started out to express anger about the warlord government's acquiescence to a treaty that threatened China's national integrity. In the end, they developed an encompassing critique of the traditional values that underlay corrupt warlord politics. Their vision of an alternative "New Culture" was summed up by the two slogans: "science" and "democracy." In 1919 these were urgent, emotional ideals that promised to liberate China from centuries of Confucian autocracy. These ideals were personified as "Mr. Science" (*Cai xiansheng*) and "Mr. Democracy" (*De xiansheng*) by young intellectuals who longed to be saved from bureaucratic politics, from arranged marriages, and from the burden of formulaic learning. By spring 1989 a new generation of Chinese students was demonstrating in the streets of Beijing. It also marched under the slogans of "science" and "democracy." This generation now quarreled with corruption inside the Communist Party. For a tragically short interval these idealistic students were convinced they could change old habits of mind. The seventieth anniversary of the May Fourth Movement gave them a dramatic opportunity to see themselves as heroes on a world stage. On the Chinese government's commemorative stamps, as well as on U.S. television, young intellectuals proclaimed fidelity to the goals of the New Culture Movement. In both settings the background is Tiananmen Square. In both, young intellectuals make speeches, distribute pamphlets, carry flags. In both a look of fierce determination is carved onto the faces of those whose modern education endowed them with an ancient responsibility.

It was Mencius, Confucius's disciple, who first codified the Chinese intellectual's duty to society in the famous adages, "Those who work with their minds are meant to rule; those who work with their brawn are meant to be ruled" and "Those who know are the first to awake; the enlightened awake the others." In spring 1989, however, neither the ancient nor the arrogant echoes of this definition of the intellectual were much noticed on the streets of Beijing. Instead, millions of ordinary citizens swelled the ranks of student demonstrators—further convincing them that this indeed was the fruition of the earlier May Fourth Movement of 1919. In the heat of the mass movement of May 1989, it was possible to ignore—momentarily—the social isolation of Chinese intellectuals. It was possible, also, to overlook for a while the echoes of the Cultural Revolution of 1966–1969. That mass movement, too, had started with millions of young people on the streets of Beijing. But then, unlike in 1989, they had been called forth by one man, Mao Zedong, and, unlike this later May, students had been impatient, even cruel to the "unbelievers." The result of that earlier frenzy of mass action, however, was the same as today: The voices of the young were drowned out, their dreams swallowed by a struggle for power among the old men of the party.

Historical memory did not fare well in the midst of mass action and dramatic commemorations. Neither the Cultural Revolution nor Mencius had much to say to a student movement wrapped up in its conviction that history was starting anew. They did not have time to take notice of the heavy burden of the past that hung over the sea of red flags in Tiananmen Square. But it was there, gloomy and ominous like the solitary black flag used to proclaim the hunger strike on May 13, 1989. It was there also even earlier—in the conference halls where older intellectuals gathered for scholarly conferences on the May Fourth Movement. These scholars were intensely aware of the burden of the past. They had known its imprint on their own lives. They had spent decades analyzing the unfinished legacy of the May Fourth Movement. And yet these seasoned academicians, too, got caught up in the passions of the student movement. The seventieth anniversary of the event of 1919 made them intensely sympathetic to the hopes embodied in the student movement of 1989. On the actual day of May 4, 1989, most of us were to be found in and around Tiananmen Square. Chow Tse-tsung, veteran U.S. scholar of the May Fourth Movement, was hoisted high on the shoulders of a new generation of students clamoring for science and democracy. It was as if history had really come full circle and a new era was about to dawn. This vision, this exhilaration was carried by the scholars into the conference halls. It is ironic that the prodemocracy demonstrations of 1989 consummated what Mao Zedong had begun in the 1950s: They made the past into a mirror for the present. Mao had placed Chinese historiography into a straitjacket using the slogan *gu wei jin yong* (use the past for the sake of the present). In spring 1989, Chinese intellectuals themselves rushed to extract didactic lessons and inspiring messages for the present out of the complex, even troubling, legacy of May Fourth. Many, to be sure, were painfully aware of the unresolved questions left over from the May Fourth era. They noted the ambivalence toward enlightenment that lingered on from the May Fourth Movement through the reforms of Deng Xiaoping. They knew that for most of the past seventy years, Chinese history belonged to men whom Nietzsche might characterize as "inventors of new noises" and not "inventors of new values." In 1989, however, the rising tempo and decibel of the prodemocracy movement promised to fulfill and to carry forward the agenda of May Fourth. For a few weeks it looked as if the distinctions between noisy and inaudible events might vanish. Today, when the divide between these two kinds of history gapes huge once again, we might well ask what would have been the fate of May Fourth if tanks had not rolled into Tiananmen Square on June 4, 1989? What if there had been no student movement at all? What if China's historical studies could have developed unaffected by this season of loud commemorations? This is the question I posed to Zhang Zhilian, eminent historian of the French Revolution at Beijing University shortly before he was to leave China to attend commemorations of the bicentennial of the event of 1789. His answer was: "Big, public occasions are good business for historians, but are not always beneficial for the development of historical scholarship. . . . Maybe history is best off when allowed to be simply historical."

Historic Commemorations

History has been wrenched out of the past throughout twentieth-century China. It has been used over and over again to explain a century of massive convulsions, a century riddled by revolution. "Revolution" is a new phenomenon in Chinese political culture that is still called by an old name: *geming*. Literally "broken mandate," this is a traditional appellation for the break of the mandate of heaven that leads one dynasty to give way to another. By 1989 China had gone through several revolutions, including the Republican revolution of 1911; the New Culture revolution of May 4, 1919; the establishment of the People's Republic in 1949, and the Cultural Revolution of 1966–1969.

With all this upheaval, one might imagine China was tired of revolution. One might imagine China ready for the language and the social experiment of reform. Instead, however, the student movement of 1989 reconsecrated the metaphor of the broken mandate. The movement had started out calling for political reforms, but it ended up as "revolutionary," first in its own eyes and later in the view of the government that condemned it as "counterrevolutionary." It was as if no other word but *geming* was available to China's political activists. It was as if everyone had forgotten the ancient Chinese curse "May you live in interesting times." History had to be historic, or of no use at all in this year of momentous commemorations. The 1989 movement was seen as fulfilling not only the "mandate" of 1919 but also the "mandate" of 1949.

Throughout spring 1989, the seventieth anniversary of May Fourth fueled talk of a new, "more revolutionary May Fourth." In 1919, 3,000 students had marched the short distance from the old, downtown campus of Beijing University to Tiananmen Square. On May 4, 1989, hundreds of thousands of students marched for eight hours from the outskirts of the city where Beijing University and other institutions of higher learning are now located. The students of 1989 marched in full view and with full support of the citizens of the capital. The momentous scale of the 1989 demonstrations led to a hyperbolic evocation of the past. Commemorations of May Fourth now had to accommodate not only the intellectuals' aspirations for science and democracy, not only the students' grievances about lack of freedom of the press and bureaucratic corruption, but also the hopes of millions of ordinary citizens aroused by activists in Tiananmen Square. In this process, the anniversary of the event of 1919 became identified with a promise left unfulfilled from China's "liberation" in 1949.

On May 12, 1989, this vision of historic commemoration was explicitly proclaimed at a "democracy salon" held on the campus of Beijing University. This "salon" (translated into Chinese as *shalong*, or sand dragon) was the seventeenth in a series of student-sponsored discussions about political reform. On this day, 500 undergraduates crowded around the grassy patch in front of a statue of Cervantes. They came to hear Bao Zongxin, a well-respected scholar of Qing intellectual history. But Bao did not speak about the past. Instead, he fired up the crowd with a series of impassioned statements: "You, your movement, has finally made China stand up! On October 1, 1949, Mao proclaimed in Tiananmen Square that China has stood up. But that was propaganda. You have made those words real."

"Liberation" became more than a metaphor in spring 1989. In the fervor of commemoration, an intellectuals' movement became linked to—and in the end, swallowed by—the language of political revolution. Time to recall the political atrocities that had surrounded the revolution of 1949, or the naive cultural radicalism of the student movement of 1919, ran out as yet another mass movement engulfed China's capital. Especially after millions took to the streets in support of students who had called for a hunger strike in Tiananmen Square, there was little room left in Chinese public life for the ambiguities of historical memory.

That spring the past had to lead straight to the present—with an inspiring message, whenever possible. Official government newspapers like the *People's Daily* commemorated the anniversary of May Fourth with bombastic editorials about the "praiseworthy patriotism" of the students of 1919. Decoded, the message to the present generation of students was simple: Be loyal to the Party, dedicate yourself to the nation's modernization program, and forget about Western ideas that only aggravate the economic crisis at hand. Students responded with a fervent defense of the right to think critically. They insisted that the contemporary economic crisis must be blamed on the Party's own corruption. They, too, asserted that the past leads up to the present as they marched under banners reading "Seventy Years Already!" and "We have waited too long for Mr. Science and Mr. Democracy!"

In the heat of the confrontation between the government and the students, the seventy-year-old May Fourth Movement could not be consigned to the past. It had to provide usable slogans in spite of warnings by a few middle-aged scholars who tried to stem the tide of present-oriented commemoration. At the Sleeping Buddha Temple conference, especially, there was a noticeable effort to take a longer view of the problem of Chinese intellectuals. Several participants sought to place the event of 1919 into a context that was quite different from that of 1989. Chen Fangzhen (from the Chinese University of Hong Kong), for example, reminded his compatriots that the original May Fourth had been the product of an extreme sort of political crisis. China in the late 1910s was in danger of disintegration at the hands of rapacious warlords and aggressive imperialists. China faced no such crisis in 1989. And yet the drama of a life-or-death crisis was reenacted with tragically augmented consequences.

At the conference sponsored by the Chinese Academy of Social Science, Chen Fangzhen went one step further. He told his fellow intellectuals that they were a transitional force, a group brought into existence by the social turmoil of twentieth-century China. Those who called themselves *zhishi fenzi* (intellectuals or, literally, knowledgeable elements), Chen argued, have a temporary mission: to voice criticism until other social groups find and express their own voice. Later, when others can speak for themselves, when the educated need no longer to be *daiyan ren* (carriers of the word for the wordless masses) then intellectuals will be superfluous. They will have no special calling in a truly modern society.

But Chinese intellectuals were not prepared to hear about their demise in the heady days of May 1989. Too much of what was going on in the streets of Beijing promised them a greater role in Chinese politics. They had every reason to hope for more public visibility as their activities drew more and more coverage from newly emancipated newspapers and television stations. This optimism was present in remarks made by the prominent philosopher Li Zehou. At both conferences, Li argued that the May Fourth promise of democracy could be fulfilled provided it became more grounded in philosophical reason and in political institutions. His new slogan, *minzhu yao kexuehua*—democracy must be more scientific—reordered and reinvigorated the old May Fourth ideals. At the same time, Li called attention to the insufficient legal foundation for democracy in China, to the absence of any constitutional guarantees for dissent.

But Li Zehou's effort to talk about the process of democratization, about its institutional prerequisites, was cut short by contemporary events. The prodemocracy movement in the streets of Beijing developed faster than middle-aged intellectuals could fathom in conference halls. Students on the streets augmented the hope and the sense of crisis. With the beginning of the hunger strike on May 13, 1989, the movement was brought to the brink of despair. Wang Dan, the student leader from Beijing University, advocated a "fight to the end" for science and democracy. Students were preparing to die. They started to write last wills and testaments, just as older intellectuals were beginning to talk about legal guarantees for dissent.

With the declaration of martial law on May 20, 1989, history appeared to have come full circle. The future of China's youth now appeared as grim as it had been in the worst nightmares of May Fourth activists. Old warnings, old pleas were now revived on the streets of Beijing. The closing lines of a 1918 story by China's foremost modern writer, Lu Xun, now echoed with a new sense of urgency. In "Diary of a Madman," Lu Xun had closed his scathing indictment of traditional autocracy with the cry: "Save the children!"[1] At the end of this May, students—the "children" from Lu Xun's bleak story about youth consumed by cannibalistic elders—roamed the faculty neighborhoods pleading: "The soldiers are coming! Teachers, teachers, please come out and save the children! Save your students!"

The teachers, now, as on the eve of the May Fourth Movement, came out in full. Nobody on the campus of Beijing University was immune to the powerful echoes of the event of 1919. Seventy years earlier, Lu Xun's generation of Beijing University teachers helped set in motion a student movement through publications such as *New Youth* magazine. They had started the assault on Confucian values that the student movement of 1919 then propagated through society as a whole. In 1989, students called out their teachers by reminding them of Lu Xun's commitment to "save the children." But the battle now was not against Confucian dogma but against the armed force of the People's Liberation Army. However "revolutionary" the meaning of May Fourth might have been, it was tragically impotent against the tanks that invaded Tiananmen Square on June 4, 1989.

By that time, May Fourth had been used too much. It was, in dark of night, used up. Young and middle-aged intellectuals alike faced a grim reality disrobed of illusions about the power of historic commemorations. They stood on the verge of a precipice described forty years earlier by the literary scholar Luo Changpei. On the eve of "liberation" in 1949, he, too, had tried to grapple with the lessons of 1919. Forty years before tanks rolled in to crush the largest movement for civil disobedience in twentieth-century China, Luo Changpei had a premonition. He voiced it mutedly in a Communist Party–sponsored volume of essays commemorating the thirtieth anniversary of May Fourth: "The old tune of May Fourth cannot be replayed. Without May Fourth, we would not have the present. If we continue to grasp forever the spirit of May Fourth, we will have no future."

The Problem of Chinese Intellectuals

The literary critic Luo Changpei did not live to see the seventieth anniversary of May Fourth. He did not have a chance to comment on the fate of Chinese intellectuals forty years after the founding of the People's Republic. But his younger colleagues did gather in early May of 1989 to assess their past and their future in light of the "old tune" of May Fourth. The most explicit statement of their concern was inscribed on the banner that hung above the conference at the Sleeping Buddha Temple: "May Fourth and the Problem of Chinese Intellectuals."

Those speaking beneath the banner were all survivors. They were victims of various criticism campaigns directed against China's educated elite from the 1950s onward. Some of the participants of the 1989 conference had been labeled "rightists" in 1957, after Mao found their expression of critical thought intolerable during the short-lived Hundred Flowers Movement. Many more had suffered when intellectuals became labeled members of the "stinking ninth" category during the Cultural Revolution. The "crime" of this group (deemed more odious than landlords, capitalists, Kuomintang sympathizers, etc.) was simply higher education. Having made a living with their minds, intellectuals were excommunicated from the sacred community of peasants and workers.

Thrown out of jobs, publicly humiliated, incarcerated in "cow pens" (as holding cells for intellectuals were known during the Cultural Revolution), these scholars had paid dearly for Mencius's ancient claim that those who labor with their minds are to rule over those who labor with their brawn. Mao had willfully, cruelly reversed the traditional Chinese veneration of the educated. By the time of his death in 1976, intellectuals had lost almost all of their former social status and much of their self-confidence as well. Rehabilitation began slowly and, predictably, from the top: Deng Xiaoping, a survivor himself, declared at the 1978 National Science Conference that the overwhelming majority of the intellectuals were indeed part of the working class. Like those who engage in physical labor, those who engage in mental labor are all socialist workers. Once renamed as workers (*gongzuo zhe*), intellectuals could hope for a little better housing, a little better pay. But their social calling—especially their right to comment critically about urgent political issues facing China in the age of reform—remained suspect in the eyes of Communist Party rulers.

In April 1986, a new face appeared on new fifty-yuan notes issued by the China People's Bank. It showed an intellectual with gray hair and tie alongside a worker and a peasant. The intellectual had replaced the soldier in the previous trinity. This was a symbolic step forward in the public rehabilitation of intellectuals. It was also a symbolic concession to the Confucian worldview that held the educated elite to be the foundation of Chinese society—along with peasants and, to a lesser extent, artisans. Soldiers, according to tradition, were the lowest, most ill regarded rung of the social hierarchy.

And yet the rehabilitation of Chinese intellectuals did not go far beyond the realm of the symbolic. Less than a year after the intellectual appeared on a bank note, China was once again in the throes of an anti-intellectual campaign. The attack mounted in early 1987 was nominally against "bourgeois liberalism," but its targets were the same critical thinkers whom Mao had sought to silence in 1957, and then again during the Cultural Revolution. The 1987 campaign followed closely on the heels of an earlier attempt to intimidate intellectuals during the 1983 campaign against "spiritual pollution." Over and over again, intellectuals were criminalized for their interest in ideas from abroad. These ideas about democracy, science, and freedom of speech had been used by Chinese intellectuals to quarrel with entrenched habits of thought on native ground. That quarrel was repeatedly squelched: in 1957, in the 1960s, in 1983, in 1987, and, most recently, with the armed assault against demonstrators on June 4, 1989.

And still the commitment to critical thought endures. In early May 1989, intellectual survivors gathered to commemorate 1919 and to ask themselves:

What had gone wrong? Conversation at conferences returned to this subject over and over again: How are intellectuals to account for their repeated victimization and powerlessness in modern Chinese history? The May Fourth Movement offered these scholars a refuge in the past. The event of 1919 anchored them in a historical moment in which teachers and students had been able to speak their minds. During the May Fourth Movement, ideas about cultural and political reform had aroused the nation as a whole. An understanding of this history promised to heal the wounds of the more recent past. It also seemed to rekindle hope for the future. The student movement exploding on the streets of Beijing accelerated this optimism. More than proclamations from Deng Xiaoping or a new face on bank notes, the confluence of a contemporary social movement and the seventieth anniversary of May Fourth offered China's battered intellectuals a genuine opportunity for self-rehabilitation.

Most of the discussions at the academic conferences sought to deepen the question of what had gone wrong between intellectuals and politics in modern China. In light of the student activism flowering on the streets of Beijing, the question became: Why have intellectuals been prevented for so long from becoming an autonomous force in Chinese society? To the intellectuals' credit, they did not simply blame Mao Zedong or Deng Xiaoping for the short-sighted policies of the Chinese Communist Party. Rather, they took this as an opportunity to examine those aspects of the Chinese intellectuals' own tradition that had kept its modern heirs from finding and expressing an autonomous voice in public life.

In seminar rooms, in hallways beyond the reach of microphones and public lectures, intellectuals dissected the ancient burden of political responsibility. Politics, in one form or another, has consumed the life of Chinese scholars from Confucius onward. Unlike European intellectuals, who had first used religion and then science as an alternative to political authority, Chinese *wenren* (literally, people of the word) had little to shield from the claims of rulers who owned both words and swords. In the midst of May Fourth commemorations, conversation drifted back to intellectual ancestors who first muted their voices for the sake of official position—or, less selfishly, for the sake of national salvation. In these conversations, it was impossible to overlook the concrete benefits that had befallen scholar-bureaucrats from the Han dynasty onward, provided they buckled down and accepted state orthodoxy. At the same time, there was also plenty of historical evidence to suggest that Chinese intellectuals had served as the moral conscience of society for centuries. Long before modern events such as the May Fourth Movement of 1919, members of the educated elite had sought to distinguish between rule by force (*zhitong*) and rule by ethical ideals (*daotong*). But for centuries as well, they have been powerless to close the gulf between the two.

Now, with a new generation of students out on the streets, the question became more urgent: Can intellectuals find and maintain a critical voice in the midst of political corruption? Will they be able to develop the seeds of a new culture sown in the May Fourth Movement and thereby edge China closer to science and democracy? In both conferences commemorating 1919, the answer was far from certain. In both settings, participants noted that the idea of enlightenment, of *qimeng*, had been overpowered repeatedly by the exigencies of national salvation (*jiuguo*). If intellectuals had been willing to forsake—or had been forced to abandon—their own ideas about political and cultural reform before 1949, what was to ensure the success of the current student movement?

Tragically, the answer from Tiananmen Square was: nothing. Without institutionalized autonomy, without legally safeguarded dissent, the current generation of students stood as naked in the face of arbitrary political authority as Chinese scholars buried in 212 B.C. by China's first emperor, Qin Shihuangdi. Unlike the ancient scholars, however, the contemporary generation of Chinese students received massive popular support. Before the tanks rolled on June 4, 1989, ordinary citizens had given students money, food, and water. Millions demonstrated in the streets, day after day, in support of hunger strikers in Tiananmen Square. They even tried to shield the demonstrators with their bodies during the first few days of martial law.

But, in the end, something overcame the students' idealism as well as the citizens' best intentions. It was not only the force of guns. The politics of crowd action, too, helped crush the student movement. This has always been the fate of intellectuals consumed by mass movements. In China, the impotence of individuals, of institutionalized groups has been reflected by millions gathered on the streets of Beijing during the Cultural Revolution, as well as in 1989. In the course of this latest movement, students repeatedly pleaded for "dialogue" with the government. But the more they pleaded, the deafer the authorities appeared to become. And as the students became more desperate, their tactics as well as their slogans became more simplistic. From beginning to end, the tragedy at Tiananmen Square was cast in terms of an old drama: injured subjects pleading for a hearing from supposedly benevolent rulers. In mid-April, for example, students kneeled for hours on the steps of the Great Hall of the People with a petition describing their grievances. And, as so often before, the rulers proved uncaring. Even before the shooting of June 4, one could foresee the tragic end to these rituals. The echoes of the Cultural Revolution were amply evident on the streets of Beijing. The government used this historical precedent to attack the students' "turmoil," to fuel popular fear of chaos. But that was not the real danger. Rather, the Cultural Revolution loomed large as a warning about how student idealism can be used and abused in the course of crowd politics. During the commemoration of May Fourth, the echoes of the Cultural Revolution could already be heard as students roamed the campus chanting ever more ardent, ever more simplistic slogans. But no one was really listening.

In the conference halls, too, commemoration displaced historical memory. At one point during our discussion at the social science academy conference, I asked: "What is the connection between the May Fourth Movement, the current student protest, and the Cultural Revolution?" Dead silence surrounded me in this seminar room filled with middle-aged intellectuals who had been victimized as members of the "stinking ninth" less than twenty years ago. A few minutes later, an old gentleman from Shanghai leaned over and whispered to me:

> Maybe there is a link after all. Maybe it is to be found in the way that both democracy and intellectuals have been ridiculed for so long. Remember the cultural conservative Gu Hongming, who was so outspoken in the late 1910s? He wore a long pigtail down his back, wrote good English, and mocked May Fourth activists by calling the proponents of democracy "demo-crazy." That is what Mao thought about intellectuals as well—crazy and dispensable. Maybe our fate is no different today. . . .

Memory in the Interstices of Commemoration

The question about the Cultural Revolution was not the only one to be met with silence around the conference table. Another concerned the intellectuals' historical memory more directly. On May 6, at the social science academy gathering, we had been talking about recent memoirs by May Fourth participants published on the mainland and in Taiwan. Scholars from both sides agreed that these personal narratives provided a meaningful alternative to politically mandated histories of the event. I asked aloud: "What about the distortions at work in personal memory as well?" Embarrassed glances crossed the small seminar room. But I went on because the issue of historical memory is a sore and important subject—at least for me: "What about the internalized censors who adjust an individual's recollections in keeping with the changing requirements of political history? What about ninety-eight-year-old Xu Deheng? This veteran of May Fourth has written a commemorative essay about May Fourth at each major anniversary for the past fifty years. Each time he has corroborated whatever version of May Fourth the Communist Party needed at the moment. What about his recollection of May Fourth printed just the other day in the *People's Daily*? As often before, he dwells on the May Fourth students' patriotism. As before, he slights their aspirations for a more democratic political culture."

The silence deepened around the conference table. Xu Deheng is an important figure in Chinese public life. He has served as head of the National People's Congress after joining the Communist Party in 1979. To call into question the veracity of his historical memory is almost as risky as to challenge the politics of Deng Xiaoping. I did not press my Chinese colleagues further. Nonetheless, the old gentleman from Shanghai again leaned over: "Xu is really too senile to write anymore, you know. His secretaries now publish stuff in his name. . . . He sounds like a windbag . . . not what you might call genuine historical memory."

What constitutes genuine historical memory in China today? I tried to ask my neighbor, but he pulled away and moved our whispering onto safer subjects. Nonetheless, this gentleman from Shanghai helped me better understand the difficulties faced by Chinese intellectuals who try to stretch the parameters of historical memory. He enabled me to better appreciate the papers presented at the conference that managed to accommodate large chunks of materials from a more genuinely remembered past. Unlike Xu Deheng, the authors of those papers wrestled with the full complexity of May Fourth. In re-remembering the event of 1919, they managed to give it a second chance, a second life as it were. This has made it possible for their colleagues to envisage a version of May Fourth that breaks through the constraints of party historiography.

One essayist, for example, dealt with the love life of Hu Shi—a major figure in the New Culture Movement of the May Fourth era. Hu became the champion of liberalism in China and a symbol of political error on the mainland after 1949. Though he lived in Taiwan, his colleagues, students, and ideas were put on trial during several campaigns directed against intellectuals. After 1979 the political venom against liberalism subsided somewhat, and Hu Shi could once again be talked about in terms of the "revolutionary literary theories" he put forth. By 1989 it was possible to explore something deeper, more personal, more complicated—Hu Shi's friendships with female intellectuals (Chinese and American) during the course of his old-fashioned marriage to an uneducated woman with bound feet.

The essay dealing with Hu Shi's inner life stretched the parameters of the remembered past, not only through new documentation from Hu Shi's letters but by going beyond the pale of political history altogether. A similar effort was palpable in an essay about Zhang Ruoming, a prominent woman student of the May Fourth era who became a major scholar of French literature. Zhang Ruoming has been more or less forgotten in Chinese public memory, but for her briefly noted political association with Zhou Enlai, the man who became premier in the People's Republic after 1949. Little else was known about Zhang Ruoming until her son began to recollect his mother's scholarly life. On the occasion of the seventieth anniversary of May Fourth, it became possible to write about Zhang Ruoming's cosmopolitanism in a way that went beyond the canons of party history.

Again, the subject and the documents brought to life details overlooked in official versions of May Fourth. The bulk of the essay about Zhang Ruoming focused on her study of André Gide—not on her role in the demonstrations of 1919, not even on her short career as a Chinese communist in France in the 1920s. It detailed her effort to interpret Gide's work according to the central theme of "narcissism"—which Zhang Ruoming wrote about with distinct appreciation. Her appreciation, in turn, evoked a positive response from Gide himself, who wrote to Zhang Ruoming in 1931: "It seemed to me in traversing your pages that I have regained consciousness of my existence. I do not think I have ever felt so well understood." Zhang Ruoming herself might have written the same thing about this May Fourth commemoration, if she had been alive in 1989. In her absence, her son's essay managed to expand public remembrance. In the interstices, as it were, he placed a recollection that did not dwell on his mother's communism in the 1920s, nor on her obsessive loyalty to the Party during the 1957 campaign against "rightist" intellectuals, nor even on her suicide out of fear and despair a year later. Instead, he used the anniversary of May Fourth to augment his contemporaries' understanding of a uniquely cosmopolitan generation of Chinese intellectuals.

Commemoration thus did not fully displace historical memory in 1989. Rather, it offered Chinese intellectuals an opportunity to tell parts of their own story in their own terms. Even as a momentous new student movement arose in Beijing, even as the passions of crowd action were engulfing the intellectuals' agenda in Tiananmen Square, recollection received its due. Far from the noise of the streets, the muted voice of memory kept history alive. Nowhere was this more apparent to me than on May 20, when I attended a ceremony commemorating the fifty-sixth anniversary of an eminent philosopher's scholarly career.

This was the day after martial law was declared in Beijing. A large lecture hall on the Qinghua University campus had been set up to accommodate hundreds of guests. Now it looked cavernous around the forty or so intellectuals who managed to get there. They had come by bicycle from universities nearby, unlike their colleagues from the social science academy downtown— whose buses were canceled at the last minute. At the center of the ceremony stood Zhang Dainian, the renowned scholar of classical Chinese thought. Everyone knew that the ceremony had been planned by former students to mark the master teacher's eightieth birthday. But such personal occasions still have to be clothed in public significance in China. Hence, the disciples fastened upon the anniversary of Zhang Dainian's teaching career at Qinghua University. The large red banner over the head table proclaimed the odd number "56" in contrast to the round, recognizably momentous "70" that had graced commemorations of May Fourth. The awkward banner and the rows of empty chairs, however, were not the only features that distinguished this gathering from those other commemorations. The whole mood had changed in the past three weeks. Now the student movement on the streets had been crushed. To be sure, no tanks yet rolled in Tiananmen Square, but an ultimatum had been given. Fear of persecution and arrest was thick among the intellectuals gathered to pay homage to Zhang Dainian.

Behind the head table hung scrolls traditionally used to honor master teachers. Classical couplets recalled the integrity of Zhang Dainian's scholarly career. A large painting portrayed an aged crane standing tall and proud on a gnarled pine branch. The bird and the pine, too, were traditional symbols for an outstanding intellectual of high moral character. These symbols were further elaborated during speeches that paid tribute to Zhang Dainian's work in classical philosophy. Several former students got up in turn to talk about the enduring influence of Zhang Dainian on their own lives. One described the lasting impression he had of Zhang's *wei ren*—his way of being fully human in a world that often denied the intellectual's humanity. This "moral achievement," his student argued, is more important than all of Zhang Dainian's considerable scholarly accomplishments. Another student emphasized his teacher's *zi zai*—his inner peace maintained through fidelity to classical moral ideals. All the speakers alluded to Zhang Dainian's suffering after he was labeled a "rightist" in 1957. All praised his ability to survive, to remain productive, to be truthful to himself under conditions that repeatedly thwarted and threatened his self-esteem.

On this day, when martial law reigned in Beijing, there was little doubt that Zhang Dainian's students were also speaking about themselves. Praising their teacher's endurance, they were trying to encourage one another to outlast yet another crackdown. None of this was explicit, of course. The symbols and the rituals of recollection sufficed for the moment. This was an intensely personal occasion. The odd setting of a fifty-sixth commemoration combined with the new situation of martial law made it more poignant.

Zhang Dainian's own speech on this occasion was subtle as well as truthful. Moved by his student's tributes, he responded with simple, modest words: "I have done nothing special over these fifty-six years. I just went on living and somehow managed to reach eighty—that is something auspicious just by itself. Throughout my life I have tried to bring together Marxism and Chinese philosophy, but I have not done it yet. . . . After 1979 [the year of Zhang's political rehabilitation], I have regained my courage and my energy. I have tried to think more independently after I turned seventy. But it has been too little, too late. Most of my life I have spent obeying and so did not accomplish enough. Still, I expect to go on with my work." As a foreign observer of this commemorative occasion, I was deeply moved by the tenacity of the bond between these intellectuals and their work. In one of the bleakest days of their shared history, they managed to come together and to hearten one another by paying tribute to the moral fortitude of one of their aged mentors. If Zhang Dainian could endure and still make significant contributions to China's understanding of truth, beauty, morality, and tradition (all major themes reflected in the titles of his recent books), others, too, might outlive the present nightmare. The key to Zhang's survival with integrity lay in his commitment to the past. It was this commitment that he had passed down to his students through his teaching and, now, through the gathering on May 20, 1989. In the very midst of what Nietzsche might have decried as loud, noisy history, Zhang Dainian and his disciples managed to recover an hour of stillness. Even as martial law was enforced outside of the gates of Qinghua University, inside intellectuals reminded themselves that the world revolves not around the inventors of new noises, but around the inventors of new values—or, as it was apparent now, around the guardians of values. Foremost among the values that Chinese intellectuals have treasured for centuries is that of historical recollection itself. In the excitement of the seventieth anniversary of May Fourth, in the heat of the passions evoked by the student movement of 1989, this treasure was almost overlooked. But never completely, never for long. The tragic end of the protests on the streets of Beijing has made historical recollection all the more precious. Now that enforced amnesia rules over Chinese public life, Confucius—the arch remem-berer—becomes ever more compelling. It was this ancient master who first encouraged intellectuals by saying "I am not someone who was born knowing the past. I love the past and am someone who seeks for it earnestly." To love the past (*hao qu*) is to hold out for the possibility that it may yet be known. To seek for it (*qiu zhi*) is to commit oneself to outlast commemorations, to outwit crackdowns, to live another day in the pursuit of truth. This remains the mission of Chinese intellectuals today.

Notes

1. Lu Xun, "Kuangren riji" (Diary of a madman), in *Lu Xun quanji* (The complete works of Lu Xun) (Beijing: People's Literature Publishers, 1981), p. 432.

6

FROM PRIESTS TO PROFESSIONALS: INTELLECTUALS AND THE STATE UNDER THE CCP

Timothy Cheek

The image the West has had of China has changed from time to time, and no doubt will change again. Of course an image to some extent reflects the viewpoint of the observer, thus distorting the reality that lies behind it. First impressions, however, are usually correct, and this holds true when two civilizations first come into contact just as much as when two people meet for the first time. . . . The first image of China formed in the West, if we discount the rationalist wisdom with which the eighteenth-century "philosophers" clothed it, was that of a mandarinate.
—Etienne Balazs, "China as a Permanently Bureaucratic State"[1]

Balazs's reflections from 1959 are a helpful reminder as Western scholars reassess their understanding of China and changes within China since the cataclysmic events of May and June 1989. The "mandarinate" does not include all Chinese intellectuals, and intellectuals are only part of the organizational and attitudinal structures that make up the mandarinate. Nevertheless, Balazs's point stands: The close relationship between members of the educated elite and the state has been a constant feature of Chinese history, including the revolutionary era, and continues to help shape the post-Tiananmen period, despite the traumatic events of 1989. We should not mistake the very real disgust individual Chinese intellectuals have expressed with the end of a *system*—that combination of ideas and institutions that make up the unwritten

I would like to thank Tony Saich for giving an earlier version of this chapter a tough, critical reading. I would also like to thank the editors of this volume for their suggestions and (even more importantly) their patience.

contract between intellectuals and the state.[2] If, as China watchers, we misread conditions in China in the 1980s, it was by extending our hopes that Chinese intellectuals in significant numbers were leaving their priestly vocations in the mandarinate and demanding a new (what some would call "modern") relationship with the state—as professionals who earn their keep in some way fundamentally separate from the government. The irony of the popular movement of 1989 and its suppression is that the wishful image of increasing professional autonomy many of us thought we saw before June has, in fact, become more of a reality precisely because of the suppression of traditional forms of loyal remonstrance (such as the petition presentations described in Chapters 4, 7, and others). As Esherick and Wasserstrom argue in Chapter 2, the 1989 popular protests were not a "democracy movement" for most of the participants in any sense that resembles democracy in the United States or Europe.[3] Few Chinese intellectuals argued for a fundamental restructuring of the political order before May 1989; many dissidents simply demanded the right to fulfill the kind of mandarin role that Chinese states (imperial, nationalist, and communist alike) have promised the intelligentsia: that of acting as advisers to those who govern.

The crackdown changed this situation. Although many still serve or hope to serve the current government, a significant group has been disestablished, forcibly alienated from the regime by its leaders, and has thus moved closer to professional autonomy. Losing one's position in the state bureaucracy does not make one instantly an independent professional. Indeed, the tragedy of mainland China's intellectuals is, as David Kelly notes, that they "remain, as a stratum, an artifact of the system they oppose."[4] However, combined with the social forces unleashed by a decade of reform—a new class of entrepreneurs, the return of inflation along with government corruption, the increased contact with foreigners and travel outside China, the increased translation of a variety of foreign books on social, economic, and literary topics—the violent reaction of the government in 1989 (and its continued repression of enemies, real and imagined) marks a major step in the punctuated evolution of China's educated elite.

Intellectuals have made a further step in the movement from priest-rentiers serving the cosmic state (Confucian or Leninist) to professionals salaried in a bourgeois society. They are not there yet, and that is one of the reasons why the popular protests of 1989 in China did not result in the dramatic change of regimes we saw in Eastern Europe (a phenomenon Chirot's chapter elucidates so well). The significance of Tiananmen is that this critical "event" has pushed that process forward. However, the mandarin vocation—which calls for a generalist serving the state through a central bureaucracy and with a unified ideology, rather than professional specialists serving the nation through a variety of separate institutions within a pluralistic range of ideologies—has not yet disappeared in China today. It is the purpose of this chapter to suggest that a greater appreciation of the "establishment" role of intellectuals will help us better understand the events of 1989 and the likely future contribution of intellectuals to China's unfinished revolution.

It is true that the CCP lost the "silent majority" of China's establishment intellectuals in 1989.[5] But if the "moral rot" (to use Chirot's term) has become increasingly apparent to leading intellectuals—starting at least in the late 1980s, with the crescendo in spring 1989, and the bitter continuing proof through repression of government critics since then—why has the "moral bankruptcy" of the regime in Beijing not become broadly apparent in China in a way sufficient to bring the regime's collapse (Chirot's thesis for Eastern Europe)? We can say that the state has lost the allegiance of many of those who are expected to staff it and propagate its policies and ideals and that alternative ideas, such as liberal democracy, are moving from the fringe of Chinese society—where such ideas certainly lay before 1989—to capture the attention of more than a few malcontents and idealists (such as the student protesters and dissident intellectuals treated in Chapters 4 and 5). Bookstores in the West are full of books on Tiananmen and especially writings by leading Chinese participants in the 1989 popular movement—from students such as Shen Tong and Li Lu to older intellectuals such as Liu Binyan and Yan Jiaqi. These valuable records, however, reinforce our propensity to overestimate the reform spirit in China. To understand the relative balance of intellectual forces for a return to full Party dominance, relaxation, or fundamental reform in China, we must see major intellectual groupings in relation to each other— students, "democratic radicals," apolitical professionals, and today's mandarins. The comparison with Eastern Europe is particularly helpful because, as Chirot describes it, three factors led to the collapse of those regimes: a loss of faith among the educated "middle classes" (which he quite helpfully describes in "cultural and educational" rather than purely economic terms) to the point that they ignored the Party-state; some range of organizational and propaganda outlets (often literature) for disaffected intellectuals to reach that audience; and, third, enough information about the outside world to enable leading intellectual speakers and the "middle-class" audience to know the state has lied to them. The power of speakers, the range of audience, and the access to examples from the outside world were all severely limited in the case of China by the nature and continuing power of the "deal" between intellectuals and the state.[6]

The Deal Between China's Intellectuals and the State

The aftermath of Tiananmen has demonstrated that the old intelligentsia-based mandarinate, its institutions and attitudes in Leninist incarnation, still exists in China today. It still attracts talented intellectuals, still has the massive support of the Party, state, and army. It will be with us for a while longer, and we would be wise, if we pretend to understand China, to familiarize ourselves with the intellectual establishment and its establishment intellectuals. As Perry points out in Chapter 7, the job allocation system in the PRC gives the state today even more control over meaningful employment opportunities for intellectuals than did the famous imperial examination system that for millennia tied Confucian elites to the state. Additionally, the work unit (*danwei*) holds sway over the lives of individuals in China, particularly urban professionals. The work unit not only dispenses one's salary, but housing, health care, and needed authorizations for travel, children's schooling, and job transfers. Despite a decade of reform, local party chiefs still control the work units of China.[7] In addition to such institutional realities, attitudes and values bind China's intellectuals to the state.

Chinese intellectuals' attitudes about their relationship to political power can be categorized on three levels: attitudes toward the state, their group, and themselves. Key attitudes shape intellectuals' behavior at each of these levels. Intellectual attitudes toward the state have been characterized by fierce *patriotism;* their behavior with superiors, peers, and subordinates reflects an acceptance of *patronage;* and their self-expressions reflect a profound elitism and sense of *paternalism.* The content of these attitudes has varied among individuals, naturally, and has changed on critical points over the past thirty years (for example, on whether the nation, the state, or the Party is most deserving of patriotic loyalty).

There have remained the three core aspects of an informal and unwritten deal between the CCP and intellectuals in the PRC.[8] This deal, which is a "social contract" in the sense that it is based on tacit understandings and shared assumptions between the Party leadership and leading intellectuals in the establishment, is fairly straightforward in principle: In return for obedient service to the Party, establishment intellectuals are promised the opportunity to serve China and to engage in intellectual pursuits. It is clear from the activities and writings of a number of the founding generation of establishment intellectuals between the 1930s and 1950s that they found the "sinification of Marxism" developed in Yan'an and embodied in Mao Zedong Thought to be not only an acceptable but actually a desirable revision of the old "contract" between intellectuals and the state under the new historical conditions of the twentieth century.[9] The praiseworthy contributions of these intellectuals during these decades shows that the deal clearly had a good side, and it was faith in the value of the contract that allowed early generations of CCP establishment intellectuals, including what Li Zehou calls the "1950s generation," to keep faith with the Party through the disasters of the 1960s and 1970s.[10] This is particularly significant in the case of the 1950s generation, as so many of those in power today (from technocrat politicians like Li Peng to heads of major academic institutions) belong to this cohort.

Under this deal with the CCP, the educated elite gave up claims to the wealth and political power of their scholar-gentry ancestors to serve what they felt was a more egalitarian and socially just government. They rejected the status of landlord and scholar-elite (*shenshi*) and accepted the status of intellectual (*zhishi fenzi*) and cadre (*ganbu*). They honored the common people (the worker, the peasant, the soldier) as never before in history and gave of their talents to raise the cultural and economic level of every Chinese. In essence they sought to select the good of the literati past and to discard the bad.

Important sociological changes also made the new establishment intellectuals serving the Communist mandarinate different from the Confucian literati. Although these intellectuals wished to continue the former role of censors (i.e., to act as loyal critics of the state), the CCP did not create an institutional equivalent to the imperial censorate.[11] In addition, intellectuals under socialism do not have the local power (i.e., lineage and local kinship organizations) that the traditional scholar-gentry had. That is, they have no estate, no monastery, no mountaintop to which to retreat when out of favor in court. This change has had ideological as well as organizational ramifications: Because the CCP does not consider passive acceptance of policy decisions a sufficient proof of loyalty, one now must speak out in favor of the state and its policies when asked to do so by the state's representatives. Intellectuals can no longer safely draw back into silence. In 1955 this was not important for Party intellectuals. In 1966 it was a matter of life and death. In the 1980s it has been a stumbling block and bone of contention for reformist intellectuals.

Generational differences have changed and will continue to change the nature and strength of the deal (first forged during the Party's Yan'an period) that binds establishment intellectuals to the Communist state, and cataclysmic events (such as those of June Fourth) have the potential to destroy the very foundation upon which the social contract is built. Nonetheless, the stability of China following the turmoil of 1989 (which contrasts so markedly with the situation in eastern Europe) demonstrates that some sort of deal between intellectuals and the state (not to mention the state and the army) still holds force. Even before June Fourth, not all intellectuals were full-fledged participants in this deal, because (as Bonnie McDougall rightly points out) throughout the Communist era there have always been members of the Chinese intelligentsia who have shied away from being "politically active." Among artists and writers (groups that have traditionally produced state ideologues and critics), for example, there have consistently been professionals who would rather steer clear of public policy issues and stick to less overtly political versions of their art.[12] However, for at least some of the politically active members of the intelligentsia, even the brutality of the crackdown of 1989 was not enough to trigger a complete repudiation of their contract with the state, in part because of the limited options available to intellectuals unprepared to take the personal and career-related risks associated with pursuing change through extralegal channels. Whether or not they felt betrayed by June Fourth and related events, establishment intellectuals in summer 1989 were faced with an unavoidable fact: There was (and still is) no functional alternative to the "Communist state" in China for the present, no nationwide, legal organization through which political alternatives could develop to parallel the Catholic church in Poland or the Lutheran church in what used to be East Germany.[13]

Although some kind of contract remains in force, the events of 1989 clearly transformed the character of the relationship between intellectuals and the state. Just how this relationship has and has not changed of late is difficult to assess with any precision at present. The rest of this chapter is devoted to putting the issue in perspective and highlighting some of the key features of the post–June Fourth contract between the intelligentsia and the state.

The Post-Tiananmen Establishment

In the months leading up to June 1989, no scholar or journalist (including myself) adequately communicated the staying power of the establishment, the limited reform goals of most reformers and students, and the profound vulnerability of all demonstrators. We ignored the power of the establishment, of the deal between intellectuals and the Party-state.[14] Nobody was running to interview General Yang Shangkun in spring 1989 or discredited "conservative" propaganda chief Deng Lichun in 1988, and only Roderick Mac-Farquhar wanted to talk to Peng Zhen (and that was about the Cultural Revolution). Mostly, we mistook *remonstrance* for *fundamental opposition*. But they were far from equivalent. Wei Jingsheng and many other heroes of the Democracy Wall Movement of the late 1970s were (and to a certain extent remain) marginal figures—of great moral significance, reflecting considerable personal courage and insight, but on the fringe of Chinese society and intellectual life.[15] For all the exciting changes in the literary world, the image McDougall has shown—that most artists and writers avoided dissent in favor of politically safe topics or cautiously remonstrated and advised the government—had not significantly changed by the end of the 1980s.[16] Among politically active intellectuals, some were drawn into a variety of think tanks and research groups under Premier Zhao Ziyang's state council and, of course, the Chinese Academy of Social Sciences.[17] Even the extreme reformers, such as Su Shaozhi (who headed the Marxism-Leninism Institute at CASS), Yan Jiaqi (who headed the Institute of Political Science at CASS), Wang Ruoshui (who remained at *People's Daily* and, though in limbo, was able to travel overseas), and even the highly critical astrophysicist Fang Lizhi (vice-president of the Science and Technology University until his purge in 1987) all tried to work through the system.[18] Wang Ruoshui is also a leading member of what Kelly calls the "counterelite" in China—reformist theoreticians who confronted the "abyss" of moral bankruptcy of the regime and over the past ten years sought to "rebuild the Marxist edifice step by step, concept by concept."[19] One goal these different groups of intellectuals shared: to revise the deal between intellectuals and the state, not to reject it.

When the crunch came and the lack of continued popular resistance (in the face of tanks) became clear, we were shocked. In retrospect we may have expected more of the popular movement than had most of its participants and then blamed its leaders for failing to live up to our exalted expectations. Western journalistic accounts of the events of 1989 and after have placed equally unrealistic expectations upon Chinese intellectuals. The unstated assumption about conditions in China today in most of these accounts is that no self-respecting intellectual would freely serve masters who called in tanks on unarmed students and citizens. Nonetheless, many intellectuals who have remained in China (including some who think of themselves as committed reformers) have been struggling to make their peace with the government. It is as mindlessly cynical to call all of these people opportunists as it is to assume that every "leader" of the popular movement is a saint. All this suggests two things: Some kind of deal between intellectuals and the state is, as I have argued above, still in force; and in order to understand this deal we may have to abandon or at least refine some of the analytical paradigms conventionally used to study politically active members of the Chinese intelligentsia.

One place to begin trying to make sense of the post–June Fourth deal between intellectuals and the state is with the pronouncements that current members of the mandarinate made in the press in 1990. These reveal a continuity of many of the features of the old deal between intellectuals and the state and also shed light on the problematic of that service. In what will strike most Western readers as a near Orwellian case of doublespeak, Su Shuangbi, an editor of Qiushi (the successor to Red Flag as the CCP's leading theoretical journal), and the theorists Ru Xin and Xing Fensi (all proponents of fundamental reform a few years ago) appeared in the June 20, 1990, issue of Guangming Daily, the leading newspaper for intellectuals, in an extended interview discussing, "Continuing the Policy of Letting a Hundred Flowers Bloom and a Hundred Schools of Thought Contend."[20] The life histories of these three intellectuals, as well as the ideas and issues they raise can help us understand how and why the "priestly" role of administrative generalists rather than the secular role of professionals still attracts some Chinese intellectuals.

Su Shuangbi was a student of Wu Han, the famous historian, and in the post-Mao period he has been a spokesman for rehabilitating his mentor (and similar colleagues, such as the Party editor-theorist, Deng Tuo) and attacking their critics, the Gang of Four.[21] Su is a product of the 1950s generation, and as he explained to one visitor, the Party gave this working-class kid the chance for education and advancement. Like Xing and Ru, Su's public announcements on reform have swung back and forth through the 1980s, following the shifts in central Party pronouncements. Thus, in spring 1986 Su was speculating— under the very same rubric of "the Hundred Flowers"—that Marxism would have to be modified and the system open for total reform, and that non-Marxist views should not be attacked as anti-Marxist ones.[22] Ru Xin, a theorist in the Institute of Philosophy at CASS, more closely follows the career pattern of the famous "humanist" theorist Wang Ruoshui, at least up to the mid-1980s. Prominent critics of "humanism" in the early 1960s, both Ru and Wang emerged in the post-Mao period as devotees of the idea. But when "humanism" was again attacked in 1983–1984, Ru Xin caved in, criticizing himself and others in typical rectification fashion.[23] Unlike Wang Ruoshui, Ru could not bring himself to risk a break with the establishment. Xing Fensi falls somewhere between the Su's apparent acceptance of the Party line and Ru's apostate humanism.

All three strike a similar tone in the June 1990 Guangming Daily interview.[24] The question of the day is, says Su for the group, "How should China build socialism?" Ideology is an important arena in that effort, and the three men address the question on many intellectuals' minds: "How should we provide correct guidance for the struggle in the ideological field?" That is, what are the rules of the game now? The overt answers are not encouraging: The words of Deng Xiaoping, enunciated by Party resolutions and the new, post-Tiananmen general secretary, Jiang Zemin, provide the guidelines. Early in the piece the three denounce both the "leftist" errors of (unnamed) earlier periods and the "rightist" errors of bourgeois liberalization.

On second reading, however, the interview is not so depressing. These men are participating in the negotiation of a revised deal between intellectuals and the state in post-Tiananmen China. These intellectuals are not free agents with many viable alternatives, but neither are they helpless. Although they make their peace with the system, they make several assertions at the same time. Repeatedly each man says there is a need for *explicit standards* as to what is or is not legitimate debate: The Party should announce and stick to such standards. Arbitrary political attacks on intellectuals is the underlying criticism of the interview. "It is necessary," says Ru Xin, "to formulate policies to protect and encourage those who are willing to study new problems." The three offer this solution to the problem: Separate academic from political debate and acknowledge and protect a separate class of theoreticians who should not be held to the more disciplined standards of publicists (i.e., propaganda work). "Theoretical study is different from publicity work," says Xing Fensi; "in theoretical study we have to proceed from what is known to what remains unknown. . . . you take risks when you make explorations. . . . We have to protect those comrades who make mistakes in making explorations . . . [otherwise] science and culture will be unable to develop." Indeed, despite the nods to current Party policy, Su Shuangbi maintains precisely the themes of his more reformist writings of 1986: Exploration and development (used to replace the now dubious "reform" in 1990) are needed and intellectuals must be free to explore (though in 1990 the limits are more clear), and non-Marxism should not be equated with anti-Marxism. What was less clear in 1986, however, was much clearer by 1990: There is but one truth, and that truth is Marxism. Su Shuangbi here demonstrates rhetorical skill worthy of his mentor, Wu Han. Su shows the dexterous flexibility of Party intellectuals that so enraged Mao. Although "upholding" Deng Xiaoping's four principles of Party dictatorship and "attacking" bourgeois liberalization, Su maintains the heart of his reform goals from 1986.

Nonetheless, these goals are limited. What these intellectuals demand are instrumental reforms, not fundamental ones. "We can only distinguish correct ideas, which conform to Marxism," says Su, "from erroneous ones, which run counter to Marxism, through calm discussions." Ru Xin tosses in the exception clause (to be utilized when conditions allow): "Marxism itself should be an open-ended theory . . . [able] to absorb useful research results of other non-Marxist schools of thought." These are precisely the ideas pushed in the 1980s by Su Shaozhi (now living in exile) when he was director of the Marxism-Leninism Institute of CASS.

The ideas and values, as well as the role for leading intellectuals, assumed in this interview maintain the priestly (read "theoretical") role for intellectuals, or that subgroup that wishes to attend to national ideological policy. By way of metaphor, we can call it Vatican II Maoism, with the socialist equivalents of folk masses and the vernacular liturgy. There is instrumental latitude, but the underlying dogma is not changed. This was first broached in the post–Great Leap period of 1961–1962 (by, among others, Wu Han). Democracy, pluralism, a release of key moral and political questions to a wide range of social groups—none of these are suggested (in fact they are rejected as "bourgeois liberalization"). Instead, instrumental themes are addressed (indeed the whole "Hundred Flowers" policy is instrumental: to "bring their [intellectuals'] enthusiasm and creativity into full play"). Su and his colleagues accept that there is one truth, but they are concerned that only imperfect humans are available for the task of revealing that liberating truth. The goal of philosophical inquiry, true since the days of Confucius himself, is good government policy. Intellectuals, particularly theorists, are qualified (by what certification is left unstated) to speak for the people on these questions in the traditional Maoist paradigm of collecting and synthesizing the ideas of the masses. "We can make a success of formulating policies," says Su, "if we pool the wisdom of the masses, hold conscientious discussions, and adopt a scientific approach." Given the lack of a viable institutional alternative to the Party, the deal outlined by Su, Xing, and Ru will likely be sufficiently attractive to a number of intellectuals to keep the system mumbling along.[25]

These values echo those expressed by an earlier generation of Party intellectuals in the aftermath of the debacle of the Great Leap Forward. Yang Xianzhen, the head of the Party School (the national cadre-training institute), clearly enunciated a version of these values by 1964, and Deng Tuo, a high official in Peng Zhen's Beijing Municipal Party organization, gave a very literate expression of these values in *Evening Chats at Yanshan* in the Beijing press during 1961 and 1962. Carol Hamrin and I have called these values "Chinese Leninism," which articulated itself in contradistinction to "Maoism" in the wake of the Great Leap. Both variants of Marxism had been integrated in the earlier, Yan'an orthodoxy.[26] The Chinese Leninism of the early 1960s is worth summarizing here because it appears to be the root set of values among the post-Tiananmen intellectual establishment, such as presented in the *Guangming Daily* interview. These values can also provide a ground for comparing and assessing the values of intellectual dissidents. It is worth remembering that the surviving elder leaders of today, such as Deng Xiaoping, Peng Zhen, and others, were closely associated with Chinese Leninist views in the past.

There are five salient aspects to the Chinese Leninist approach to political life.[27] First, in the realm of *theory* or ideology, acceptance of Marxism meshed with ancient Chinese attitudes about orthodoxy: the need for one absolutist moral ideology and the need to assert publicly its infallibility. The Chinese Leninist approach has come to rely on a relatively orthodox version of Marxism-Leninism in comparison with Mao's voluntarism. In the realm of *political organization,* Chinese Leninists, like most of the Chinese leadership, have assumed the traditional statist belief that political institutions should dominate culture and society. They have accepted the Leninist concept of the Party as the vanguard and have viewed its domination of all aspects of Chinese society as a good and necessary thing. However, Chinese Leninists have placed a premium on Party discipline and social order. They have been painfully aware of human imperfection, technical limitations, and the probability of error in the process of social transformation. Thus they support differences of opinion within the Party in the name of scientific experimentation.

In *social policy,* Chinese Leninists have had little tolerance for criticism from the larger society. Subgroup interests are to be taken into account by realistic investigation, strict discipline, strong moral training, and rational decisionmaking by Party officials acting on behalf of the people—not by non-Party organizations. In the realm of *professional activity,* Chinese Leninists have relied on specialists and technocrats. Leading intellectuals have been well recompensed for their efforts. The general population is assumed to be the passive recipients of their ministrations. In the realm of *private life,* this approach has acknowledged the legitimacy of personal interests and family concerns, so long as they do not interfere with the broad social policies of the Party. This personal latitude is granted not on pluralistic grounds but from a somewhat deterministic social philosophy that posits that ownership and control over the means of production (now in the hands of the vanguard Party) automatically determines the future of China's political institutions, culture, and thought. The Chinese Leninist approach acknowledges the importance of individual thinking, particularly the role of "thought reform" (*sixiang gaizao*), as an indispensable companion of economic development in the achievement of socialism. However, thought reform has been seen as a rational transformation based on an appreciation of scientific history, not as a cataclysmic emotional experience.

This excursion into the values of the post-Tiananmen establishment and its antecedents has sought to demonstrate that the establishment is alive and well, having survived the trauma of spring 1989. In exchange for the yoke of orthodoxy, intellectuals are offered a kinder and gentler plower and once again the opportunity to till the fields of history. It is, on the intellectual and moral level, a "velvet prison" as appealing to intellectual idealism as the velvet prison described by Miklós Haraszti for Hungary.[28] If we find it incredible for intellectuals to explain away the tragedy of June 1989, we need only recall how quite respectable intellectuals such as Wu Han, Deng Tuo, or Yang Xianzhen explained away a much greater tragedy twenty-five years ago after the Great Leap Forward.[29]

Returning to Chirot's model for intellectual change in Eastern Europe, we can say that the continued attractiveness of the priestly vocation in China's socialist state has limited (not eradicated) the loss of faith in the system and the growth of alternate organizations that contributed to the collapse of Communist regimes in Europe in 1989. However, what of the *audience*

(Chirot's cultural and educational middle class) that serves as a sort of social base for radical ideas and invidious foreign comparisons with the native regime? There are still enough priests, like Su, Ru, and Xing, and there are new deacons and acolytes (He Xin, for one, has volunteered), but is there still a congregation of the faithful among China's intellectuals?

The answer to this question lies outside the scope of this chapter and has yet to be studied in great depth. There are some indications, though, and the prognosis is sobering. The forces that delimit reform activities of top intellectuals (or opinionmakers), such as the constraints of patriotism or loyalty to the Party and patronage, also affect lower-level "audience" intellectuals. Additionally, preliminary research shows a great diversity among Chinese intellectuals—not only by generation but by occupation, gender, attitude toward Westernization, personal political history, income, and the much-noted technical-humanist divide.[30] One empirical study of political attitudes of Chinese intellectuals was made in 1987 by the Public Research Institute at the Chinese People's University. Analyzed by expatriate Chinese in the United States, this detailed survey of some 1,200 Beijing urban residents tested respondents on their attitudes toward, knowledge of, and participation in reform. The results showed "radical" reform intellectuals to be but 7 percent of this already politically active base population. The majority were "emulators" of current policy (34 percent) or less informed but economically well-to-do "optimists" (13 percent).[31] That the majority of respondents were reformists of one sort or another suggests guarded optimism that some time in the future there may be an audience in China to parallel the one that served Eastern European reformers so well in 1989.

Intellectuals: Types, Roles, and Spheres of Activity

It is now time to turn more explicitly to the issue of conventional paradigms raised earlier and ask: Is there a better way to conceptualize intellectual activity in the public arena that might help us understand the relationship between intellectuals and the state in China? Over the past twenty years, there has been a cottage industry devoted to typologies of Chinese intellectuals—radicals (Maoists) vs. liberals (and later reform radicals), Marxian-Confucians vs. establishment radicals, establishment intellectuals vs. Maoists, and, more broadly, typologies such as inquisitors, technocrats, critical intellectuals, and dissidents.[32] Our inability to comprehend fully the role of China's intellectuals in the popular movement of 1989 and our failure to predict events, before, during, and since highlight the weaknesses in our understanding of current intellectual activity in China. I am no more likely than the next student of Chinese intellectual life to provide insightful and accurate typologies of key kinds or groups of Chinese intellectuals. What I can offer from my experience is the suggestion that it may be more fruitful to think of various Chinese intellectuals not in terms of types, but in terms of their *roles*, and furthermore in terms of *spheres of activity*.

Many of the intellectual types scholars identify can more usefully be seen as roles individual intellectuals may occupy serially or concurrently. In 1987 Merle Goldman and I suggested three such roles: as ideological speakers for the state, a role that dominated the career of the Party theoretician Ai Siqi, for example; as academic and professional elites, roles a number of Chinese intellectuals have endeavored (with mixed success) to separate from political life in the PRC; and as critical intellectuals, that dangerous modern role of Confucian censor and May Fourth iconoclast.[33] The focus on roles was an improvement over static "types," but our categories only concentrated on the politically relevant activities of Chinese intellectuals.

If we follow the career of one of China's modern mandarins—be it that of the former literary czar Zhou Yang or humanist theorist Wang Ruoshui or the infamous astrophysicist democrat Fang Lizhi or less extreme characters such as the economist Sun Yefang or Party propagandist Deng Tuo—we find that our concern with their political views and activities blots out large sections of these people's lives. In addition to seeing these people in terms of their political roles, we must attempt to account for *all* their activities, not just their overtly political ones. A focus on key realms or spheres of intellectual activity may help us to understand the various roles intellectuals play in Chinese politics. Such a concentration produces a more inductive study of intellectual behavior, demanding that a researcher gather information on all domains of public (and, if possible, private) activity in order to frame the significance of the political portion of an intellectual's career. My research on Deng Tuo introduced me to this reality—large amounts of his time were taken up in aesthetics, poetry writing, antique collecting, and Ming and Qing social history. Colleagues researching other Party intellectuals, such as Mary Mazur on Wu Han, report a similar breadth of activity.[34] Although we are a long way from a complete picture of these circles of activities in the lives of leading intellectuals, not to mention statistical data on large numbers of intellectuals, we can still identify three important areas of public activity generally undertaken in greater or lesser degree by all Chinese intellectuals.

Tu Wei-ming has suggested that we think of the behavior of Chinese intellectuals in terms of three overlapping spheres of activity: the realms of *zheng* (politics or governance), *xue* (learning or study), and *dao* (an almost untranslatable ethical and religious term often rendered as the "Way," but which I prefer to think of as the search for "transcendence").[35] The value of Tu's distinction among the spheres of *zheng, xue,* and *dao* stems not only from the rootedness of these concepts in Chinese culture and the models of intellectual activity available to current Chinese intellectuals (Tu developed his analysis from the ideas of his teacher, Confucian scholar Tang Junyi), but also from the ability of these spheres of activity to relate seeming opposite "types." Thus, both establishment intellectuals, like Su Shuangbi, and current dissidents, like Yan Jiaqi, operate primarily in the "political" sphere. Similarly, autonomous professionals and dependent state advisers are types found active in the "academic" sphere. In the "transcendent" sphere we find not only those engaged in public ethics and propaganda work (which, as we recall from the ancient injunction "wen yi zai dao" [literature carries the *dao*], includes most fiction and film) but also those engaged in religion, a fairly dormant activity until recently. It is fruitful to think about the ways in which Su Shuangbi and Fang Lizhi (normally seen as government spokesman and heroic dissident, respectively) are similar; how state planner and private economic consultant share professional skills; and how state propaganda and religious ceremonies parallel each other.

The real strength of this focus on the spheres of activity is that it calls on us to recognize the breadth of intellectual activity behind politically active intellectuals and requires us to contextualize activities in each arena for individual intellectuals. The results can add depth to our understanding of intellectual life and politics in China and can occasionally change our basic view of some intellectuals. I offer two examples, one from the past and one from the present.

Deng Tuo was a politically active intellectual in the CCP from 1930 (when he joined the Party) until his suicide under political duress in 1966, in the early months of the Cultural Revolution. He is famous in China as an intellectually talented, level-headed, and moderate Communist official. He is noted in Western and Japanese studies of China as a "liberal" or "Marxian-Confucian" who had the courage to denounce the errors of the Party after the failures of the Great Leap Forward. The key data for this picture are Deng's own set of over 150 essays from 1961–1962, *Evening Chats at Yanshan*.[36] However, sustained research on the totality of Deng's life (his historical writings in the 1930s and 1950s, his service as editor of leading CCP newspapers in the 1940s and 1950s, and his political falling out with Mao in the late 1950s) and the range of his intellectual activities in the years around 1960 greatly modify this picture. Not only are implications that Deng rejected the CCP (strongly made in earlier studies) simply not true, but it is apparent that Deng perceived himself to be a true, loyal Communist. His criticisms were given to improve, not remove, the Party. More fundamentally, his own perception of authority turns out to have been grounded not in his administrative rank (though he respected due rank and position) but in his *aesthetics*. Activities that at first seemed irrelevant, or tangential, to his political work now seem central to his identity as a "culture bearer." His historical forays into the niceties of Chinese history, culture, poetry, and art (which make up the bulk of Deng's *Evening Chats*, far outnumbering the overtly political essays that had formed the basis of Western views of his ideas) are blatant demonstrations of his qualifications for this literatus (*wenren*) status. Rootedness in the wisdom of Chinese culture not only suited the times (resurgent national pride to compensate for the depressing results of the Great Leap and the anxiety of the emerging Sino-Soviet split) but provided a fulcrum outside Mao Zedong Thought on which to lever the Party and China toward the goals of wealth and power and human dignity for the individual. This is nothing short of an attempt to "re-sinify" Marxism-Leninism in an elitist, intellectual, and rationalist manner in explicit contradistinction to the populist, anti-intellectual, and charismatic "re-sinification" of the Leap itself. It was an attempt, supported by a segment of the Party (especially Peng Zhen), to revive an attractive deal for intellectuals to participate in the government (or to serve its policies directly) following the dispiriting attacks on intellectuals since 1957. It was the Chinese Leninist deal, described earlier in this chapter.[37] Attention to the other circles in Deng Tuo's life—his academic and transcendent activities—has brought the political role of his aesthetics starkly into view.

Fang Lizhi is an example well known to most Westerners. An outspoken critic of the current regime, Fang has been called both "China's Tom Paine" and "China's Andre Sakharov."[38] He was purged from the CCP in January 1987 for "promoting bourgeois liberalization" among students. His case became famous when he took refuge in the U.S. embassy in Beijing shortly after the 1989 massacre. Fang has rightly been viewed as a critic of the regime, as one advocating fundamental democratic reform. But how he came to his views and what he hoped to achieve before he was dismissed from his post are less clear.

Sustained research on Fang's life by James Williams, who devotes much of his attention to Fang's activities in the seemingly "nonpolitical" spheres of physics and astrophysics, has refined our understanding of the scientist-dissident in important ways.[39] First, Fang came to his "radical" democratic ideas based on his experience as a scientist in the 1960s and early 1970s, with little reference to Western political theory. He was originally interested in laser physics but withdrew from any applied science in the wake of the Cultural Revolution. He turned to the theoretical field of astrophysics and cosmology. His hopes for academic autonomy were dashed in 1972 when his innocuous-sounding article "A Solution of the Cosmological Equations in Scalar-Tensor Theory, with Mass and Blackbody Radiation" became the object of heated political attack. Williams explains Fang's fateful error: By following the standard big bang model of cosmic evolution accepted by international physics circles, Fang and his colleagues had violated a basic tenet of dialectical materialism in that they proposed the universe may be finite in space and time. Insofar as Engels had declared the universe to be spatially and temporally infinite, and that the assertion of a finite universe provided arguments for the existence of that opiate of the masses, a God, such a proposition was tantamount to idealist heresy.

Throughout the 1970s and 1980s, Fang was periodically attacked for his calls for "science over politics." In *response* to these attacks, particularly by propaganda chief Hu Qiaomu, Fang extended his defense of professional autonomy to a critique of CCP science policy and from there to a general critique of CCP rule and the political order in China. In this he took advantage of the greater space for professional work outside the "sphere" of politics, as the three spheres of activity spread out, away from the extreme overlap of the Cultural Revolution years. Thus, Fang's famous democratic ideas evolved out of his mundane commitment to his profession and his defense of it from political attacks. The focus on the changing relationship of the three spheres of activity between 1967 and the 1980s helps draw our attention to these factors.

The fight between Fang and more conservative Party reformers can be seen as a fight over the role of intellectuals: Fang wants politically independent critical intellectuals, the Party leaders want politically engaged advisers. Fang explicitly rejects the idea that democracy, or any other social good, can be "bestowed" by the Party or government, and he advocates the basic values of a democracy based on humanism and individual rights and responsibilities. Fang's role as democrat is not limited to ideas. He represents an important sociological development in the PRC—the rise of autonomous professions. As a critic, Fang presents himself as a citizen, not as a politician or government official. His authority for speaking, he claims, is his education in *science*, not "philosophy" (by which he means orthodoxy, Marxism–Leninism–Mao Zedong Thought). His failure, as of this date, to find an audience inside China powerful enough to maintain a public profile in opposition to the current regime indicates that the social base for a polity in which an authority other than the Party and Marxism-Leninism is publicly legitimate has not yet emerged.

It is important to see Fang's efforts as an emerging democrat in the five-decade-long tradition of Party intellectuals pushing for greater individual autonomy and humanism within the corporatist polity of the Party-state. Since the establishment of state power by the CCP in the Yan'an area in the late 1930s, Party intellectuals have sought to negotiate and revise the deal offered by the CCP (the deal being to advise, staff, and propagandize). Each new set of "troublemakers" (who, like Fang, were all Party members) sought a degree of *autonomy* in their service to the state. Each sought that fulcrum in a different sphere of intellectual activity outside the political sphere.

In the early 1940s, Wang Shiwei and other left-wing writers claimed the right to criticize policy in public based on the romantic inspiration of the revolutionary artist. Literature that was, in essence, transcendent of the mundane reality of political bickering, said Wang Shiwei, gave the artist the moral authority to monitor and criticize politicians.[40] In the early 1960s, Deng Tuo, among others, sought such leverage in the moral cultivation derived from the study and practice of China's traditional arts and culture. This role as "culture bearer" drew from an intersection of the academic and transcendent spheres of activity. In the 1980s Fang, drawing purely from the academic sphere, made his fulcrum science, the rational and incremental thinking of the scientific method as embodied in twentieth-century international physics. With the claim of science, Fang could maintain his establishment stance (as vice-president of Science and Technology University and member of several government advisory committees) yet use a more effective pivot than his forebears of the 1940s and 1960s: Scientific method remains both more central to the current orthodoxy and less subject to dismissal (as "foreign" or "feudal") than claims to artistic insight or aesthetic moral cultivation. The sorry fact of the matter is, of course, that none of the three fulcrums has served to shift the Party-state very far in the desired direction.

Fang's efforts to influence politics add another important development in the tradition of Party intellectuals who push for reform. He does not presume to speak "for" or "to" the "people." If Fang appears arrogant when he calls intellectuals the vanguard of the proletariat, his stance is, in fact, more humble than previous establishment reformers or current incumbents, such as Su Shuangbi. He claims to speak only for his own group, intellectuals. He addresses them and calls on them to act. He is not an "interest politician" in the U.S. sense; he speaks for what he sees is the public good: fair government, individual freedom, public responsibility. He cares about other groups in China but is content to let them speak up for themselves. Because he is in a privileged position, Fang feels he and other intellectuals should speak first (especially when such outspokenness is dangerous), but that is all. This is a form of democratization new among Chinese intellectuals who have, otherwise, continued the traditional Confucian pretense to minister to and speak for the "people."[41]

Finally, the political context in which the three spheres of intellectual activity reside is not static. The Chinese "political order" has changed markedly in the course of the past several decades. During the first years of CCP rule, it became harder and harder to separate *xue* and *dao* activities from politics. By 1967, at the height of the Cultural Revolution, the concern with orthodoxy became so great that there was virtually no space left for autonomous scholarly and religious or ethical pursuits. As Mao put "politics in command," the *zheng* sphere swallowed up *xue* and *dao* activities.

In the 1980s, however, the centrifugal forces of the "four modernizations" and de-Maoification triggered a move in the opposite direction: Political concerns still shaped all others, but autonomous space for *xue* and *dao* pursuits gradually grew. The picture resembled that of the 1950s in many ways. There was certainly some integration of academic activity in politics (as in Zhao Ziyang's think tanks), but the boundaries of the three spheres were not coterminous. The key difference between the 1950s and 1980s was the direction of change. In the former decade, the realms of intellectual activity were moving toward a *zheng*-dominated "unity," whereas in the latter period the shift was toward diversity, especially in the provinces.

It is too soon to tell whether or not the trend toward comparatively autonomous *xue*, *dao*, and *zheng* spheres seen in the 1980s will continue in the 1990s. This will certainly be important to watch, for a continuation of this trend could play a key role in fostering the growth of the kind of "civil society" to which the authors of other chapters in this volume direct our attention. The conceptualization of intellectual activity sketched above, besides letting us put the issue of "civil society" into a slightly different perspective, can also help us minimize our misperceptions of changes in two significant domains: the institutionalization of knowledge and the creation and dissemination of ideology. Intellectuals are key, but not sole, actors in both domains. If we can place *individuals* into a detailed context of their political, academic, and transcendent activities (not to mention private concerns, which in the case of Chinese intellectuals, sadly, remains for the most part out of our sight), and if we can situate individuals' roles in a historical context (identifying the integration or conflation of the three spheres)—then we might move a step closer to figuring out what is going on in China.

Priests, Professionals, and the Price of Autonomy

To be of use, the three circles of intellectual activity that Tu Wei-ming has suggested should help us understand the conundrum that permeates this essay: Are intellectuals in China moving from the "priestly" deal of the early PRC to a "professional" contract in China's polity, or not? I think the answer is yes, but that the going will be painfully slow, much slower than Poland's thirty-year rise from reassertion of Party-state authority in 1956 to a democratically elected government today. Still, when the circles of activity are as disassociated as they are now, intellectuals are confronted with de facto "secularization" of academic and transcendent activities (and "demoralization" of political activity) by dint of the disbelief of political assertions on the part of the intended audiences. The circles, then, simply help us keep in focus the *contexts* of intellectual endeavor both at the individual and (by specific period) polity level. In the shift toward disengagement from the priestly mandarin role, context is important: 1967 would have been a terrible time to try it, the social anomie of the 1930s made it a frustrating time to try it, and the 1990s look to be a promising time to push ahead.

More than propitious circumstances are necessary to make this change, however. Chinese intellectuals will need to conceptualize their separation from the state, the end of their mandarin role. They must articulate, and then fight to protect, their *autonomy* from political direction. Among Chinese critics I have seen numerous expressions of the latter, but only fitful expressions of the former, with Fang Lizhi being a key example. According to George Konrad, Hungarian intellectuals by the late 1980s had made this shift, choosing to speak for their own group rather than continuing the seductive role as voice of the people.[42] They have accepted liberal democratic electoral institutions as the imperfect but preferable mechanism for articulating the will of the masses. "The price of autonomy" for Chinese intellectuals will be not only to let go of their priestly vocation as have their Eastern European colleagues, but to become as irrelevant as Western intellectuals in their nations' politics. Late Qing intellectuals like Liang Qichao inadvertently handed away their traditional Confucian role as legitimators of the state to a new and ill-defined political entity, the *qun* (masses).[43] The founding generation of establishment intellectuals in the PRC recaptured the role of state legitimators, but ever since the antirightist movement of 1957, they paid "the price of engagement."[44]

It remains to be seen if intellectuals will be ready to pay the "price of autonomy" in the 1990s. Will they be willing to forgo their role as interpreters of Communist orthodoxy, or even of its reform into something else, and once again hand authority back to "the people" (now *renmin*) in practice as well as in theory, via the institutions and values of a free society? The search for "socialism with Chinese characteristics" would seem to have failed. Can China's intellectuals now contribute to the complex process of creating a workable "democracy with Chinese characteristics"? Can they resist the siren calls of participation as mandarins in an unelected bureaucratic state and instead accept the less august role of opinion makers in an open market of ideas in which other groups can make key political and administrative decisions? The lesson from Tiananmen, for me, is that this transformation will have to be undertaken on the basis of reforming the still very powerful intellectual establishment in the PRC—both the political institutions of the state and the mental attitudes of the intellectuals. As ever, China's hope will have to be found within itself.

Notes

1. Etienne Balazs, *Chinese Civilization and Bureaucracy*, ed. Arthur F. Wright, trans. H. M. Wright (New Haven: Yale University Press, 1964), p. 13.

2. On the traditional pull of state service on Chinese intellectuals (and its limitations during an era of weak government), see Jerome Grieder's discussion of the Republican era (1911–1949), in *Intellectuals and the State in Modern China* (New York: Free Press, 1981); on this pull over five generations, see Wang Gungwu, *The Chinese Intellectual— Past and Present* (Singapore: Graham Brash, 1983).

3. Thus, to speak of the events of 1989 as a "democracy movement" reflects the wishful thinking of Western observers and the sloganeering of some Chinese activists. For this reason I prefer the term "people's movement," which Tony Saich adopts in his edited volume, *Perspectives on the Chinese People's Movement: Spring 1989* (Armonk, N.Y.: M. E. Sharpe, 1990), or the still more neutral terms such as "1989 protest movement" that contributors to the present volume use. For further discussion of the limits of democracy as a motivating force behind the protest movement, and descriptions of specific ways in which calling the events part of a "democracy movement" can obscure key differences in the political agendas of students and other social groups, see Lee Feigon, *China Rising: The Meaning of Tiananmen* (Chicago: Ivan R. Dee, 1990); Jane Macartney, "The Students: Heroes, Pawns, or Power-Brokers?" in George Hicks, ed., *The Broken Mirror: China After Tiananmen* (London: Longman, 1990), pp. 3–23; and, in this volume, Elizabeth Perry's essay (Chapter 7) on the elitist "casting" of the political theater in and around Tiananmen Square. For a contrary view that articulately defends the use of the term *democracy* in this context and, more importantly, stresses the need to study the spiritual as well as economic factors involved (on this point I agree), see David Kelly, "Chinese Intellectuals in the 1989 Democracy Movement," in Hicks, *The Broken Mirror*.

4. Kelly, "Chinese Intellectuals," esp. pp. 46–47.

5. We see this in part in the personal memory of Chinese intellectuals sprouting in the cracks of the official Party-directed commemoration of the May Fourth anniversary in 1989, as recounted by Vera Schwarcz in this volume. Most China scholars have also seen it in the personal comments of our Chinese colleagues in the year since the crackdown. A small, but telling, example is the mailing of *neibu* books. *Neibu* books are ostensibly "internal circulation" books that foreigners are not supposed to see (because the books contain more frank information that our bourgeois ideology is bound to distort to China's detriment). Although many such books are simply academic studies or document collections with little security value and can easily be purchased in China by foreigners, it has been illegal to mail them out of China. Since June 1989, the number of *neibu* books received from the Chinese post by scholars I know in the United States and Europe has increased dramatically. I cannot but conclude that the flaunting of this petty regulation (in the spirit of disseminating information) is an

indicator of general distaste for the government among clerks and office workers. Indeed, even a senior cadre known for his "leftist" views (supportive of the policies of the general current regime) refused a request to return from retirement after June 1989, so strong was his disgust with the military crackdown. My thanks to Tony Saich for raising this example.

6. Naturally, service in the establishment institutions of the PRC does not by itself demonstrate that an intellectual has *actively* consented to such a "deal." We can imagine a range of participation extending from tacit consent to active negotiation.

7. For an insightful analysis of the role of such "basic units" in relation to other control mechanisms in PRC society, see Lowell Dittmer, *China's Continuous Revolution: The Post-Liberation Epoch, 1949–1981* (Berkeley: University of California Press, 1987), pp. 53–57ff.

8. This analysis is pursued in Timothy Cheek, "Habits of the Heart: Intellectual Assumptions Reflected by Chinese Reformers from Deng Tuo to Fang Lizhi," in Shaochuan Leng, ed., *Changes in China: Party, State, and Society* (Lanham, Md.: University Press of America, 1989), pp. 117–143. Studies of lower-level institutions, such as factories, suggest that similar understandings (about expressions of patriotism, or loyalty to the Party, and patronage) extend to the working classes. See Andrew G. Walder, *Communist Neo-Traditionalism* (Berkeley: University of California Press, 1986). Thomas Gold follows similar themes in his study of daily life in post-Mao China, "After Comradeship: Personal Relations in China Since the Cultural Revolution," *China Quarterly*, no. 104 (December 1985), pp. 657–675.

9. This is my conclusion based on the biographies of numerous leading Party intellectuals, including Yang Xianzhen, Deng Tuo, Wu Han, Jian Bozan, Sun Yefang, and Wang Ruowang, as well as a younger generation: Bai Hua, Liu Binyan, and Wang Ruoshui—all of whom have biographies in either Carol Lee Hamrin and Timothy Cheek, eds., *China's Establishment Intellectuals* (Armonk, N.Y.: M. E. Sharpe, 1986), or in Merle Goldman, with Timothy Cheek and Carol Lee Hamrin, eds., *China's Intellectuals and the State: In Search of a New Relationship* (Cambridge: Harvard Council on East Asian Studies, 1987).

10. I follow the general definition of political generation (based on the formative political experiences of individuals between age seventeen and twenty-five) used by Michael Yahuda, "Political Generations in China," *China Quarterly*, no. 80 (December 1979), pp. 796–805. Li Zehou's valuable depiction of revolutionary generations has been expanded in English in Li Zehou and Vera Schwarcz, "Six Generations of Modern Chinese Intellectuals," *Chinese Studies in History*, 17, 2 (Winter 1983-1984), pp. 42–56. See also Wang, *The Chinese Intellectual*. I am fully aware that later cohorts (such as the generations of the Cultural Revolution and post-Mao reform period) have greatly different mixes of values compared to the two eldest generations. Nonetheless, for reasons elaborated below, the *institutional* realities of China today limit the younger generations, who have moved beyond their elders in the "alienation" process, whereas the mental constructs of the deal that the intellectuals and the state struck in the 1940s and 1950s continue to limit the actions of the older intellectuals generations and those younger folk who adopt similar attitudes. Chirot, in Chapter 11 (on Eastern Europe), also notes the faith in the Communist system held by intellectuals of the 1940s and 1950s.

11. The profound dangers involved in trying to play the role of censor between the 1930s and 1950s are well documented in Merle Goldman, *Literary Dissent in Communist China* (Cambridge: Harvard University Press, 1967).

12. This point is made emphatically in Bonnie McDougall's conclusion, "Writers and Performers, Their Works, and Their Audiences in the First Three Decades," in

Bonnie S. McDougall, ed., *Popular Chinese Literature and Performing Arts in the People's Republic of China, 1949-1979* (Berkeley: University of California Press, 1984), pp. 269–301, esp. pp. 270–271.

13. See for example, Tony Saich, "The Chinese Communist Party and the Future," *China Information*, 4, 4 (Spring 1990), p. 29.

14. Some did take note of this, at least in passing. See, for example, Carol Hamrin's 1987 conclusion to Goldman, *China's Intellectuals and the State*, pp. 275–304, esp. pp. 285ff. Nonetheless, those of us who study "establishment intellectuals" from the 1950s and 1960s used to joke in 1988 and early 1989 that our subjects were finally historical. We no longer think so. Interestingly, Chirot's chapter concludes in an analogous (but reverse) fashion, declaring that specialists on communism failed to predict events of 1989 in Eastern Europe because they focused too much on the power of the Communist establishment and did not consider the moral and ideological power of intellectual discussions popular in those countries.

15. Many reformist intellectuals have made denigrating remarks to Western scholars about these working-class activists as "unlettered boat rockers" upsetting the emerging reform deal for intellectuals. A public example is the famed translator Yang Xianyi, who quickly recanted his public dismissal of Wei Jingsheng at a conference in Britain after shocked protests from scholars there.

16. Perry Link's collections of literature and debates from the post-Mao period give me this impression. See particularly his introduction, which covers the continuing Party controls on literature in the 1980s, in *Roses and Thorns* (Berkeley: University of California Press, 1984). The same limitations can be seen in philosophical debates, as reflected in the *Chinese Philosophy Yearbook;* see Bill Brugger and David Kelly, *Chinese Marxism in the Post-Mao Era* (Stanford: Stanford University Press, 1990), p. 18. There have certainly been trenchant criticisms of the status quo in Chinese periodicals and books. My point is: How much of an audience did such critics have before 1989 and what could those who might agree with fundamental criticism of the system do? See the excellent collection of critical Chinese writings from the 1980s, Geremie Barmé and John Minford, eds., *Seeds of Fire: Chinese Voices of Conscience* (New York: Hill & Wang, 1988).

17. The key reform think tank was the Development Center (short for the State Council Research Center for Economic and Technological and Social Development) headed by Ma Hong. This and other groups, such as the Reform Institute and Rural Development Center, were organized under Zhao's reform-minded state council and offered intellectuals the opportunity to directly influence state policy. See Carol Lee Hamrin, *China and the Challenge of the Future: Changing Political Patterns* (Boulder: Westview, 1989), esp. pp. 231ff.

18. All four men have been expelled from the Party, alienated by the regime from the deal. Still, as late as winter 1990, both Su Shaozhi and Liu Binyan, who are now in exile, maintained (much to the chagrin and anger of the expatriate Chinese student movement) that the Party will likely continue and that reformers will have to work through it if China wishes to avoid a period of bloody confusion (personal communications with Su and Liu). Both men have stuck their heads out to change the current system, so I take these comments as an indication of their reading of the institutional realities of China today.

19. See Brugger and Kelly, *Chinese Marxism*, esp. p. 3. The ideas of counterelite and the "abyss" come from Kelly's earlier essay, "The Emergence of Humanism," see note 23, below.

20. Translated in Foreign Broadcast Information Service: China (FBIS-CHI), 90-134 (July 12, 1990), pp. 25–29. The title of the monthly central Party theory journal, *Qiushi*, is literally "seek truth," just as *Pravda* means "truth."

21. See for example his collection of essays, Su Shuangbi, *Jieji douzheng yu lishi kexue* (Class struggle and historical science) (Shanghai: Shanghai Renmin chubanshe, 1982).

22. Su Shuangbi, "Guanyu kaizhan 'baijia zhengming' de jige wenti" (Several questions on the promotion of "A Hundred Schools of Thought" contend), *Guangming Ribao*, April 30, 1986, p. 3; translated in FBIS-CHI (May 19, 1986), pp. K7–11.

23. See David Kelly, "The Emergence of Humanism: Wang Ruoshui and the Critique of Socialist Alienation," in Goldman, *China's Intellectuals and the State*, esp. pp. 164 and 178. The classic model of rectification (*zhengfeng*) criticism and self-criticism in historical and political context is analyzed in Frederick Teiwes, *Politics and Purges in China: Rectification and the Decline of Party Norms*, 2d ed. (Armonk, N.Y.: M. E. Sharpe, 1992).

24. Quotations taken from translation in FBIS-CHI-90-134 (July 12, 1990), pp. 25–29.

25. Geremie Barmé gives the controversial example of He Xin, who went back into government service after June 1989; see Barmé's introduction to "A Word of Advice to the Politburo—Text by He Xin," *Australian Journal of Chinese Affairs*, no. 23 (January 1990), pp. 62–63. He's and Barmé's conversation continues in the next issue of that journal, no. 24 (July 1990), pp. 337–345.

26. See Carol Lee Hamrin, "Yang Xianzhen: Upholding Orthodox Leninist Theory," in Hamrin and Cheek, *China's Establishment Intellectuals*, pp. 51–91; and Timothy Cheek, "Deng Tuo: A Chinese Leninist Approach to Journalism," in ibid., pp. 92–123.

27. This analysis is fully developed in Timothy Cheek and Carol Lee Hamrin, "Collaboration and Conflict in the Search for a New Order," in Hamrin and Cheek, *China's Establishment Intellectuals*, pp. 6–11

28. Miklós Haraszti, *The Velvet Prison: Artists Under State Socialism* (New York: Basic Books, 1987).

29. See Hamrin and Cheek, *China's Establishment Intellectuals* and Goldman, *China's Intellectuals and the State*. These volumes document elder intellectuals' criticism of the Great Leap, in Chinese Leninist fashion, behind closed doors in various Party meetings and indirectly through Aesopian language in the press.

30. See Lynn T. White III, "Thought Workers in Deng's Time," in Goldman, *China's Intellectuals and the State*, pp. 253–274; and Lynn T. White III and Cheng Li, "Diversification Among Mainland Chinese Intellectuals," in King-yuh Chang, ed., *Mainland China After the Thirteenth Party Congress* (Boulder: Westview, 1990), p. 466.

31. Jianhu Zhu, Xinshu Zhao, and Hairong Li, "Public Political Consciousness in China," *Asian Survey*, 30, 18 (October 1990), pp. 992–1006.

32. In order, types put forward by: Merle Goldman, *China's Intellectuals: Advise and Dissent* (Cambridge: Harvard University Press, 1981); Peter J. Moody, *Opposition and Dissent in Contemporary China* (Stanford: Hoover Institution Press, 1977); Hamrin and Cheek, *China's Establishment Intellectuals;* and a thoughtful paper by Frederic Wakeman, Jr., "Chinese Intellectuals Since the Cultural Revolution" (presented at the New England China Seminar, Harvard University, March 7, 1983).

33. Goldman, *China's Intellectuals and the State*, pp. 3–10.

34. Timothy Cheek, "Broken Jade: Deng Tuo and Intellectual Service in Mao's China" (manuscript); Mary Mazur's study of Wu Han's life can be found in her forthcoming University of Chicago Ph.D. dissertation.

35. Tu has often mentioned the three circles in his public lectures. I had an extended conversation with him on this topic in December 1981 at Harvard.

36. Analyses by Moody, *Opposition and Dissent*, and Goldman, *China's Intellectuals*.

37. Such is the argument I seek to defend in *Broken Jade*. See also, Cheek and Hamrin, "Collaboration and Conflict."

38. "China's Tom Paine Speaks Out on Democracy," *Washington Post*, November 19, 1987, pp. C1 and C4; Orville Schell, "China's Sakharov," *Atlantic Monthly*.

39. The following discussion on Fang draws from the research and translations of James H. Williams. See his "Fang Lizhi's Expanding Universe," *China Quarterly*, no. 123 (September 1990), pp. 459–484; his translations and analysis of Fang's scientific writings in "The Expanding Universe of Fang Lizhi: Astrophysics and Ideology in People's China," *Chinese Studies in Philosophy*, 19, 4; and Fang Lizhi, *Bringing Down the Great Wall: Writings on Science, Culture, and Democracy in China*, trans. and ed. James H. Williams (New York: Alfred A. Knopf, 1991).

40. See Wang Shiwei, "Statesmen and Artists" (1942) translated as "Politicians, Artists" by Gregor Benton in *Wild Lilies—Poisonous Weeds: Dissident Voices from People's China* (London: Pluto Press, 1982), pp. 175–178; and Timothy Cheek, "The Fading of Wild Lilies: Wang Shiwei and Mao Zedong's 'Yan'an Talks' in the First CPC Rectification Movement," *Australian Journal of Chinese Affairs*, no. 11 (January 1984). For more details on the Wang Shiwei case and its continuing relevance to Chinese intellectuals today, see Dai Qing, *Wang Shiwei and "Wild Lilies": Rectification and Purges in the Chinese Communist Party, 1942–1944* (Armonk, N.Y.: M. E. Sharpe, 1991).

41. For an articulately argued contrary view that sees Fang as a self-interested speaker on behalf of a disgruntled elite only, see Richard C. Kraus, "The Lament of Astrophysicist Fang Lizhi: China's Intellectuals in a Global Context," in Arif Dirlik and Maurice Meisner, eds., *Marxism and the Chinese Experience* (Armonk, N.Y.: M. E. Sharpe, 1989), pp. 294–315, esp. p. 306. In "Habits of the Hearts," pp. 131–132, I also argued that Fang reflected nondemocratic paternalistic values. In view of Williams's research, I no longer hold that view.

42. Conversation with George Konrad during his stay at Colorado College, Colorado Springs, fall 1988.

43. Frederic Wakeman, "The Price of Autonomy: Intellectuals in Ming and Ch'ing Politics," *Daedalus*, no. 2 (1972), pp. 67ff.

44. This is what I argue in the revision of my dissertation on Deng Tuo; see Cheek, *Broken Jade*.

7

CASTING A CHINESE "DEMOCRACY" MOVEMENT: THE ROLES OF STUDENTS, WORKERS, AND ENTREPRENEURS

Elizabeth J. Perry

Of all the momentous political upheavals in 1989, few captured wider attention and sympathy than the Chinese protests that spring. Taking full advantage of the international media (then focused on Beijing to cover first the Asian Development Bank meetings and then the Gorbachev summit), the demonstrators engaged in a style of political showmanship that seemed tailor-made for their new global television audience: festive marches complete with colorful banners and contemporary music, somber hunger strikes punctuated by the wail of ambulance sirens, even a twenty-seven-foot "goddess of democracy" guaranteed to strike a resonant chord in foreign viewers.

Undoubtedly this adept handling of symbolic politics contributed to the widespread publicity and enthusiasm that the events in China elicited around the world. The revolutions in Eastern Europe later in the year were surely stimulated in part by the Chinese example. And yet whereas the Berlin Wall came tumbling down, the walls surrounding Tiananmen Square stand more heavily fortified than ever. International opinion was obviously not sufficient to break a Chinese regime whose leadership operated according to its own

An earlier version of this essay appeared in Daniel Chirot, ed., *The Crisis of Leninism and the Decline of the Left: The Revolutions of 1989* (Seattle: University of Washington Press, 1991). This revised version is printed with the permission of the University of Washington Press. The author would like to thank participants in the "Revolutions of 1989" conference (Seattle, October 1990) for their helpful comments.

political logic. Moreover, despite the apparent sophistication of the young Chinese protesters in dealing with the international media, their movement also remained for the most part within a distinctly Chinese political tradition. The shared assumptions of rulers and rebels served to reinforce preexisting authority relations, ensuring that China's protest movement did not become its revolution of 1989.

Why No Revolution in 1989? The Standard Explanations

When compared to the head-spinning transformations in Eastern Europe, the Chinese outcome has been tragically anticlimactic. To account for this difference, two sorts of explanations are commonly given. The first, ironically enough, points to China's *revolutionary heritage*. In contrast to the communism in most of Eastern Europe, Chinese communism was the outcome of a hard-fought civil war. Having been won from within rather than imposed by alien tanks, the Chinese system was said to enjoy a considerably higher level of popular legitimacy than its East European counterparts.

In the early 1960s, Chalmers Johnson highlighted China's (and Yugoslavia's) indigenous revolutionary experience—which he termed "peasant nationalism"—as an explanation for the emergence of the Sino-Soviet rift.[1] At that time it seemed that nationalist revolutions had engendered independent and dynamic variants of socialism: Maoism in China, Titoism in Yugoslavia. Today, however, that same revolutionary heritage (lingering on in Cuba, Vietnam, and to some extent North Korea as well) reputedly acts as a brake on further political transformation.

If legitimacy was once the product of a revolutionary past, however, it is surely being eroded by a repressive present. Presumably, then, this explanation for contemporary political stagnation is a short-lived one; as the reservoir of popular support is drained by the heavy-handed tactics of obsolescent polities, the aging rulers' claim to revolutionary legitimacy is rendered less and less convincing.[2]

A second type of explanation would seem to have more staying power. This is the view that stresses the *peasant nature* of China. Mired in poverty and ignorance, the 800 million rural dwellers are held responsible for China's political impasse. The tendency to lay the blame for tyranny at the feet of the peasantry is a familiar theme in social science analysis on both the left and the right. Marx claimed that Louis Napoleon's rise could be attributed to those French "potatoes in a sack," a notion that parallels the explanation many a modernization theorist has proffered for Third World dictatorships. Among Chinese intellectuals, this line of reasoning has been especially pronounced. Mao's cult of personality—and the resultant tragedies of the Cultural Revolution and its aftermath—are said to have sprung from the benighted peasantry's undemocratic messianic yearnings. It was these peasants, we are told, who were so attached to the anthem of the Cultural Revolution: "The East is red; the sun is rising. China has given birth to a Mao Zedong. He works for the people's happiness; he is our great savior." The same adulation that had propped up imperial despots for thousands of years was now being transferred to Communist tyrants—first Mao and then Deng Xiaoping. Little wonder that democracy advocates like Fang Lizhi allude to the need to limit peasant political participation; democracy demands an enlightened citizenry—something that in China only the intellectuals claim to be.[3]

The use of peasants as convenient scapegoats is an old practice among Chinese thinkers. Whenever political change failed to occur in the desired manner, the fault could always be said to lie with the backward inhabitants of the countryside. In fact, however, most of China's twentieth-century political follies have been centered in the cities, where intellectuals themselves have played a central role. Certainly this was true for the Cultural Revolution; not ignorant peasants but educated students proved the most zealous disciples of Chairman Mao. In the post-Mao period as well, intellectuals were a bastion of support for Deng Xiaoping through much of the 1980s. History might well have taught them better. In 1957 Deng had taken charge of implementing the notorious antirightist campaign that ruined the careers of hundreds of thousands of the nation's finest intellectuals.[4] In 1979–1980 Deng's harsh crackdown on the Democracy Wall Movement again indicated his intolerance for intellectual criticism. Yet despite this record of repression, Chinese intellectuals continued to express great enthusiasm for Deng Xiaoping. To a greater degree than the peasants (most of whom have, after all, benefited materially from Deng's agrarian reforms), it is the intellectuals whose complicity in despotism seems based less on realistic interests than on traditional patterns of authority.

Intellectual Traditionalism

To explain the weaknesses of China's 1989 protests, one must not stop with the country's revolutionary heritage or peasant population. Rather, the very people who launched the Tiananmen protest—urban intellectuals—were perhaps the greatest fetter on its further development. The seemingly cosmopolitan and contemporary style of the demonstrations masked a deeper reality that was essentially Chinese.

Educated Chinese have tended to identify closely with the regime in power, as Cheek argues (Chapter 6). For much of imperial history, this identification was of course institutionalized in the examination system; the highest honor for a Confucian scholar was to win official position by an outstanding examination performance. Although a vigorous tradition of remonstrance did develop among Chinese intellectuals, it remained for the most part within officially prescribed channels. In contrast to early modern Europe, an alienated academy did not emerge in China until the twentieth century under foreign tutelage. The May Fourth Movement of 1919 revealed the explosive potential of this new critical stance, but it was a short-lived enlightenment indeed. The tendency for subsequent generations of Chinese intellectuals to invoke the May Fourth model—most recently on the seventieth anniversary of that historic occasion—reflects nostalgia for a truncated event rather than the completion of its critical mission.[5] Contemporary intellectuals have fallen into the trap of trying to "replay the old tune of May Fourth" that the literary critic Lo Changpei so presciently warned against on the eve of liberation in 1949 and that Schwarcz describes in Chapter 5. In endeavoring to imitate the May Fourth exemplar, recent generations of intellectuals have been guilty of the same "emperor-worship mentality"—characterized by submission to a familiar pattern of ceremonial politics—against which the May Fourth Movement was directed.

A dramatic example of this recycling of tradition was seen on April 22, 1989, a day of government-scheduled memorial services for former Party General-Secretary Hu Yaobang. As they had on many previous occasions (e.g., the Qingming remembrance for the late Premier Zhou Enlai thirteen years earlier, which sparked the momentous Tiananmen incident of April 5, 1976), students managed to convert an official ceremony into a counterhegemonic performance.[6] The inversion of state rituals has been used to considerable effect by protesters in other parts of the world as well, of course.[7] In taking charge of the occasion (in the Chinese case by claiming control of the official site for such events: Tiananmen Square), the demonstrators are able to challenge the legitimacy of the regime and gain a forum for conveying their own political messages. Yet a striking feature of the April 22 counterceremony was its adherence to traditionally sanctioned modes of behavior. Three student representatives attempted—in the age-old manner of Chinese scholarly remonstrance—to present a petition demanding an explanation for the ouster of Hu Yaobang and a meeting with the current premier, Li Peng. Denied entrance to the Great Hall of the People, the young emissaries suddenly fell to their knees and began to kowtow. Embarrassed officials eventually opened the doors, allowing the students to present their petition to a low-ranking functionary who summarily rejected the demands.[8] The obsequious demeanor of the petitioners was a stark reminder of the degree to which contemporary intellectuals remain bound to traditional styles of protest.

Perry Link, a specialist in Chinese literature who was an eyewitness to the memorial demonstration, offers an insightful account:

> The students knelt on the steps of the People's Hall and asked the Premier, "Will you just come out and see us, just give us your acknowledgement of our trying to be patriotic and trying to help?" From our point of view the demand for dialogue with somebody might not really have punch. But for them it was really important, and in fact I can view that whole square through those thrilling days of April and May as a Beijing Opera Stage . . . in that morally charged Beijing Opera sense . . . when one after another unit would come out, and say, "Here we are with our banner." This to me meant two things. It meant literally, "We have shown up," but it also meant, "We have presented ourselves in this drama."[9]

The presentation of banners representing one's unit was both a theatrical convention and part of the standard protest repertoire.[10] It was, moreover, a tradition not confined to Beijing. When a delegation of graduate students from the Shanghai Academy of Social Sciences attempted on May 25 to present their banner to the Shanghai Garrison Command,[11] the scene was reminiscent of the Shanghai workers' militia presentation of their banner to Chiang Kaishek following a major labor uprising in spring 1927.[12] In all these instances, the protesters were in effect seeking recognition from the ruling authorities of their unit's place on the political stage.

The Limits of Tradition

To be sure, the protesting units had changed somewhat since the Republican period. Though schools remained central, gone now were the native-place associations, guilds, and professional societies that had served as the building blocks of urban unrest during the first half of the twentieth century. Thanks to the reordering that took place under communism, in 1989 many of the participating groups were the *danwei* (or units) created by the state itself. In fact, at one point members of more than ten organs directly under the Central Committee of the Chinese Communist Party—including the propaganda department—could be counted among the marchers.[13]

The incestuous relationship between state and society that had developed as a consequence of communism rendered familiar forms of protest ineffective. Although *danwei* could serve as a vehicle to mobilize millions of people for a Tiananmen demonstration, because these units (whether schools, factories, or Party organs) were ultimately dependent on the state for their very survival, they could easily be *de*mobilized once the state leadership was united in its determination to take action. The frailty of "civil society" in contemporary Chinese cities, even when compared to the late imperial and Republican scene,[14] has made much of the old protest repertoire anachronistic. Lacking autonomy from state domination, urbanites restage the pageant of May Fourth without the *social* power that invigorated the initial performance.

The actors in the most recent rendition of this continuing drama were certainly capable of putting on an exciting show. In their contribution to this volume, Esherick and Wasserstrom characterize the 1989 protest as "street theater: untitled, improvisational," but following "a historically established 'repertoire' of collective action." They rate Wuer Kaixi's performance in the May 18 dialogue with Li Peng as "one of the best acts" in this "instance of political theater"; costuming, timing, and props were all exquisitely handled.

But if the theatrics were first-rate, the politics were less impressive. A particularly disappointing feature of this self-styled "democracy" movement was its fickle search for patrons. Hu Yaobang, posthumous hero to the students of 1989, had been vilified in the huge demonstrations that broke out during his tenure as general-secretary just a few years earlier. In winter 1986–1987, a popular protest slogan had called for the overthrow of Hu Yaobang, comparing him unfavorably to the Gang of Four of Cultural Revolution notoriety.[15] Yet once Hu was ousted in January 1987, and particularly after his death from a heart attack on April 15, 1989, he became a martyr to the movement. Hu's successor as general-secretary, Zhao Ziyang, now suffered the wrath of the students. Whereas Hu had been criticized for his buffoonery, Zhao was attacked for the corruption of his children.[16] Even so, when Zhao Ziyang deigned to visit the hunger strikers in Tiananmen Square on May 19, he became an instant hero, with students clamoring for his autograph. And just as soon as Zhao was deposed, he too attained martyrdom.

Although it would be grossly unfair to accuse the 1989 activists of anything close to the degree of adulation that surrounded Mao's cult of personality during the Cultural Revolution, nevertheless the longing for heroes remained disturbingly evident. Among many young intellectuals, this tendency found expression in support for the doctrine of "New Authoritarianism" (*xin quanweizhuyi*), which looked to a political strongman—in the tradition of Chiang Kaishek in Taiwan or Park Chung-Hee in South Korea—to push forward with economic reform. There were important differences among advocates of this doctrine,[17] but a number of its adherents played a leading role in the early stages of the 1989 demonstrations.[18] To them, state strengthening was the sine qua non of democracy—an argument that, as Andrew Nathan has shown, has been common among Chinese "democrats" since the late nineteenth century.[19] But whereas earlier generations lived under imperial and Republican regimes that were indeed too weak to effect the economic and political transformation of which young activists dreamed, the current dilemma is of an entirely different sort. Genuine change will almost certainly require breaking, not buttressing, the state's control.

The students' deference to state authority was seen in their demand for dialogue—for a place on the political stage, as it were. Xinhua News Agency reported on April 30, "Dialogue has become a household word here as millions of Beijing residents watched last night and tonight the television program of the dialogue between Yuan Mu, the spokesman for the State Council, and the college students."[20] Dramatic as it was, the demand for dialogue was also an admission of the hold that the state continued to exert; protesters wanted a role in the official political pageant, which for them remained the only real show in town. As French correspondent Geremie Barmé observes, "students and intellectuals alike have craved above all for some form of official recognition, their own place at the helm of the ship of state."[21] In sharp contrast to their counterparts in Eastern Europe, Chinese urbanites certainly had not "simply . . . [begun] to turn away from the state, by refusing to take it seriously," as Chirot notes in Chapter 11.

Perhaps the most distressing aspect of the demand for dialogue was the limited cast of characters included in the request. Perpetuating a Confucian mentality that assigned to intellectuals the role of spokespeople for the masses, students assumed that they were the only segment of society whose voice deserved to be heard. The disregard for peasants and workers was a prejudice that intellectuals shared with state leaders. As Young argues in Chapter 1, Deng Xiaoping—like Chiang Kaishek and Yuan Shikai before him—was a reformer who viewed the Chinese peasantry as an obstacle to the fulfillment of national objectives. When each of these reformers turned repressor, he pointed to the "backward" peasants as the reason why China's march toward representative government would have to be postponed. Similarly, in last year's "democracy" movement, students were reportedly "horrified at the suggestion that truly popular elections would have to include peasants, who would certainly outvote educated people like themselves."[22] As a young intellectual in Wuhan explained, "While the people support our aims of stamping out corruption, they just don't understand the ideas of freedom and democracy."[23]

Confucian Moralism

From the perspective of the students, peasants and workers appear motivated by crass materialism, whereas their own politics are selflessly pure. The link to Confucian morality is evident here. When hunger strikers wrote out their last testaments—vowing to sacrifice their very lives for their beliefs—they joined an ancient tradition of scholar-martyrs dating back to the third century B.C. (on this point, see Chapters 2 and 3).

The intense moralism of the Tiananmen protesters has been noted by many analysts. Lee Feigon writes of the hunger strikers: "By fasting they hoped to contrast the *moral righteousness* of their behavior with that of the corrupt and despotic government against which they protested."[24] Dorothy Solinger highlights the "proclivity to *moralize* and demand high behavioral standards from rulers."[25] And Esherick and Wasserstrom (see Chapter 2) point out that the statements of the protesters were filled with "*moral* statements of resolve" (emphasis added).

In this respect, the Chinese case would seem to fit comfortably into Daniel Chirot's interpretation of the revolutions of 1989; the cause was essentially moral. Chirot's chapter in this volume links "the endless corruption, the lies, the collapse of elementary social trust, the petty tyranny at every level" to a moral backlash. Similarly, at the height of the Chinese protests, Fang Lizhi offered the following analysis: "The corruption is so obvious now. People see it every day in their factories and offices. Everybody understands what is going on. The blatant profiteering of state officials is now the focal point of the movement because it is this profiteering that has directly led to the failure of the economic reform."[26] An attitude survey conducted in Beijing at about the same time provided support for Fang's assertions; the overwhelming majority of respondents saw anticorruption as the most important goal of the movement and predicted that corruption was the most likely precipitant of future unrest in China.[27] A startling indication of this moralism was the nostalgia for Chairman Mao that surfaced during the spring protests.[28] One popular ditty expressed the general sentiment: "Mao Zedong's son went to the front lines [and was killed as a soldier in the Korean War]; Zhao Ziyang's son smuggles color television sets."

The 1989 demonstration was, in David Strand's words, "a morality play done in Beijing opera style."[29] As a morality play, it shared many features of the East European scenario. But its Beijing opera style limited the stars of the show to the Confucian elite: scholars and officials. Indeed, the criticisms that Mao's wife Jiang Qing had leveled against the Beijing opera during the Cultural Revolution could be applied with equal force to last year's Tiananmen drama: The plot followed a standard format that denied heroic roles to workers and peasants.

Rank-and-File Participation

That the ordinary populace is in fact fully capable of dramatic action is revealed not only by its revolutionary history but by its recent behavior as well. In the post-Mao era, despite major gains for agriculture under the reforms, unrest in the Chinese countryside has been remarkably prevalent.[30] Significantly, this rural protest is accompanied by a strong resurgence of folk religion; many of the incidents have involved shamans, ancestral temples, "jade emperors descended to earth," and the like. Undoubtedly the popular religion of the contemporary countryside differs significantly from its pre-1949 forerunners; the socialist experience has left a visible imprint on the mentality of today's peasantry.[31] But regardless of how old or new these practices may be, they suggest the fuzzy outlines of a "civil society" in the sense of a domain of public interaction not fully controlled by the state. The drive to institutionalize this domain (as seen in the privately financed rebuilding of local earth-god temples or rewriting of lineage genealogies, for example) further attests to the efforts of the rural populace to carve out a niche of independence from state authority. We are not, of course, seeing here a Chinese Solidarity or Neues Forum. Yet we are witnessing the consolidation of organizational forms that have for centuries provided a foundation for popular protest.[32] When they join state officials in dismissing these practices as "feudal superstition" (*fengjian mixin*), contemporary intellectuals mirror the prejudice of their Confucian forefathers as well as of the ruling regime. In failing to take seriously the peasantry's capacity for collective action, would-be democrats deny themselves a powerful and essential ally.

Equally damaging to the democratic project has been the exclusion of other key social groups: entrepreneurs and workers in particular. With the liberalization of marketing under the post-Mao reforms, an explosion in entrepreneurship occurred. Enticed by the profits to be made in commercial activity, hundreds of thousands of peasants and town dwellers rushed to join the burgeoning ranks of the *getihu*, or independent entrepreneurs. Their transactions gave new life to the realm of nongovernment economic activities that G.W.F. Hegel, Karl Marx, and Antonio Gramsci all viewed as central to the emergence of civil society. The importance of the growth of this commercial class for the advent of democratic politics has often been posited. In Barrington Moore's memorable formulation, "No bourgeoisie, no democracy." The defense of property and profits encourages ordinary citizens to fight for the freedoms associated with liberal democracy.[33]

The support provided by Chinese entrepreneurs for the student protests in 1989 was in fact substantial. In Shanghai on May 21, "hundreds of people with 'entrepreneur' banners staged a sit-in" in sympathy with the students.[34] Unlike most Chinese, the independent *getihu* could engage in political action without fear of sanctions from their work units. Many of them were, moreover, financially well off. Their largess proved crucial in sustaining the student movement. As one private entrepreneur recalled, "Whenever the *getihus* passed by one of the students' donation checkpoints, they would stop to give money—from ten, several tens to a thousand or even tens of thousands of dollars, to show that the *getihus* were sincere from the bottom of our hearts."[35] Such monetary contributions made possible the purchase of battery-operated megaphones for the student leaders.[36] One of the largest of the new private enterprises, the Stone Corporation, is estimated to have donated tens of thousands of dollars' worth of sophisticated equipment—including facsimile machines—to the protesters.[37] As military intervention grew imminent, the Flying Tiger Brigade of *getihu* on motorbikes delivered news of troop movements to the students. After the crackdown, the pedicabs of the *getihu* carried off the casualties.

Despite this crucial help, the entrepreneurs received from the students the same disparaging appellation that the regime used to discredit them. Intellectuals and officials alike referred publicly to the *getihu* as *xiansan ren*—idle drifters.[38] In Communist China as in Confucian China, commercial elements are scorned as rootless, amoral figures who cannot be trusted.[39] (Significantly, the Chinese societies where merchants *have* flourished—Taiwan, Singapore, and Hong Kong—are also societies where the link between state and scholar was broken by colonialism.)[40] The recent experience of Taiwan in particular establishes the catalytic role that the commercial middle class can play in the democratization process. Chirot (see Chapter 11) similarly points to the centrality of the East European middle class in the upheavals of 1989. In denigrating this key social element, Chinese students undervalued the contributions of one of the most enthusiastic supporters of their cause.

Another group in the Tiananmen drama relegated to a role well beneath its actual performance ability was the urban working class. A review of Chinese popular movements of the past century reveals the extraordinary power of a worker-student alliance. The May Fourth Movement of 1919, which began as a demonstration by 3,000 students in Beijing, became a historical watershed only after it had been joined by tens of thousands of Shanghai workers in a general strike the following month. It was this participation by labor that persuaded the government to disavow the terms of the Versailles treaty that threatened to turn China's Shandong Province into a virtual colony of Japan. And it was this same worker activism that in 1921 persuaded young student organizers to establish a Communist Party dedicated to the proletarian cause. Four years later the influence of this new party was seen in the momentous May Thirtieth Movement of 1925—again precipitated by a worker-student protest against imperialism—which marked a high point of Communist strength in the cities. Although subdued by Chiang Kaishek's "white terror" of repression against the Left in spring 1927, the urban coalition regained force after the Japanese invasion of 1937. Fueled first by anti-Japanese sentiment and then, after 1945, by anti-Americanism, worker-student nationalism was a key ingredient in the Communist victory of 1949.[41]

The founding of the People's Republic, although ushering in a self-proclaimed "dictatorship of the proletariat," certainly did not spell the end of labor unrest. In fact, every decade has brought a new round of widespread strikes. In 1956–1957, the Hundred Flowers Movement saw a major outburst to protest the inequities of the First Five-Year Plan.[42] In 1966–1967 the Cultural Revolution prompted another explosion of labor protest.[43] In 1974–1976 resentment against the austere policies of the Gang of Four resulted in a further display of working-class dissatisfaction.[44] And in 1986–1988, strikes erupted at factories across the country to protest the inflationary consequences of the post-Mao reforms.[45] In contrast to the pre-1949 situation, however, the contemporary upheavals elicited little enthusiasm from students. To be sure, much of the explanation for the separation of worker and student politics in the socialist era can be attributed to the effectiveness of state controls.[46] But a certain amount of the responsibility must also be assigned to the intellectuals' disdain for a working class whose aspirations are dismissed as crass "economism."

That workers are actually attracted to larger social causes than many intellectuals give them credit for is shown in their reaction to recent student demonstrations. When tens of thousands of students marched in Shanghai during winter 1986–1987 to demand freedom of expression and an end to police brutality, an even larger group of workers gathered in support. Although a tight police cordon was formed to prevent anyone without valid student identification from entering the center of the demonstration, sympathetic workers stood just outside the police lines yelling, "Younger brothers, your elder brothers support you!" and tossing in bread and cigarettes as a gesture of solidarity. The immediate precipitant of this massive demonstration was the police beating of a college student during a concert by a U.S. rock group in Shanghai. When fellow students erupted in fury, the mayor of Shanghai (now secretary general of the Communist Party), Jiang Zemin, went to the campus of the injured student to offer an explanation. The police, he assured his audience, had mistaken the young concert-goer for a worker; had they only realized he was an intellectual, such heavy-handed treatment would never have been applied. Most members of the campus community reportedly found nothing improper in the mayor's line of reasoning.[47]

Many workers, increasingly disadvantaged by the post-Mao industrial reforms, had ample cause for concern about government policy. For one thing, double-digit inflation was threatening their standard of living. For another, the reforms promised to put more money into industrial reinvestment at the expense of workers' housing and bonuses. "Economistic" as such issues may be, they could form the backbone of a lively protest. Moreover, workers were no less aware or intolerant of corruption and petty tyranny than other Chinese. In short, the basis for a potent worker-student alliance seemed to exist. As in the pre-1949 era, such an urban coalition might have been constructed on the foundations of both *consumer* identity and *citizen* identity. As consumers, urbanites could unite against the debilitating effects of runaway inflation (also a central issue during the general strikes of May Fourth and the Civil War years). As citizens, they could condemn government corruption (again an issue, along with imperialism, in all the major pre-1949 urban movements). Orthodox historiography notwithstanding, it was not *class* identity (or protest against on-the-job exploitation) that had fueled the massive worker strikes of early twentieth-century China. Labor was accustomed to performing on a larger stage than the narrow confines of the workplace.[48]

In spring 1989, workers again sought to play a major role in the drama unfolding in Tiananmen Square. On April 20, laborers from a number of Beijing factories made speeches at the square, proclaiming that "workers and students should work together for the introduction of a more democratic and less corrupt system."[49] Fearing the dangers of growing working-class participation, especially as the May Fourth anniversary drew near, the Beijing city government issued an order forbidding any worker to take leave of absence between April 25 and May 5.[50] At this same time, Deng Xiaoping—explaining that "the movement might soon spread to workers and peasants, as in Poland, Yugoslavia, Hungary, and the Soviet Union"[51]—arranged for two divisions of the Thirty-eighth Army to be called into the city. But the leadership's fears of a worker-student coalition were in fact ungrounded. As Anita Chan and Jonathan Unger have observed, until the very end of the movement, "the students had disdainfully tried to keep the workers at arm's length."[52] This was literally the case, with students linking arms to prevent workers from joining directly in their ranks.[53] As the member of one working-class family observed, "The workers could see that participation was being strictly restricted by the students themselves, as if the workers were not qualified to participate. . . . the issues that the students raised had nothing to do with the workers. For example, Wuer Kaixi in his speeches only talked about the students. If he had mentioned the workers as well, appealed to the workers, appealed to them in a sincere manner, the workers might really have come out in a major way."[54] Only during the last week of May, beleaguered by the growing threat of military suppression, were student delegations sent to the major factories to seek support.[55]

Considering the lack of student initiative, the extent of worker participation was really rather remarkable. In late April an unofficial workers' group calling itself the Beijing Workers' Autonomous Association issued a statement condemning inflation and the gap between wealthy government leaders and the ordinary people. The group called for wage raises, price stabilization, and publication of the incomes and material possessions of Party and government officials and their families.[56] A month later, claiming a membership of more than 6,000 workers, the association's goal was "to set up a nationwide non-Communist union along the lines of Poland's Solidarity trade union."[57] At this time it issued a stinging attack, in cynical Marxist language, on official corruption and its deleterious consequences for the Chinese working class:

We have carefully considered the exploitation of the workers. Marx's *Capital* provided us with a method for understanding the character of our oppression. We deducted from the total value of output the workers' wages, welfare, medical welfare, the necessary social fund, equipment depreciation and reinvestment expenses. Surprisingly, we discovered that "civil servants" swallow all the remaining value produced by the people's blood and sweat! The total taken by them is really vast! How cruel! How typically Chinese! These bureaucrats use the people's hard earned money to build luxury villas all over the country (guarded by soldiers in so-called military areas), to buy luxury cars, to travel to foreign countries on so-called study tours (with their families, and even baby sitters)! Their immoral and shameful deeds and crimes are too numerous to mention here.[58]

To fight such "typically Chinese" bureaucratic corruption, the autonomous union pledged to support the student hunger strikers and to "promote democratization in alliance with students and citizens from all walks of life."[59]

Pressured by this competition from an unofficial labor association, the official All-China Federation of Trade Unions (ACFTU) began to assume a more active role in responding to working-class concerns. On May 1 (International Workers' Day), the president of the ACFTU conceded that government-sponsored unions "should fully support workers in their fight against corruption."[60] Thanks to this encouragement, workers became more involved in the demonstrations. On May 17, as the hunger strike entered its fifth day,

Millions of workers, peasants, and clerks from government organs, personnel from cultural and publishing circles and from the press took to the streets to show they supported and cared for the students. . . . Particularly noticeable were the massive marching columns of workers. They came from scores of enterprises such as the Capital Steel Corporation, the main factory of the Beijing Internal Combustion Engines, Beijing Lifting Machinery Factory and the state-run Number 798 Factory. The demonstrating workers were holding banners and placards carrying slogans stating: "Students and workers are bound by a common cause" and "Workers are grieved seeing students on hunger strike."[61]

The next day the ACFTU took the bold step of donating 100,000 yuan (about $27,000) for medical aid to students in the sixth day of their hunger strike. Explained a spokesperson for the federation, "We workers are deeply concerned about the health and lives of the students."[62] The same day, the Shanghai Federation of Trade Unions added its voice in support of the movement: "Workers in the city have expressed universal concern and sympathy for the patriotism of students who are demanding democracy, rule of law, an end to corruption, checking inflation, and promoting reform. The municipal council of trade unions fully affirms this."[63]

There were limits beyond which the official unions could not go, however. On May 20, a crowd of workers gathered in front of the ACFTU offices to demand that the unions order a national strike.[64] Three days later, after the declaration of martial law, Beijing television announced: "In the last few days, there have been rumors in some localities saying that the All-China Federation of Trade Unions has called for a nationwide general strike. A spokesman for the Federation said that this is merely a rumor with ulterior motives. The spokesman emphatically pointed out that the ACFTU has recently stressed that the vast number of staff members and workers should firmly stay at their posts and properly carry out production work."[65] By the end of the month, Ruan Chongwu, a former minister of public security, had been appointed to the post of labor minister. His brief was "to ensure that workers remain loyal to the party and government—and that they not take part in activities that challenge the regime."[66] Reported the Hong Kong press, "A top priority with Mr. Ruan and the restructured leadership of the trade unions federation will be to prevent nonofficial unions from being organized."[67]

In the drive to recapture control of labor, three leaders of the Beijing Workers' Autonomous Association were detained by the police on May 30. Also rounded up were eleven members of the Flying Tiger Brigade—the contingent of 300 motorbikers, at least 200 of whom were independent entrepreneurs—which was providing information on troop deployment to the students.[68] Once again workers and other nonstudents were being made to pay the price for a movement in which they had played only supporting roles.[69] Even so, many continued to defy the authorities. On June 9 at a huge demonstration and memorial service in Shanghai for victims of the June 4 massacre, among the marchers were about 1,000 workers holding high a banner that read "Shanghai Autonomous Federation of Labor Unions."[70]

Conclusion

The tragic ending to China's uprising of 1989 is explained neither by the salience of its revolutionary ideology nor by the silence of rural inhabitants. If the persistence of "tradition" served as a brake on political transformation, the relevant tradition was not that of the committed revolutionary or the conservative peasantry. Ironically, it was the very instigators of the Tiananmen protest—the urban intellectuals—who appeared most wedded to a limiting legacy. In their *style of remonstrance* (presenting petitions and banners and demanding dialogue with the authorities), their *search for political patrons* (emphasizing the need for state strengthening and switching quickly from one "hero" to the next), and above all their *stress on moralism* (contrasting their own selfless martyrdom to the crass materialism of the masses), the students evinced a brand of political behavior and belief replete with the stigmata of the past.

The traditionalism of student protesters was not due to some immutable Confucian culture, forever lurking like a sea monster beneath the surface of China's political waters—waiting to seize and sink any unsuspecting would-be democrat who happened to swim by.[71] Rather, the intellectuals' political proclivities were shaped by the close links between state and scholar that persist in contemporary China.[72]

Though the Confucian examination system was abolished in 1905, the Communists instituted a *fenpei* (allocation) system whereby the state assigns college graduates to jobs commensurate with their scholastic records, political loyalties, and of course personal connections. Even more than under the imperial regime, the socialist state exercises a virtual monopoly over meaningful job opportunities for intellectuals. Little wonder, then, that these intellectuals—even in the act of protest—should evidence such state-centric tendencies. It was only during the Republican interregnum, when the state's hold over the scholar was effectively eased, that a different sort of student protest emerged. That "May Fourth Tradition," which held sway from 1919 until the founding of the PRC in 1949, was a brilliant but brief chapter in the history of Chinese popular protest. Occurring during an unusual period of state retrenchment (at least with respect to control over intellectuals), the protests of that generation demonstrated an unprecedented independence and enthusiasm for active alliance with workers, peasants, and merchants. It was these qualities of autonomy and mass involvement which imbued the collective action of the Republican era with such social fire. By contrast, contemporary intellectuals who attempt to resuscitate the spirit of May Fourth are hampered by the inability to liberate themselves from the hegemonic claims of the state and thereby embrace the interests of other social elements. As a consequence, their rendition of the May Fourth drama is much less powerful—politically, if not necessarily theatrically—than pre-1949 performances.

The omnipresence of the Chinese Communist state, even more than its Confucian forerunner or its East European counterparts, has inhibited the florescence of "civil society" and rendered the formation of cross-class coalitions correspondingly difficult and dangerous. Accordingly, Andrew Walder cautions against interpreting the Tiananmen upheaval "as a direct expression of the growth of an independent society. Such independence was greatly restricted in China relative to Poland, Hungary, and the Soviet Union."[73] But if the answer lies not in a developed "civil society," how *do* we explain China's recent turmoil? For Walder, "the key to the 1989 upheaval appears to be the splintering of the central leadership and the Party-state apparatus after the initial student protests of April."[74] There is considerable merit in Walder's emphasis on elites and political institutions. As we have seen in the case of the All-China Federation of Trade Unions, elements of the state did indeed play a significant role in facilitating the protest movement of 1989. At the same time, however, we must not underestimate the potential for self-generated political action by nonstate entities. The traditions of Chinese civil society are admittedly weaker and different from those of Eastern Europe. Absent in China are the Catholic church of Poland, the old democratic parties of Hungary, or the dissident intellectual circles of the Soviet Union and Czechoslovakia. Yet there is evidence that recent reforms have encouraged the resurgence of meaningful traditions of extrastate economic and associational behavior in China, just as in Eastern Europe. Today's independent entrepreneurs, practitioners of folk religion, and members of autonomous labor unions are all building on patterns of collective identity and action with proven records of resisting state domination in the Chinese context. These practices may well lack the democratic character of the institutions of civil society in Eastern Europe.[75] But as Strand has noted, "When Chinese seek to revive a democratic tradition, it is a tradition of movements, not institutions, they are drawing upon."[76] And China's merchants, peasants, and workers—as well as students—can rightfully lay claim to a vital part of that inheritance.[77]

In accounting for the timing of the 1989 protest movement, it is clear that the efforts of the Chinese state to undertake reform have played a major hand in encouraging dissent on the part of both political elites and ordinary citizens. Although the relationship between reform and revolution is poorly understood, it is obviously significant. As the history of modern China shows, reform is often the harbinger of revolution. The 1911 Revolution that toppled the imperial system followed upon the Hundred Days' reform and New Policies of the ailing Qing dynasty. The reformist New Life Movement of Chiang Kaishek's Kuomintang heralded the imminent demise of the Nationalist regime. Serious reforms exact substantial costs on at least some sectors of both state and society. Furthermore, they raise expectations to levels that can seldom be attained. Most important, reforms are admissions by the regime of its own inadequacies. As a result, they encourage widespread disbelief. This is especially unsettling in Communist systems, where claims to ideological truth have been so central. When the leadership publicly repudiates many of its past practices, it invites ordinary citizens to engage in open criticism as well.

The uprising of 1989 was a dramatic expression of the Chinese people's appetite and aptitude for political criticism. Influenced by forty years of socialism as well as by international cultural currents, the demonstrators staged an innovative performance. Dunce caps from the Cultural Revolution, rock music from Taiwan, headbands from South Korea, and a hunger strike from Gandhi's India all contributed a seemingly contemporary and cosmopolitan flavor. Yet in its core values the student movement was in fact remarkably traditional. Thanks to the special bond between state and scholar that had persisted for so long under the imperial system and was reconstituted (on different terms, to be sure) under the socialist system, Chinese students engaged in an exclusionist style of protest that served to reinforce preexisting authority relations. At the same time, however, other social groups showed themselves ready to reclaim the true spirit of the May Fourth Movement—in which a fledgling civil society had challenged a troubled Chinese state on both moral and material grounds.

Notes

1. Chalmers Johnson, *Peasant Nationalism and Communist Power: The Emergence of Revolutionary China, 1937–1945* (Stanford: Stanford University Press, 1962).

2. Of course, powerholders in Beijing see the situation differently. Jiang Zemin, general secretary of the Chinese Communist Party, offered five reasons why his country would not go the way of eastern Europe: (1) The CCP is armed with Marxism–Leninism–Mao Zedong Thought and has grown strong through armed struggle; (2) the

Chinese military is armed with Maoism and led by the CCP; (3) Chinese socialism was created by the Chinese people themselves and not forced upon them by the Soviet Red Army; (4) China is not surrounded by capitalist countries, and (5) Marxism has been sinicized by Mao Zedong and Deng Xiaoping and is thus not subject to a Soviet type of reform movement. Quoted in *World Policy Journal*, December 22, 1989, p. 20.

3. Richard C. Kraus, "The Lament of Astrophysicist Fang Lizhi: China's Intellectuals in a Global Context," in Arif Dirlik and Maurice Meisner, eds., *Marxism and the Chinese Experience* (Armonk, N.Y.: M. E. Sharpe, 1989), pp. 294–315.

4. On Deng's role in the antirightist campaign, see David Bachman, *To Leap Forward: Bureaucracy, Economy and Leadership in China, 1956–57* (New York: Cambridge University Press, 1991), ch. 8.

5. Vera Schwarcz, *The Chinese Enlightenment: Intellectuals and the Legacy of the May Fourth Movement of 1919* (Berkeley: University of California Press, 1986), pp. 283–291. Schwarcz argues convincingly that the incompleteness of the May Fourth enlightenment is linked to the tension in twentieth-century China between commitment to cultural criticism and commitment to national salvation. Those who raised the most serious criticisms have been open to the charge of being unpatriotic.

6. Examples of this technique during the Republican period can be found in Jeffrey N. Wasserstrom, *Student Protests in Twentieth-Century China: The View from Shanghai* (Stanford: Stanford University Press, forthcoming).

7. See Charles Tilly, *The Contentious French* (Cambridge: Harvard University Press, 1986), for a discussion of comparable protest behavior in France.

8. Lee Feigon, *China Rising: The Meaning of Tiananmen* (Chicago: Ivan R. Dee, 1990), p. 146; Foreign Broadcast Information Service (FBIS) (April 27, 1989), pp. 11–12.

9. Perry Link, *Chinese Writers Under Fire*, pp. 21–22; quoted in David Strand, "Civil Society and Public Sphere in Modern China: A Perspective on Popular Movements in Beijing, 1919–1989," *Working Papers in Asian/Pacific Studies* (Durham, N.C.: Duke University Press, 1990), pp. 30–31.

10. On the continuity with earlier student movements, see Jeffrey Wasserstrom, "Student Protests in the Chinese Tradition, 1919–1989," in Tony Saich, ed., *Perspectives on the Chinese People's Movement: Spring 1989* (Armonk, N.Y.: M. E. Sharpe, 1990). At least since the May Fourth Movement, groups of students had paraded with banners naming their alma mater as they marched from school to school, calling on those at other institutions to join in the task of saving the nation.

11. Wu Mouren et al., *Bajiu Zhongguo minyun jishi* (Annals of the 1989 Chinese democracy movement) (New York: privately published, 1989), p. 446.

12. Jean Chesneaux, *The Chinese Labor Movement, 1919–1927* (Stanford: Stanford University Press, 1968).

13. FBIS (May 18, 1989), pp. 49–50.

14. On the earlier situation, see William Rowe, *Hankow: Conflict and Community in a Chinese City, 1796–1895* (Stanford: Stanford University Press, 1989); Susan Mann, *Local Merchants and the Chinese Bureaucracy, 1750–1950* (Stanford: Stanford University Press, 1987); and Mary Rankin, *Elite Activism and Political Transformation in China* (Stanford: Stanford University Press, 1986).

15. Personal observation, Shanghai, December 1986. The slogan was: "Dadao Hu Yaobang; Ningyuan Sirenbang!" (Down with Hu Yaobang; better the Gang of Four!).

16. A son who had allegedly used his family connections to make huge profits from an illicit trading company in Hainan was the cause of much of the public hostility.

17. The Beijing variant, formulated by Rong Jian and others close to Zhao Ziyang, argued for a coercive government to carry out radical liberalization of the economy. The southern variant, as formulated by Xiao Gongqin at Shanghai Normal University,

favored a more gradual reform program. See Xiao Gongqin, "Lun guodu quanweizhuyi" (On transitional authoritarianism), *Qingnian xuezhe*, 2 (1989).

18. Feigon, *China Rising*, ch. 6.

19. Andrew J. Nathan, *Chinese Democracy* (Berkeley: University of California Press, 1985).

20. FBIS (May 1, 1989), p. 50.

21. Geremie Barmé, "Blood Offering," *Far Eastern Economic Review*, June 22, 1989, p. 39. As Barmé explains this phenomenon: "The traditional role of the scholar-bureaucrat dovetailed neatly with the Stalinist talk of engineers of the human soul."

22. Mary S. Erbaugh and Richard C. Kraus, "The 1989 Democracy Movement in Fujian and Its Consequences," *Australian Journal of Chinese Affairs*, 23 (1990), p. 153.

23. Eddie Yuen, "Wuhan Takes to the Streets" (unpublished paper, 1990), p. 11. However, as Yuen notes (pp. 10, 12), hundreds of workers did in fact participate in the Wuhan protests by attending demonstrations and driving out in factory trucks after their work shifts were over.

24. Feigon, *China Rising*, p. 196 (emphasis added).

25. Dorothy Solinger, "Democracy with Chinese Characteristics," *World Policy Journal* (Fall 1989), p. 625 (emphasis added).

26. *South China Morning Post*, May 22, 1989, p. 23.

27. *China Information*, 4, 1 (1989), p. 4.

28. Feigon, *China Rising*, p. 206. The carrying of Mao posters was one expression of this phenomenon.

29. Strand, "Civil Society and Public Sphere," p. 16.

30. Elizabeth J. Perry, "Rural Collective Violence: The Fruits of Recent Reform," in Elizabeth J. Perry and Christine Wong, eds., *The Political Economy of Reform in Post-Mao China* (Cambridge: Harvard University Press, 1985).

31. For this argument, see Helen Siu, *Agents and Victims* (New Haven: Yale University Press, 1989). See also Elizabeth J. Perry, "Rural Violence in Socialist China," *China Quarterly*, no. 103 (September 1985), pp. 414–440.

32. On rural religion as a basis for antistate rebellion, see Susan Naquin, *Millenarian Rebellion in China: The Eight Trigrams Uprising of 1813* (New Haven: Yale University Press, 1976). On kinship and village as organizational bases of rural protest, see Elizabeth J. Perry, *Rebels and Revolutionaries in North China, 1845–1945* (Stanford: Stanford University Press, 1980).

33. Barrington Moore, Jr., *Social Origins of Dictatorship and Democracy* (Boston: Beacon Press, 1966), ch. 6. For a dissenting view, see Nina P. Halpern, "Economic Reform and Democratization in Communist Systems: The Case of China," *Studies in Comparative Communism*, 22, 2/3 (1989).

34. Wu, *Bajiu Zhongguo minyun jishi*, p. 355.

35. *Jiushi niandai* (The nineties) (December 1989), pp. 15–16, quoted in Anita Chan and Jonathan Unger, "Voices from the Protest Movement, Chongqing, Sichuan," *Australian Journal of Chinese Affairs*, 24 (July 1990), p. 264.

36. Feigon, *China Rising*, p. 183.

37. Ibid., p. 184.

38. Interviews with participants, Seattle, April–May 1990. An exception was the dissident writer Wang Ruoshui, who argued for an affinity of interests between intellectuals and entrepreneurs. See the interview with Wang in *Jiushi niandai* (The nineties) (April 1989), p. 37.

39. On public disdain for the *getihu*, see Thomas B. Gold, "Guerrilla Interviewing Among the *Getihu*," in Perry Link, Richard Madsen, and Paul Pickowicz, eds., *Unofficial*

China: Popular Culture and Thought in the People's Republic (Boulder: Westview, 1989), pp. 175–192.

40. In Taiwan, the role of intellectuals was further weakened after the KMT takeover via a land reform that undermined their traditional economic base and (by compensating dispossessed landlords with stock in nascent industries) converted the intellectuals themselves into members of the bourgeoisie.

41. Suzanne Pepper, *Civil War in China* (Berkeley: University of California Press, 1980).

42. François Gipouloux, *Les cents fleurs dans les usines* (Paris: L'Ecole des Hautes Etudes en Sciences Sociales, 1986).

43. Hong Yung Lee, *The Politics of the Chinese Cultural Revolution* (Berkeley: University of California Press, 1978).

44. Lowell Dittmer, *China's Continuous Revolution* (Berkeley: University of California Press, 1988).

45. Interviews at the Shanghai Federation of Trade Unions, Shanghai, May 1987 and September 1988.

46. See Andrew Walder, *Communist Neo-Traditionalism: Work and Authority in Chinese Industry* (Berkeley: University of California Press, 1986). Walder provides an insightful discussion of the operation of state controls in state-owned factories. In my view, however, he underestimates the possibility of autonomous worker protests.

47. Personal observations and interviews, Shanghai, December 1987–January 1988.

48. Elizabeth J. Perry, *Shanghai on Strike: The Politics of Chinese Labor* (Stanford: Stanford University Press, forthcoming).

49. FBIS (April 20, 1989), p. 18.

50. FBIS (April 26, 1989), p. 17.

51. Feigon, *China Rising*, p. 153.

52. Anita Chan and Jonathan Unger, "China After Tiananmen," *Nation*, January 22, 1990, pp. 79–81. See also Henry Rosemont, Jr., "China: The Mourning After," *Z Magazine* (March 1990), p. 87. Rosemont notes that for the first four of the six weeks of demonstrations, students kept their distance from workers. Workers were primarily concerned with inflation and job security, issues that did not gain student attention.

53. Feigon, *China Rising*, p. 203.

54. Chan and Unger, "Voices," p. 273. Similar sentiments were expressed in an open letter to the students from a Beijing worker. See Mok Chiu Yu and J. Frank Harrison, eds., *Voices from Tiananmen Square* (Montreal: Black Rose Books, 1990), pp. 111–112.

55. FBIS (May 26, 1989), p. 52.

56. The founding manifesto of the union can be found in Yu and Harrison, *Voices*, p. 107. See also FBIS (April 28, 1989), p. 11.

57. FBIS (May 30, 1989), p. 9; FBIS (May 31, 1989), p. 44.

58. Yu and Harrison, *Voices*, p. 109.

59. Ibid., p. 114.

60. *China Daily*, May 1, 1989, p. 1.

61. FBIS (May 18, 1989), p. 49.

62. Ibid., p. 76.

63. FBIS (May 22, 1989), p. 91.

64. Ibid., p. 45. See also Yu and Harrison, *Voices*, p. 114.

65. FBIS (May 23, 1989), p. 58. Whatever the ACFTU leadership may really have felt about a general strike, theirs was one of the last government/Party units to express support for martial law. See FBIS (May 30, 1989), p. 9.

66. FBIS (May 30, 1989), p. 9.

67. Ibid.

68. FBIS (May 31, 1989), p. 44.

69. On the detention of additional workers and entrepreneurs in early June, see FBIS (June 2, 1989), p. 11. Wuhan also saw more severe treatment for workers than for students. See Yuen, "Wuhan," p. 13. Rosemont states that at least forty-two workers were executed after the June 4 crackdown, whereas no student executions had been reported. Rosemont, "China," p. 87.

70. Wu, *Bajiu Zhongguo minyun jishi*, p. 787. Members of the Workers' Autonomous Union and a handful of small radical workers' groups had assisted Shanghai students in erecting barricades on the morning of June 4. Official workers' militia (composed largely of Party members and cadres) dismantled these barriers on June 8, however. See Shelley Warner, "Shanghai's Response to the Deluge," *Australian Journal of Chinese Affairs*, 24 (July 1990), pp. 303, 312.

71. The "unchanging China" argument can be found in Lucian Pye, *The Spirit of Chinese Politics* (Cambridge: MIT Press, 1968); Richard Solomon, *Mao's Revolution and Chinese Political Culture* (Berkeley: University of California Press, 1971); and Lucian Pye, "Tiananmen and Chinese Political Culture: The Escalation of Confrontation from Morality to Revenge," *Asian Survey*, 30, 4 (April 1990), pp. 331–347. Pye and Solomon argue for a unitary Chinese culture (across time and social class) instilled during childhood socialization experiences.

72. In Taiwan, where the bonds between state and scholar were weakened first by Japanese colonialism and then by the KMT takeover, intellectuals have found it easier to make common cause with other social elements, especially entrepreneurs. This has been apparent in the development of the Democratic Progressive Party, the main opposition party to the ruling KMT. It is also seen in the active participation of intellectuals (along with virtually all other social groups) in Taiwan's recent stock-market boom.

73. Andrew G. Walder, "Political Upheavals in the Communist Party-States," *States and Social Structures Newsletter*, 12 (Winter 1990), p. 8. See also Walder, "The Political Sociology of the Beijing Upheaval of 1989," *Problems of Communism* (September-October 1989), pp. 39–40.

74. Ibid.

75. For this interpretation, see Chapter 2 by Esherick and Wasserstrom.

76. Strand, "Civil Society and Public Sphere," p. 3.

77. This is not to say that protests by peasants, workers, and entrepreneurs were invariably less exclusionist than student protests. We can, of course, point to numerous examples of labor unrest or rural uprisings that eschewed alliance with outside forces. But in contrast to the student movement, these were not self-proclaimed "democracy" protests. The argument here is simply that a successful effort at democratization must incorporate the interests of a diverse array of social elements. Another important source of potential allies left untouched by the students in 1989 were the national minorities. Disaffection in Tibet, Xinjiang, and elsewhere might well have been creatively addressed by student leaders—several of whom (including, most notably, Wuer Kaixi) were themselves of minority descent. However, any overt expression of sympathy with minority aspirations for freedom would have immediately elicited charges of lack of patriotism (not only from the government, but most likely from many ordinary Han Chinese as well).

8

GENDER AND THE CHINESE STUDENT MOVEMENT

Lee Feigon

During the protests of 1989, Chinese students and intellectuals proclaimed themselves untainted by the wrongful doctrines of past feudal rulers as well as present Communist ones. Even when activists became confused and divided about how to carry out their movement, they retained the conviction that China's problems stemmed from a failure to break with repressive and outdated familial values and other features of the oldest of the "ancien régimes" Young discusses in Chapter 1. But did the students really escape the hold of "feudal" values? Were they in fact as "untainted" as they claimed to be?

My goal here is to examine these questions by focusing on one particular issue: patriarchal practices and ideas. Elsewhere in this volume, other authors highlight the role that various kinds of entrenched patterns of thought and action had upon those who sought to create yet another "new" China in 1989. Thus, for example, Perry draws attention to the assumption of cultural superiority that many intellectual and student activists exhibited when dealing with members of other social classes, and Esherick and Wasserstrom highlight the influence long-standing scripts for collective action and patterns of political behavior had upon the protesters of 1989. But what of the beliefs and modes of behavior relating to gender that the students inherited? Were students more or less successful in breaking with the past when patriarchal structures as opposed to democratic political procedures or social egalitarianism were at stake? Were they even interested in challenging the status quo concerning issues of gender and sexuality?

Despite the enormous amount that has been written about the events of 1989, questions such as these have rarely been asked. Standard works on the topic, such as the accounts discussed in this volume's concluding essay, generally have little or nothing to say about the topic of gender. Rey Chow has written a provocative essay, "Violence in the Other Country: China as Crisis, Spectacle, and Woman," that uses concepts of "otherness" developed by feminist literary critics to look at the way foreign observers treated the bloodshed of 1989.[1] Dru Gladney has presented a conference paper on the symbolism of the protests, which has a good deal to say about the importance of gender and sexuality.[2] Works such as these are, however, rare indeed. This is unfortunate, if hardly surprising, because all of the various "ancien régimes" that the students claimed to be rejecting have been patriarchal in one way or another. Looking at student beliefs and practices relating to gender can thus tell us a great deal about the political and cultural assumptions they shared with the rulers whose authority they sought to undermine.

Breaking with the Past

There are some grounds for thinking that the students of 1989 were a good deal less patriarchal than the regime they challenged. It was, after all, a woman, Chai Ling, who spearheaded the protest movement during its final stages. Invariably described in both Western and Chinese accounts as frail-looking, Chai's role in the student movement belied the description. In early May, when the movement was flagging, she went to the campus of Beijing University. Her passionate speech single-handedly convinced several hundred students to add their names to the list of those willing to begin a hunger strike in Tiananmen Square. Thanks in large part to this and other speeches, she became one of the top student leaders, sharing the spotlight with Wang Dan and Wuer Kaixi. Later she became commander-in-chief of the Tiananmen forces.

She remained in Tiananmen to the end. Not until the wee hours of the morning of June 4 did she lead the students out of the square. A few days after the massacre, Chai Ling, from her hiding place, taped a ringing and defiant condemnation of the government that her followers have listened to over and over again inside and outside China. Her words have served both as an inspiration to those who continue to struggle against the Chinese government and as a generally credible account of what happened on the evening of June 4.[3] Almost a year after the movement was crushed, she captivated Chinese audiences again. Her escape from China, long after most of the other well-known dissidents had exited the country, offered hope that the struggle for democracy in China would continue.

Chai Ling's prominence in the movement—as well as that of other woman leaders, especially the older graduate student Wang Chaohua—could easily lead to the conclusion that in spring 1989, Chinese students attempted to redefine the status of women in modern China. Even for those not especially concerned with feminist issues, Chai Ling signified the possibility of opening a radical new chapter in Chinese history, one that would break with the chauvinist and patriarchal Han culture of China's past. The leadership role played by Chai Ling, not to mention Wuer Kaixi, a Uigher from China's northwestern Xinjiang Province, indicated student repudiation of China's traditional male Han ruling culture. This impression was reinforced because both Chai Ling and Wuer Kaixi often criticized traditional gender and family relationships in their discussions of the movement. Their emphasis on cultural and social issues set them apart from earlier activists, who stressed political and intellectual matters.

Safely in exile in the United States in fall 1989, Wuer Kaixi dramatically articulated this attitude at a scholarly conference in Boston called to celebrate the movement. At the conference, he sang a popular Chinese rock song and suggested that Chinese rock and roll influenced students' ideas more than any of the theories of aging intellectuals on democracy. A few weeks later in a conference in New York, Wuer Kaixi declared that democracy for Chinese students implied sexual liberation.[4]

Chai Ling has been less controversial but hardly less emphatic in her insistence that Chinese students struggled for changes in cultural and social relationships. Since her dramatic escape from China approximately a year after the June 4 massacre, Chai Ling has several times noted that what she saw in families throughout China while she was in hiding convinced her that democratic values would come to her country after changes occur in the authoritarian structure of the Chinese family. As she put it in an interview with *Ms.* magazine: "The government, the family, it's all connected. The Chinese family has an unequal structure. There is always a tyrant—sometimes the father, sometimes the mother. Sometimes it's the son, because the parents have no chance to succeed, so they put all their expectations on the son. And when he grows up, he doesn't know how to be equal or respect others. He builds another such family. And so on up through society, such relationships, such hierarchy."[5]

In exile, with her marriage to fellow activist Feng Congde threatened, she has related the lack of democracy in China to the inequalities between men and women in Chinese society. In the *Ms.* interview, she notes: "There are some men who work for the democracy movement in the daytime but beat their wives at night. If democracy is just a concept and not a style of living, it's useless." She also somewhat cryptically contends that: "In the movement, it's traditional wisdom that's represented by a woman, wisdom and love."

Power and Gender: Familiar Patterns

As important as Chai Ling was within the movement, both as a leader and as a symbol of changing gender relations, it should not be forgotten that she was one of only a very few women leaders of the Chinese struggle for democracy in 1989.[6] In spite of her prominence, males still dominated the upper levels of the movement, both in composition and tone. This situation may have been an improvement over the present Chinese government, where none of the 19-member Politburo and only 10 of the 175-member Central Committee of the

Chinese Communist Party are women, but it did not mark a radical new
chapter for gender relations in China. In short, to adopt the dramatic metaphors Esherick and Wasserstrom and Perry use in their chapters, stars such
as Chai Ling aside, in both the official and subversive acts of political theater
performed in 1989, women were relegated for the most part to traditional
kinds of supporting roles.

The men in the student movement, though enlightened about many of the
inequalities of Chinese society, were not particularly enlightened about the
role of women in society. There were two generations of student leaders, as I
have contended elsewhere.[7] The first generation, especially the graduate
students from the Party History Department at People's University, launched
the initial demonstrations after the death of Hu Yaobang. They had thought
deeply about the difficulties of the movement and the problems of communi-
cating democratic ideals to a patriarchal Chinese society. These men, and they
were all males, proved remarkably prescient about the shortcomings of their
fellow students. But they did not see other issues as clearly: To the extent that
gender issues even entered my conversations with them, they did so in a few
lighthearted, patronizing remarks about the number of "pretty girls" taking
part in the demonstrations. In the minds of these People's University student
leaders, like those of the former revolutionaries they opposed, changes in
gender relations would have to wait until they resolved what they considered
the more important and immediate problems affecting the Chinese people as
a whole.

Surprisingly, few of the women leaders, either at People's University or
any other school, acted offended by this attitude. Under prodding from Robin
Morgan of *Ms.*, Chai Ling allowed: "Next time it's human rights for women."[8]
But as a number of recent studies have demonstrated, throughout this century
the Chinese women's movement has been told to wait until "next time" to
resolve its problems.[9] In Chapter 7 Perry has argued that Chinese intellectuals
have a long tradition of identifying "closely with the regime in power."
Women intellectuals do not differ from their male colleagues in this regard.
They have bought into a system in which it has been taken for granted that
one should not raise issues like gender discrimination while supposedly more
important issues are on the agenda. Talk of sexual discrimination, it has been
alleged, would alienate worker and peasant allies. Because women intellectuals
in China, like their male counterparts, have benefited from what seemed to
be a special relationship between the government and the intelligentsia, they
have willingly put off gains in their own position until "next time," accepting
the government's or the Party's claim that "this time" more pressing problems
exist.

In spring 1989 not once did I see a poster or hear a speech discussing
gender discrimination in China. Moreover, neither Chai Ling nor any of the
other women leaders at the time criticized the way virtually all the top male
Chinese student leaders reveled in the sexual clout that went with their
prestige and power. Almost all the male leaders enjoyed the attentions of
female groupies. Wang Dan, identified as the "intellectual" of the movement

and the best-known leader in addition to Wuer Kaixi and Chai Ling, openly bragged to at least one reporter about the love letters he received from admirers. Although some of the stories of Wuer Kaixi and women may perhaps be dismissed as government propaganda, his calls for breaking with old ideas of sexual chastity seemed more a reaction to social prudery than a sensitivity to women's issues. Wuer Kaixi had girlie pin-ups on the wall of his headquarters at Beijing Teacher's College. He boasted about his drinking ability and thought nothing about appointing his "girlfriend" as secretary to screen his calls.

Wuer Kaixi served as a particular target for government efforts to discredit student leaders as corrupt and decadent. He was labeled a "playboy." Numerous articles appeared in the Chinese papers about his supposedly corrupt and indecent behavior. Although some of these charges might have a factual basis, the government (and for that matter some rival leaders) may have found it easy to single him out for particular criticism because his Uigher heritage makes him susceptible to traditional Chinese stereotypes of so-called barbarian behavior.

In China barbarians have often been associated with a kind of eroticism and sexual vitality thought to be lacking in Han Chinese. Even contemporary artists and writers have used these stereotypes as a way of criticizing the dominant ethos in Chinese society. As Esther Yau has pointed out, for instance, the recent film *Sacrificed Youth* dwells on the supposed sexual vigorousness of Dai women as a way of challenging prim Han standards.[10] At a time when Chinese men have questioned their own virility as a result of their subordination to an oppressive authoritarian model, this proof of their sexual power can, as Yau argues, be an important way of establishing an identity independent of the government.[11] In this context, the flaunting of masculine sexuality by Wuer Kaixi and the other male student leaders may be interpreted as a political act, demonstrating their strength and independence from the restrictive values of the government. Similarly, as I have discussed elsewhere, the student fascination with *liumang* (hoodlum) elements and modes of behavior shows their defiance of the conventions of a society they oppose.[12]

But where does this leave the women of the movement? Many of the women activists also embraced their own sexuality and what some might consider a kind of frivolous femininity as a way of breaking with tradition. Early in the movement, even in the most dangerous and tiring marches and parades, women students wore high heels, tight T-shirts, and other attire obviously meant to make them appear sexually appealing. One young man grinningly informed me that the women were using their sexual lures to convince male students to join the demonstrations. His point was probably overstated; the women dressed so as to demonstrate their own sexual potency and beauty, not necessarily to entice men into the movement.

But it is true that the women's behavior was certainly open to differing interpretations. On the one hand there seemed to be the degrading notion that one role for women in the movement was to be sexually available to men. (This was implied in the remark mentioned in the paragraph above and in other comments I occasionally heard.) On the other hand, however, women also showed a sense of pride in their bodies and a liberation from the constraints of the old society, especially the traditional double standard for men and women.

Young argues persuasively that the "ancien régime" that both the students and the government claimed to oppose was, among other things, a combination of the supposed feudalism of the Qing and the austere communism of the Maoist era. For the students, one aspect of this "ancien régime" was the puritanical morality and isolationism associated with the first few decades of the revolution. Reacting against this order, students looked to the West, especially Western movies, pulp novels, and magazines, for an image of sensuality and liberation that they associated with democracy. After all, if, as the Deng regime has implied throughout much of the last decade, the austere poverty of the Chinese countryside has produced China's backwardness, then the apparent materialist sensuality of the West must mean modernization. In any event, it's fun, not least of all because their elders have been cautioning Chinese youth against this kind of decadence for years.

Before and during the movement, often somewhat shocking pornography sold openly on many campuses. During the movement, it became almost a formula for student leaders to proclaim their sexual prowess. In his speech in New York, Wuer Kaixi associated the movement with sexual liberation, and in his autobiography Shen Tong discusses his first sexual experiences, assuming that by doing so he shows himself to be modern and liberated.[13]

Similar attitudes prevailed among the women. For those raised in a society that had once recommended cold showers and loose underwear as a way of coping with teenage problems, this sensuality appeared a welcome change. However, it also often resulted in stereotypes of subordination as bad as or worse than those many women thought they were leaving behind.

The students were evidently attempting to define for themselves a realm of individual expression. This was particularly important for women because of the subordination they routinely experienced in both the public and private realms. The woman writer Wang Anyi has commented on this phenomenon, suggesting that in a society in which women have been compelled to work as well as to do their traditional household chores, they already feel they have been "made too equal." Wang Anyi's views are that "what women in China want is to have the freedom to express their femininity, including the freedom to wear skirts, put on make-up, and stay at home to take care of their child."[14]

This desire to dress up or stay at home and take care of their children, though certainly understandable, also demonstrates the way even modern and independent Chinese rebel women still often receive their cues from the official policies of the Chinese state. By the 1980s, a slew of articles and official pronouncements implied that problems of chronic unemployment could be eased if female workers who are "physically weaker than men" and pose "problems" for enterprises would stay at home to tend to household chores.[15] Rather than directly confront this concept, women students embraced an image of women as a gender more focused on personal, interior problems. To the consternation of even those in official circles, who generally endorse this view, they have shown their rebellion by pushing this self-image to an extreme. They have flaunted their sexuality and highlighted their physical differences from men.

Before the movement began, Wang Anyi, who generally sanctions what she considers the return to femininity, worried about the radicalness of this rebellion. "Nowadays," she complained to an interviewer, "university students are really wild, it's fashionable to be sexually liberated."[16] Pressured by changing government attitudes on the one hand and a desire to imitate what they believed to be the fashionable and independent Western woman on the other, many Chinese women became confused about the right behavior. A typical example presented itself to me in early 1989, when I went to the house of a friend, whose college-student daughter came in wearing tight leather hot pants of the sort worn by urban U.S. prostitutes. "Doesn't she look fashionable," her proud mother exclaimed. "She looks just like an American co-ed."

Unfortunately, by spring 1989 this misguided effort to make a modern feminine statement obscured the few genuinely revolutionary protests that had occurred in the months before the demonstrations. Women had begun to demand that the government do something about increasingly sexist job and wage discrimination. The campaign for a "one child per family" policy, many complained, had resulted in girl babies' again being killed in the countryside by parents who wanted boys; women demanded that it be stopped. Why, some asked, were women in particular being urged to stay home and not work? In the universities, many grumbled that highly qualified women were dismissed from jobs to make way for men and that young women graduates had an impossible time finding good employment.

Not only did the mass protests of April–June subordinate these cries for gender equality, but for some urban intellectuals the macho aspects of the movement may have given them the freedom to express more blatant sexist sentiments than had been the case before. In the middle of the demonstrations, for example, an acquaintance sought my help in getting his new son-in-law into a graduate school in the United States. It puzzled me because his daughter seemed a better candidate than her husband. When I mentioned my concerns, suggesting at the same time that I would much rather help the daughter (whom I had known for a number of years) than the son-in-law (whom I didn't know), my friend laughed and admitted he would like his daughter to study some day in the United States, but then he also candidly acknowledged that he didn't want a wife to precede her husband to the United States.

Even Chai Ling sometimes appeared to see herself as simply a stand-in for the men who should have been in her position. During the movement, word circulated over and over that Chai Ling had assumed her role as a leader because she was seen as a kind of compromise candidate who could get the macho, quarreling men to put aside their arguments temporarily. The male leaders argued belligerently with one another over who had the final word in the movement, sometimes even engaging in physical struggles for control of the microphones at public news conferences. In distinction to this, Chai Ling pandered to an image of herself as a mother figure, calling the students her "children." In the *Ms.* interview, Chai Ling said that she "did not seek leadership. The group chose me. Maybe because they couldn't agree on anyone else and I had less ego than the men. Maybe they made a bad choice. . . . But if someone more suitable is found I would not mind stepping down."[17]

The idea that women are not suited for men's jobs has become commonplace again in Chinese society in recent years. It is a view sanctioned, as I have mentioned, by the official establishment. Not surprisingly, women activists in the movement accepted this idea—certainly not unique to Chinese society—even justifying it by claiming that although women are not particularly powerful within society as a whole, they rule the home. Chai herself suggests that women aren't like men, because "men become journalists, professors, politicians, and just work, work, work. They lose themselves. They know only power, knowledge, politics."[18] She does, it's true, then add that Chinese women are now beginning to fight for their own role within the society, but then she continues that "if Chinese men could realize women's love and wisdom in their actions, the world would be more balanced."[19]

Many of the men in the movement who were Chai's rivals for power dismissed her as someone who couldn't be taken seriously because of these "womanly" qualities. Shen Tong, for instance, whose own role in the movement did not become generally known either in China or abroad until he came to the United States and hired the William Morris Agency to represent him, dismisses her as "an idealist" but one whose "ideals were based very much on emotion and not on a real philosophy."[20] Wuer Kaixi describes her similarly. The insecurity of these male leaders was apparent from their constant need to brag about their ability and influence. Chai Ling had the opposite problem. In spite of her immense powers of persuasion and obvious intelligence, she spent much of her time bemoaning her powerlessness to affect what was happening. At times it almost appeared she felt more secure when she could think of herself as the traditional, helpless female, although that was clearly not what she was.

The Goddess as Symbol and Gesture

Both the strengths and difficulties that women like Chai Ling had in the movement are represented in the symbol of Chinese womanly values constructed by the students, the goddess of democracy. Its creators have acknowledged that their original intent was to copy the U.S. Statue of Liberty. But after considering it they decided that they needed to adapt it to the Chinese vernacular. They used as a model a preexisting figure of a Chinese peasant man grasping a wooden pole in both hands. The bottom part of the staff was cut off and the top part changed into a torch, so only the hand above the man's head grasped this symbol of freedom. The students then lengthened the hair, added breasts, and feminized the facial features, transforming the male figure into a woman.

By specifically changing a male figure into a female one, the students made it clear that it was important for them to have a woman as their image of defiance. As a "goddess," the statue resembled Chinese folklore figures. She was Chai Ling's idea of woman as "traditional wisdom." But at the same time, the statue was a representation of the U.S. symbol of liberty. As such, she personified the proud, independent Western woman many Chinese students wanted to imitate. And the significance of the statue didn't stop there. Its creators have suggested that they intended to imitate "the Russian school of revolutionary realism, and specifically the style of the woman sculptor Vera Mukhina, whose monumental statue of A Worker and Collective Farm Woman, originally placed atop the Soviet Pavilion at the 1937 Paris World's Fair, is still much admired in China; the head of the farm woman in this work was the inspiration for the face and head of the Goddess."[21]

This image of the goddess as a fecund and strong Soviet farm woman contrasts powerfully with the impotence of the feeble old men who ran the Chinese government. In their youth the present leaders of the Chinese government had also looked to Soviet models (indeed in this light the goddess appears a reincarnation of the poster art and sculpture of the 1950s and even, as Esherick and Wasserstrom argue in Chapter 2, the icons of the Cultural Revolution era), so the image of the statue was a particularly apt way of demonstrating the extent to which the old men had failed to live up to even their own measurements. The goddess exemplified the potency of students no longer cowed by that government. At a time when word of Gorbachev's reforms was sweeping China, she reminded the government of how far it was falling behind both the West and the Soviet Union.

The goddess also demonstrated the hollowness of this conception of feminine strength, however, and inadvertently highlighted the dependence of the student movement on the Chinese government. The students initially built the goddess for what they planned would be a departing gesture against a government that clearly had the upper hand. They intended to leave the statue behind when they bowed to the inevitable and vacated the square at the end of May. Then after the sculpture arrived in the square, the students changed their minds and remained in place. It appears that what was in reality a helpless although stirring symbol falsely heartened them; they waited immobilized in the square with their goddess as the government garnered its forces against them.

Perhaps it is unfair to say so, but in the end it appeared that the goddess emphasized student impotence against a government they had mocked for being run by feeble old men. The symbol, constructed from papier-mâché, offered nothing concrete for either women or democracy in China. Like the choice of Chai Ling, she was a "fragile" compromise decided upon because those who were running the revolution could agree on no other alternatives. The first tanks into the square easily toppled and beheaded the goddess. Like much else about the movement, the statue looked impressive but offered little resistance to the old order.

The weakness of their symbol may aptly demonstrate the ambivalence Chinese women intellectuals felt toward the government concerning gender issues as well as democracy. Although it is undeniably true that the status of women as a whole has been set back as a result of the reforms, women intellectuals have probably been affected less by this than most other elements in the society. Pressure on women graduates to accept jobs inferior to those of their male counterparts or not to work at all has mounted, but women intellectuals have generally done better than their worker or peasant counterparts, whose jobs in factories have been eliminated and whose freedoms and opportunities have been increasingly restricted throughout the period of reforms. Although women intellectuals may be angered by gender-based job discrimination and may shudder at the reemergence of female infanticide in the countryside, most women students have little incentive to make common cause with their less fortunate counterparts.

This lack of unity on gender issues is significant not only in and of itself but also because it helps explain why the movement failed. The failure to take a strong position on the issue of gender roles did not sink the movement. But the fuzzy thinking that characterized the student approach to gender issues also clouded their understanding of issues like democracy and economic reform. As was the case with gender issues, the students often struggled against a government whose authority and logic had a much greater hold on them than they admitted. On gender issues as on other matters, students allied themselves with workers but failed to appreciate their concerns; as Perry argues in Chapter 7, the gap between these groups weakened the movement.

In 1989, students did not comprehend the extent to which they had accepted governmental attitudes that men were strong in the world of government and politics and women in the household. They failed to appreciate the sufferings and concerns of peasant and worker women. But this may change, as the results of gender-based job discrimination hit the universities. However flawed, the examples of leaders like Chai Ling and Wang Chaohua send a powerful message to women about their potential as leaders. In light of the failure of the movement, some women have now begun to think about their place as women in the movement and may work more militantly on this in the future. The first step would be for male activists like Wuer Kaixi or Shen Tong to undergo the same kind of introspection. There is little evidence that any of them has begun to reconsider his own actions. But the revolution is still young, and the new generation may have a very different attitude.

Notes

1. Rey Chow, "Violence in the Other Country: China as Crisis, Spectacle, and Woman," in Chandra Mohanty et al., eds., *Third World Women and the Politics of Feminism* (Bloomington: Indiana University Press, 1991).

2. Dru Gladney, "Bodily Positions and Social Dispositions: Sexuality, Nationality and Tiananmen" (paper presented at the Institute of Advanced Study, Princeton, April 26, 1990).

3. For a translation of this statement, as well as transcripts of interviews with Chai Ling conducted during the month preceding June 4, see Han Minzhu, ed., *Cries for Democracy* (Princeton: Princeton University Press, 1990), pp. 197–199, 214–215, 327–328, and 361–366.

4. For further discussion of Wuer's activities and speeches in autumn 1989, see Richard Bernstein, "To Be Young and in China: A Colloquy," *New York Times*, October 7, 1989, p. 11, and Dru Gladney, "The People of the People's Republic: Finally in the Vanguard?" *Fletcher Forum of World Affairs*, 12, 1 (Winter 1989-1990), pp. 62–76.

5. Robin Morgan, "Chai Ling Talks with Robin Morgan," *Ms.* (September-October 1990), p. 15.

6. One sign of this is that Chai and Wang Chaohua were the only two women included in the government's list of the twenty-one most-wanted protesters, the full text of which can be found in Wu Mouren et al., *Bajiu Zhongguo minyun jishi* (Annals of the 1989 Chinese democracy movement) (New York: privately published, 1989), pp. 833–835. There were female leaders in provincial student movements, as the picture of a Shanghai activist in Han, *Cries for Democracy*, p. 171, indicates. The caption to this photograph, however, reminds readers that "relatively few female students assumed leadership roles in student organizations."

7. Lee Feigon, *China Rising* (Chicago: Ivan R. Dee, 1989).

8. Morgan, "Chai Ling," p. 16.

9. Among the books that in one way or another discuss this problem are: Margery Wolf, *Revolution Postponed: Women in Contemporary China* (Stanford: Stanford University Press, 1985); Kay Ann Johnson, *Women, the Family and Peasant Revolution in China* (Chicago: University of Chicago Press, 1983); Judith Stacey, *Patriarchy and Socialist Revolution in China* (Berkeley: University of California Press, 1983); Patricia Stranahan, *Yan'an Women and the Communist Party* (Berkeley: Center for Chinese Studies, 1983); Phyllis Andors, *The Unfinished Liberation of Chinese Women, 1949-1980* (Bloomington: Indiana University Press, 1983); Elisabeth Croll, *Feminism and Socialism in China* (New York: Schocken Books, 1980); and Elisabeth Croll, *Chinese Women Since Mao* (Armonk, N.Y.: M. E. Sharpe, 1983). For a more positive assessment of the commitment Chinese revolutionaries have had toward eliminating patriarchy, see Ono Kazuko, *Chinese Women in a Century of Revolution, 1850-1950*, ed. Joshua A. Fogel (Stanford: Stanford University Press, 1989).

10. Esther C.M. Yau, "Cultural and Economic Dislocations: Filmic Phantasies of Chinese Women in the 1980s," *Wide Angle*, 11, 2 (1989), pp. 15–16.

11. Ibid., p. 18.

12. Feigon, *China Rising*.

13. See Shen Tong and Marianne Yen, *Almost a Revolution* (Boston: Houghton Mifflin, 1990).

14. W. L. Chong, "Love and Sexuality: Themes from a Lecture by Woman Writer Wang Anyi," *China Information*, 3, 3 (Winter 1988-1989), p. 65.

15. A comprehensive analysis of the (often mixed) messages Chinese women receive through the official press, as well as an important discussion of the way these same women use letters to the editor and other forms of writing to respond to these messages, can be found in Gail Hershatter and Emily Honig, *Personal Voices: Chinese Women in the 1980s* (Stanford: Stanford University Press, 1988).

16. Alice de Jong and Anne Sytske Keyser, "A Talk with Woman Novelist Wang Anyi," *China Information*, 3, 3 (Winter 1988-1989), pp. 67–68.

17. Morgan, "Chai Ling," p. 15.

18. Ibid., p. 14.

19. Ibid., p. 15.

20. Shen and Yen, *Almost a Revolution*, p. 276.

21. Tsao Hsingyua, "The Birth of the Goddess of Democracy," in Han, *Cries for Democracy*, p. 344. For other discussions of the symbolism of the goddess that highlight the implications of the statue's gender, see Gladney, "Bodily Positions and Social Dispositions," and Chow, "Violence in the Other Country."

9

SOCIALIST ETHICS AND
THE LEGAL SYSTEM

Ann Anagnost

For many, the Beijing massacre of 1989 marked the moment when the mask of power slipped, revealing the bloated face of a regime morally and ideologically corrupt. Did this disclosure show that the Party's claim to represent the popular will was unequivocally hollow? Was the deployment of murderous force the unmistakable expression of power devoid of conscience or commitment to some larger ideological goal? Or does this interpretation perhaps simply play into the currently prevailing discourse that proclaims the collapse of socialisms around the world as "the end of history," in which any alternatives to a capitalist world order are by definition no longer credible?[1] Such a perspective is most revealing in what it takes for granted. What goes without question here is that ideology is no longer a necessary category of analysis for understanding the post-Mao period. In most portrayals of this era, pragmatism reigns. The Party's ideological practice is seen as a manipulative tool or, even more vexingly, as mere empty posturing. Ideology is dismissed as a dead issue or at most a retrograde activity tarnished by the excesses of high Maoism. Although the Party continues to devote great energy to ideological work (*sixiang gongzuo*), this effort does not figure importantly in how Western scholars study the changing structure of power in the post-Mao period.[2]

I would like to redress this neglect by suggesting that ideology is critically important for understanding not just the crisis of legitimacy posed by the

I wish to thank the University of Illinois Research Board, the University of Illinois Hewlett Summer Awards for International Research, and the Stanford Humanities Center for fellowship support for research and writing. I also wish to thank Gail Kligman and Elizabeth Perry for their comments on earlier versions of this essay.

events of 1989 but the entire reform period as well. The Party's ideological practice underlies its self-construction as a unified agent building a strong and prosperous nation, despite internal divisions over how such a social plan is to be achieved. This vision of the Party's role has been actively pursued in the ideological sphere throughout the post-Mao period, despite the apparent withdrawal of the Party from control over the economic sphere. In ideology the Party constructs its will; it informs the motivations of the Party leadership in ways that cannot be ascribed simply to a will to power. It is essential to understanding how the Party's inability to open itself to dialogue with dissenting voices led to the tragedy of Tiananmen.

To explore this issue further, I must step back from a discussion of the student movement and the discourse of democratic reform among intellectuals and instead look more closely at the Party's efforts to promote democratic institutions at the local level in rural China. Specifically, I focus on the village compact (*xianggui minyue*), which has been promoted throughout the reform period as a model for democratic self-government in the Chinese countryside. These compacts are sets of locally drafted regulations that address a wide range of social concerns. As instruments of local government, they occupy an ambiguous place between the Party's ideological practice and a newly developing legal system. This ambiguity arises in no small part from the compacts' heterogeneous nature. They were designed to broaden democratic participation at the local level by limiting the arbitrary power of local officials, particularly in the economic realm. And yet because they also address concerns about social disorder, the village compacts have become to some extent the very means to reconstitute the power they were intended to circumscribe.

This structural ambiguity complicates the dichotomies governing the debates on democratic reform: the oppositions between Party and state and between Party and masses. The village compact is primarily an ideological instrument; it promotes the values of an authoritative center. But it also supplements a developing legal system presumably "outside" ideology. Do these compacts, then, belong to the Party's ideological program or to the legal system pertaining to the state? Moreover, the compact is a "democratic" form of self-government drafted by the people themselves. And yet the initiative to draft them clearly comes from the Party organization. Are they thus part of state or society? These questions suggest how notions of "democracy" (*minzhu*) and democratic institutions have become a contested domain in Chinese political discourse of the last decade. They also challenge our prevailing notion of democracy as predicated on the existence of an autonomous social sphere, in which diverse parochial interests may be articulated through the institutions of civil society.[3] The village compact as an instrument of self-government, inculcated under Party tutelage, lies within an ambiguous space between state and society. Its being "between" decenters our received categories of analysis and forces us to reframe our questions.

Indeed, the Party quite consciously uses the village compact to bridge the widening gap between Party and masses. It is touted as one of a number of "new" methods to improve the Party's prestige at the local level. And yet in many respects this very concern over the mounting post-Mao crisis of the Party's relationship to the "masses" attests to the Party's will to merge its consciousness with the hearts and minds of the people, a goal continuous with Maoist ideological practice. In this sense, the village compact is essentially a hegemonic practice in that it represents the Party's efforts to rebuild, from the ground up, its exclusive claim to political leadership as representing the popular will. The Party enlists this willed consent of the people by engaging in "educative" and "formative" activities that position individuals as subjects within its discourse. These activities take the form of models promoted for emulation by local communities. The village compact is one such model, as is the "civilized village" (*wenmingcun*) model that often encompasses the compact.

These models promote the reconstruction of the "ethical community" threatened by the divisive forces unleashed by the economic reforms. This emphasis on community has historical resonance with the Chinese past, both with a Confucian moral order and a Maoist collective sensibility, but its present significance must be placed in the context of China's current dilemmas. I argue that "community" is a key factor in the post-Mao construction of socialism in that it offers an "alternative modernity" against the destruction of community implicit in capitalist development. In recent debates about civil society, the ethical community is proposed as a category that can mediate the opposition between the modern regulative state and the normalized individual.[4] I would like to suggest that the concept of ethical community as it is deployed in Party discourse and practice can be in itself "normalizing." However, the modality of this normalizing process is quite different from that of the Western disciplinary state as described by Michel Foucault. It is not the law of the average but the law of the model that governs the disciplinary practices of the Party. The Party's notion of ethical community is based on the definition of rectitude, of ideological uniformity, and this emphasis implicates it in the construction of a totalizing power that suppresses dissenting voices from within.

This raises the issue of representation. Again, although the Party's claim to exclusive leadership is not new, the way in which it is structured must be placed in the historical specificity of the reform period. I argue that with the muting of the class subject, the Party's claim to leadership must be based on an even more totalizing construction of the people as a unified body for whom the Party is the head and voice, stifling legitimized avenues for dissenting voices.[5] This monological closure could only be confronted by people's reclaiming their voices on the streets.

The Problem of Ideology

In my discussion of the village compacts as an ideological practice, I must first define more precisely what I mean by ideology. At one level, I am referring to the conscious practice of the Party to direct and reform everyday practice in accord with its values and goals. The compacts are presented quite explicitly as a means for reconstituting the Party's authority under new circumstances. However, I am also addressing the issue of ideology at a broader level that focuses less on its instrumental aspects, as a technology of persuasion or control. At this broader level, ideology is not something that the Party leaders are outside of or that is subject to their self-interested manipulation, but it encompasses a social vision, defines the leaders' interests and motivations. At the same time, I am not referring to an organized and coherent set of ideas that goes by some label such as Marxism or socialism but to the imaginary envisioning of a unified will, a single historic mission, despite the Party's internal fragmentation. Moreover, this social vision is very much formed by the historical specificities of the Chinese encounter with modernity in the last two hundred years, and the terms of its discourse must be placed within the trajectory of that struggle.

As a system of representations, ideology is not understood here as something that people are conscious of having. It is not so much a "set of ideas" at the level of conscious intellection as a set of "images that precisely encourages people to 'see' their specific place in a historically peculiar social formation as inevitable, natural and a necessary function of the 'real' itself."[6] This "seeing" precedes or underlies the way in which subjects "think about" social reality; it is experienced at the level of common sense or what goes without saying. Ideological analysis must therefore focus on the discursive apparatuses (institutions, modes of textual production, practices) that work on the conception of the self and the social order so as to call or solicit (in Althusser's term, "hail") an individual into a specific form of social "reality" as a subject. One's subjectivity is a recognition of oneself in that representation. Therefore, ideology is not something that we have at a conscious level; it is what positions us as subjects within a social "reality." Finally, if ideology is not a coherent system of ideas but allows contradictory discourses to coreside within the individual, subjectivity is also partial and contingent. This notion of a split subject—never finally determined but always in process—is especially pertinent to the issue of the political subjectivity of the local Party officials who are the active agents of the Party's ideological initiatives. Much of the complex interweaving that occurs between the institutions and discourses of the Party-state and those of the local community is a process internal to the subjectivity of the local Party officials, poised as they are between Party and community.

Defining ideology as I have above enables us to situate the post-Mao reforms in the context of a continuing ideological project of the Party, despite the disillusionment of many with Maoist ideology and practice. The Party possesses a certain supra-individual subjectivity that struggles to represent itself as internally coherent. It has never ceased to construct itself as a unified agent in pursuit of a social vision. Nor has it ceased to engage in activities that demonstrate its concern with the ideological sphere. The important question, for the post-Mao period, is the relationship of the Party's social vision to popular notions of its proper role. In what sense is the Party's ideological vision and practice hegemonic, in the Gramscian sense of a pervasive "structure of feeling" and value that enlists popular consent to be ruled?[7] I would argue that this relationship is terribly complex and difficult to objectify in scholarly analysis. It must be captured at multiple sites of the exercise of power, resistance, negotiation, and accommodation.

One of these sites, as I have already suggested, is the village compact. I argue below that the compacts are indeed effective as a hegemony-producing practice. However, in suggesting this, I do not deny that a serious rupture has developed between the Party and masses. This the Party itself has acknowledged and articulated as critical to the redefinition of its role throughout the reform period. And yet in discussing the nature of this rupture, one must be specific in terms of social groupings within the larger polity. In other words, we must de-objectify what goes by the name of "the masses": What lines of division become obscured in using such a totalizing abstraction to represent the popular will? These compacts are largely directed at rural populations, although urban groups such as factories and shops are also known to have them. It may be that they resonate more effectively with rural people's concerns about social order and social equity than they do with urban people's interests.[8] This may be true even if they are also found to be intrusive and oppressive. Hegemony does not necessarily imply a seamless convergence of will between rulers and ruled but indeed may result in an uneasy accommodation between the two.

We can nevertheless recognize such hegemony-producing efforts as effective, even in an atmosphere of cynicism and disaffection. Havel defines the "post-totalitarian" condition as one in which the voice of power no longer convinces but is still able to enlist the complicity of its subjects in staging the appearance that it does.[9] This complicity is enlisted by more subtle forms of political terror as well as the redistributive power of the state to imbue the social will with a fetishism of the commodity that is in some respects more total than that of capitalism. If the post-Mao era may be defined as post-totalitarian, the period following June Fourth must count even more so. And yet it would seem that such complicity would not be possible without some accurate reflections between the social vision of the Party and that of society, although this mirroring may vary among the diverse social groupings of Chinese society, between country and city, between intellectual and worker. It is precisely the points of resistance, negotiation, and accommodation that must be mapped in order to understand the continuing hegemonic power of the state, despite its wanton exercise of murderous force.[10] How else may we explain the apparent success of the Party's attempts to impose its interpretations of the events of 1989? The most powerful image of this discourse (as earlier chapters have suggested) is the specter of social disorder, the quintessential image of which is the disorder (*luan*) of the Cultural Revolution. It should not be surprising, therefore, that the discourse that calls the institution of village compacts the "establishment of a socialist spiritual civilization" (*shehuizhuyi jingshen wenmin jianshe*) has been cranked up to an even more frenzied level in the aftermath of the crackdown.

The construction of a socialist spiritual civilization centers on the promotion of socialist ethics (*shehui daode*) that underlie the Party's continuing effort to intervene into everyday practice—to make behavior conform to an ideal model, to reform society. However, the post-Maoist composition of this effort has fundamentally changed in ways that reflect a shifting conception of the relationship between base and superstructure. "Ideology" no longer figures as a powerful force in which subjective will can overcome an underdeveloped material base (a Maoist fantasy now repudiated as "superstructural determinism"); it is now conceived of as a stabilizing force in the face of the profound dislocations of the economic reforms. In other words, although the economic base provides the motor for modernization, ideology becomes a brake on the social disorder arising from the economic reforms.

The village compact, therefore, becomes a powerful means through which local levels of Party organization can demonstrate their will to take charge of the ideological sphere, too often neglected in the eagerness to produce economic results. Indeed, ideological work is continually being reaffirmed as a necessary complement to the economic reform. The "two civilizations," "material civilization" (*wuzhi wenming*) and "spiritual civilization" (*jingshen wenming*), must be "grasped together." The "construction of a socialist spiritual civilization" authorizes the Party's intervention into everyday life. And yet this project bears a complex relationship with the Party's apparent withdrawal from certain areas formerly assigned to the sphere of politics, so that other kinds of institution building might take place. Part of the discourse of the post-Mao political reform is the establishment of a legal apparatus in which the arbitrary power of local officials can be made more subject to the "rule of law."[11] For instance, the village compact may demarcate the new parameters of economic practice to protect peasant households. The polyvalent character of these compacts both constrains and empowers rural cadres; these compacts are, therefore, an active site for the renegotiation of power at the most basic level of society.[12]

The Village Compact

The village compact, as a model for community reform, first appeared in the early 1980s. A recent handbook on propaganda work identifies village compacts as part of the civic education movement that started in 1982.[13] In that same year, a *People's Daily* commentary marked the beginning of a national campaign to draft village compacts.[14] This commentary, however, accompanied a report of a model brigade in Yunnan Province that had drafted their compact in 1981.[15] In at least one other instance, a village compact in Fujian was described in the early 1980s as having a twelve-year history.[16] In any case, from 1982 on, the village compact was quickly incorporated into a succession of officially defined models for local political and social reform. As early as 1982, for example, the drafting of a village compact was listed as one of the ten criteria for achieving model status in a "civilized village" campaign in Hebei Province.[17] Beginning in 1986, the village compact was associated with the "construction of socialist spiritual civilization."[18] These compacts also figure importantly in recent campaigns to increase peasant understanding of the law.

Despite their seeming ubiquity in post-Maoist models for ideological work, it is difficult to determine how often compacts are put into practice. Successful campaigns to draft compacts initiated by various levels of the Party organization are not infrequently reported in the press, but it is unclear to what extent they are enforced once the campaign is over. And yet one recent account mentions the village compact as part of the normal functioning of local government.[19] Can we assume, then, that the village compact is an intrinsic part of post-Mao local government that has managed to evade much notice in the Western-language literature on the Chinese reforms because of the way we ask our questions? Or is its importance primarily imaginary? As for many areas of policy implementation, no blanket statement may be made. The degree to which compacts are implemented and enforced probably varies from one local area to another depending on the activism and ambition of local officials at all levels. No doubt this variability depends on perceptions by the local leadership (or their superiors) of the need to reaffirm social order. At the same time, their relative effectiveness depends in no small part on the specific politics of the local community. These issues are important for any micro-level analysis of their working. However, for the purposes of this chapter, I must pose questions of a more global nature in terms of how these compacts are represented in the post-Mao discussions of the Party's role.[20]

Already we see from the contexts in which it is promoted that the village compacts occupy a somewhat ambiguous status between the ideological practice of the local Party organization and the legal system. They provide a punishing specificity to areas of everyday life that are too trivial or too pervasive to be dealt with adequately by the state legal apparatus. They have a quasi-legal status in that they are intended to address issues such as family quarrels, interpersonal disputes, the fulfillment of state contracts, vandalism, and petty theft—matters of social order beyond the scope of the law or the present capacity of the legal system. Ideally, village regulations play only a supplementary role to keep China's immature legal system from becoming overloaded; often, however, they appear to substitute for it in places where legal institutions do not yet exist.

In the case of Housuo Brigade (Yunnan), featured in the 1982 commentary introducing the village compact model, brigade leaders felt that the legal agencies of the state were inadequate to resolve a number of local problems. In 1981 they drew up a sixteen-point compact to handle petty theft, the private use of collective land, the destruction of crops by unpenned draft animals, and other issues. Prior to the drafting of this compact, those who attempted to address these issues had met with derision or reprisals. The injured party had no recourse because these disputes were considered outside the reach of the law. The village compact stipulated problems for resolution mainly through education and persuasion, with small fines imposed when necessary. Public criticism and social pressure would give the compact its "invisible binding force." "The people become their own legislators and policemen. Offenders cannot escape the people."[21]

The ambiguous status of the village compacts is reflected in the effort made to clarify what differentiates them from state law. In a recent handbook for disseminating legal knowledge in the countryside, the distinction is defined with great care. It states that such compacts (*gongyue*) or regulations (*shouze*) are stipulated by the twenty-fourth article of the constitution as a "democratic form" in the construction of "a socialist spiritual civilization." They are drawn up by the people themselves, not by a national legislative body. Their jurisdiction is limited to the community that drafted them and their "binding force" depends on education and criticism, supplemented when necessary by economic sanctions.[22] Whereas the law depends on the guarantee of coercion, the compacts must depend on the force of public opinion and social consciousness. The village compacts are therefore distinguished from state law in terms of their institutional status and their enforcement. And yet when policy is promoted through this extralegal means, it confuses the boundary between politics and law. For example, village compacts are subject to revision to bring them into line with current policy. Zhongzhen Brigade (Fujian) was designated a "civilized village" in 1982. Its success was largely attributed to its compact, which had been in existence since 1970, making it the earliest compact in my sample. This compact originally contained six articles but had undergone three major revisions in the intervening years, once to add sanctions for promoting birth policy in 1975 and once to remove regulations that reflected "leftist" influence. By 1982 the brigade had also achieved the distinction of being named as an advanced unit in public security.[23]

Village compacts are supposed to be drafted and implemented by local communities, usually at the village or township level by the newly constituted village committees (*cunwei*). They are often touted as a model for self-government, as a basic democratic process of the masses. But it is also evident that village compacts are usually initiated and implemented under the leadership of local Party organizations and personnel. In Housuo Brigade, for example, the initiative clearly came from the local Party leadership. In Huang Shu-min's account, the Party secretary himself wrote the local laws and ordinances, presiding over litigations and dispensing justice.[24]

Yet the initiative to draft compacts can also come from above. Indeed, the village compact becomes an important sign that the construction of a socialist spiritual civilization has been "grasped firmly" and therefore figures importantly in the accumulation of political capital at a number of levels in the Party organization. For instance, the Party committee of Shangwang Commune in Yuncheng County (Shanxi) instructed all of its brigades to draw up compacts.[25] In Jiyuan County (Henan) the program was implemented on a countywide scale, resulting in compacts in 485 brigades of the county's thirteen communes.[26] The measure was used in this case to correct a rapidly deteriorating social order plagued by an increasing number of disputes over water and land, theft, fighting, and other problems. The compacts were reported as especially effective in reducing the number of civil disputes referred upward from the commune level to the county authorities.[27] Following this success in the countryside, the county began to encourage similar compacts in urban units such as factories, shops, and schools.

Responsibility for ensuring the observance of the compact is not always solely in the hands of the local Party secretary. It is often shared, at least ostensibly, with persons of a certain moral standing who may be outside the Party organization. The surveillance that these compacts entail is therefore represented as coming not from the Party but from the "people," demonstrating the compacts' linkage of the Party and local society. This participation of extra-Party personnel seems to have gathered emphasis as time passed. For example, in 1982 a campaign to promote village compacts was initiated in Binhai County (Jiangsu). Each brigade was instructed to organize a supervisory group composed of the assistant Party secretary, the youth league secretary, the heads of public security and the women's association, and the person in charge of dispute mediation. This group was to undertake a monthly investigation and use a system of rewards and punishments to ensure compliance. In addition, commune and county authorities were to subject local communities to a periodic scrutiny according to a set annual schedule of major and minor evaluations.[28] It is unclear how many of these group members, if any were not Party members.

However, in the years since this early initiative, there has been a proliferation of new organizational forms created to address the problem of enforcing village compacts as well as improving the general moral atmosphere of the community. These new forms are variously titled: "social ethics appraisal committees" (*shehui daode pingyi hui*), "village people's educational activities group" (*cunmin jiaoyu huodongzu*), "councils on weddings and funerals" (*hongbai xishi lishihui*) (to discourage ostentatious family rituals), or "civilization committees" (*wenming zu*). These groups are generally composed of a mix of Party personnel and persons of communally recognized high moral standing, selected under the direction of the local Party organizations.

For example, Fengcheng County in Liaoning Province instituted the above-mentioned "village people's educational activities group."[29] These committees are made up of three to five members who take decimal units of ten households each as the object of their educational activities. The group members are elected by the people at large or are selected by the Party branch in consultation with the masses. They tend to fall into six categories: Party members, youth league members, retired village cadres, people of high moral character, women "heads of household,"[30] and individuals of proven ability. These small groups are intended to carry out propaganda and educational activities, mobilize the masses for public works, resolve conflicts, transmit information, provide mediation services, and carry out other functions. Their primary means of enforcement are limited to persuasion and the exertion of personal influence.[31] This widening of participation beyond the local Party apparatus is promoted as a way to narrow the gap between the Party and the people. By enlisting individuals locally regarded as having a high ethical standard, the Party is clearly trying to legitimate its claims to popular support for its leadership. Where this wider participation is actively practiced, one might speculate that it could have an important moderating influence on the ability of local officials to abuse their power by means of the compacts.

Indeed, this issue of abuse provides some of the most convincing evidence of how these compacts may actually operate on the ground. Occasionally, there is documentation of the ways in which the compacts may fall short of the model or, even more interesting, the ways in which they provide new opportunities for the abuse of power by local officials. In traditional China attempts by the imperial state to use compacts as an instrument of ideological control often ran afoul of local lineages and other parochial interests. In its present incarnation, the emphasis on the voluntary and mass character of these compacts also leads to situations in which they represent local interests. In some cases this may merely reflect some form of accommodation between the state and the local community. In other cases the compact has gone beyond the attempt to define ambiguous areas of state policy to become in itself a vehicle for the expression of opposition. For example, a number of production teams in Xinyi County (Guangdong) had provisions in their village compacts that seriously contradicted the national birth policy. These deviant regulations allowed couples to have children (up to five or more) until they produced a son.[32]

Of course, the use of compacts to enforce local birth quotas is also widely practiced, usually by exacting fines for out-of-plan births. Yet these fines may vary greatly. Cadres who are overly dependent on heavy fines to enforce village regulations are criticized in the press as unimaginative and lazy. Education and persuasion are the preferred means of enforcement but require time and energy in pursuit of uncertain gains. Moreover, the fines do not seem to act as a deterrent but as a tax on out-of-plan births. The unabashed readiness of those who have to pay for their extra children implies that the ability of more prosperous households to afford the fine may be a new form of conspicuous consumption in the countryside. This points to new dimensions of resistance to the allocative power of the state in which its penalties become the basis for status enhancement. At the same time, it suggests a potent (and, one suspects, deeply felt) marker of class differentiation.

Because of this capacity to deviate from the model, local compacts do come under scrutiny from higher levels of the Party organization. In the campaign to draft compacts in Binhai, a minority of cases encountered certain problems. This led to a countywide campaign for revision in which the county authorities specified six areas of deviation: (1) The compacts did not fit the local situation but indiscriminately used models from other localities; (2) they did not have a mass character but were imposed by the local leadership; (3) they were unable to deal with the real problems of the community; (4) they were not complete but left out important areas that needed specification; (5) there were regulations that were not in accord with national policy or law; and (6) some of the regulations were not appropriate in form to allow for developmental change.[33]

Despite these attempts to correct deviations in local compacts, the results obtained in their implementation invariably conform to some degree to the local structures of power. The attempts of the state to assert its authority through such institutions almost inevitably results in the bending of these institutions to local political realities. This is especially true in a political climate that shies away from confrontation and struggle with entrenched local interests at the expense of more universally defined state objectives. The other difficulty is the purely formalistic observance of the compacts to preserve a buffer between state and local society that allows them to coexist with the pretense of compliance.

However, in addition to the need to rectify the content of village compacts, another area comes up in discussions of their shortcomings. This is the abuse of power when local officials overstep their authority in enforcing village regulations. The dimensions of such abuse were compellingly described in one especially detailed commentary in the *Peasant Gazette*.[34] The use of physical coercion to enforce the compacts was deplored. A minority of cadres "with a weak concept of the law" were described as using the charters for arbitrarily seizing or imprisoning people, searching their homes, and confiscating their property. The implicit sanctioning of cadre use of corporal punishment was also censured. In one township charter, the fine for striking a cadre was 20 to 50 yuan, but there was no stipulation for punishment when a cadre beat a village resident.[35]

Overdependence on fines was also deplored, as were overly punitive measures. The editorial cited a compact from one township in which twenty-nine out of fifty articles stipulated a total of thirty different fines ranging in amount from 1 to 4,000 yuan.[36] If a village resident cut thatch in a neighboring village, the fine was 5 yuan. If the fine were not immediately forthcoming, another fine of 300 yuan, called an "attitude penalty," was added. Moreover, in what appears to be a bizarre display of punitiveness, the malefactor was required to treat forty people to a free meal, and the misdoer's pig, sewing machine, bicycle, and desk clock were confiscated. One wonders how often such sanctions were enforced or whether their excessiveness on the books was merely intended to deter potential offenders.

And yet in at least one case reported in the same editorial, sanctions that were far less stringent provoked an act of ultimate protest. A peasant who had illegally cut two trees was fined 80 yuan, according to village regulations. Reportedly, he was unable to pay this amount and hanged himself instead. His death brought the case to the attention of higher-level authorities, who arrested the local officials, holding them responsible for the suicide.[37] This case was used to illustrate that village cadres themselves are subject to the rule of law when they overstep the limits of their powers (ill-defined as they are). Still, this case also begs the question why this unfortunate peasant had no other legal recourse to bring his wrong to the attention of the higher authorities. The editorial's failure to discuss the absence of avenues of appeal highlights the dubious democratic character of the compacts in practice.

The Problem of History

The idea of a village compact to ensure social order has a long history.[38] The community compact emerged out of the Neo-Confucian revival of the eleventh century. It was then intended to be a voluntary institution of self-government and ideological education through ritual. The early advocates of the community pact meant for it to include pledges for mutual aid, respect for elders, discouragement of heterodox practices, and encouragement of good deeds. Observance of these pledges was to be effected through public loss of face. By the end of the Ming, the compact had become part of the effort to reconstitute communities in a period when other systems of administrative control had broken down (e.g., the *lijia* system).[39] In the Qing, the village pact gradually took the form of a periodic exhortatory lecture (*xiangyue*) performed on a semimonthly basis by local gentry leaders. Present dismissal of the *xiangyue* as a perfunctory ritual may have been influenced by its desuetude in the nineteenth century, as Western observers often noted. However, Victor Mair has suggested that the sustained political stability and apparent ideological uniformity of the eighteenth century may have been enhanced by the village lecture system.[40]

Attempts to revive the pact as a means of national renewal through local self-government were made by the Neo-Confucian visionary Liang Shumin in the 1930s. The pact's purpose was to "scrutinize and perfect each person's moral character."[41] But at this point the compacts were not just aimed at the creation of the ethical community; they were also envisioned as an effective force for modernization by providing the organization for mass mobilization and political participation. The development of the "small groups" (*xiaozu*) for political study in Maoist practice shares many similarities with the principles of Liang's community pact system in that both were intended to be the "primary instrument of horizontal and vertical integration of the political community and mass mobilization for specific social and economic reforms."[42]

The ideological practices of the post-Maoist state strikingly parallel these Neo-Confucian and Maoist technologies of governing. How should we interpret these apparent continuities? It has been a popular exercise of late to demonstrate the degree to which the modern Chinese state embodies the heavy historical burden of its past.[43] To privilege these continuities as somehow causal in producing China's "backwardness" is to commit the Orientalist error of rendering China as an inert object of history, held back from achieving a "modernity" that is defined by its developmental distance from the West. I attempt instead to demonstrate how historically available resources are put to heretofore unimagined uses specific to the construction of a post-Maoist "social imaginary." In so doing, I hope to follow Foucault's dictum to be sensitive to the ruptures within the apparent continuities of history in order to understand how power operates within a specific conjuncture of social and historical forces.[44]

The use of village compacts in the Ming and in Liang's rural experiments provides interesting parallels to the present in which prior structures of administrative control have been displaced and the resulting vacuum has prompted the reaching back into history for resources to fill it.[45] The interesting point is that these historical antecedents of the village compact are never mentioned. On the contrary, the compacts are consistently portrayed as an organizational *innovation* of "the masses." If this could be understood as a revival of old forms, it would have to be called a crypto-Confucian revival: Despite the resemblance of these compacts to older forms, they are represented as a rupture in the Party's own practice, opening it to forms of self-regulation that derive from the people themselves.[46] The premise of this break forces us to look more closely at what these compacts signify in the present discursive construction of a post-Mao polity. And indeed their status as a signifying activity may be, in some respects, more important than their operation at the level of the "real."

The Narrative of Progress and the Ethical Community

What, then, are the true categories of universal history? State and civil society? public and private? social regulation and individual rights?—all made significant within the grand narrative of capital as the history of freedom, modernity, and progress? Or the narrative of community—untheorised, relegated to the primordial zone of the natural, denied any subjectivity that is not domesticated to the requirements of the modern state, and yet persistent in its invocation of the rhetoric of love and kinship against the homogenizing sway of the normalized individual?[47]

How may we situate the issues raised by the village compact within the debates on the "emergence" of civil society in China in the post-Maoist period? These debates in Chinese studies borrow terms derived from parallel discussions on the status of civil society during the disintegration of the Eastern European socialism, to which Chirot alludes in Chapter 11. In both cases, civil society is marked by its absence or its weak development.[48] This posing of a "lack" in terms of a Western standard should, one would think, immediately alert one to the dangers of Eurocentric theorizing. Moreover, the definition of civil society that appears dominant in this discourse appears to be overly narrow, an impoverishment of the theoretical richness of this concept within the Western philosophical tradition. Civil society appears reduced in liberal philosophy to the notion of a sphere of discourse and practice autonomous from the state. In the discussions of civil society in China, this notion is even more rigorously narrowed to some notion of the regulation of society by the market, free of interference from the state. Civil society therefore "emerges" with the loosening hold of the state on economic practice, leading to autonomous associations that can represent the parochial interests of sovereign individuals. And yet some have suggested the impossibility of any clean separation of the institutions of state and civil society in China, finding them so tightly fused as to resist any attempt to prize them apart analytically.[49]

The village compact is problematic in this debate. On the one hand, it represents efforts to achieve a separation between state and society. On the other, it is a vehicle for the Party's educative efforts. This dual character of the compact is not necessarily contradictory, if one takes a Gramscian perspective on the institutions of civil society as the space in which the educative and formative activities of the state are practiced.[50] Civil society, in this sense, approximates what Althusser calls the "ideological state apparatuses" that include schools and religious and secular associations that both are constructed by a dominant ideological discourse and construct that discourse in reproducing it.[51] The village compact is not merely regulatory, nor perhaps even predominantly so; it is pedagogical (in the sense of the "pedagogical will" of the state).[52] Its goal is to allow the values of the Party to permeate all of society—to create an ideological uniformity that can legitimate the Party as the sole representative of the people. The compact expresses a will, therefore, for a particularly close relationship between Party and masses, and this will has grown in urgency along with the mounting consciousness of a crisis in this relationship.

The model for the proper relationship between the Party and the masses is expressed metaphorically in the language promoting the village compact and other models. For instance, a report from Guangdong promoted a comprehensive program to disseminate legal knowledge as one of "five links" in a comprehensive plan to improve ideological work in a county-level initiative.[53] Similar efforts have been described as a "lever," a "baton," a "magic sword," or a "bridge" that could bring the intentions of the higher-ups down to the masses and transmit the needs and voice of the masses upward. This ideal of unobstructed flow is captured by the image of how these efforts work to "resensitize the deadened 'nerve endings'" of Chinese rural society.[54] These methods provide a therapeutic antidote to the perceived apathy or even "paralysis" of local Party organizations. These parallel chains of signifiers representing society both as machine and as body link socialism with the idea of the harmonious society "in touch with itself through all its parts, delivered from the dysfunctions of a system in which the various sectors of activity each obeyed specific norms and in which their interdependence remained at the mercy of the vicissitudes of the market."[55] Socialism, therefore, defines itself profoundly in terms of its capitalist double. In place of the "invisible hand" of the market, it seeks to put in place an organizing rationality (the Party) that is conscious to itself as "the head of the body" even as it seeks to merge its consciousness and identity with "the masses." This ideal of a merging of consciousness between the Party and masses is deeply constitutive of Maoist revolutionary practice.[56] The depth of this concern for the educative function of the Party is perhaps specific to revolutionary socialisms, such as those of China and Cuba, that embody a national narrative, unlike the socialisms of Eastern Europe under the shadow of the Soviet Union. Moreover, it is a feature continuous with the Maoist era that has gone unrecognized in the context of apparent ruptures elsewhere. For if it is an error to mistake superficial continuities as proof of the weight of the past on the present, it is equally an error to mistake superficial discontinuities as true ruptures. In this sense, the village compact may indeed be a historical resource to reconstitute a power only apparently in retreat, a power that conceives of itself as the legitimate voice of the people, that sees itself as both socialist and modern in its self-constitution as a managerial rationality governing all aspects of the social body.

The particular terms in which this rationality manifests itself is in the management of the social disorder produced by the economic reforms. The figure of chaos (*luan*) that confronts the present as the "only" alternative to the Party may have a long pedigree in Chinese history, but its current figuration is distinctly colored by the experience of the Cultural Revolution. The chaos of this period is represented as the product of social division. Class warfare did not galvanize a single will of the people but instead fragmented into anarchic and highly localized struggles for dominance among competing factions. In the prevailing narrative about that time, the greatest legacy of the Cultural Revolution is recognized to be ideological disunity and a general disenchantment with politics. A more compelling portrayal is of a period when any sense of community, even between class equals, became completely eroded by the corrosive effects of political terror. It should not be surprising that Huang Shu-min's Party Secretary Ye points to the year 1970 as a turning point in the character of social conflict. Political conflict gave way to civil conflicts (adultery, theft, gambling).[57] And although this cessation of political conflict was regarded with general relief, the prevalence of victim crimes throughout the 1970s and 1980s is generally attributed to the breakdown of social order that occurred during the Cultural Revolution. Perhaps it is significant that Zhongzhen Brigade's village compact cited above for its longevity was also drafted in the early 1970s. In this period, concern for social order was clearly being recast in very different terms as the imperative for social stability established its priority. The irony, of course, is that although the rhetoric of class struggle was used to mask other kinds of contradictions in the Maoist period, class differences are now repudiated when they lead to acts of retribution redefined as the "victimization" of newly prosperous peasant households by their envious neighbors and kin. The class subject, so carefully constructed in the revolutionary practice of the Maoist era, has now been muted in deference to a new construction of the social order and the meaning of economic difference.

This class subject had been given its voice in Maoist rituals. "Speaking bitterness" (*suku*) provided a narrative form that positioned individuals as subjects by means of marking social divisions and contradictions. These narratives provided a new language with which to speak of the pain and oppression of a society torn apart by abstract historical forces impossible to comprehend in any concrete form. The power of these narratives lay in their ability to represent these impersonal, macro-level forces as embodied by concrete class enemies, to give these enemies a recognizable face within a knowable community. These narratives of division have now been partially effaced by a post-Maoist rhetoric that refuses to grant a class character to the new contradictions and conflicts emerging in rural society under the reforms. Instead, the danger emanates from "outside" or from those who have been contaminated by contact with the outside. Hence, the cultural manifestations of "bourgeois individualism," despite its class label, are perceived as a danger from without that threatens the social solidarity of the masses as a unified body. This new emphasis on social unity may seem similar in some respects to a Confucian ideal of communal order. However, its present articulation bears the traces of a recent history in which social divisions wore a class label. The well-ordered Confucian community was based on the premise of social division conceptualized in terms of a moral hierarchy of ranks and status bound together by ties of obligation and reciprocity rather than in terms of conflict. Social harmony rested on the proper performance of one's social role as defined by one's rank and status. These divisions were understood as permanent, corresponding to a cosmic order that could not be transcended. To a certain extent, the evolution of class statuses under Mao replicated a model of community also based on social division, but one that was, of course, conflictual in essence. Class division was envisioned as something that would be transcended in the achievement of socialism; in practice, however, it tended to be perpetuated as a status system that governed the allocation of the goods of a postrevolutionary social order. In the post-Mao period, social status is yet again quite differently conceived. Although economic difference is acknowledged, it is regarded as transitional, a state of affairs that will be superseded by a socialist order in which common prosperity is the ultimate goal.

Nevertheless, individual prosperity provokes resentment among those who lag behind, for whom the Maoist discourse of class is only partially effaced. The obligations of wealth, when they are expressed in the discourse of the Party, do not involve maintaining social distinctions but seeking to erase them. Wealthy households are praised for helping others to get started on the road to prosperity. They may even be recruited as Party members for their generosity. However, this call to share one's prosperity with others can also operate as a thinly veiled justification for exploitation. Witness the vegetable farmer in the film *All Under Heaven* who allows his less fortunate neighbors to help out in his fields without giving them a set wage. Wages come in the form of small gifts so that the transaction is viewed as reciprocity rather than the exploitation of labor. The village compacts fit into this new moral order by rephrasing social conflict in terms of interpersonal conflict rather than class conflict. They are able to negotiate the various dimensions of difference proliferating in Chinese rural society with the economic reforms without appealing to the divisive notion of class. Contradictions among the people require resolution not through struggle but through persuasion and mediation or, if necessary, appeal to law.

Could not these compacts be a recuperation of the idea of community so damaged by the political disturbance of the past? And if this is so, to what extent does this idea of the self-governing ethical community, domesticated to the requirements of the modern state, come into conflict with a more subterranean subjectivity that reconstitutes community in its invocation of love and kinship undisturbed by the normalizing regimes of the Party? Indeed, recent scholarship suggests the continuing vigor of unofficial constructions of community through gift giving, ritual, and work.[58] Many of these practices are precisely the signs of social disorder targeted by the village compacts for its reforming influence.

The meaning of "chaos" in present political discourse must therefore be situated historically in relation to the divisiveness of class conflict during the Cultural Revolution and the erosion of community norms governing everyday life. But "chaos" as a cautionary feature does not end there, for it also defines a profound difference between socialism and capitalism. The association of chaos with the blind regulation of the market cannot be reduced simply to a "primordial" Confucian disdain for the market (or even to a generalized pre-industrial prejudice against the market as the domain of illicit gain). It has to be understood in terms of the link between socialism and capitalism as ideologically grounded categories bound in a mutually defining relationship that constructs a present "reality." In this regard, the village compacts define a domain of the pedagogical practice of the Party that explicitly sets the willed ethical practice of a socialist state in juxtaposition to the moral vacuity of states governed by the immoral logic of the market. The proper role of the Party, then, is to actively inculcate a "socialist spiritual civilization" that can contain the forces unleashed by the newly defined freedoms of the marketplace and harness them for more constructive goals. Therefore, even when it is widely acknowledged that the model of the "civilized village" is something that may exist in form only, without substance, this cynicism does not necessarily imply that the Party should abandon efforts that the general population may still perceive as intrinsic to the Party's role.[59]

Exemplary Rule

Undoubtedly, the norm is related to power, but it is characterized less by the use of force or violence than by an implicit logic that allows power to reflect upon its own strategies and clearly define its objects.[60]

We are unable to fix the village compacts into a firmly defined category of analysis because it lies between our received categories. Are these compacts politics or law? Do they represent the will of the Party or the masses (are they state or society)? In this section of the essay I take up the first of these ambiguities, which has to do with the nature of these compacts as a disciplinary technology that rules through the imposition of norms consensually agreed upon. The second ambiguity is also closely related to this theme of willed consent; I deal with this issue of representation in the subsequent section.

The first issue has to do with the disciplinary nature of the compacts. They represent the Party's will to reform everyday practice, to ensure the extension of its norms throughout society. And yet this disciplining is represented as a retreat of the Party's sovereign power and its replacement with more participatory local politics. Moreover, the power of the norm does not derive here from the invisible orchestration of labor and the biological processes of the body that arose with capitalism, but as a willed and highly self-conscious form of social engineering. The compacts are marked by a concern for ordering social life, but this social order is not an end in itself because it is placed within a narrative of progress that aims to channel and magnify an ethic of production. This productivity is intended to transform society itself, as evidenced by new mobilities within the rural economy. In this sense, the re-creation of the ethical community does not mean the continued existence of the closed community encysted within the collective organization of the Maoist era. But with the opening up and fragmentation of these communities, the newly "liberated" economic actors must now be subsumed within the ethical community as it is promoted in a more global sense. The compacts are then a disciplinary intervention at a time when the organization of labor and production have been otherwise dispersed in the encouragement of a petty commodity economy.

The village compacts would thus seem to fall within the definition of *biopower* that Foucault describes as "a power bent on generating forces, making them grow, and ordering them." This is a power that contrasts with the murderous display of juridical force that "seizes things, time bodies, and ultimately life itself," preferring instead "to incite, reinforce, control, monitor, optimize, and organize the forces under it." It juxtaposes the sovereign's "power of life and death" with the rationality of the modern state as "managers of life and survival."[61] Foucault distinguishes two poles around which bio-power organizes itself: the body as a machine that can be rendered docile through the discipline of work and everyday life and the population as a body politic that defines the rationality of the state in its efforts to improve its "quality," by regulating and intervening into its biological processes. The post-Mao Chinese state consciously aspires to this regulative ambition, perhaps more than any other modern state. It is clearly expressed in the Party's determination to "improve the quality of the people" that suffuses its educative efforts. One need only look at China's birth policy to get a sense of the size of this ambition in which "the large-scale phenomenon of population" becomes the site where power is exercised.[62] And yet the operation of biopower in the Chinese context seems somehow radically different from the Western disciplinary state that Foucault was writing about.

The village compacts, with their aim to intervene into everyday practice, are disciplinizing, for example, and yet the way in which these compacts control differs from the procedures of industrial capitalism. The application of a discipline is contingent on the existence of a norm that can act as a standard of measure or evaluation. Indeed, Foucault suggests that the development of biopower resulted in the growing importance of the norm over the deployment of juridical power. "Such a power has to qualify, measure, appraise, and hierarchize, rather than display itself in its murderous splendor."[63] It is perhaps here, in the operation of the norm, that we can begin to see where these two modes of discipline begin to differ.

The function of the normative in Foucault's sense is the distribution of values around an average. This definition of the norm, however, is of relatively recent derivation in Western technologies of discipline, developing within the historical specificity of a maturing system of capitalist production. François

Ewald has detailed its origins as the quintessential medium of communication in the homogeneous space/time of capitalist production. The norm is "the means through which the disciplinary society communicates with itself."[64] It engineers the "controlled insertion of bodies into the machinery of production."[65] But this was not always true. Until the beginning of the nineteenth century, the norm implied a "principle of valorization" directly linked to the notion not of the average, but of rectitude. In the transformations of industrial capitalism, the play of oppositions specified by the norm shifted from an ideal of rectitude and its antithesis to the "normal" versus the abnormal or the pathological.[66] Ewald draws our attention to how this "law of the average" gave rise to a positivism that is both objectifying and emptied of signification:

> [Facts] do not signify, they simply are. . . . they are comprehended solely in terms of probability, the statistical category. The statistical category operates as a system of classification rather than as an identifying denomination. The average man is a "fictional entity," not a real individual, nor a model or original that serves as the standard for all men but the reference point common to them all. . . . He is society itself as it sees itself objectified in the mirror of probability and statistics.[67]

However, in China the norm is a common standard or model rather than the average. In the norm as model, categories are not neutral systems of classification but identifying denominations that signify values in a moral system that is prescriptive rather than normative.[68] In much of the literature defining the construction of a socialist spiritual civilization, the traditional opposition between *zheng* (rectitude) and *wai* (heterodoxy or crookedness) is refigured into the post-Maoist narratives of the model. These narratives relate transformations of entire communities to "civilized village" status from a disvalued state, a "quarrelsome village," a "war chaos village," or a "pirate village." The intensity of these designations clearly puts the normative value of what is "civilized" into a system of moral signification.

This moral dimension of the village compacts means that they do not operate as law in the Western sense—as an objective structure "outside of politics." Their intention is to stipulate not crimes but areas of ethical concern, demarcating the boundaries between correct and incorrect behavior by means of persuasion and exhortation through models. In this sense these regulations participate in a Chinese conception of law that differs from a Western notion of law as in the Roman *lex*, as something legislated or decreed.[69] Historically, Chinese conceptions of law (*fa*) were predicated on the idea of the model— that which has been codified in harmony with cosmic principles and to which one must conform. Léon Vandermeersch finds that he must translate *fa* as "law-model."[70] In the socialist context, the model is defined in harmony with a transcendent order as well, but with a utopic social vision promised by the laws of historical materialism.

In noting the differences between these two constructions of the norm, I am not trying to argue that one is more "modern" than the other but am merely taking into account their sociohistorical specificity. Nor am I trying to make an argument for an essential "Chineseness" intrinsic to this way of operating, despite striking antecedents in the Chinese past of similar technologies of control.[71] Both of these caveats are all the more necessary in that the specific modes of discipline that I describe here are becoming superseded in the Chinese academy, where Western modes of disciplinary practice are rapidly holding sway in the importation of a highly empirical, positivistic Western social science theory, which represents itself as the indispensable condition of the "modern" and therefore empowering.[72]

In looking at the village compacts, we see something that apparently operates in similar ways to Foucault's concept of the panopticon, which distributes individuals across a grid, exposing them to a central gaze. This grid is composed of the decimal units of surveillance and control, the creation of bureaucratic categories marking degrees of compliance that isolate the objects of the Party's normalizing practice. However, there are some important differences. For Foucault, the norm exercises its influence invisibly and anonymously as a "natural" state in society; the abnormal is an "unnatural" state against which the technologies of normalization must be mobilized.

In China the "natural" state of being is devalued as outside the moral prescription of the state, a raw material to be worked on by the projection of a conscious will to transform society from its present state of backwardness. The opposition between "civilized" and "uncivilized" (see Chapter 3) becomes the basis of a projected transformation of the social body as a whole (rather than the normalizing of the individual, even when these technologies are applied directly to the individual subject). Power is not disseminated in quite the same form Foucault describes for the modern European state. It is not anonymous, invisible, and silent, but personal, extravagantly visible, and accompanied by the hushed buzz of voices or the clamor of gongs and drums. The disciplines of the body—its bearing and demeanor, its productivity and reproductivity—are influenced by means of a direct "address" by the Party as a transcendent authority that bears a recognizable face in the person of the local Party secretary. In order to apply its force, the Party *must* be visible, as it lacks the orchestrating power of capitalist organization, by which discipline can be applied through the production process. The orchestration of bodies, practices, spaces is done at the level of conscious signification, where it can also be consciously resisted. Despite this difference in the operation of the norm, is there anything less "modern" about this power, in its representation of itself as the triumph of a rational will over darkness and in its dreams of effecting a profound transformation of space and time and the practices that inhabit them, according to a logic of production that puts to flight a magical understanding of the world?

But underneath the level of representations, within the realm of practices, we see a much more complicated picture in which the model of normative rule collides with the juridical use of force. The compacts assume the form of willed consent but operate by means of the arbitrary exercise of power. In practice, the compacts may provide the means whereby local cadres can reconstitute their power in the face of their declining direct control over production. The delegation of power to local officials carries with it a high tolerance for abuse in the form of forcible seizure of body and property—the crude methods of "local emperors."

Foucault suggests that the dawning of the modern disciplinary state came with the consciousness of a "badly regulated distribution of power" in which officials in the lower jurisdictions could ignore procedure and exercise their power arbitrarily without sufficient supervision.[73] This dysfunction was the result of a monarchical "superpower"—an overconcentration of power at the center. What the reformers of the late eighteenth century wanted was a new economy of power that would render "it more constant and more detailed in its effects, to increase its efficiency, to punish less and punish better."[74] In other words, they wanted to disseminate power more effectively throughout the system.

This reforming zeal is analogous to the Party's tradition of rectification, which targets the commandist and "patriarchal" tendencies of local cadres. But this personalization of power in the Party secretary is not just the unevolved product of a feudal past, it is also very much a legacy of the tactics of guerrilla war and revolution that were repeatedly reprised in the Maoist period as a highly effective mobilization strategy. This personal power is defined as abuse, and yet the center depends on it to distance itself from the deployment of force. In other words, it is a feature of the distribution of power in contemporary Chinese politics that has been actively reproduced throughout the socialist period. In the current debates about whether local Party officials still retain power in the wake of decollectivization, the questions we ask should perhaps employ a conception of a mobile power that can take into account the changing loci of its exercise. This suggests a more radical reading of the death of that hapless peasant as a protest against his excessive punishment—suicide defines perhaps the only limits of a power that hides its murderous force in the guise of willed consent. And yet even this act of ultimate protest is swept up to provide grist for the mill of power's self-representation.

The Problem of Representation

In its guise as the willed consent of the ruled, the village compact suggests a Party contemplating its own loss of prestige and engaging in a desperate effort to recuperate its one-time identification with the masses. How do the compacts allow the Party to reconstitute itself as a monolithic power under the guise of democratic form? I argue that this process entails a certain misrepresentation of the popular will. The Party speaks for "the People-As-One," an imaginary unity that knows no division.[75] In post-Mao political discourse, "the masses" are represented as a unified subject in the dual meaning Gayatri Spivak notes: as both a "speaking for," in the sense of political representation, as well as a "re-presenting" or "speaking of" a subject that is constructed in the very process of "speaking for."[76] This representation of "the people" is central to understanding how the Party has attempted to reconstitute its monological voice in the face of divisive forces, the reemergence of class divisions under the new reforms.

The Party points to institutions like the village compact as a democratic form.[77] The designation of these compacts as *yue* (which can be translated as "contract" but can also mean "to bind or restrict") is based on an idea that is said to have originated with Liu Bang: that law is something agreed on by both sides, rulers and ruled.[78] This sounds almost Gramscian in its emphasis on willed consent. In this sense, village compacts become an important site for the negotiation between power and resistance, and for the hegemony-producing process of interweaving the values of the state with the institutions of the local community. The institutions of horizontal surveillance and policing that the compacts entail imply that the "people" have internalized their subjection and call it "their own." And yet the way in which this assertion is made is by a fetishization of the Party's authoritative voice.

The Party's authority rests on its presumption to speak as the voice of the people. The authorship of the model is clearly that of the Party, but the Party is continually rediscovering these models as creations of the people. The Party appears in a state of perpetual surprise at this creative energy. The masses lead and the Party propagates and promotes the best effects of these popular impulses. If the process of suture is when the subject recognizes him- or herself in the discourse of the other so that an identification is formed, then the process I am describing here is a curious inversion of this.[79] The state continually sees its own reflection mirrored in these models and it misrecognizes itself as the other, in that the models are identified with the creativity of the people. This misrecognition allows the state to take up these models as representing the will of the masses; it underpins the Party's assumption of the delegation to it of the popular will. The Party authorizes itself to "represent," in the sense of "speaking for," the people as a unitary social body. Any dissent with the Party's will must therefore come from "outside the people."[80]

In appropriating for itself the voice of "the people," the Party allows no legitimate space for whatever individual voices or collectivities lie within that construction to speak for themselves. The reclaiming of that voice is perhaps only possible when "the people" can in some fashion become their own signifier. The students and workers massed on Tiananmen Square and in other urban spaces in spring 1989 were proportionally a small fraction of China's total population. Nevertheless, their sheer numbers created a strong aggregate effect: A sea of heads filling a "public space" is powerful metonymy for an alternative voice of the "people" that comes from without the Party, however fragmented or faint that voice might be.

Afterword: Spring 1989

On the afternoon of June 5, I joined the crowd gathered in the Drum Tower Square. For days, this Nanjing intersection had been the terminus for massive street processions in support of the democracy protesters in Beijing. During the day, a loudspeaker was installed high in the limbs of a tree bordering the square to announce news from Beijing and to rebroadcast the Voice of America coverage of the protests. At night, it was carried with some ceremony on a cart back to the campus of Nanjing University for safekeeping. On this day, people had come to the square to mourn and to hear news of the crackdown. The square and all the thoroughfares leading up to it were filled with people as far as the eye could see. I stationed myself on a slope directly behind the loudspeaker, allowing me to look over the crowd. At one point, a uniformed public security officer pushed his way slowly through the crowd toward the loudspeaker.

Only that morning I had been awakened at 5:30 by a broadcast cry for help. The campus loudspeaker station had been silenced when its wires were cut by a trio of plainclothes thugs (*bianyi*) generally assumed to be in the employ of the public security bureau. A crowd had gathered outside the dorm where the two loudspeakers were housed during the night. The mood of the crowd waiting for the thugs to show their heads was buoyant. When they tried to run, the crowd gathered itself up and began to press forward to prevent their escape. I found myself crushed against a stone pillar.

Now again, in this renewed threat to the loudspeaker on the square, a roar swelled from the crowd as it gathered itself up and propelled the officer backward. The crowd, as a supra-individual body, gloried in the sense of its own power. As rumors spread that army tanks were ringing the city, this elation was guaranteed to be short-lived. But for a moment, the crowd had the giddy experience of confronting—and overpowering—its own fetishized presence in the uniformed authority of the state.

For me, this image of the crowd reclaiming its power and the state in retreat is a necessary complement to the more widely publicized image of that lone, quixotic figure confronting the line of tanks on the streets of Beijing. It restores a sense of what is possible in spite of the crushing weight of a power that can only imagine itself as total.

Notes

1. The "end of history" concept and its presumed relevance for making sense of 1989 is discussed in Wasserstrom's Afterword to this book.

2. Some ideological flare-ups have of course been duly noted, most notably the campaigns against "spiritual pollution" in 1983 and against "bourgeois individualism" in 1987, but they were largely directed at intellectuals and had little impact on the wider Chinese society. The "civic morality" (*wujiang simei*) campaign has been perhaps the most sustained Party initiative in the ideological sphere in both urban and rural China, though it has not been regarded very seriously by Western scholars. For an important exception, see Arif Dirlik, "Spiritual Solutions to Material Problems: The Socialist Education and Courtesy Month in China," *South Atlantic Quarterly*, 81 (Autumn 1982), pp. 472–501.

3. Discussions of the emergence of civil society as autonomous from the state focus primarily on the zone of economic practice in the period of reform. This commonsense

understanding of civil society as reduced to the economic sphere, governed by its own laws, is attributed to Marx's reworking (and impoverishment) of Hegel's concept of civil society. In Marxist theory, Gramsci restored much of the richness to Hegel's concept that was lost by Marx. See Charles Taylor, "Modes of Civil Society," *Public Culture*, 3, 1 (Fall 1990), p. 99, n. 2.

4. Partha Chatterjee, "A Response to Taylor's 'Modes of Civil Society,'" *Public Culture*, 3, 1 (Fall 1990), pp. 119–134.

5. In suggesting that the Party was unable to open itself to dialogue with dissenting voices, I do not mean to imply that there were no voices from within the Party that heartily supported the idea of dialogue. In the months following Tiananmen, we have seen the suppression of such voices from within the Party.

6. James H. Davanagh, "Ideology," in Frank Lentricchia and Thomas McLaughlin, eds., *Critical Terms for Literary Study* (Chicago: University of Chicago Press, 1990), p. 310.

7. Raymond Williams uses the phrase "structure of feeling" to capture a sense of "meanings and values as they are actively lived and felt" and that have a variable relationship to formal or systematic beliefs. Raymond Williams, *Marxism and Literature* (Oxford: Oxford University Press, 1977), p. 132.

8. At the same time, however, we must be aware of speaking of "the peasantry" as an undifferentiated mass. There is a world of difference between peasant families in the Jiangnan, with their home computers, and those in the mountainous interior of Fujian, for whom the post-Mao economic transformations of the coastal area are only distant echoes.

9. Vaclav Havel, "The Power of the Powerless," in Jan Vladislav, ed., *Vaclav Havel, or Living in Truth*, (London: Faber and Faber, 1986).

10. For example, it is instructive that in the Chinese human rights discourse of 1989, no mention was made of reproductive rights. On the contrary, population control was singled out as one of the critical problems that must be addressed by the state, as part of its proper rationality and role. This could only be understood in terms of the Party's success in convincing intellectuals and urban people of the absolute necessity of a birth policy of unprecedented stringency.

11. I don't mean to suggest that law and ideology are discrete domains. Law itself is inscribed within a system of representations that work ideologically. I am opposing them here in terms of the categories used in the state's own discourse.

12. This suggestion comments on the current debate as to whether the power of local cadres has been increased or diminished by the economic reforms. See, for example, Jean Oi, *State and Peasant in Contemporary China* (Berkeley: University of California Press, 1989), and Victor Nee, "Peasant Entrepreneurship and the Politics of Regulation in China," in Victor Nee and David Stark, eds., *Remaking the Economic Institutions of Socialism* (Stanford: Stanford University Press, 1989), respectively. This debate needs a more Foucauldian notion of power as a highly protean aspect of human relations that is constantly reconstituting itself through displacement, much as the forms of resistance intrinsic to all power relations also redefine themselves. This construction of power underlies my argument below.

13. Sun Meiyao, ed., *Xuanchuan gongzuo shiyong shouce* (A practical guide to propaganda work) (Beijing: Hongqi chubanshe, 1988), p. 198.

14. Li Zhenxi and Bai Yukun, eds., *Zhongguo baokan ciyu* (New Chinese press terms) (Beijing: Huayu jiaoxue chubanshe, 1987), p. 255.

15. *Renmin ribao* (People's daily), February 11, 1982, p. 1.

16. See the discussion below of Zhongzhen Brigade.

17. *Fujian ribao* (Fujian daily), June 7, 1982.

18. In September of that year the Party Central Committee passed a resolution on a guiding policy for the establishment of a socialist spiritual civilization.

19. Huang Shu-min, *The Spiral Road: Change in a Chinese Village Through the Eyes of a Communist Party Leader* (Boulder: Westview, 1989).

20. This approach also shows that this essay is drawing primarily from documentary sources in the Chinese media and not on fieldwork. My 1991 field research will allow me to offer a more institutional analysis of how these compacts operate.

21. *Renmin ribao* (People's daily), February 11, 1982, p. 1.

22. Du Xiachuan and Xu Xiuyi et al., eds., "Are Village Charters the Same as Law?" *Nongmin falü zixun* (Peasant legal counseling) (Beijing: Zhongguo renmin gongan daxue chubanshe, 1988), pp. 1–2.

23. This brigade, located in Xiandu Commune in Hua'an County, was a land-poor brigade. As such it was permitted to develop its brigade industries and had a dozen or so collective factories employing about 40 percent of the brigade's labor force. The strength of its collective economy made this brigade a county-level model. For a discussion of the advantages such land-poor brigades had in being allowed to develop a more diversified economy in the years prior to 1978 and the difficulty such models posed for emulation by brigades better endowed with land, see Norma Diamond, "Model Villages and Village Realities," *Modern China*, 9, 2 (1983), pp. 163–181. For accounts of Zhongzhen Brigade, see *Fujian ribao* (Fujian daily), June 6, 1982, and December 30, 1982, and *Zhongguo nongminbao* (Chinese peasant gazette), April 1, 1982. The achievement of the "civilized village" status is in accord with later accounts that draw attention to the achievement of material well-being as a necessary prior step to achieving "socialist spiritual civilization."

24. Huang, *The Spiral Road*, p. 107. Of course, the Party secretary in this case was perhaps atypical in the sense that he had formerly been public security head before he became Party secretary. As the public security head who succeeded him was too busy in entrepreneurial activities, Party Secretary Ye took over those responsibilities, which were already familiar to him. At the same time, however, he indicated to Huang that some members of the community felt that he was overstepping the limits of his authority in taking on public security work. See below for other patterns of distributing the responsibility for ensuring observance of the compacts.

25. *Zhongguo nongminbao* (Chinese peasant gazette), February 28, 1982, p. 1.

26. *Renmin ribao* (People's daily), April 7, 1982, p. 1.

27. This concern with excessive litigation has a familiar resonance with the concerns of the late imperial state.

28. The campaign to promote the compacts specified three areas of particular concern: (1) problems of civil disorder that were otherwise hard to reach by the legal apparatus, such as gambling, petty theft, feuding, and feudal superstition; (2) problems of civic morality, interpersonal relations, and regard for the public welfare; and (3) problems in the economic realm, such as conflicts over collectively owned tools and draft animals and failure to adhere to the economic plan. *Nongcun gongzuo tongxun* (Rural work report) (April 1983), p. 42.

29. *Nongcun gongzuo tongxun* (Rural work report) (July 1988), pp. 42–43.

30. From what I can gather, these women are household heads because of the absence of their husbands, who have taken jobs in nearby cities.

31. For references to the other group titles mentioned above, see *Nongmin ribao* (Peasant daily), July 15, 1987; *Nongmin ribao*, July 15, 1987, p. 2; and *Renmin ribao* (People's daily), May 27, 1986, p. 5.

32. *Zhongguo nongminbao* (Chinese peasant gazette), September 27, 1981, p. 1.

33. *Nongcun gongzuo tongxun* (Rural work report) (April 1983), p. 42.

34. *Nongmin ribao* (Peasant daily), September 12, 1986, p. 3.

35. In speaking of physical punishment, the editorial also urged local officials to abolish any "lineage regulations" or "family rules" that might incite lineage feeling or that represent lineage power. It cited one lineage with the surname of Li that had drafted lineage regulations. In addition to fines, physical punishments were also stipulated. These, the editorial insisted, are bizarre and "very uncivilized."

36. The editorial only obliquely addressed the issue of fiscal responsibility in collecting the fines. It cited unfavorably the regulation of one township that stipulated that the money collected was to go to the level of government responsible for levying them. In cases involving more than one level of government, it was to be divided up proportionally. I interpret this as an expression of disapproval for using the collection of fines as revenue. With fines amounting to several thousand yuan, this would not be an insignificant issue. One also wonders whether the collection of fines might not also be a disguise for the taking of bribes. The above-mentioned phenomenon of using fines as a "tax" on out-of-plan births suggests this possibility.

37. *Nongmin ribao* (Peasant daily), September 12, 1986, p. 3.

38. See Kung-chuan Hsiao, *Rural China: Imperial Control in the Nineteenth Century* (Seattle: University of Washington Press, 1967), and Timothy Cheek, "Contracts and Ideological Control in Village Administration: Tensions in the 'Village Covenant System' in Late Imperial China" (paper presented at the annual meeting of the Association of Asian Studies, Washington, D.C., March 1984).

39. Cheek, "Contracts and Ideological Control," p. 25.

40. Victor H. Mair, "Language and Ideology in the Written Popularizations of the Sacred Edict," in David Johnson, Andrew J. Nathan, and Evelyn S. Rawski, eds., *Popular Culture in Late Imperial China*, (Berkeley: University of California Press, 1985), p. 357. In their chapter on political theater, Esherick and Wasserstrom mention the "public lecture" (*xiangyue*) of the Qing as one of the rare instances of public speaking in late imperial China, but one that "quickly atrophied." They attribute this absence of public speech to a mistrust of clever speech. Confucian officials "preferred the authority of the written word." This putative "graphocentrism" positions Chinese culture oppositionally to the "logocentrism" of the West and its metaphysics of presence. See Jacques Derrida, *Of Grammatology*, trans. Gayatri Spivak (Baltimore: Johns Hopkins University Press, 1976). However, I question this absence of public speech genres, especially given the stunning display of public narrative in the process of revolution and in the constitution of a socialist political culture. What were the pre-revolutionary antecedents of the "speaking bitterness" narratives? Did these appear de novo or from Leninist prototypes? I also question this absence in the context of the rhetorical strategies of local officials to persuade individuals to conform to the model. Repeatedly in accounts of ideological work, the approach of the ideological worker to the recalcitrant subject is through "heart to heart talk" (*tanxin*). Public speech certainly took different forms in China. As harangue or as spoken appeal, it was structured primarily in terms of hierarchy as speech delivered by moral superiors to their inferiors. Surely, in a society in which literacy was so circumscribed, modes of persuasive speech were a necessary bridge between those whose moral superiority was cultivated through familiarity with the classic texts and those who lacked access to the written word. Mair's treatment of popularizations of the Sacred Edicts as "pseudopopular" works suggests this was the case with the *xiangyue*. Ann Anagnost, "Who Is Speaking Here? Discursive Boundaries and the Politics of Representation in Socialist China," in John Hays, ed., *Boundaries in Chinese Thought and Practice* (London: Reaktion Press, 1991), addresses the issue of subjectivity and speech genres in Chinese socialist political culture.

41. Guy Alitto, *The Last Confucian: Liang Shu-min and the Dilemma of Modernity* (Berkeley: University of California Press, 1979), p. 289.

42. Cheek, "Contracts and Ideological Control," p. 42.

43. Although this Orientalism is characteristic of some Western scholarship on China, it has also been adopted by certain Chinese intellectuals as a means of criticizing the Party's monopoly of rule in "cultural" terms rather than political ones. The celebrated television series "He Shang" (River elegy), is perhaps the best-known example of this auto-Orientalist critique. For a brief general discussion of the concept of "Orientalism," see the Afterword to this volume.

44. Michel Foucault, "Nietzsche, Genealogy, History," in Donald F. Bouchard, ed., *Language, Counter-Memory, Practice* (Ithaca, N.Y.: Cornell University Press, 1977).

45. This notion of reaching back for historical resources to fill an institutional vacuum in some ways parallels the current discussion of the postsocialist resurrection of the institutions of civil society by those Eastern European societies endowed with such traditions.

46. When Cheek was doing his research on late imperial community pacts during the early 1980s, Chinese historians assured him that such pacts were no longer used under socialism (Cheek, personal communication). These scholars may indeed have been unaware of the revival of the pact as an institution of local political reform.

47. Chatterjee, "A Response," p. 132.

48. The degree of the "lack" varies in the case of Eastern Europe, depending on the relative affinity of national traditions with the history of Western Europe, most notably the Czech (as opposed to the Slovak) political institutions and traditions.

49. Helen Siu, "Socialist Peddlers and Princes in a Chinese Market Town," *American Ethnologist*, 16, 2 (May 1989). Siu's work is exemplary in her mapping of many of the dimensions of this interweaving.

50. Gramsci understood civil society as an element not of the structural sphere but of the superstructure. Civil society is therefore "the ensemble of organisms commonly called 'private'" that carries out the hegemonic functions of the dominant group throughout society. In this sense, civil society is distinguished from "political society" or "the state," which exercises direct domination. In this wider definition, civil society comprises not just all material relations but "all ideological-cultural relations . . . the whole of spiritual and intellectual life." See Norberto Bobbio, "Gramsci and the Concept of Civil Society," in John Keane, ed., *Civil Society and the State: New European Perspectives* (London: Verso, 1988), pp. 82–83.

51. Louis Althusser, "Ideology and Ideological State Apparatuses (Notes Towards an Investigation)," in Althusser, *Lenin and Philosophy and Other Essays* (New York: Monthly Review Press, 1971), pp. 127–186.

52. Homi K. Bhubha, "DisseminNation: Time, Narrative, and the Margins of the Modern Nation," in *Nation and Narrative* (London: Routledge, 1990).

53. These five links were "Party liaison households" or Party members who link with targeted backward elements to engage in intensive ideological education, a "legal education" program, a program to build cultural facilities, Party schools to train cadres for night schools for peasants, and a program for building the rural infrastructure (water control, road repair, and electrification) to be tied into the ideological efforts. *Nongcun gongzuo tongxun* (Rural work report) (July 1987), p. 22.

54. *Nongcun gongzuo tongxun* (Rural work report) (July 1988), pp. 42–43.

55. See Claude Lefort, "The Image of the Body in Totalitarianism," in John B. Thompson, ed., *The Political Forms of Modern Society* (Cambridge: MIT Press, 1986).

56. See Arif Dirlik, "The Predicament of Marxist Revolutionary Consciousness: Mao Zedong, Antonio Gramsci, and the Reformulation of Marxist Revolutionary Theory," *Modern China*, 9, 2 (April 1983), pp. 182–211.

57. Huang, *The Spiral Road*, p. 109.

58. For gift giving, see Mayfair Yang, "The Gift Economy and State Power in China," *Comparative Studies in Society and History*, 31, 1 (January 1989). For ritual, see Helen Siu, "Recycling Rituals: Politics and Popular Culture in Contemporary Rural China," in Perry Link et al., eds., *Unofficial China: Popular Culture and Thought in the People's Republic* (Boulder: Westview, 1989), and Ann Anagnost, "The Politics of Ritual Displacement," in Laurel Kendall et al., eds., *Communities in Question: Religion and Authority in East and Southeast Asia* (forthcoming). For work, see Lisa Rofel, "Hegemony and Productivity: Workers in Post-Mao China," in Arif Dirlik and Maurice Meisner, eds., *Marxism and the Chinese Experience* (Armonk, N.Y.: M. E. Sharpe, 1989), and Mayfair Yang, "Between the State and Society: The Construction of Corporateness in a Chinese Socialist Factory," *Australian Journal of Chinese Affairs*, 22 (July 1989).

59. And yet Huang Shu-min's account illustrates at least one instance where the promotion of a socialist spiritual civilization was recognized as unequivocally hollow. Huang, *The Spiral Road*, pp. 168–169.

60. François Ewald, "Norms, Discipline, and the Law," *Representations*, 30 (Spring 1990), p. 139.

61. Michel Foucault, *The History of Sexuality*, vol. 1, *An Introduction*, trans. Robert Hurley (New York: Vintage, 1980), pp. 136–137.

62. Certainly the use of abortion to ensure that birth quotas are met fits Foucault's sense of biopower not so much as the right to take life or let live as "the power to *foster* life or *disallow* it to the point of death." Foucault, *History of Sexuality*, vol. 1, p. 138, emphasis in the original.

63. Foucault, *History of Sexuality*, vol. 1, p. 144.

64. Ewald, "Norms, Discipline, and the Law," p. 141.

65. Foucault, *History of Sexuality*, vol. 1, pp. 140–141.

66. Ewald, "Norms, Discipline, and the Law," p. 140.

67. Ibid., p. 145.

68. This was also true of the categories that made up the class-status system of the Maoist period. See Jean-François Billeter, "The System of Class-Status," in Stuart R. Schram, ed., *The Scope of State Power in China* (London: School of Oriental and African Studies, 1985).

69. Léon Vandermeersch, "An Enquiry into the Chinese Conception of the Law," in Schram, *Scope of State Power in China*.

70. Vandermeersch, "An Enquiry," pp. 21–22. Esherick and Wasserstrom suggest in their chapter that the Confucian concept of "ritual" (*li*) corresponds to a Geertzian notion of ritual as both "models for and models of" what people believe. They therefore contrast this sense of *li* (ritual) with *fa* in the Legalist sense as "law or coercive control." However, the word *fa* has a much broader spectrum of connotation than the more narrowly circumscribed Legalist term that opposes Confucian ritual (*li*). It can mean model, method, way, standard, or even occult practice, as well as law. Also, the relationship of *fa* with the rectification of names, that is, names fixed by the law, also would have implications for language as the model for a transcendent reality.

71. This caution addresses the problem of talking about difference without essentializing that difference so that culture becomes reified as an explanatory variable. This issue is essential to how our language of rationality fixes the other into a stable category making possible a relation of domination.

72. To some extent, this new discursive domain within the academy represents an increasing autonomy of intellectual thought from the language of the Party, as I discovered in 1989 when I tried to put my newspaper vocabulary to work in explaining my research goals to Chinese colleagues. They found my language inappropriate for scientific work. At the same time, Elizabeth Perry (personal communication) suggests

that Chinese and Western social science constructions of the "norm" confront each other in designation of the "typical" unit as the proper object of scholarly study. In Chinese, *typical* translates as *dianxing* in the sense of corresponding to a type or model, whereas Western social science operates in terms of the typical as "the average," which in Chinese would translate as *yiban*.

73. See Michel Foucault, *Discipline and Punish: The Birth of the Prison*, trans. Alan Sheridan (New York: Vintage, 1979), p. 80.

74. Foucault, *Discipline and Punish*, pp. 80–82.

75. Lefort, "The Image of the Body in Totalitarianism."

76. See Gayatri Spivak, "Can the Subaltern Speak?" in Cary Nelson and Lawrence Grossberg, eds., *Marxism and the Interpretation of Cultures* (Urbana: University of Illinois Press, 1988), pp. 275 and passim. Spivak suggests that this difference is akin to that between a proxy and a portrait.

77. Esherick and Wasserstrom's chapter draws attention to how the Chinese term for democracy configures "the people" as an undifferentiated mass undivided by contending interests or voices in the realm of political representation. See Ann Anagnost, "The Politicized Body," *Stanford Humanities Review* (1991), for a detailed discussion of how individual subjects become subsumed within this mass identity in the rituals of the Party.

78. Cheek, "Contracts and Ideological Control."

79. I am adapting here a specular logic and a concept of suture used in contemporary film theory. See Kaja Silverman, *The Subject of Semiotics* (New York: Oxford University Press, 1983).

80. Lefort, "The Image of the Body in Totalitarianism."

10

THE ROLE OF THE CHINESE AND U.S. MEDIA

Stephen R. MacKinnon

In scholarly analysis of the events of spring 1989, the Chinese press is usually discussed as a tool manipulated by factions within the CCP and the student movement, whereas the U.S. press is pictured as swayed by familiar sympathetic symbols like the goddess of democracy. So far, serious historical analysis of the political role of either country's media has been lacking. In the case of the Chinese press, there is acknowledgment of its importance as a hesitant cheerleader of the democracy movement, having given the signal (by publication of Zhao Ziyang's May 4 speech and coverage of student marches) that sparked two weeks of mass demonstrations involving entire urban populations. Suppression of the Chinese press after May 20 is said to have prefigured the tragic outcome of June 4. Yet the place of journalism in the history of twentieth-century Chinese protest is underanalyzed. Likewise, media analysts often depict U.S. coverage in 1989 as naive, skillfully manipulated by the demonstrators, and having failed to probe the systemic forces that produced the tragedy.[1] As I argue in this chapter, the intertwined histories of both the Chinese press and U.S. reporting on China are directly relevant to an understanding of the political forces that led up to the Tiananmen incident.

In reconstructing Chinese political history since June 4, 1989, scholars have focused on the underdevelopment of a civil society in relation to the state's domination of the public sphere of political discourse.[2] How popular protest movements of the twentieth century were ritualized and ultimately controlled by the state has held center stage, with the history of the modern Chinese press treated as a sideshow. Similarly, U.S. coverage of China in the 1930s and 1940s is seen as censored and manipulated by those in power—or by their opponents, as in the case of Edgar Snow, Nym Wales, Harold Isaacs, Agnes Smedley, and others, who are portrayed as having been won over by student protestors and communist guerrilla leaders.[3] Yet it was the forceful persistence of an outspoken, Chinese-language, treaty-port press during the 1930s and 1940s under editors like Zou Taofen, Cheng Shewo, and Chen Bosheng that brought a mass following to the student demonstrations of the mid-1930s. Likewise in the 1980s, without such publications as *World Economic Herald* (Shijie jingji daobao), *Scientific and Technology Daily* (Keji ribao), or the muckraking reporting and sophisticated political analysis of Liu Binyan and Wang Ruoshui, the mass movements of 1989 would have been unlikely. In the same way, U.S. reporting on China in the 1930s laid the groundwork for the emotional, contradictory U.S.-China relationship of the 1940s, just as the China-lobby journalism of Henry Luce in the 1940s laid the groundwork for the Asian cold war relationships of the 1950s and later. Today it is hard to overestimate the effect in political terms of U.S. media penetration of Chinese cities, as reflected in the present regime's concerned (albeit inept) attempts to counter such influence.

Since Deng Xiaoping initiated reforms in the late 1970s, the Chinese press had been liberalizing rapidly. *Xinwen gaige* (journalism reform) was the catchall phrase for reforms running from technical changes like the introduction of computers to structural changes in press financing, advertising, and censorship.[4] The growth in the number of officially sponsored publications through the 1980s makes the point statistically. By 1987 2,578 newspapers of many varieties were being published, in contrast to the low of 46 during the depths of the Cultural Revolution (1966–1969). Tone and content changed, with prominence given to readers' letters, investigative reporting, and human interest stories. Behind all this was a new professionalism tied directly to the rapid expansion of journalism training and the ideas of Western journalism educators (particularly Americans). The latter saturated Chinese media institutions with U.S. definitions of objectivity, curriculum, critical analysis, textbooks, writing techniques, and so on. By spring 1989 the Chinese press was in the midst of a flowering of free expression the likes of which had not been seen since the 1930s and 1940s. Not surprisingly, the continuing political crackdown since June 1989 has been aimed at controlling the press and limiting U.S. influence. In future political struggles a critical battleground undoubtedly will be issues of a free press and Western (mainly U.S.) models.

Available works in English on the history of the Chinese press in the twentieth century are few. The most important is *Chinese Democracy* (1986), in which Andrew Nathan ties the Chinese press to the theory and practice of democracy in China.[5] Nathan focuses first on the roots of the modern press during the early 1900s by discussing the polemical writings of figures like Liang Qichao. Then he leaps to the Democracy Wall episode of the late 1970s, skipping the period in between almost altogether. Yet the 1930s and 1940s were the most creative and courageous decades in the history of the Chinese press. The fluidity and freedom of the times were comparable to that of the 1980s for the Chinese press in Taiwan, Hong Kong, and mainland China. A key link between the two periods, the 1930s to 1940s and the 1980s, is the symbiotic relationship between the U.S. and Chinese press at both times.

The best-known aspect in the history of the Chinese press in the 1930s is its sometimes lethal restriction—or censorship—by Chiang Kaishek's government.[6] But official censorship was not a constant. It varied in strength from year to year and region to region. From 1930 to spring 1933, Shanghai was a freer place for journalists than during the following three years. Although publishers and writers were arrested and assassinated, the pattern was erratic and seemingly arbitrary. Leading figures such as Zou Taofen and Cheng Shewo saw papers shut down but usually escaped arrest. In 1936 Xian was an island of relatively free expression—especially about the need for a war with Japan—because of the presence of Zhang Xueliang and the Manchurian army. Two years later, when Hankou was the wartime capital, the Chinese press was freer and more vibrant than at any other time before or since. Communist, Kuomintang, Trotskyist, and independent publications proliferated.[7] In subsequent years, Japanese censorship blanketed the coastal cities and was complete by the time the Pacific War broke out in 1941. Likewise, after Chiang Kaishek moved to Chongqing, his regime became progressively more repressive of the press (both Chinese and Western). He virtually closed down the Communist press after the New Fourth Army incident during winter 1942.

Chiang's chief censor and sometime minister of information through much of the 1930s and 1940s was Hollington Tong (Dong Xianguang).[8] Tong was a University of Missouri journalism school graduate who prided himself on an American approach to journalism and good rapport with U.S. journalists. In the early 1930s he had worked closely on Shanghai English-language publications with the young journalists Harold Isaacs, Tilman Durdin, and Edgar Snow. He understood the importance of image making, applying U.S. media techniques to information control in China.[9] Between 1937 and 1945, Hollington Tong frustrated the U.S. reporters, whom he censored heavily, precisely because of his strong Western credentials.

As Chiang's chief censor, Hollington Tong was outmaneuvered at times by courageous editors. When their papers were closed down by the authorities in Nanjing or Beijing, these editors founded new publications in the foreign concession zones of Shanghai and continued their defense of civil liberties of intellectuals as well as criticism of the Nanjing government's reluctance to confront the Japanese. The most widely known among those who dodged official censorship was Zou Taofen, who was educated at the U.S. missionary college of Yanjing University—an outpost of the journalism school of the University of Missouri. Through publications like *Xin shenghuo* (New life), he mobilized people for the anti-Japanese street demonstrations of the mid-1930s. Moreover, Zou personally led the assault of a new "civil society" on the public sphere. In 1935 he founded the National Salvation Association (Jiuguo Hui), resulting in his arrest—along with five other notables—in the "six gentlemen incident." The event sparked national demonstrations of protest that in turn led to Chiang Kaishek's being kidnapped and turned over to the CCP during the Xi'an incident of December 1936. The experience radicalized Zou, who thereafter developed close ties to the Chinese Communist Party.[10]

Cheng Shewo was more of a political maverick and is less well known today than Zou Taofen. But in the 1930s, Cheng's papers had a wider circulation. He represented a prototype of the scrappy, entrepreneurial editor-publisher whom one finds today in Hong Kong, Taiwan, and overseas Chinese communities. In 1930 Cheng toured the United States. The highlight of his visit was a long stay at Hollington Tong's alma mater, the University of Missouri School of Journalism, where Cheng attended lectures and gave talks on Chinese journalism. The U.S. experience seemed to embolden Cheng. He was one of five founders in 1932 of the League of Civil Rights (Zhongguo Minquan Baozhang Tongmeng) and almost lost his life because of it. In 1934 Cheng was arrested and his papers shut down. Cheng moved his papers from Nanjing and Beijing to Shanghai (and in 1938 to Hong Kong). In the pages of the *Li Bao* (1935–1940), he challenged the Kuomintang on Japanese policy and continued to defend civil liberties. The key to Cheng Shewo's survival as a publisher was consistent patronage from individuals or factions (whom he paid off financially) within the ruling party. During most of the 1930s, Cheng was protected by Ye Chucang and Li Shizeng, cabinet-level officials in the Nanjing government. Yet at the same time, Cheng's papers were staffed by talented young Communists like Sa Kongliao and Zhang Youyu. Like Zou Taofen, Cheng was much more than a mouthpiece or tool. Through their publications and actions in the public sphere, these editors led the challenge to Kuomintang or Communist monopoly of political dialogue.[11]

The historical literature on U.S. press coverage of China in the twentieth century is sparse, consisting mostly of memoirs and a sprinkling of analytical studies. U.S. reporting about the Chinese Communists has received most of the attention, no doubt because of the controversies in the early 1950s concerning "who lost China." In conducting research for an oral history of reporters who covered China for major U.S. dailies during the 1930s and 1940s, I found that the connection between reporters and their Chinese colleagues was crucial to an understanding of the larger context or network within which the U.S. journalist operated.[12] Chinese journalists served in major staff positions and as chief sources for U.S. journalists: Teddy White of *Time* relied upon Cheng Defang; Peter Rand of the *New Yorker* depended upon Yang Chao; Hank Lieberman of the *New York Times* turned to Gong Peng and Qiao Guanhua. Of course the urban elite backgrounds and politically leftist sympathies of their Chinese colleagues and staff colored the kinds of stories U.S. reporters filed during the 1930s and 1940s. There was one place and year when the Chinese influence was especially pronounced: the wartime capital of Hankou in 1938. This was a crucial period in shaping positive first impressions of Chinese Communists and reinforcing the strong anti-Japanese and pro-Chinese nationalist sympathies of U.S. reporters who became the major interpreters of events in China from 1938 to at least 1947. Moreover, views developed in the crucible of Hankou affected the military as well as diplomats like Joseph Stilwell and John Davies, whose subsequent policy actions would shape the postwar debate on U.S.-China policy.

The symbiotic relationship between the Chinese and U.S. press of the 1930s and 1940s is illustrated further by the intertwined careers of F. Mc-

Cracken ("Mac") Fisher and Liu Zunqi. Fisher studied journalism and Chinese at Yanjing University in Beijing from 1931 to 1933. In 1935 Fisher participated with Edgar Snow in the December 9 demonstrations over Chiang Kaishek's Japan policy. By 1938 Fisher was in Hankou as United Press International bureau chief covering the war against Japan. In 1941 he moved to Chongqing, Chiang's wartime capital, and after Pearl Harbor became head of the Office of War Information (OWI), where he recruited and trained most of the U.S. journalists who would cover China for the next twenty years. Fisher's Chinese chief of staff in Chongqing was Liu Zunqi, arguably one of twentieth-century China's most important journalists.[13]

A fluent speaker and writer of English, Liu Zunqi was also a graduate of the journalism school at Yanjing. After graduation in 1932, Liu worked closely in Shanghai with Harold Isaacs and Agnes Smedley on the *China Forum*, a path-breaking, English-language anti-KMT weekly. Liu had been a secret member of the CCP since the late 1920s. Eventually he was arrested in the mid-1930s but managed to escape and make his way to the guerrilla areas in the northwest. In 1941 the party sent him to Chongqing, where he was recruited by Fisher, who had known him at Yanjing but was unaware of Liu's Party membership. From the key position as chief of the Chinese staff, Liu oversaw and facilitated the work of U.S. journalists in China during the war. It was Liu, for example, who arranged for the visits to Yan'an by U.S. journalists in 1944. Like Hollington Tong on the Kuomintang side, Liu applied U.S. techniques and know-how behind the scenes to improve the image of and contact with the Chinese Communists. After the war Liu worked in Shanghai and Hong Kong for the Chinese press. In the 1950s he was one of the founders of the *Guangming ribao* (a national daily) in Beijing. Then in 1957 he was branded a rightist because of his outspokenness and U.S. connections. Not until the late 1970s did Liu resurface as the founding father of China's only English-language daily, *China Daily*, recruiting staff heavily from those who had been rightists in the 1950s and who had worked earlier with U.S. reporters in Shanghai, Hankou, Chongqing, Yan'an, and elsewhere. (It is ironic that Fisher suffered a parallel fate to Liu at the time: Fisher's career was effectively derailed by McCarthyism and questions about earlier familiarity with Liu Zunqi.)[14]

In the 1980s the Sino-U.S. relationship in journalism became close again. With the revival of pre–Cultural Revolution schools at Fudan (Shanghai) and the People's University (Beijing) and the creation of new graduate schools, notably the institutes of journalism at the new Chinese Academy of Social Sciences and Xinhua News Agency, U.S. textbooks and foreign experts were heavily relied upon in the classroom. Extensive exchanges were conducted with major journalist training programs in the United States, beginning with the University of Missouri's journalism school. A national foundation was created to honor the memory and work of journalists Agnes Smedley, Edgar Snow, and Anna Louise Strong. Chinese bookstalls were flooded with trans-lations of U.S. works in all fields—from mysteries, romances, and science fiction to more serious works on psychology and history, and biographies of major journalists like Walter Lippmann. A best-seller was Alvin Toffler's *Future Shock*. The response in the United States was similarly enthusiastic. Deng Xiaoping was named *Time* magazine's man of the year twice (1979 and 1986)—a distinction he shares with Chiang Kaishek. Leading Chinese journalists were invited to study and lecture under the sponsorship of newspapers, universities, and foundations like Luce. Satellite news-report exchanges were instituted, and the number of correspondents in each country (with restrictions relaxed) annually increased until 1989.

A major result in terms of the Chinese press was the sweeping reforms described earlier, most of which went in a Western direction. These reforms, however, never broke the Communist Party's monopoly of the media. Prominent antirightist campaign victims of the 1950s, like Liu Binyan, were restored and able to publish penetrating exposés of the extensive corruption, political and otherwise, of the Party-run bureaucratic system. But by the middle of the decade, Liu was criticized and, when he refused to recant, dismissed from the Party and forced into exile by 1988. Media reform thus paralleled the ups and downs of the popular movement for democracy, from the Democracy Wall demonstrations of 1978–1979 to the Beijing uprising of May 1989.[15]

As in the 1930s, the key to survival in the 1980s for a Chinese journalist or editor was patronage within the ranks of the Party elite. A major figure in the liberalization of the *People's Daily* (for whom Liu Binyan worked) was vice-editor An Gang, who had a direct line to Party Secretary Hu Yaobang. An Gang's Party pedigree ran back to Communist-led New Fourth Army units in his home province of Anhui during the war against Japan (1937–1945). An Gang spearheaded the application of high technology (computerization and new presses) to production at the *People's Daily* as well as the creation of its overseas edition. He founded the paper's most profitable ancillary publications: two weekly magazines focusing on the marketplace and political cartoons, respectively. An Gang also played a major role with Liu Zunqi in the establishment of the *China Daily*, which became a pacesetter in the use of photocopy and computerized production.

In the end, however, An Gang went too far too fast. In 1985 he headed a team that financed the preparation of a two-hour video documentary that contrasted China's economic backwardness to the development of Japan and the West—exactly the same theme as that of "He Shang"(River elegy), which would scandalize the Party elders during summer 1988. After Hu Yaobang fell from power in January 1987, An Gang was mysteriously beaten up on the street. He retired from the leadership of the new commercially successful and self-sufficient newspaper *Jinji ribao* (Economic daily), of which he had been editor-in-chief and founder. By 1989 An Gang had virtually disappeared from the scene.[16]

The major difference between the 1980s and the 1930s–1940s, of course, is the effectiveness of Communist Party controls over the media in the later period. There have been no treaty-port alternatives to state publications in the People's Republic of China; underground opposition media never developed as in Eastern Europe. Journalists like Liu Binyan and An Gang chose to dissent within the system as "establishment intellectuals" (see Chapter 6).[17] Yet in the long run, given the growing fragility of the Communist state in China, this distinction may not be so important. Like Zou Taofen and Cheng Shewo in the 1930s, Liu Binyan and An Gang in the 1980s were perceived by the government as having challenged the state's monopoly over political discourse in the public sphere. Despite setbacks, the confidence-building experience and examples of Liu and An, as well as the plethora of semi-independent publications that flowered for a time in the 1980s, may well do more to transform Chinese politics by the end of the twentieth century than have street demonstrations.

The travails and growing sophistication of the Chinese press during the 1980s was reflected in improving U.S. coverage of China. At the beginning of the decade, U.S. reporting was remarkably homogeneous and derivative of the Chinese view, blaming the Cultural Revolution for all of China's contemporary ills.[18] As in the 1930s and 1940s, U.S. reports on China retained a strong urban bias (in the overestimation of success in population control efforts, for example). By the end of the decade, however, sustained access to reliable sources and experience gave greater variety and depth to the coverage, notably in the work of Orville Schell (feature writer mostly for the *New Yorker* and *Atlantic*), Frank Ching (*Wall Street Journal*), Mike Chinoy (Cable News Network), Nicholas Kristoff and Sheryl WuDunn (*New York Times*), and Jonathan Mirsky (U.S. writer for British publications). Thus, taken as a whole, even television reporting of the events of spring 1989 was comparatively sophisticated. Teams of academic and diplomatic analysts were enlisted for interpretation of events on an unprecedented scale. The results compared favorably, for example, with reporting on Indochina from 1965 to 1975 or coverage of the Persian Gulf crisis in 1990 and 1991.

Finally, just as during the late 1940s, serious divisions over U.S. policy have opened up between Washington policymakers and reporters covering China. Following the events of June 4, 1989, the more experienced journalists in the field have reported more hostilely and cynically on policy paralysis in Beijing and the obsession with security and control of Deng's regime. Their empathy for the suppressed Chinese intellectual resembles that of counterparts like Theodore White and Anna Lee Jacoby in the 1940s. A major diplomatic figure like the U.S. ambassador to China, Winston Lord, has risked a career by breaking with the president over policy. Splits in Congress over most-favored-nation trading status for China and the Chinese government's human rights violations reflect mixed editorial opinion in the regional press. But as Harry Truman reluctantly supported Chiang Kaishek in the late 1940s, George Bush continues lukewarm backing of an unpopular Deng Xiaoping for global geopolitical reasons.

On balance U.S. influence on the Chinese press may be greater than the reverse, given the importance of the ideal of a free press to the Chinese democratic movement since the turn of the century. But it is worth remembering that the U.S. journalists covering China inevitably reflect the prejudices and concerns of their Chinese co-workers. Current features of U.S. press reporting in some ways resemble those of the 1940s: poor coverage of rural conditions, strong coverage of the urban-educated elites, and genuine empathy for political dissenters. What may be more important by the end of the century is the leading contribution of both media to the creation of a civil society in China or a political dialogue and legitimacy outside a state-dominated public sphere. In the 1980s the Chinese and U.S. press demonstrated that the struggles for press freedom in China of the 1930s and 1940s had not been an empty exercise.

The liberalization of the Chinese press in the 1980s and its interaction with U.S. media had a dual effect: It provoked a crackdown yet demonstrated the potential of an unbridled press to mobilize the urban masses against the state and give form to a new body politic. By 1989 even more threatening to the Communist Party's domination of the media was the renewed and growing Chinese journalistic commitment to a higher kind of loyalty: to truth outside the state. Exercise of such rights had led in the United States to Richard Nixon's impeachment in the mid-1970s. For two momentous weeks in mid-May 1989, the Chinese press pursued their Fourth Estate rights—with sadly different results. Tragic as the outcome was in the short run, however, this flexing of journalistic muscle may well have prefigured an even more critical role for the media in the years ahead.

Notes

1. Seth Faison, "The Changing Role of the Chinese Media," in Tony Saich, ed., *Perspectives on the Chinese People's Movement: Spring 1989* (Armonk, N.Y.: M. E. Sharpe, 1990), pp. 144–162; Michael J. Berlin, "Chinese Journalists Cover (and Join) the Revolution," *Washington Journalism Review* (September 1989), pp. 33–37; James C. Thomson, "Jilted Again: The U.S. Media's Courtship with Democracy in China," *Gannett Center Journal* (Fall 1989), pp. 91–103; and Yi Mu and Mark V. Thompson, *Crisis at Tiananmen* (San Francisco: China Books, 1989), esp. pt. 3 on the press.

2. David Strand, "Protest in Beijing: Civil Society and Public Sphere in China," *Problems of Communism*, 29, 3 (May-June 1990), pp. 1–19; and Andrew Nathan, *China's Crisis: Dilemmas of Reform and Prospects for Democracy* (New York: Columbia University Press, 1990). See also Esherick and Wasserstrom (Chapter 2) in this volume.

3. Kenneth Shewmaker, *Americans and Chinese Communists, 1927–45: A Persuading Encounter* (Ithaca: Cornell University Press, 1971).

4. Judy Polumbaum, "Tribulations of China's Journalists After a Decade of Reform," introduction to Chin-Chuan Lee, ed., *Voices of China: Politics and Journalism* (New York: Guilford Press, 1990); Won Ho Chang, *Mass Media in China: The History and the Future* (Ames: Iowa State University Press, 1989).

5. Andrew Nathan, *Chinese Democracy* (Berkeley: University of California Press, 1985).

6. Lee-hsia Hsu Ting, *Government Control of the Press in Modern China, 1900–1949* (Cambridge: Harvard University Press, 1974).

7. Chinese sources summarized in *Wuhan kangzhan shiyao* (Important events in Wuhan during the War of Resistance) (Hubei, 1985). See also Guo Moruo, *Hong Boqu* (Tianjin, 1959), a book of poems celebrating the Hankou spirit.

8. On Hollington Tong and his U.S. background, see his memoir, *Dateline China* (New York: Rockport Press, 1950).

9. An interesting parallel is the strong U.S. influence on Chiang Kaishek's reformed police structure under Dai Li; see Frederic Wakeman, "Policing Modern Shanghai," *China Quarterly* (September 1988), pp. 408–440.

10. Parks Coble, "Chiang Kaishek and the Anti-Japanese Movement in China: Zou Taofen and the National Salvation Association, 1931–37," *Journal of Asian Studies*, 44, 2 (February 1985), pp. 293–310.

11. Cheng Shewo, *Baoxue Zashu* (Journalism miscellany) (Taipei, 1957); *Xinwen Yanjiu Ziliao* (Materials on the study of journalism), vols. 26–29 (Beijing, 1985); *Zhongguo Minquan Baozhang Tongmen* (The Chinese League of Civil Rights) (Beijing, 1979); and Wesley S. Palmer, "Cheng Shewo and Chinese Journalists in the 1920s and 1930s" (M.A. thesis, Arizona State University, 1988).

12. Stephen R. MacKinnon and Oris Friesen, *China Reporting: An Oral History of American Journalism in the 1930s and 1940s* (Berkeley: University of California Press, 1987).

13. MacKinnon and Friesen, *China Reporting*; and F. McCracken Fisher Papers, Arizona State University, Hayden Library.

14. MacKinnon and Friesen, *China Reporting*, pp. 196–199; Harold R. Isaacs, *Re-encounters in China: Notes of a Journey in a Time Capsule* (Armonk, N.Y.: M. E. Sharpe, 1985), pp. 95–110; and E. J. Kahn, Jr., *The China Hands: American Foreign Service Officers and What Befell Them* (New York: Penguin, 1976).

15. Liu Binyan, *A Higher Kind of Loyalty* (New York: Pantheon, 1990).

16. I worked for *People's Daily* for two years (1979–1981) and at the Chinese Academy of Social Sciences in 1985, during which time I had close contact with An Gang. Thereafter I followed An Gang's career through students who worked under him at the *Economic Daily*.

17. Literature on this subject is abundant; the best recent work is Timothy Cheek and Carol Lee Hamrin, eds., *China's Establishment Intellectuals* (Cambridge: Harvard University Press, 1986).

18. The first wave of reporters after 1979 produced books that were remarkably similar in terms of viewpoint and conclusions about China. Two even have the same title. See Fox Butterfield (*New York Times*), *China: Alive in the Bitter Sea* (New York: Times Books, 1982); John Fraser (*Toronto Globe*), *The Chinese: Portrait of a People* (New York: Summit, 1980); David Bonavia (*Times of London*) *The Chinese* (New York: Penguin, 1980); Jay Mathews and Linda Mathews (*Los Angeles Times*), *One Billion: A China Chronicle* (New York: Random House, 1983); and Richard Bernstein (*Time*), *From the Center of the Earth: The Search for Truth About China* (Boston: Little, Brown, 1982).

11

WHAT HAPPENED IN
EASTERN EUROPE IN 1989?

Daniel Chirot

The world knows that in Eastern Europe communism collapsed in 1989, and that the USSR set out on a path that not only promises the end of socialism but threatens its very territorial integrity. But knowing this does not explain why it all happened. Nor are the implications of all these revolutionary events as clear as the immediate, short-run strategic effects that follow from the dissolution of the Warsaw Pact and the Council for Mutual Economic Assistance.

There are many ways of looking at the "revolution of 1989." As with other great revolutionary events—the French Revolution of 1789, the European revolutions of 1848, the Bolshevik Revolution of 1917, or the Chinese Revolution of 1949—economic, political, cultural, and social analyses offer only partial insights because everything was interconnected. Yet no single analysis can entirely absorb all aspects of such cataclysmic events. Even after 200 years, the French Revolution is still a subject for debate, and novel interpretations remain possible. And if the political controversy generated by that revolution two centuries ago has cooled somewhat, for well over a century and a half it remained a burning issue at the center of European and world politics.[1] We should not be surprised, then, if over the next several decades the events of 1989 form the basis of much passionate political and scholarly debate.

This essay was originally prepared for inclusion in Daniel Chirot, ed., *The Crisis of Leninism and the Decline of the Left: The Revolutions of 1989* (Seattle: University of Washington Press, 1991). It is reprinted here with the permission of the University of Washington Press. The author would like to thank Tim McDaniel for his helpful comments on the chapter.

Having said this, I should add that for those of us interested in social change, revolutionary periods offer the most important fields of observation. We cannot, of course, conduct controlled laboratory experiments that suit the needs of our research. But in fact revolutions are large-scale social experiments. Though they are neither tailored to scholarly ends nor by any stretch of the imagination controllable, they are the closest we can come to those major scientific experiments that have shaped our understanding of the physical world. Great revolutions, then, are better windows into how societies operate in the long run than almost any other type of historical event. So, aside from being immediately and keenly interested in the events that have taken place in Eastern Europe in 1989 because these are reshaping the international political order, we also have a fascinating, unexpected, revealing glimpse into how seemingly stable, enduring social systems fail and collapse.

The Underlying Causes

Economic

There is no question that the most visible, though certainly not the only, reason for the collapse of Eastern European communism has been economic. It is not that these systems failed in an absolute sense. No Eastern European country, not even Romania, was an Ethiopia or a Burma, with famine and a reversion to primitive, local subsistence economies. Perhaps several of these economies, particularly the Romanian and to a more limited extent the Polish one, were headed in that direction, but they had very far to fall before reaching such low levels. Other economies, in Hungary, but even more in Czechoslovakia and East Germany, were only failures by the standards of the most advanced capitalist economies. On a world scale these were rich, well-developed economies, not poor ones. The Soviet Union, too, was still a world economic and technological power despite deep pockets of regional poverty and a standard of living that was much lower than its per capita production figures would indicate.[2]

There is no need to go over the defects of socialist economies in detail. These have been explained by the many excellent economists from these countries, particularly the Poles and Hungarians, the two most famous of whom are Wlodzimierz Brus and János Kornai.[3] The main problem is that investment and production decisions were based largely, though not entirely, on political will rather than on domestic or international market pressures. In order to overcome the force of the domestic market, which ultimately meant consumer and producer wishes and decisions, the quantities and prices of goods and services were fixed by administrative order. To exclude external market forces, which might have weakened domestic guidance of the economy, foreign trade with the advanced capitalist world was curtailed and strictly controlled, not only by fiat but also by maintaining nonconvertible currencies. The aim of curtailing the power of market forces was achieved, but an inevitable side effect was that under these conditions it became impossible to measure which firms were profitable and which production processes were more or less efficient. There were no real prices.

As the inefficiencies of socialist economies became evident, it proved impossible to reform them largely because the managers were so closely tied to the ruling political machinery. They were able to lobby effectively to steer investments in their direction, regardless of the efficiency of their enterprises. Success as a manager was measured by the ability to produce more, maintain high employment, and attract politically directed investment, not by producing more efficient, more marketable goods. Equally important was that the very concept of profit as a measure of efficiency was foreign to these managers.[4]

Such systems developed inevitable shortages of desired goods. This was partly because production was so inefficient that it kept the final output of consumer goods lower than it should have been at such high levels of industrialization. It was also because the crude ways of measuring success, in terms of gross output, slighted essential services and spare parts, so that the very production process was damaged by shortages of crucial producer goods and services.

But whereas in some cases it was possible to carry out reform, most notably in agriculture and some services (the outstanding successes were the Chinese decollectivization of agriculture after 1976 and the Hungarians' ability to privatize some services and small-scale agricultural production), in industries the power of the Communist Party and its managers was simply too strong to effect real change. The sincere commitment to full employment and the maintenance of low food prices further damaged efficiency.[5]

None of this would have made the slightest sense without the ideological base of communism. Some critics of Communist economic arrangements have argued that the system was simply irrational. In strict economic terms, it may have been, but that hardly explains its long life. The key is that political will was ultimately the primary determinant of economic action, and this will was based on a coherent worldview developed by Lenin, Stalin, and the other Bolshevik leaders. This view then spread to other Communist leaders and was imposed on about one-third of the world's population.

Lenin was born in 1870, and Stalin in 1878 or 1879. They matured as political beings in their teens and early twenties, when the most advanced parts of the world were in the industrial heartland of Western Europe and the United States—in the Ruhr or in the newly emerging miracles of modern technology in the U.S. Midwest, from Pittsburgh and Buffalo to Chicago. It is not mere coincidence that a century later these areas and others like them, including the major steel and shipbuilding centers of Britain or the coal and steel centers of northern France and Belgium, became giant rust belts with antiquated industries, overly powerful trade unions, and unimaginative, conservative, bureaucratic managers. It has been in such areas, too, that industrial pollution has most ravaged the environment, and where political pressures resistant to free trade and the imposition of external market forces were the fiercest in the advanced countries. But in 1900 these areas were progressive, and for ambitious leaders from a relatively backward country like Russia, they were viable models.

Lenin, Stalin, and all the other Bolshevik intellectuals and leaders (Leon Trotsky, Lev Kamenev, Grigory Zinoviev, Nikolay Bukharin, and so many others) knew that this was what they ultimately had to emulate. They felt, however, that they could make it all happen more quickly and more efficiently by socialist planning than by the random and cruel play of market forces. Despite the inherent inefficiencies of socialism, these astonishing, visionary men—in particular Stalin—actually succeeded. The tragedy of communism was not its failure but its success. Stalin built the institutional framework that, against all logic, forced the Soviet Union into success.[6] By the 1970s the USSR had the world's most advanced late nineteenth-century economy, the world's biggest and best, most inflexible rust belt. It was as if Andrew Carnegie had taken over the entire United States, forced it to become a giant copy of U.S. Steel, and the executives of the same U.S. Steel had continued to run the country into the 1970s and 1980s.

To understand the absurdity of this situation, it is necessary to go back and take a historical look at the development of capitalism. There have been five industrial ages so far. Each was dominated by a small set of leading high technology industries located in the most advanced parts of the industrial world. Each has been characterized by a period of rapid, extraordinary growth and innovation in the leading sectors, followed by slower growth, and finally a period of relative stagnation, overproduction, increasing competition, declining profits, and crisis in the now aging leading sectors. It was precisely on his observations about the rise and fall of the first industrial age that Karl Marx based his conclusions about the eventual collapse of capitalism. But each time, one age has been followed by another as unexpected new technologies have negated all the predictions about the inevitable fall of profits and the polarization of capitalist societies into a tiny number of rich owners and masses of impoverished producers.

The ages, with their approximate dates, have been:

1. the cotton-textile age, lasting from about the 1780s into the 1830s and dominated by Great Britain;
2. the rail and iron age, which went from the 1840s into the early 1870s and was also dominated by Britain;
3. the steel and organic chemistry age, from the 1870s to World War I, during which new industries based on the production and utilization of electrical machinery were developed and in which the U.S. and German economies gained the lead;
4. the age of automobiles and petrochemicals, from the 1910s to the 1970s, during which the United States became the overwhelmingly hegemonic economy;
5. the age of electronics, information, and biotechnology, which began in the 1970s and will certainly run well into the first half of the twenty-first century; in this last age, it is not yet certain which economies will hold sway, though certainly Japan and the European Community are well on their way to replacing the United States.[7]

Transitions have been difficult. Depressions and political turmoil from the 1820s to the 1840s, in the 1870s and 1880s, and in the 1920s and 1930s can be explained, at least in good part, by the difficult effects of the passage from one age to another. World War I—or, more precisely, the mad race for colonies in the late nineteenth century and the European arms race (especially the naval competition between Germany and Britain)—was certainly a function of the shifting economic balance within Europe. World War II resulted from the unsatisfactory outcome of the first war and from the Great Depression of the 1930s. The shocks from the latest transition to the fifth industrial age have been mild by comparison, but the difficulties that attended past transitions produced many predictions about the imminent collapse of capitalism that seemed reasonable at the time.[8] This brief bit of economic history has to be connected to the events of 1989.

The Soviet model, that is, the Leninist-Stalinist model, was based on the third industrial age, the one whose gleaming promises of mighty, smoke-filled concentrations of chemical and steel mills, huge electric-generating plants, and hordes of peasants migrating into new factory boomtowns mesmerized the Bolshevik leadership. The Communist Party of the Soviet Union found out that creating such a world was not easy, especially in the face of stubborn peasant and worker refusal to accept present hardships as the price for eventual industrial utopia. But Stalin persuaded the Party that the vision was so correct that it was worth paying a very high price to attain it. The price was paid, and the model turned into reality.[9]

Later, the same model was imposed on Eastern Europe. Although sheer force ensured that the East Europeans accepted the model, it must also be said that the local Communists, many of whom were only a generation younger than Stalin, had faith in Stalin's vision, particularly those who came from more backward countries. In Romania Nicolae Ceausescu held on to it until his last day in power. It was based on his interpretation of his country's partial, uneven, and highly unsatisfactory drive for industrialization in the 1930s, when he was a young man just becoming an active Communist.[10] To a degree we usually do not realize because the country remained so heavily agricultural, this was Mao's vision for China, too.[11] In 1991 the last practitioner of the Stalinist plan was Ceausescu's contemporary and close ideological ally, Kim Il-Sung of North Korea.

In the Soviet Union, the more backward areas of Eastern Europe, the already partly industrial areas of China (especially on the coast and in Manchuria), and North Korea, the model worked because there were numerous peasants to bring into the labor force; because this type of economy required massive concentrations of investments into huge, centralized firms; and because, after all, the technology was pretty well worked out. Also, producer goods were more important than consumer goods at this stage. It is worth remembering, too, that these were all areas where industrialization had begun before communism, either because of local initiatives, as in Russia or most of Eastern Europe, or because of Japanese colonial investments, as in North Korea and Manchuria. (I should note, in passing, that the model is particularly harmful for very backward economies that have no industrial base to begin with. Thus, whatever successes it may have had in East Asia and Europe, it has produced nothing but disaster when tried in Africa or Indochina.) But if the Stalinist model may be said to have had some success in creating third-age industrial economies (based on steel, organic chemistry, and electricity), it never adapted well to the fourth age of automobiles, consumer electrical goods, and the growth of services to pamper a large proportion of the general population. This is why we were able to make fun of the Soviet model, even in the 1950s and 1960s, because it offered so few luxuries and services. But the Soviets and those who believed in the Stalinist-Leninist model could reply that though they did not cater to spoiled consumers, the basic sinews of industrial and military power, the giant steel mills and power-generating plants, had been built well enough to create an economy almost as powerful as that of the United States.

Alas for the Soviet model, the fifth age turned out to be even more different. Small firms, very rapid change, extreme attention to consumer needs, reliance on innovative thinking—all these were exactly what the Stalinist model lacked. Of course, so did much of the United States' and Western Europe's rust-belt industry (chemicals, steel, autos), but even as they fought rearguard actions to protect themselves against growing foreign competition and technological change, these sectors had to adapt because market pressures were too intense to resist. Their political power was great but, in capitalist societies open to international trade, not sufficient to overcome the world market. In the Soviet case, such industries, protected by the Party, and viewed as the very foundation of everything that communism had built, were able to resist change, at least for another twenty years. That was what the Brezhnev years were—a determined effort to hold on to the late nineteenth-century model the Bolsheviks had worked so hard to emulate. So in the 1970s and 1980s, their relative backwardness went from being amusing to being dangerous. The Soviets and East Europeans (including the Czechs and East Germans) found themselves in the 1980s with the most advanced industries of the late nineteenth and early twentieth centuries: polluting, wasteful, energy intensive, massive, inflexible—in short, huge rust belts.[12]

Of course, it was worse than this. It was not just the adherence to an outdated, rigid model, but all of the well-known failures of socialism that prevented adequate progress. The strains of keeping out the world market, of excluding knowledge about what was going on in the more successful capitalist world, became more and more difficult. It also threatened to intensify backwardness. What had been possible in the early stages of communism, when the leadership was fresh and idealistic about the possibilities of creating a more perfect world, became increasingly problematic with the growing awareness and cynicism about the model's failure.

But the Soviet and East European leaders in the Brezhnev years were very aware of their mounting problems. Much of their time was spent trying to come up with solutions that would nevertheless preserve the key elements of Party rule, Soviet power, and the protection of the new ruling class's power and privilege. The Soviets urged their East European dependencies to overcome their problems by plunging into Western markets. That was the aim of détente. China, of course, followed the same path after 1978. This meant borrowing to buy advanced technology and then trying to sell to the West to repay the debts. But as we now know, the plan did not work. The Stalinist systems were too rigid. Managers resisted change, using their political clout to force ever greater investments into obsolete firms and production processes. In some cases, most notably Poland and Hungary, foreign loans started to be used simply to purchase consumer goods to make people happier, to shore up the crumbling legitimacy of regimes that had lost what youthful vigor they had once possessed and were now viewed simply as tools of a backward occupying power. This worked until the bills came due and prices had to be raised. Societies with little or no experience with free markets responded to price increases with political instability. This was truest in Poland, but it became a potential problem in Hungary (and China) because it created growing and conspicuous social inequities between the small class of new petty entrepreneurs and the large portion of the urban population still dependent on the socialist sector.[13] (Kornai and others have explained why the partial freeing of the market in economies of shortage creates quasi-monopolistic situations favoring the rapid accumulation of profits by those entrepreneurs able to satisfy long-repressed, immense demand.)[14]

What had seemed at first to be a series of sensible reforms proved to be the last gasp of European communism. The reforms did not eliminate the rigidities of Stalinism, but they spread further cynicism and disillusionment, exacerbated corruption, and opened the Communist world to a vastly increased flow of Western capitalist ideas and standards of consumerism. They also created a major debt problem. In this situation, the only East European leader who responded with perfect consistency was Ceausescu: He reimposed strict Stalinism. But neither Romania's principled Stalinism, Hungary's semi-reformism, nor Poland's inconsistency and hesitation worked.[15]

Political and Moral Causes of Change

Although economic problems certainly contributed to the downfall of communism, the changing moral and political climate of Eastern Europe was the primary catalyst of the destruction. There is no better way to approach this topic than by using the old concept of legitimacy. Revolutions only occur when elites and some significant portion of the general population—particularly intellectuals, but also ordinary people—have lost confidence in the moral validity of their social and political system.

Never before in advanced industrial countries, except at the end of major, catastrophic wars, has the basic legitimacy of the system collapsed. And if some serious questions were raised in Germany after World War I, France in 1940, or Germany and Japan in 1945, no successful revolutions occurred there. It would be laughable to claim that Eastern Europe's economic crisis in the 1980s approached such levels of massive crisis as those brought about by utter defeat in international war. In times of peace and relative stability in societies with a strong sense of their nationhood and with functioning infrastructures, police forces, armies, and governments, to have had such revolutionary situations developing in the absence of foreign invaders or international crises and without precipitating civil wars, famines, or even depressions would be unprecedented. No mere recitation of economic problems can provide sufficient explanation.

To see how this loss of legitimacy occurred, it is necessary to go back to the beginning. In the mid- to late 1940s, at least among cadres and a substantial number of young idealists, communism had a considerable degree of legitimacy, even where it had been imposed by force, as in all of Eastern Europe. After all, capitalism seemed to have performed poorly in the 1930s, the liberal European democracies had done little to stop Hitler until it was too late, and Stalin appeared to be a leader who had saved the Soviet Union. The claim that Marxism-Leninism was the "progressive," inevitable wave of the future was not so far-fetched. In fact, many intellectuals throughout Europe, East and West, were seduced by these promises.[16] In the Soviet Union itself, as in China after 1949, communism benefited from the substantial nationalist accomplishments it had to its credit. Foreigners had been defeated, national greatness reasserted, and for all of the problems faced by these regimes, there was clear economic growth and extraordinary progress.[17]

The repressions, terror, and misery of life in the early 1950s soured some believers, but after Stalin's death, reform seemed possible, and after all, the claims made about rapid urbanization, industrialization, and the spread of modern health and educational benefits to the population were true. Not 1956, when the Hungarian revolution was crushed, but 1968 was the decisive turning point. That was when the implications of the Brezhnev policy became clear: Fundamental political reform was not going to be allowed. It must be said in Brezhnev's defense that what happened in 1989, both in Eastern Europe and in China, has proved that in a sense he and his policy of freezing reform were perfectly correct. To have done otherwise would have brought about an earlier demise of communism. Economic liberalization gives new hope for political liberalization to the growing professional and bureaucratic middle classes and to the intelligentsia. It further increases the appeal of liberal economic ideas as well as of democracy. The demand for less rigid central control obviously threatens the Party's monopoly on power.

Whatever potential Communist liberalism may have had in the Prague spring of 1968, the way in which it was crushed and the subsequent, gradual disillusion with strictly economic reform in Hungary and Poland in the 1970s brought to an end the period in which intellectuals could continue to hope about the future of communism. But this was not all. The very inflexibility of Communist economies, the unending shortages, the overwhelming bureaucratization of every aspect of life created a general malaise. The only way to survive in such systems was through corruption, the formal violation of the rules. That in turn left many, perhaps almost all, of the managerial and professional class open to the possibility of blackmail and to a pervasive sense that they were living a perpetual lie.[18]

Then, too, the original imposition of the Stalinist model had created tyranny, the arbitrary rule of the few. One of the characteristics of all tyranny, whether ideological and visionary, as in this case, or merely self-serving and corrupt, is that it creates the possibility for the dissemination and reproduction of petty tyranny at every level. With tyrants at the top, entire bureaucracies become filled with tyrants below, all behaving arbitrarily and out of narrow self-interest. The tyrants at the top cannot hope to enforce their will unless they have subservient officials, and to buy that subservience they have to allow their underlings to enjoy the fruits of arbitrary power. In any case, such tyranny becomes the only model of proper, authoritative behavior.

This is one of the recent explanations given for the widespread, almost uncontrolled spread of purges in the USSR in the 1930s and of course for the ravages of the Chinese Cultural Revolution decade from 1966 to 1976. Once the model is set from the top, imitating that behavior becomes a way of ensuring survival for officials. But even beyond this, a tyrannical system gives opportunities for abuse that do not otherwise exist, and lower-level officials use this to further their own, narrow ends. (This is not meant to suggest that in some way the tyrants who ruled such systems, and their immediate followers, can be absolved of responsibility for the abuses; it does imply that the way in which tyrannies exercise power is necessarily deeply corrupt.)[19]

Daily exposure to petty tyranny, which at the local level rarely maintains the ideological high ground that may have inspired a Lenin, Stalin, Mao, or even a Ceausescu, also breeds gradual disgust with corruption and the dishonesty of the whole system. In the past, peasants subjected to such petty tyranny may have borne it more or less stoically (unless it went too far), but educated urbanites living in a highly politicized atmosphere where there were constant pronouncements about the guiding ideological vision of fairness, equality, and progress could not help but react with growing disgust.[20]

In that sense, the very success of communism in fostering a more urban, more educated, more aware population also created the potential for disintegration. The endless corruption, the lies, the collapse of elementary social trust, the petty tyranny at every level—these were aspects of life less easily tolerated by the new working and professional classes than they might have been by peasants. (This remains, of course, the advantage of the Chinese Communists; they can still rely on a vast reservoir of peasant indifference and respect for authority as long as agriculture is not resocialized.)[21]

The whole movement toward the creation of alternate social institutions, free of the corruption and dishonesty of the official structures, was the great ideological innovation of what began to emerge in Poland in the 1970s and 1980s as the movement toward the creation of a "civil society." Traditional revolutionary resistance, taking to the streets, planning covert military actions, and assassinations might be fruitless because they could only bring down a heavy military intervention by the Soviets. But simply by beginning to turn away from the state, by refusing to take it seriously, Polish and then other Central European intellectuals exposed the shallowness of communism's claims and erased what little legitimacy Communist regimes still had. It is because of his early understanding of this fact and his excellent descriptions of how this new ideology grew in Central Europe that Timothy Garton Ash has justly earned his fame.[22]

Certainly, in the Soviet Union all these forces were at work, too, but the patriotism engendered by superpower status (though it has turned out that this was largely Russian not "Soviet" pride and patriotism), the sheer size of the military, and the long history of successful police terror and repression kept the situation under better control than in much of Central Europe. Yet combined with the slow erosion of legitimacy, there was also the fundamental economic problem alluded to above, namely, the failure to keep up with the rapidly emerging fifth industrial age in Western Europe, the United States, and, most astonishingly for the Soviets, in East Asia.[23]

There is no doubt that in the mid-1980s, after Solidarity seemed to have been crushed in Poland, with the Soviets massacring Afghan resistance fighters, with Cuban troops successfully defending Angola, with Vietnam controlling all of Indochina, it seemed to the rest of the world that Soviet military might was insurmountable in countries where the Soviet system had been imposed. But underneath, the rot was spreading. So the question is not, "What was wrong with Eastern Europe?" or "Why was communism so weak?" Every specialist and many casual observers knew perfectly well what was wrong. But almost none guessed that what had been a slowly developing situation for several decades might take such a sudden turn for the worse. After all, the flaws of socialist economic planning had been known for a long time. Endemic corruption, tyranny, arbitrary brutality, and the use of police force to maintain Communist parties in power were hardly new. None of these answers the question, "Why 1989?" Almost all analysts thought that the Soviet system would remain more or less intact in the USSR itself and in Eastern Europe for decades more. To understand why this was not to be requires a shift in analysis from a discussion of general trends to a review of some specific events in the 1980s.

The Events of the 1980s

No single event can explain what happened, but if there was a series of developments that began to unravel the entire system, it has to be located in the interaction between events in Poland in the early 1980s and a growing perception by the Soviet leadership that their own problems were becoming very serious.

As late as 1987 and throughout most of 1988, most specialists felt that the Soviet elite did not understand the severity of their economic situation. Although Gorbachev and many of the Moscow intellectuals almost certainly did, there was some question about the lesser cadres and even many of the top people in the government. But as Gorbachev's mild reforms failed to have a beneficial impact, as the original influence of his policy of openness, encouragement, and anti-alcoholism ran into sharply diminishing returns, the

Soviet economy began to slip back into the stagnation of the late Brezhnev years.[24]

Serious as rising discontent in the Soviet Union might have seemed to Gorbachev, this would not have been enough had it not been for the direct military implications of the Soviet's inability to keep up with the developments of the fifth industrial age. If the Soviet nuclear deterrent was unquestionably safe and effective in preventing any possibility of a frontal attack by the United States, the growing gap between Western and Soviet computer and electronic technology threatened to give NATO (and ultimately Japan) a striking advantage in conventional weapons. This is almost certainly why the Soviets were so worried about the "Star Wars" antiballistic missile system not simply because the illusion of an effective defense was likely to unbalance the nuclear arms race. Pouring billions into this kind of research was likely to yield important new advantages in lesser types of electronic warfare that could be applied to conventional air and tank battles. This would nullify the Soviet's numerical advantage in troops and machines and would threaten Soviet military investments throughout the world.[25]

Given the long-standing recognition by the major powers that nuclear war was really out of the question, a growing advantage by the capitalist powers in electronic warfare had the potential to transform any future local confrontation between Western and Soviet allies into a repetition of the Syrian-Israeli air war of 1982. From the Soviet point of view, the unbelievable totality of Israel's success was a warning of future catastrophes, even if Israel's land war in Lebanon turned out to be a major failure.[26]

There was one other, chance event that encouraged change in the Soviet Union by revealing to the leadership the extent of the country's industrial ineptitude: the 1986 nuclear plant accident at Chernobyl. Unlucky as the catastrophe was, it served to confirm what was already suspected. Many such massive industrial and environmental accidents had happened before in the Soviet Union, with little effect on Soviet policy. But on top of everything else in the late 1980s, Chernobyl served to galvanize Gorbachev and his advisers.[27]

Meanwhile, in Eastern Europe, the Communist orthodoxy imposed under Brezhnev was seriously threatened in Poland. Rising discontent there had made Poland ungovernable by the mid-1980s. It seemed that Hungary would soon follow. Economic reforms were not working, the population was increasingly alienated, and though there was no outward sign of immediate revolt, Wojciech Jaruzelski's regime had no idea of how to bring the situation back under sufficient control to be able to carry out any measures that stood a chance of reversing the economic decline and regaining the trust (rather than the mere grudging and cynical acceptance) of the population.[28]

In retrospect, then, the events in Poland in the late 1970s, from the election of a Polish pope, which galvanized the Poles and created the massive popular demonstrations that led to the creation of Solidarity, to the military coup that seemed to destroy Solidarity, had set the stage for what was to happen. But the slow degeneration of the situation in Poland, or in all of Eastern Europe, would not have been enough to produce the events of 1989 had it not been for the Soviet crisis. Nonetheless, had there been no breakdown of authority in Poland, and a looming, frightening sense of economic crisis and popular discontent in Hungary and probably in the other Eastern European countries, too, the Soviets would certainly have tried to carry out some reforms without giving up their European empire. The two aspects of the crisis came together, and this is why everything unraveled so quickly in the late 1980s.[29]

Gorbachev must have realized that it was only a matter of time until there was an explosion—a bread riot leading to a revolution in Poland or a major strike in Hungary that would oblige the government to call out the army. The problem was that neither the Polish nor Hungarian army was particularly reliable. The special police could always be counted on, but if they were overwhelmed, it would be necessary to call in Soviet troops. This the Soviet economy could not bear if it was also to reform itself enough to begin to meet the challenges of the fifth industrial age, especially if this involved increasing trade and other contacts with the advanced capitalist countries.

I believe that some time in 1988 Gorbachev decided that it was necessary to head off the danger before it was too late to prevent a crisis.[30] I cannot prove this because the documentation is not available, but I am almost certain that because of this decision, in discussions with the Poles there emerged the plan to allow partially free elections and the reopening of talks with Solidarity. The aim would be to relegitimize the regime and give it enough breathing room to carry out economic reforms without risking strikes and massive civil disobedience. The idea of roundtable talks between Solidarity and the regime were proposed in a televised debate between Lech Walesa and a regime representative on November 30, 1988. The talks themselves began on February 6, 1989.[31] They did not work. Everyone—Gorbachev, the Communist parties of Eastern Europe, foreign specialists, and intelligence services in NATO and the Warsaw Pact—vastly underestimated the degree to which the moral bankruptcy of communism has destroyed any possibility of relegitimizing it.

There was something else, too, an event whose import was not fully appreciated in the West and that remains almost unmentioned. In January 1989, Gorbachev tried an experiment. He pulled almost all of the Soviet army out of Afghanistan. The United States and the Pakistani army expected this to result in the rapid demise of the Communist regime there. To everyone's surprise, it did not. I think that this might have been an important card for Gorbachev. He could point to Afghanistan when his conservative opponents, and especially his military, questioned his judgment. Afghanistan was proof that the Soviets could partially disengage without suffering catastrophe, and that in some cases, it might even be better to let local Communists handle their own problems. I suspect that a rapid victory by the anti-Communist guerrillas in Afghanistan would have slowed progress in Eastern Europe, if not ended it entirely.[32]

We know how rapidly event followed event. Despite the patently unfair arrangements for the Polish election designed to keep the Party in power, the electorate refused to tolerate Communist control any longer, and Party rule collapsed. Because the Soviets had agreed to the process and wanted at almost any cost to avoid a war of invasion, they let Poland go. Once it became obvious that this was happening, the Hungarians set out on the same path.[33]

Then, partly out of a well-timed sense of public relations, just before George Bush's visit, the Hungarians officially opened their border with Austria. In fact, the border had no longer been part of any iron curtain for a long time, but this move gave thousands of vacationing East Germans the idea that they could escape to the West. We know that this set off a mass hysteria among East Germans who had given up hope of reform and whose demoralization and disgust with their system led hundreds of thousands to want to flee. They rushed to West German embassies in Budapest and Prague and began demonstrating in East Germany, particularly in Leipzig and Dresden.[34]

The failure of communism in East Germany, in many ways, represents the ultimate failure. Here was a country that was not poor, where there were 200 automobiles for every 1,000 inhabitants, and where for years Western, particularly West German, sympathizers had said that communism was working by producing a more communal, more kindly Germany than the harsh, market-driven, materialistic West German Federal Republic. It was just wishful thinking.[35]

It is known that head of state Erich Honecker ordered repressive measures. During summer 1989, Chinese officials had visited East Berlin to brief the East Germans on how to crush prodemocracy movements. But during his early October visit to East Germany, Gorbachev had publicly called for change and let it be known that the Soviets would not intervene to stop reform.[36]

By October, ambulances were readied to cart away the thousands of dead and injured in Leipzig and perhaps Dresden that were sure to be produced by the crackdown. This was prevented. Most accounts credit a local initiative in Leipzig led by the conductor Kurt Mazur, though the central Party machinery, taken in hand by Egon Krenz, also played a pacifying role. It is likely that an appeal was made to the Soviets and that the local Soviet military commander said he would not intervene. Knowing this, the East German Communist Party simply overthrew Honecker rather than risk physical annihilation.[37]

East Germany was no China, despite Honecker's claim that it would be. It had no reserve of ignorant, barely literate peasant boys to bring into the breach, and its economy was far too dependent on the West German connection to risk a break. So once repression was abandoned, the system fell apart in a few weeks. With East Germany crumbling, the whole edifice of Communist rule in Eastern Europe simply collapsed. On November 9 the Berlin Wall was opened. It was no longer possible to maintain it when the government of East Germany was losing control over its population, and the rate of flight was increasing at such a rapid rate.

East Germany was always the key Soviet position in Europe.[38] It was on the internal German border that the cold war began, and it was there that the military might of the two superpowers was concentrated. When the Soviets abandoned the East German hard-liners, there was no hope anywhere else in Eastern Europe. The Bulgarians followed in order to preserve what they could of the Party, and the day after the Berlin Wall was opened, Todor Zhivkov resigned after thirty-five years in power. This was surely no coincidence. A week later, demonstrations began in Prague, and within ten days, it was over. Only Ceausescu resisted.[39]

Enough is now known about Ceausescu's Romania so that it is unnecessary to give much background. Only three points must be made. Ceausescu himself still held on to the Stalinist vision. Aside from the possible exception of Albania (which began to change in spring 1990),[40] there was only one other Communist country in which the model was so unquestioned: North Korea. In fact, Ceausescu and Kim Il-Sung long considered themselves close allies and friends, and their style of rule had many similarities. Yet in Romania, and probably in North Korea as well, this model turned sour about two decades ago, and pursuing it meant economic stagnation, a growing gap between reality and ideology, and the progressive alienation of even the most loyal cadres.[41]

Second, Romania was the most independent of the Warsaw Pact European countries and so felt itself less dependent on Soviet support. But though this brought considerable legitimacy to the Romanian regime in the 1970s, when partial independence was thought to be grounds for hope, by the late 1980s that hope had failed, and intellectuals as a growing number of ordinary urban people alike had noticed that the Soviet Union had become more progressive than Romania.[42] In southern Romania, they listened to Bulgarian television and radio, and when they heard that even there (for the Romanians, Bulgaria has always been a butt of jokes as a backward, thick-headed, peasant nation) there were reforms, it must have had a considerable impact. In the north and west, Romanians could pick up the Hungarian and Yugoslav media and so be informed about what was going on elsewhere. In the east, of course, they had the example of the Soviet Union and of Romanian-speaking Soviet Moldavia, where, for the first time since the 1940s, people were freer to demonstrate than in Romania itself. I should add that aside from broadcasts from these neighboring countries, Radio Free Europe, too, played a major role in educating Romanians about what was going on elsewhere in Eastern Europe. The point is that, again unlike China, it proved impossible to keep the news about the world out of the reach of the interior.

Finally, and this is much less known than other aspects of Romania's recent history, even at its height, the Ceausescu regime relied very heavily on the fear of Soviet invasion to legitimize itself. There was always the underlying assumption that if there were too much trouble, the Soviet tanks would come in, and was it not better to suffer a patriotic Romanian tyrant than another episode of Soviet occupation? Once it became clear, in 1989, that the Soviets were not going to march, the end was in sight. It was only because Ceausescu himself was so out of touch with reality, and because he had so successfully destroyed his Communist Party by packing it with relatives and sycophants (like Kim Il-Sung) that no one told him the truth, and he was unable to manage the more peaceful, gradual, and dignified exit of his Bulgarian colleague, Zhivkov.[43]

So in the end communism collapsed. The ramifications are far from clear, and there is no way of knowing how things will develop in the Soviet Union. But come what may in the USSR, it is certain that the Soviet empire in Eastern Europe is dead and that there are almost no foreseeable circumstances that would make the Soviet army invade any of its former dependencies. We cannot be sure what directions the various revolutions of Eastern Europe will take, though it is safe to predict that there will be important differences from country to country. On the whole, it is also possible to be somewhat optimistic about the future of Eastern Europe, or at least its northern, "Central European" parts, if not necessarily of the Balkans and the Soviet Union. Why this is so I leave to my concluding remarks, in which I try to draw together some of the lessons Eastern Europe has taught us about revolution and social change in general.

On the Causes of Revolution in Advanced Societies

Eastern Europe and the Traditional Causes of Revolution

Most widely accepted sociological models of revolution provide limited help in explaining what happened in Eastern Europe in 1989. There was no sudden fall in well-being after a long period of improvement. If the Polish, Hungarian, and Romanian economies were deteriorating (at very different rates), the East German and Czechoslovak ones were not yet causing immediate problems. People felt deprived when they compared their lives to those available in Western Europe, but this had been true for well over three decades. In Poland, as a matter of fact, the sharpest period of economic deterioration was in the early 1980s, and though the situation had not improved much since then, it could be assumed that people were getting used to it.[44]

In Poland there was a prolonged period of protest marked by open explosions in 1956, 1968, 1970, 1976, and of course 1980–1981. As time advanced, Poles learned to organize better and more effectively. But this gradual mobilization and organization seemed to have been decisively broken by the military seizure of power. In fact, there is good evidence that the Communist Party and police had learned even more from the long series of protests than the protesters themselves and had become very adept at handling trouble with just the right level of violence. Certainly in the early 1980s, the Jaruzelski regime was able to impose peacefully a whole series of price increases that in the past had provoked massive, violent uprisings.[45]

Only in Hungary was there much open mobilization of protest in the late 1980s, and that only in the last couple of years. Much of it was over ecological and nationalist issues that did not take the form of direct antiregime activity. In fact, the Communists even supported some of this activity.[46] None of the other countries had much open dissent. At most, in Czechoslovakia a few, seemingly entirely isolated intellectuals had organized themselves, but they had no followers. In East Germany the Protestant churches had supported some limited draft protests and a small peace movement, but the regime had never been directly threatened. In Bulgaria only a tiny handful of intellectuals ever made any claims to protest. In Romania there had been some scattered outbreaks of strikes in the late 1970s and a major riot in one city, Brasov, in 1987, but there, even intellectual protest was muted, rarely going beyond certain restricted literary activities.[47]

The international position of the East European countries was not at stake either. Although in the Soviet Union it is clear that key elites, particularly in the KGB, saw the impending danger to the USSR's international strength, in Eastern Europe no one cared about this kind of issue. None of the elites saw their countries as potentially powerful nations, nor was their national existence threatened by any outsiders except the Soviets. And that threat, present since 1945, was now so highly attenuated as to be almost absent. That the Soviets were unpopular in Eastern Europe was a given, and a very old one, but there was no new risk of further intervention or damage because of these countries' weakness.[48]

Perhaps, however, the debt crisis in Poland and Hungary (and in Romania, because it had provoked such harsh and damaging countermeasures by Ceausescu) was the equivalent of visible international failure that exposed the incapacity of the regimes. But though this remained severe in Poland and Hungary in the late 1980s, elsewhere the problem was not particularly acute.[49]

Nor can a very strong case be made for the rise of an economically powerful new class that was fighting to gain political power. Political and economic power was firmly in the hands of what the Yugoslavian critic Milovan Djilas had called the "New Class," but that class, the professional party cadres, had been in charge for four decades, and it seemed neither highly dissatisfied nor in any way revolutionary. The leadership of the revolutions, if there was any, was in the hands of a few intellectuals who represented no particular class.[50]

Poland, of course, was different. There, an alliance between the Catholic church, the unionized working class, and dissident intellectuals was very well organized, and it had almost taken power in 1980. But the days of Solidarity seemed to have passed, and the regime reasserted visible control. Virtually none of the Polish opposition thought it had much chance of success in an open, violent confrontation. So even in Poland, this was not a traditional revolution. The opportunity for that had passed with the successful imposition of martial law.[51]

What happened was that the moral base of communism had vanished. The elites had lost confidence in their legitimacy. The intellectuals, powerless as they seemed to be, disseminated this sense of moral despair and corruption to the public by their occasional protests and veiled commentaries, and the urban public was sufficiently well educated and aware to understand what was going on. The cumulative effect of such a situation, over decades, cannot be underestimated. Those who had had hope in the 1940s or 1950s were replaced by those who had never had hope and who had grown up knowing that everything was a lie. Educated youths, not just in the universities but those who had only gone through high school, knew enough about the rest of the world to know that they had been lied to, that they had been cheated, and that their own leaders did not believe the lies.[52]

What took everyone by surprise was the discovery that the situation was not all that different in the Soviet Union. Nor could anyone foresee the kind of panicked realism, combined with astounding flexibility and willingness to compromise, shown by Gorbachev. In the end, this was the reason that all of this happened in 1989 rather than in the 1990s, but sooner or later, it would have happened anyway.

Eastern Europe Compared to Other Modern Revolutions

This brings up a serious issue. It has long been assumed that modern methods of communication and the awesome power of tanks, artillery, and air power would prevent the kind of classical revolution that has shaken the world so many times since 1789. Even relatively inefficient regimes, such as the Russian autocracy or the KMT in China, fought successfully against revolution until their armies were decisively weakened by outside invaders. In China's case, it took the Communists two decades to build the strong army that finally won power for them, and they probably would have failed had it not been for the Japanese invasion.[53]

Many utterly corrupt, weak African, Asian, and Latin American regimes have held on to power for a long time with little more than mercenary armies whose loyalties are purchased by allowing them to loot their own countries. This is what goes on in, for example, Burma, Guatemala, and Zaire. Cases where such regimes were overthrown show that it takes long years of guerrilla organization and warfare to carry out revolutions, and then the chances of success are slim. If revolutions occurred in Fulgencio Batista's Cuba and the Somozas' Nicaragua, in Uganda Idi Amin held on until he foolishly provoked Tanzania into attacking him. If "Baby Doc" Duvalier was frightened into leaving office in Haiti, even by 1991 it was not clear that the Duvalier system had been removed.[54]

Finally, even anticolonial wars, when the overwhelming majority of populations have sympathized with revolutionary movements, have been long, bloody events when the colonizers have chosen to fight back, as did the Dutch in Indonesia, the French in Indochina and Algeria, or the British in Kenya and Malaya (where, however, the Malay population rallied to the British side against the Chinese revolutionaries). A particularly startling case was the Bangladesh war, when massive popular opposition to Pakistani rule still needed help from an Indian military invasion to get rid of the Pakistani army.[55] Only internal military coups, as when the Ethiopian or, much earlier, the Egyptian monarchies were removed, seem to make for relatively easy revolutions.[56]

But none of these types of revolutions fit what happened in Eastern Europe. Even if the Romanian case is included, the total level of bloodshed was minuscule compared to other revolutions. There were certainly no military coups. In Romania there was almost certainly cooperation between the army and the population but no direct coup, and that was the only case where the army was involved at all. But compared to any African, Latin American, or almost any non-Communist Asian dictatorship, the East European Communist regimes were overwhelmingly strong. They had large, effective, loyal secret police forces; an abundance of tanks and soldiers led by well-trained (though not necessarily enthusiastic) officers; excellent internal communications; and no threat of external, hostile invasion. Only in Romania was the army thoroughly alienated. Again, we are left with the same explanation: utter moral rot.

Few observers have noticed a startling parallel between events in Eastern Europe in 1989 and in Iran in 1979. There, too, the shah should have been stronger. But despite numerous deaths in the final days, and months of rioting before the shah's departure in January, many were taken by surprise by the overwhelming lack of legitimacy of the regime. Even the newly prosperous middle classes and the young professionals, who had much to lose if the shah were overthrown, failed to back him.[57] Although this is not a suitable place to discuss Iranian society and politics in the 1960s and 1970s, it is evident that the rapid modernization and urbanization of the society helped its intellectuals disseminate their feelings of disgust about the shah's regime, with its empty posturing, lies, torturers, corruption, and lack of redeeming moral values.

We can wonder, of course, to what extent the rising intellectual and professional classes in urban France in 1787 to 1789 felt the same way about the French monarchy, church, and aristocracy, and the extent to which such feelings played a decisive role in unleashing that revolution. We know that in Petrograd and Moscow from 1915 to 1917, whatever the level of popular misery, the professional and middle classes felt a good bit of disgust at the corruption and lack of morality at the imperial court.

The lesson may be that we need to combine some Marxist notions of class with an understanding of John Rawls's theory of justice as fairness in order to understand what happened in Eastern Europe. Economic modernization did, indeed, produce a larger middle class (not in the sense of bourgeois ownership, of course, but in the cultural and educational sense, as well in its style of life). That class was in some ways quite favored in Communist regimes. But because of the flaws of the socialist system of economic management, it remained poorer than its West European counterpart and even seemed to be falling further behind by the 1980s. This is the Marxist—or class and material basis—of what happened.

But what is more important is that, almost by definition, the educated middle classes are well informed and can base their judgments about morality on a wider set of observations than those with very limited educations. The artistic and literary intellectuals who address their work to these middle classes in a modern society helped them understand and interpret the immorality of the system and so played a major role. They needed receptive audiences, but it was their work that undid Eastern European communism.

Without the social changes associated with the economic transformations that took place in Eastern Europe from 1948 to 1988, these revolutions would not have taken place. But it was not that new classes were striving for power so much as that a growing number saw through the lies on which the whole system was based. That is what utterly destroyed the will to resist on the part of those in power. Once these conditions were set, the massive popular discontent with material conditions, particularly among the working classes in the giant but stagnating industries that dominated Communist economies, could come out into the streets and topple these regimes.

Models and Morals

In exploring the revolutions in Eastern Europe, we should keep three points in mind. First, the fundamental reason for the failure of communism was that the utopian model it proposed was obviously not going to come into being. Almost everything else could have been tolerated if the essential promise were on its way to fulfillment. But once it was clear that the model was out of date and its promise increasingly based on lies, its immorality became unbearable. Perhaps in the past, when other ideologically based models failed to deliver their promises, systems could still survive because the middle classes and the intellectuals were present in smaller numbers. But in advanced societies, the original economic problems spelled out above, the absurdity of basing a whole social system on an outdated industrial age, was more than an economic mistake. It undermined the whole claim to scientific validity that lay at the very heart of Marxism-Leninism.

Second, much of the standard of morality that created such a revolutionary situation in Eastern Europe was based on the middle classes' interpretation of what was going on in Western Europe. This is one reason why, despite all the economic and political troubles that are sure to accumulate in the near future in Eastern Europe, there is some reason for optimism. Western Europe is no longer the warlike set of competing imperialistic powers it was when the Eastern Europeans first began to look at the West as their model in the nineteenth century and through 1939. All of Western Europe is democratic, its various countries cooperate well with one another, and on the whole they have abandoned their imperialistic pretensions. This means that, as a model, Western Europe is a far healthier place than it was in the past. It does not mean, however, that all future revolutionary intellectuals and scandalized middle classes will look to Western Europe or to the United States as their model. After all, the Iranians looked to Islam, and it is only because Eastern Europe has long been so close to Western Europe that it automatically looks in that direction.

Third, we must come to realize that in the twenty-first century there will still be economic problems, political instability, and revolutions. But more than ever, the fundamental causes of revolutionary instability will be moral. The urban middle and professional classes, the intellectuals and those to whom they most directly appeal, will set the tone of political change. Regimes to which they do not accord legitimacy because these regimes are seen as unfair and dishonest will be shaky. When these classes can be persuaded to defend their own narrow material interests, when they accept immoral and unfair behavior, then regimes, no matter how corrupt, will be safe. But it would be foolish for regimes that are defending essentially unjust social systems to rely too much on the continued acquiescence of their middle classes and intellectuals.

But many of us who study social change must be reminded that we barely know how to study moral perceptions and legitimacy. We have been so busy observing material changes—which are, after all, more easily measured and perceived—that we do not know where to look to sense the moral pulse of key classes and intellectuals. In some ways, the lesson of Eastern Europe has this to offer, too: Sometimes literature written for what seems to be a handful of people is a better measure of the true state of mind of a society than public opinion polls, economic statistics, or overt political behavior.

An alternative "civil society," places where people could interact freely and without government interference, where they could turn their backs on the Party-state's corruption, was in the making in Eastern Europe before 1989. This alternative civil society was the creation of intellectuals, novelists, playwrights, poets, historians, and philosophers like Vaclav Havel, Miklos Haraszti, Adam Michnik, György Konrad, and hundreds of other, less famous ones. In a sense, in their literature and pamphlets, in their small discussion circles, they imagined a future that most of their people could only dimly perceive and that hardly anyone believed possible.

Vladimir Tismaneanu, in an article entitled "Eastern Europe: The Story the Media Missed," points out that most Western observers never grasped the significance of this creation of an alternative "civil society."[58] That is not quite correct because even before 1989 those most closely following the intellectual life of East-Central Europe were aware of what was going on and were writing about it. Garton Ash was the best known, but a few other scholars saw it, too.[59] On the whole, however, most of the specialists on communism were too hard-headed, too realistic, and even too dependent on social science models to take such highly intellectualized discussions seriously. After the fact, it is easy for us to say this. Before the fact, almost none of us saw it.

Notes

1. Because of its second centennial anniversary in 1989 this has been a particularly busy period for the publication of new works on the French Revolution. That the event still generates considerable excitement is shown by the controversies about Simon Schama's hostile critique of the revolution, *Citizens: A Chronicle of the French Revolution* (New York: Knopf, 1988). A more positive evaluation is Eric J. Hobsbawm's *Echoes of the Marseillaise: Two Centuries Look Back on the French Revolution* (New Brunswick: Rutgers University Press, 1990). A lively review essay about recent books on the revolution is Benjamin R. Barber's "The Most Sublime Event," *Nation*, March 12, 1990, pp. 351–360.

2. A review of the condition and prospects for the East European economies can be found in John R. Lampe, ed., "Special Issue on Economic Reform," *Eastern European Politics and Societies*, 2, 3 (Fall 1988). Though the articles in this issue emphasize the region's economic problems, not all are pessimistic, and none predicted the astounding

political changes that were to begin within months of publication. The same is true of a slightly older but still recent review of Eastern Europe's economies, with some comparative chapters on other socialist economies in Ellen Comisso and Laura Tyson, eds., *Power, Purpose, and Collective Choice: Economic Strategy in the Socialist States* (Ithaca: Cornell University Press, 1986). A surprisingly positive account of the Soviet economy published a few years ago by Ed A. Hewett also seemed to soften the nature of the crisis, even though Hewett gave an excellent account of the many problems facing the Soviets. See his *Reforming the Soviet Economy: Equality Versus Efficiency* (Washington, D.C.: Brookings Institution, 1988).

3. Janos Kornai, *Economics of Shortage*, 2 vols. (Amsterdam: North Holland, 1980), and Wlodzimierz Brus, *Socialist Ownership and Political Systems* (London: Allen and Unwin, 1977).

4. The popular resistance to accepting capitalist profits should not, after all, be surprising. Karl Polanyi's seminal work, *The Great Transformation* (Boston: Beacon Press, 1957), showed how difficult it was for the British to accept the notion that market forces should regulate the economy in the early nineteenth century. By now, the capitalist West has had almost two centuries to get used to this dramatic change in the organizing principles of society, and it has only been in the last few decades that resistance to the market has waned in Western Europe. That Eastern Europe, especially the Soviets, should view markets with suspicion is understandable. Among the many discussions of this, Geoffrey Hosking's new book, *The Awakening of the Soviet Union* (Cambridge: Harvard University Press, 1990), is particularly good. He writes, "How many times over the last year or two have I heard Soviet citizens use the word 'speculator' to disparage private traders or co-operatives providing at high prices goods and services seldom available at all in the state sector? This sullen egalitarianism dovetails neatly with the interest of the party-state apparatus in retaining their network of controls and hence their grip on the economy" (p. 132).

5. On China, see Nicholas Lardy, *Agriculture in China's Modern Economic Development* (Cambridge: Cambridge University Press, 1983), pp. 190–221. On Hungary, see Tamas Bauer, "The Hungarian Alternative to Soviet-Type Planning," *Journal of Comparative Economics*, 7, 3 (1983), pp. 304–316. See also Ellen Comisso and Paul Marer, "The Economics and Politics of Reform in Hungary," in Comisso and Tyson, *Power, Purpose, and Collective Choice.*

6. Though the story is now well known, it is worth reviewing the nightmarish quality of this success. For a good account, see the essays in Moshe Lewin, *The Making of the Soviet System* (New York: Pantheon, 1985).

7. The attempt to fit the industrial era into such straightforward stages oversimplifies its economic history. Walt W. Rostow identifies nine "trend periods" in his *World Economy: History and Prospect* (Austin: University of Texas Press, 1978), pp. 298–348. My industrial ages group together his first and second periods (1790–1848); take his third period (1848–1873) as a distinct age; group together his fourth and fifth periods (1873–1920) and his sixth, seventh, and eighth periods (1920–1972); and consider his ninth (starting in 1972) as the beginning of a new industrial age. I rely more on the history of technology provided by David S. Landes in his *Unbound Prometheus: Technological Change and Industrial Development in Western Europe from 1750 to the Present* (Cambridge: Cambridge University Press, 1969), and by the various authors in Carlo M. Cipolla's edited series, *The Fontana Economic History of Europe*, vols. 4–6 (Glasgow: Fontana/Collins, 1973–1976), than on price data and business cycles. I explain my reasoning more fully in Daniel Chirot, *Social Change in the Modern Era* (San Diego: Harcourt Brace Jovanovich, 1986), pp. 223–230. The point, however, is not to argue about precise periodization but to recognize that there are different technologies,

different types of social organization, and different models of behavior at different stages of the industrial era. The forceful maintenance of an outdated model is one of the main reasons for the backwardness of Soviet-type economies.

8. Polanyi's *Great Transformation* was one such prediction. So was Lenin's in *Imperialism, the Highest Stage of Capitalism* (New York: International Publishers, 1939). For an account of the ideological effects of the Great Depression of the 1930s on Eastern Europe, see Daniel Chirot, "Ideology, Reality, and Competing Models of Development in Eastern Europe Between the Two World Wars," *Eastern European Politics and Societies,* 3, 3 (1989), pp. 378–411.

9. Alexander Erlich, *The Soviet Industrialization Debate* (Cambridge: Harvard University Press, 1960). Whether or not this strategy was necessary remains a subject of debate in the Soviet Union, where Stephen F. Cohen's book on Bukharin has been greatly appreciated by the Gorbachev reformers because Bukharin was the most important ideological opponent of the Stalin line. See Cohen's *Bukharin and the Bolshevik Revolution: A Political Biography, 1888–1938* (Oxford: Oxford University Press, 1980). For Eastern Europe, however, the issue is moot.

10. Vladimir Tismaneanu, "The Tragicomedy of Romanian Communism," *Eastern European Politics and Societies,* 3, 2 (1989), gives the most recent, and best short account of the origins and development of the Romanian Communist Party from the prewar period until 1989 and explains Ceausescu's role in determining its fate.

11. Lardy, *Agriculture in China's Modern Economic Development,* pp. 130, 155, 158, and 165.

12. Hosking quotes the Soviet reform economist Otto Latsis, who put it this way: "They build irrigation channels which bring no increase in agricultural production. They produce machine tools for which there are no operators, tractors for which there are no drivers, and threshing machines which they know will not work. Further millions of people supply these superfluous products with electricity, ore, oil, and coal. In return they receive their wages like everyone else, and take them to the shops. There, however, they find no goods to buy, because their work has not produced any." And Hosking also quotes Soviet Premier Nicolai Ryzhkov: "We produce more tractors in this country than all the capitalist countries put together. And yet we don't have enough tractors" (*Awakening of the Soviet Union,* p. 134).

13. Kazimierz Poznanski ascribes the failure of the Polish reforms in the second half of the 1970s to political pressure rather than to economic mismanagement, but it would be fruitless to argue about which came first. See his "Economic Adjustment and Political Forces: Poland Since 1970," in Comisso and Tyson, *Power, Purpose, and Collective Choice.*

14. Comisso and Marer, in their article "The Economics and Politics of Reform in Hungary," cover this and the other major contradictions in the Hungarian economic reforms, pp. 267–278.

15. On the debt crisis and Eastern Europe, see Laura D'Andrea Tyson, "The Debt Crisis and Adjustment Responses in Eastern Europe: A Comparative Perspective," in Comisso and Tyson, *Power, Purpose, and Collective Choice.* On Romania, see Ronald H. Linden, "Socialist Patrimonialism and the Global Economy: The Case of Romania," in Comisso and Tyson, *Power, Purpose, and Collective Choice.*

16. Jan Gross stresses this in "Social Consequences of War: Preliminaries to the Study of Imposition of Communist Regimes in East Central Europe," *Eastern European Politics and Societies,* 3, 2 (1989), pp. 213–214. There is no way of quantifying the extent to which youthful enthusiasm helped Communist cadres take power and effectively transform their societies in the late 1940s and early 1950s, but the phenomenon is attested to by numerous literary sources describing the period. Even such bitter anti-

Communists as Milan Kundera in *The Joke* (New York: Harper & Row, 1982) verifies this. Had there never been a substantial body of energized believers, it is unlikely that the sheer force of Soviet military could have held all of Eastern Europe in its grip. Yet as Gross and others—for example, Elemér Hankiss, "Demobilization, Self-Mobilization, and Quasi-Mobilization in Hungary, 1948–1987," *Eastern European Politics and Societies*, 3, 1 (1989)—have pointed out, Communist regimes worked hard to destroy social cohesion and any type of genuine solidarity, so that in the long run it was inevitable that the enthusiasm of the early intellectual believers would be curbed and debased. As for Western, particularly French, Marxism, Tony Judt believes that it also contributed to the legitimacy of Eastern European Communist regimes. See his *Marxism and the French Left* (Oxford: Oxford University Press, 1986), pp. 236–238. Thus, the rise and demise of Marxism in Eastern and Western Europe are not wholly separate phenomena but fed on each other.

17. The best-known explanation of communism as nationalism is Chalmers Johnson, *Peasant Nationalism and Communist Power: The Emergence of Revolutionary China, 1937–1945* (Stanford: Stanford University Press, 1962), esp. pp. 176–187. Johnson explicitly compares Yugoslavia to China. To varying degrees, but most strongly in Poland, Czechoslovakia, and Albania, the Communists were able to make similar claims as national saviors after 1945 elsewhere in Eastern Europe. In East Germany, Hungary, Bulgaria, and Romania, they could at least claim to represent the substantial leftist nationalist sentiments that had been silenced during the period of Nazism or the German alliance.

18. Again, it is difficult to quantify feelings of moral revulsion. But the sense of all-pervasive corruption and self-disgust can be grasped in all of the literature of Eastern Europe, starting in the 1950s and becoming ever more obvious with time. A particularly somber view is given by Petru Dumitriu's *Incognito* (New York: Macmillan, 1964).

19. Though he certainly exaggerates the role of local officials, this is a central theme in J. Arch Getty's revisionist view of the Stalinist purges in his *Origins of the Great Purges: The Soviet Communist Party Reconsidered, 1933–1938* (Cambridge: Cambridge University Press, 1985). On the Chinese Cultural Revolution, see Hong Yung Lee, *The Politics of the Chinese Cultural Revolution* (Berkeley: University of California Press, 1978). Although such events could not have begun without central direction, they could not have been carried out without local officials trying to ingratiate themselves by imitating the top. But this very process led to widespread cynicism and corruption, and so had to undermine the long-term legitimacy of communism.

20. James C. Scott's argument about how the violation of a "moral economy's" sense of justice leads to revolts is based on observations of peasants, but it actually applies even more to urban intellectuals and professionals. It is now evident that they also have a "moral economy," though one tied to their own sense of self-worth rather than to their subsistence. See *The Moral Economy of the Peasant: Rebellion and Subsistence in Southeast Asia* (New Haven: Yale University Press, 1976), particularly pp. 157–192.

21. Yet it is difficult to believe that China will not follow the same course as Eastern Europe in future years. The crisis of the Democracy Movement in spring 1989 was caused by all the same factors that led to the collapse of communism in Eastern Europe: the contradictions of economic reform in a system still run by Communist officials, growing corruption, loss of faith in the official ideology, and increasing disgust with the endless hypocrisy of those in power. The main difference, of course, was that China in 1989 was much less developed, much less urbanized than the Eastern European countries and also much more insulated from the effects of the economic and political crisis in the Soviet Union. For a brief review of the events in China and their causes, see Jonathan D. Spence, *The Search for Modern China* (New York: Norton, 1990), pp. 712–747.

22. His major essays from the late 1980s have been collected in Timothy Garton Ash, *The Uses of Adversity* (New York: Random House, 1989).

23. Kazimierz Poznanski, *Technology, Competition and the Soviet Bloc in the World Market* (Berkeley: Institute of International Studies of the University of California, 1987).

24. Each new report from the Soviet Union makes the picture of the Brezhnev years and the prognosis for the future seem bleaker. For years, the CIA reports painted a bleaker picture than the official Soviet reports, but recently Soviet economists have said that even the CIA reports were too optimistic. As an example of what is now known about the state of the Soviet economy and how it reached its present crisis, see Bill Keller, "Gorbachev's Need: To Still Matter," *New York Times*, May 27, 1990, section 1, pp. 1, 6. None of this is new to academic specialists such as Marshall Goldman, who discusses it in *USSR in Crisis: The Failure of an Economic System* (New York: Norton, 1983).

25. That scientists did not believe the extravagant claims made by the proponents of the "strategic defense initiative" is clear. See, for example, Franklin A. Long, Donald Hafner, and Jeffrey Boutwell, eds., *Weapons in Space* (New York: Norton, 1986), particularly the essay by Hans Bethe, Jeffrey Boutwell, and Richard Garwin, "BMD Technologies and Concepts in the 1980s," pp. 53–71. Yet the Soviets were very troubled by it, and it was Gorbachev's political genius that figured out that U.S. funding for military research could only be reduced in the context of a general move toward disarmament, and this necessitated a reversal of traditional Soviet foreign policy that would reassure the West. For an appreciation of Gorbachev's policy in an otherwise harshly critical article, see Elena Bonner, "On Gorbachev," *New York Review of Books*, May 17, 1990, p. 14. In general, it seems to me that the Soviets' fear that their conventional warfare capabilities would be undermined by the West's technological superiority has been relatively neglected in most of the discussion about arms control. It has, however, been noted by experts. See Alan B. Sherr, *The Other Side of Arms Control: Soviet Objectives in the Gorbachev Era* (Boston: Unwin Hyman, 1988), pp. 38 and 63.

26. Chaim Herzog, *The Arab-Israeli Wars* (New York: Random House, 1982), pp. 347–348. That the Soviets remained concerned by this is shown by statements in Alexei Arbatov, Oleg Amirov, and Nikolai Kishilov, "Assessing the NATO-WTO Military Balance in Europe," in Robert D. Blackwell and F. Stephen Larrabee, eds., *Conventional Arms Control and East-West Security* (Durham, N.C.: Duke University Press, 1989), pp. 78–79.

27. Hosking, *Awakening of the Soviet Union*, pp. 56–60.

28. The desperate and almost comical attempts made by the Jaruzelski regime to create new organizations and institutions that would reimpose some sort of political and social coherence and bring society back into the system are explored very well by George Kolankiewicz in "Poland, and the Politics of Permissible Pluralism," *Eastern European Politics and Societies*, 2, 2 (1988), pp. 152–183. But even Kolankiewicz thought that the attempt to include broader segments of the population, and particularly the intellectuals, in officially defined institutions might meet with partial success. In the event, it turned out that these desperate inclusionary policies failed, too.

29. Timothy Garton Ash, "Eastern Europe: The Year of Truth," *New York Review of Books*, February 15, 1990, pp. 17–22. A collection of Garton Ash's new essays on 1989 appears in *We the People: The Revolution of '89, Witnessed in Warsaw, Budapest, Berlin and Prague* (Cambridge: Granta/Penguin, 1990).

30. In summer 1988 it certainly became obvious that the forces of political and social disintegration in the Soviet Union were starting to get out of hand, too, and this no doubt influenced Gorbachev greatly. See the essays of Boris Kagarlitsky in *Farewell*

Perestroika: A Soviet Chronicle (London: Verso, 1990), particularly "The Hot Summer of 1988," pp. 1–29.

31. The whole process is well documented by the Polish publications, particularly, issues of *Rzeczpospolita, Polityka, and Trybuna Ludu*. I thank Dieter Bingen of Cologne's Bundesinstitut für Ostwissenschaftliche und Internationale Studien for helping me understand the sequence of events in Poland during this period.

32. Bill Keller, "Getting Out with Honor" (February 2, 1989), in Bernard Gwertzman and Michael T. Kaufman, eds., *The Collapse of Communism* (New York: New York Times, 1990), pp. 10–12. This book is a collection of relevant articles published in the *Times* during 1989.

33. In Gwertzman and Kaufman, *Collapse of Communism*, see John Tagliabue, "Solidarity May Win 40 Percent of Parliament" (February 19, 1989), pp. 20–21; "Stunning Vote Casts Poles into Uncharted Waters" (June 5, 1989), p. 121; "Warsaw Accepts Solidarity Sweep and Humiliating Losses by Party" (June 8, 1989), pp. 121–123; and "Jaruzelski, Moved by 'Needs and Aspirations' of Poland Names Walesa Aide Premier" (August 19, 1989), pp. 130–132. To this must be added the August 17, 1989, article from Moscow by Bill Keller, "In Moscow, Tone Is Studied Calm," pp. 132–133.

34. In Gwertzman and Kaufman, *Collapse of Communism*, see Henry Kamm, "East Germans Put Hungary in a Bind" (September 1, 1989), pp. 154–156; and Serge Schmemann, "East Germans Line Émigré Routes, Some in Hope of Their Own Exit" (October 4, 1989), p. 158, and "Security Forces Storm Protesters in East Germany" (sent from Dresden, October 8, 1989), p. 159.

35. Thomas A. Baylis, "Explaining the GDR's Economic Strategy," in Comisso and Tyson, *Power, Purpose, and Collective Choice*, esp. the optimistic conclusion, pp. 242–244. A conventionally favorable summary of how East German Communist labor relations worked is found in Marilyn Rueschemeyer and C. Bradley Scharf, "Labor Unions in the German Democratic Republic," in Alex Pravda and Blair A. Ruble, eds., *Trade Unions in Communist States* (Boston: Allen and Unwin, 1986). Judging by the comments from these and other similar studies, East Germans should not have behaved the way they did in 1989.

36. In a speech on October 7 in the GDR, Gorbachev said, "Life itself punishes those who delay." Quoted in Timothy Garton Ash, "The German Revolution," *New York Review of Books*, December 21, 1989, p. 14. Then, on October 25 in Helsinki, he said that the Soviet Union did not have the moral or political right to intervene in the affairs of Eastern Europe. This was interpreted by his spokesman, Gennadi I. Gerasimov, as the replacement of the Brezhnev Doctrine by the "Sinatra Doctrine" (after the song, "I Did It My Way"). Bill Keller, "Gorbachev in Finland, Disavows Any Right of Regional Intervention" (October 25, 1989), in Gwertzman and Kaufman, *Collapse of Communism*, pp. 163–166.

37. Garton Ash, "The German Revolution," p. 16.

38. Christopher Jones, "Gorbachev and the Warsaw Pact," *Eastern European Politics and Societies*, 3, 2 (1989), pp. 215–234.

39. Serge Schmemann, "East Germany Opens Frontier to the West for Migration or Travel; Thousands Cross," *New York Times*, November 10, 1989, p. 1. Clyde Haberman, "Bulgarian Chief Quits After 35 Years of Rigid Rule," same issue of the *Times*, p. 1. Timothy Garton Ash, "The Revolution of the Magic Lantern," *New York Review of Books*, January 18, 1990, pp. 42–51. The Czech Communist regime fell on November 24.

40. Louis Zanga, "Albania Decides to End Its Isolation," *Soviet/East European Report* of Radio Free Europe/Radio Liberty, May 1, 1990, p. 4. Then, after partial liberalization was announced in Albania, and a *New York Times* reporter was allowed in, there was

this story by David Binder, "Albanian Youths Split on Pace of Change and Leader's Sincerity," New York Times, May 27, 1990, section 1, p. 9.

41. The Ceausescu regime began to move in this direction in the early 1970s, though the full ramifications of the return to autarkic Stalinism did not become entirely obvious until the early 1980s. For an explanation of the changes in the early 1970s, see Ken Jowitt, "Political Innovation in Rumania," Survey, 4 (Autumn 1974), and Daniel Chirot, "Social Change in Communist Romania," Social Forces, 57, 2 (1978), pp. 495–497. Jowitt noted Ceausescu's references to his "beloved friend" Kim Il-Sung and to the sudden demotion of a young reform Communist who had built up well-educated, technocratic cadres and who was expected to become increasingly important. That was Ion Iliescu, the man who was to become the first post-Communist president of Romania. Jowitt again emphasized the similarity of the North Korean and Romanian regimes in "Moscow Centre," Eastern European Politics and Societies, 1, 3 (1987), p. 320. For a brief description of what Romania was like by 1988, see Daniel Chirot, "Ceausescu's Last Folly," Dissent (Summer 1988), pp. 271–275. In North Korea, despite the many similarities with Romania, decay was not as advanced in the late 1980s, perhaps because, as Bruce Cumings has suggested, Kim's autarkic Marxist patrimonialism was more in tune with Korean historical and cultural tradition than Ceausescu's was with Romania's past. See Bruce Cumings, "Corporatism in North Korea," Journal of Korean Studies 4 (1982-1983), particularly p. 277, where Cumings quotes Ken Jowitt's quip about Romania and North Korea being examples of "socialism in one family." Since then, that quote had been widely repeated without being attributed.

42. One of the best accounts of what was going on in Romania was written by the Romanian dissident Pavel Campeanu, "Birth and Death in Romania," New York Review of Books, October 23, 1986. That article was written anonymously. His "Revolt of the Romanians," New York Review of Books, February 1, 1990, was signed. See also, Daniel N. Nelson, Romanian Politics in the Ceausescu Era (New York: Gordon and Breach, 1988), pp. 213–217.

43. There could hardly be a better demonstration of how removed Ceausescu had become from reality than the way in which he was overthrown. The shock on his face as the crowd he was addressing began to jeer him on December 21, 1989, was captured on television. More than this was the unbelievable ineptitude of his attempt to escape. Some highly placed Romanians have told me that Ceausescu realized in the last few days that changes had to be made, and that he was hoping to reassert his full control before starting to reform. But it is quite clear that despite the years of growing misery and the alienation of all Romanians outside the Ceausescu family, he still believed he had enough legitimacy to carry on. His surprise may have come about because the demonstration against him was probably instigated by elements in the army and from within the Securitate itself. The reports in the New York Times on Romania from December 22 to December 25, 1989, give the essence of the story without, however, clarifying what still remains, much later, a murky sequence of events.

44. The famous J-curve theory of James Davies predicted that a growing gap between rewards and expectations would lead to revolutions; see his article, "Toward a Theory of Revolution," American Sociological Review, 27, 1 (1962). Ted Gurr expanded on this and other "psychological explanations" of revolution in Why Men Rebel (Princeton: Princeton University Press, 1970). These would be, at best, weak explanations of what happened, except, of course, for the obvious point that many people must have been dissatisfied for regimes that were essentially intact to fall so quickly. There is no obvious reason why discontent should have been any higher in 1989 than five, ten, or twenty years earlier.

45. Michael Bernhard has shown that in fact the Party-state machine in Poland learned from the events of the 1970s and of 1980, and that Jaruzelski was able to

impose martial law, raise prices repeatedly, and avoid the political turmoil that had occurred earlier. "The Strikes of June 1976 in Poland," *Eastern European Politics and Societies,* 1, 3 (1987), pp. 390–391. Both the opposition and the regime became more sophisticated with time, but by the mid-1980s the regime had won. The prevailing political attitude, according to many and on the whole fairly reliable surveys done in Poland, was growing apathy toward all political issues. See Jane L. Curry, "The Psychological Barriers to Reform in Poland," *Eastern European Politics and Societies,* 2, 3 (1988), particularly p. 494. David S. Mason's *Public Opinion and Political Change in Poland, 1980–1982* (Cambridge: Cambridge University Press, 1984) consistently shows this, but also that the turn in the J, that is, the growing gap between a deteriorating reality and high expectations created by the growth of the early 1970s, took place in the late 1970s and in 1980. As the 1980s unfolded, peoples' expectations fell into line with reality, the excitement of 1980–1981 replaced by the apathy and hopelessness of martial law. See particularly pp. 42–53 and 222–232.

46. Hankiss, "Demobilization, Self-Mobilization, and Quasi-Mobilization," pp. 131–139.

47. Vladimir Tismaneanu, quoting Vaclav Havel, points out that the dissidents in these countries made up a "minuscule and rather singular enclave." *The Crisis of Marxist Ideology in Eastern Europe: The Poverty of Utopia* (London: Routledge, 1988), p. 166. In his chapter on intellectual dissidents (pp. 160–182), however, Tismaneanu, is prophetic in noting that the refusal of the intellectuals to accept the lies of communism can destroy these systems precisely because they are ultimately based on ideas. This, in fact, was the entire premise of the dissident intellectuals, particularly in Poland, Czechoslovakia, and Hungary.

48. The analysis of conflicts between states trying to reform in order to keep up their power in the international arena and obstructionist traditional elites makes up an important part of Theda Skocpol's theory of revolution in *States and Social Revolutions* (Cambridge: Cambridge University Press, 1979). Classes more committed to reform, then, play an important role in conducting revolutions. But however much merit this argument has in explaining the classical French, Russian, and Chinese revolutions, it seems to have little bearing on what happened in Eastern Europe in 1989. It may, however, have considerable bearing on the future of politics in the Soviet Union.

49. Przemyslaw T. Gajdeczka of the Word Bank claimed in 1988 that the debt problem was more or less under control and that international lenders gave only three countries poor ratings: Poland, Romania, and Yugoslavia. "International Market Perceptions and Economic Performance: Lending to Eastern Europe," *Eastern European Politics and Societies,* 2, 3 (1988), pp. 558–576.

50. That rising classes cause revolutions is at the heart of the Marxist theory of revolution. An interesting twist to this was suggested by György Konrad in *Intellectuals on the Road to Class Power* (Brighton: Harvester Press, 1979). Intellectuals were identified as the rising class that helped put the Communists into power and were becoming the ruling class. But intellectual dissidents in Eastern Europe represented no class, were not numerically large, and were held together by a common moral position, not their position in the economic structure. Zygmunt Bauman identified their role more correctly by pointing out that they were more the carriers of national consciousness and morality than a class as such. "Intellectuals in East-Central Europe: Continuity and Change," *Eastern European Politics and Societies,* 1, 2 (1987), pp. 162–186.

51. Only in Poland could it be said that Charles Tilly's theory about revolutions, that organization of the revolutionary groups counts most, works at all. But even in Poland, the height of organizational coherence in Solidarity was reached in 1980. To the limited extent that Poland fits Tilly's theories about mobilization, that cannot

explain the loss of nerve and collapse in the other Communist regimes. See Tilly's *From Mobilization to Revolution* (Reading: Addison-Wesley, 1978).

52. Thus, the first step of what Jack A. Goldstone has called the "natural history" approach to the study of revolutions, based largely on the 1938 work of Crane Brinton, turns out to describe some of what happened in Eastern Europe, too: "Prior to a great revolution, the bulk of the 'intellectuals'—journalists, poets, playwrights, essayists, teachers, members of the clergy, lawyers, and trained members of the bureaucracy—cease to support the regime, writing condemnations and demanding major reforms." Goldstone, "The Comparative and Historical Study of Revolutions," *Annual Review of Sociology*, 8 (1982), pp. 189–190. See also Crane Brinton, *The Anatomy of Revolution* (New York: Vintage, 1965). But most recent theorists of revolution have not taken this observation as anything more than a symptom of deeper class and structural conflicts, and none seems to have believed it could be the prime cause of revolutions. Goldstone's own theory that rapidly rising demographic pressures explain revolutions has much validity in premodern history (pp. 204–205); it has no bearing on Eastern Europe.

53. See Johnson, *Peasant Nationalism*, pp. 31–70.

54. It would be pointless to extend the number of examples because there are so many. For some African cases, see Robert H. Jackson and Carl G. Rosberg, *Personal Rule in Black Africa: Prince, Autocrat, Prophet, Tyrant* (Berkeley: University of California Press, 1982), particularly chapter 6, "Tyrants and Abusive Rule," about the incredible misrule of Idi Amin of Uganda and Macias Nguema of Equatorial Guinea. For Haiti, Robert I. Rotberg's classic study, *Haiti: The Politics of Squalor* (Boston: Houghton Mifflin, 1971) remains excellent. The tyranny in Burma and the revolution of 1988 (the ultimate effects of which are still pending, despite the repression that took place during that year) are discussed by Bertil Lintner in *Outrage: Burma's Struggle for Democracy* (Hong Kong: Review Publishing, 1989).

55. Leo Kuper, in *Genocide* (New Haven: Yale University Press, 1981), estimates that up to three million Bengalis were killed as the Pakistani army tried to reverse the overwhelming electoral victory of the independence-minded Awami League (pp. 78–80). Of course, it was not just the army but a general collapse into anarchy and interethnic warfare that contributed to the high death toll, but the point is that despite all this, as in Cambodia in 1979 or Uganda also in 1979, the nightmare perpetrated by the government in control against the wishes of the large majority of the population could only be overthrown by outside military intervention (p. 173). By these standards, the European colonial powers, however brutal they may have been, seem to have been more prone to give in to a combination of moral arguments against what they were doing and simple calculations of the costs and benefits of their colonial wars. None of these cases shed much light on what happened in Eastern Europe. After all, the last case of large-scale killing in Eastern Europe was by the Soviets in Hungary in 1956.

56. Ryszard Kapuscinski's *The Emperor* (London: Picador/Pan, 1984), about the fall of Haile Selassie, makes that emperor seem very much a Ceausescu-like figure—out of touch with his population and with his own elite. But some have pointed out that Kapuscinski's book may have been as much about his native Poland under Edward Gierek as about Ethiopia. The violence that followed the first, peaceful stage of the Ethiopian revolution, however, is unlikely to be repeated in Eastern Europe, though it is a chilling reminder of what happens when a disintegrating multiethnic empire tries to hold itself together at any cost.

57. Tim McDaniel has pointed out the extraordinary analogy between the Russian Revolution of 1917 and the Iranian one of 1978–1979. In both cases, autocratic modernizing regimes, despite some real successes, managed to alienate almost all elements in the society. In the case of Iran, this was even more startling because, as in Eastern

Europe, there was no major defeat, just a collapse. See McDaniel, *A Modern Mirror for Princes: Autocratic Modernization and Revolution in Russia and Iran* (Princeton: Princeton University Press, 1991).

58. Vladimir Tismaneanu, "Eastern Europe: The Story the Media Missed," *Bulletin of the Atomic Scientists* (March 1990), pp. 17–21.

59. For example, Tony R. Judt in a paper delivered at the Woodrow Wilson Center in Washington, D.C., during summer 1987 and published as "The Dilemmas of Dissidence: The Politics of Opposition in East-Central Europe," *Eastern European Politics and Societies*, 2, 2 (1988). The journals *Telos* and *Cross-currents*, run by scholars from Central Europe, were aware of what was going on, as were some other equally specialized publications in Europe. But before the events of 1989, very few scholars or intellectuals paid much attention to such publications, and even most specialists, especially those in the policy-related fields, hardly took them seriously.

AFTERWORD:
HISTORY, MYTH, AND
THE TALES OF TIANANMEN

Jeffrey N. Wasserstrom

During the emotional days that followed June 4, 1989, it seemed as though there were only two ways to tell the story of the Chinese protests and the crackdown that ended them. One could follow the CCP authorities and denigrate the protests as "counterrevolutionary riots," deny that a massacre had taken place, and claim that soldiers were the only martyrs worthy of the name. Alternatively, one could follow the accounts of protesters and foreign eyewitnesses, which told of unarmed innocents whose demands for democracy and dialogue were answered with a brutal assault by tanks and guns. The differences between these two kinds of narratives initially seemed enormous, irreconcilable, and unambiguous to Western observers. The tale the authorities told appeared a cynical fabrication designed to justify an abhorrent act, a myth that should concern us only because it might mislead certain sectors of the Chinese population. The other version, by contrast, appeared a straightforward statement of fact; uncritical acceptance of it laid the groundwork for what one sinologist called a "remarkable and truly moving unanimity on the issue of China."[1]

The question of how the story of 1989 should be told no longer seems so clear-cut. Foreigners concerned with China still tend to agree on certain key points: The protesters had valid grievances; a massacre did indeed take place

I am grateful to Paul Cohen and Henry Rosemont, Jr., for their valuable criticisms of an earlier version of this essay and to Anne Bock for giving the final draft a careful reading. I also want to thank Joe Esherick for getting me to think seriously about the implications of calling 1989 a "tragedy."

in Beijing; and many more protesters and bystanders than soldiers were killed on June 4. The initial "unanimity on the issue of China," however, now appears to have been little more than widespread agreement that the Chinese government's crackdown and subsequent campaign of arrests and disinformation were abhorrent acts. There has certainly been no clear consensus concerning U.S. foreign policy. Writers associated with widely differing points on the political spectrum have attacked Bush's decision to maintain essentially normal relations with the Beijing authorities as unconscionable.[2] As previous chapters have indicated, China scholars have also disagreed with each other on a variety of interpretive issues, relating to everything from how "democratic" the protesters were to how important factional struggles within the CCP were in shaping the movement.

In retrospect, it has also become obvious that the Chinese authorities were not the only ones to distort or mythologize history in 1989. Western journalists played a key role in getting accurate information out of and back into China, for example, but (as many scholars before me have noted) they also created their own share of myths.[3] Although MacKinnon is right in his chapter to draw attention to the academic training and experience writers like Orville Schell brought to their coverage of the protests, many members of the foreign press corps had only a limited familiarity with the Chinese context and at best a passing knowledge of Chinese history. Western journalists also had limited access to certain kinds of data and locales (even the best were seldom able to develop extensive contacts outside of Beijing), and were hindered by the constraints of time (in the case of broadcasters) and space (in the case of print journalists) that their media imposed. These factors, coupled with a desire to make the situation in China readily intelligible to a mass audience at home, resulted in coverage that was often misleading.

Television commentators tended to concentrate so intently upon protests in and around Tiananmen Square during the weeks leading up to the June Fourth bloodshed, for example, that they obscured the fact that significant (although often unfilmed) demonstrations were taking place simultaneously in other parts of the country. Then, in the immediate aftermath of the massacre, some Western reporters were too quick to give credence to a variety of rumors (that tens of thousands had died in the city center, that Li Peng had been shot, etc.). Foreign media also reinforced the distorted image of the movement as a single-city event by giving very limited attention to the violence in Chengdu and other provincial capitals. As a result of wishful thinking and a desire to find easily graspable analogies for a complex series of events, foreign reporters also tended to leave viewers with an overly simplistic and mythologized picture of the protesters, by acting as if labeling the protests a "democracy movement," a Chinese version of "people power" or "Solidarity," or a modern-day Boston Tea Party said all that needed to be said. That the student activists of 1989, like their predecessors of the Republican period (1911–1949), frequently emphasized different sets of symbols and slogans when appealing to foreign as opposed to domestic audiences, and proved remarkably adept at telling Westerners what they wanted to hear, contributed to this mythmaking process.[4]

The mythologizing did not stop, furthermore, when the camera crews and network anchors left Beijing. Scholars, propagandists, dissidents, pundits, and diplomats have continued to create new myths and perpetuate old ones. The tendency in the West to reduce the history of the nationwide protests to the story of the (admittedly critical) events that took place in Beijing has if anything intensified since June 1989, and this (rather than my own views) accounts for the use of the phrase "tales of Tiananmen" in the title of this chapter. The Chinese authorities have spent the last two years distributing a wide variety of written and visual treatments of the 1989 "turmoil" that attempt to "prove" the veracity of Deng Xiaoping and Li Peng's fairy-tale version of events. And Chinese dissidents have been guilty at times of passing off hagiography as critical analysis where the martyrs of 1989 are concerned.

Thanks to these and other kinds of mythmaking, there is now no simple way to separate myth from history when dealing with the protests and repression of 1989. This is hardly surprising. The distinction between the two realms is always problematic at best. It becomes especially so when, as Paul Cohen notes in a perceptive essay on treatments of the Boxers, the events in question "resonate with themes of broader historical scope," involve the "most important and controversial unresolved issues" in a nation's past, and touch upon symbols and values that members of a culture prize or fear most fervently.[5] This was certainly the case with the protests of 1989. As earlier chapters by Young and Schwarcz have shown, virtually every major theme in twentieth-century Chinese history reappeared in some form in the rhetoric and action of 1989, as the protesters and the government's spokespersons alike claimed to speak for treasured values such as patriotism, progress, democracy, and revolution and tried to link their opponents to negative images associated with feudalism, despotism, subjugation, and chaos. Foreign journalists, who often presented the protests to the outside world as a simple fight between noble "democrats" and "Communist dictators," ensured that the events would resonate with a somewhat different (but equally potent) set of symbols and ideals.

Historical analogies contributed still further to the mythologization process. Both the students and their opponents insisted from the start that their actions be understood in the light of history. This has made it harder rather than easier, however, to treat the events historically. As Vera Schwarcz suggests, the past actors to whom the students most frequently compared themselves (the heroes of the May Fourth Movement) were already enshrined as mythic figures to be commemorated rather than remembered. And, as Ernest Young shows, the images from the past that the authorities invoked to discredit the students—visions of Qing "feudalism," KMT villainy, and Maoist excesses—were equally mythologized ones. Broadcasts that showed banners inscribed with the words of larger-than-life Western heroes (Patrick Henry, Martin Luther King, Jr., and Abraham Lincoln) and carried narrations that compared the occupation of Tiananmen Square to events like Woodstock and the Prague spring of 1968, meanwhile, led foreign viewers to locate the events within a different (but no less mythic) historical framework.

Mythmaking and Mythbreaking

How, then, should a scholar interested in 1989 deal with the mythic quality of so many of the narratives of Tiananmen? One way to proceed is to try to demythologize the stories of a specific type of mythmaker. In an article defending Bush's China policy, for example, Richard Nixon claims that those opposed to a realpolitik approach have committed the sin of "romanticizing" the realities of Chinese communism. Henry Kissinger has argued in a similar vein that those who disagree with Bush have insisted upon reducing the complex events of 1989 to a "simple morality play" and let "emotion" cloud their judgment. The picture they draw of Deng Xiaoping as a tyrant, he argues, is a "caricature" that does not do justice to the man.[6]

Left-wing and right-wing critics of U.S. foreign policy have used similar language to make the opposite point: that is, that the so-called realpolitik that Nixon and Kissinger defend is itself based on myths and misunderstandings. Fervent anti-Communists have described this policy as one based upon "fantasies," "fictions," and "wishfulness."[7] In her tellingly titled "The Romance of *Realpolitik*," Miriam London expands on this theme, arguing that Western views of Communist China have been distorted for decades by a variety of "illusions" put forth by an unholy alliance of self-proclaimed "China experts" with leftist leanings, liberals like John K. Fairbank (whose sentimentality has led him to underestimate the perfidy of the CCP), and hypocritical anti-Communists like Kissinger (who has been "seduced" by the "charm" of leaders like Zhou Enlai into suspending his principles where China is concerned). Writers of these three types, she claims, have continually obscured the irredeemably evil nature of Dengist as well as Maoist forces, something that only a few clear-sighted analysts such as the Belgian sinologist and former diplomat Simon Leys never lost to view.[8] From the opposite end of the political spectrum, in a powerful recent essay Arif Dirlik and Roxann Prazniak argue that Leys actually has a great deal more in common with both Fairbank and Kissinger than London and others think. Leys and Fairbank share a common sentimental attachment to the Chinese people (as opposed to the Chinese state), Dirlik and Prazniak claim, and both Leys and the defenders of realpolitik share an uncritical conviction that capitalism will inevitably defeat socialism and thus save China, an assumption that leads them to simplify complex events.[9]

A different set of attempts to demythologize the events of 1989 focuses on specific aspects of the protests or the crackdown rather than particular kinds of mythmakers. Sarah Lubman's "The Myth of Tiananmen," for example, was an early effort to show that the actions of the student protesters were often less fully "democratic" than some of their own wall posters and the more enthusiastic Western reporters would have had us believe.[10] Various works (including earlier chapters by Perry and Feigon) have expanded upon this theme, attempting to "strip [the students] of their halos" while leaving them "their humanity," as George Hicks puts it when introducing a piece in this vein by Jane Macartney.[11] In "Who Died in Beijing, and Why," Robin Munro turns from student actions to those of the government as he looks at one particular episode, the night of June 3 and morning of June 4, that "remains shrouded in myth."[12] This important piece criticizes not only the Chinese government's disinformation campaign but also the myths perpetuated by foreign journalists, such as the idea that most of those who died were students (when most were members of other social classes) and that much of the violence took place in Tiananmen Square itself (when the main killing fields were elsewhere).[13]

Yet a third type of demythologizing work focuses on issues of ethnocentricism. Works such as Harold Isaacs's classic study of perceptions of China and India, *Scratches on Our Minds*, provide one kind of starting point. Isaacs argued that Americans have tended to view the Chinese as either diabolically cruel and clever heathens (the Fu Manchu image) or as hardworking and honest souls who were remarkably like us in many ways (the image popularized in works such as Pearl Buck's *The Good Earth*).[14] Isaacs based his work on interviews with Americans alive in the 1950s, but his main themes have much broader chronological and geographical relevance. European Enlightenment thinkers, after all, were divided over the question whether those who ruled China were perfect rationalists or unrestrained despots. *Scratches on Our Minds* also has contemporary relevance, as the last few decades have witnessed the continuation of what Bill Brugger aptly describes as the Western "sunshine-horror" syndrome in respect to China: Foreign observers begin with unrealistic hopes for each new regime, then in time come to view this same regime as utterly despotic.[15] Western views of individual Chinese leaders and the Chinese populace (as opposed to Chinese regimes) have veered between equally extreme poles. Miriam London's satirical comment that, on the eve of Nixon's first visit to China, "experts" often treated the Cultural Revolution-scarred PRC as if it were a land filled with "happy, relaxed and motivated people, somewhat like our Pennsylvania Amish, only better," indicates that Pearl Buck–style imagery lives on. The language she uses to describe Mao Zedong (a "cruel despot," an "executioner of millions," a "merciless dictator" reigning over a "dark age" of "oppression and despair") and Zhou Enlai (Mao's "wily supporter," whom Simon Leys claimed could tell "blatant lies with angelic suavity" and "stick a knife in your back [with] disarming grace"), meanwhile, is uncomfortably reminiscent of pulp novelist Sax Rohmer, the creator of Fu Manchu.

These positive and negative stereotypes were alive and well before 1989, but (as others have noted) the events of April through June breathed new life into them. In the wake of June Fourth, the same Western analysts who had once treated Deng Xiaoping as a hardworking modernizer began to recast him into a contemporary version of Fu Manchu. "Sunshine"-filled pictures of Deng's China—as a land in which a billion Chinese were being converted to capitalism as smoothly as missionaries had once hoped they could be converted to Christianity—gave way to images colored by "horror." In spite of this new pessimism, however, the images of China as a land filled with honest souls waiting to be converted to our ideals did not disappear. The burden of fulfilling Western hopes was simply shifted to the shoulders of a new generation: the protesters.[16]

Some of those concerned with ethnocentrism and 1989 have been less interested in Western views of China per se than with Western treatments of radically "other" cultures in general. For them, Edward Said's work rather than Isaacs's provides the critical starting point. Said's theory of "Orientalism" is based on the premise that what those in the United States and Europe have called the "Orient" is in fact a Western construction imposed upon the East. Adopting a position of cultural superiority, Western specialists have treated Asia as a reverse mirror image of the "Occident" and attributed to it a series of exotic and usually negative values.[17] Some sinologists have argued that Said's work (the main focus of which is the Middle East) is either overly schematic or needs at least to be modified to have relevance for China. As recent events have reminded us, there has always been much less "sunshine" and more "horror" in Western views of the Middle East as opposed to China. What Edward Graham has referred to as China's own highly developed ideology of "barbarianism" (a view of other cultures as inferior, dangerous, and lewd, which Watson examines above and which Feigon alludes to in his chapter when discussing official attempts to discredit Wuer Kaixi) also makes it something of a special case.[18] Many sinologists have found Said's general arguments compelling, nonetheless, and some have used his concept to examine Western treatments of 1989. In a provocative recent essay, for example, Rey Chow insightfully combines Said's ideas with concepts derived from recent work in feminist literary theory and a discussion of the colonialist imagery of films such as *King Kong*, to explore the assumptions and implications of foreign press coverage of Tiananmen.[19]

The various kinds of demythologizing efforts outlined above all have their merits. My approach below is somewhat different, however, for I try to cast my net wider than previous writers—including even Dirlik and Prazniak, whose essay attacks not only the myopia of those with "an obdurate conviction in the evilness of communism" but also the short-sightedness of those who see the students as pure democrats or invoke Fu Manchu–style imagery to criticize the CCP.[20] My working assumption is that there are bound to be mythic elements to all of the narratives of Tiananmen, from the most blatantly propagandistic pamphlets issued by the Chinese government to the most carefully documented works of scholarship—the preceding chapters in this volume by no means excepted.

Rather than set out to demythologize one set of texts and present another as opaquely "realistic" accounts, therefore, my aim is to see how a wide range of myths created and perpetuated by a variety of very different kinds of authors work. As a result, in the pages that follow, I treat all of the accounts of what took place in China in 1989 as though they were works of fiction. This premise frees me to use ideas derived from literary criticism to look at how these stories are structured, paying particular attention to the distinction between tragedy and romance that Northrop Frye develops in his classic *Anatomy of Criticism*.

Tragedy, Romance, and Northrop Frye

Frye's work is particularly attractive here for several reasons. First, in his discussion of the different "generic plots" of tragic, romantic, comic, and ironic narratives, he is primarily concerned with forms of literature that are either explicitly mythological (Homeric odes, the Wagnerian *Ring* cycle), have heroes imbued with mythic qualities (Shakespeare's historical plays), or involve quests of mythic proportions (like that of Don Quixote).[21] The events of 1989 certainly involved figures who had already attained mythic stature (Deng Xiaoping was twice named *Time's* "man of the year" and Fang Lizhi had been called "China's Tom Paine"), and Western journalists (such as the two who subtitled their book on the events "An Eyewitness Account of the Chinese People's Passionate Quest for Democracy") also tended to present the protests as an epic struggle.[22]

Another attraction is that Lynn Hunt and Hayden White, two leading proponents of what Elizabeth Perry refers to in her Introduction as "neoculturalist" analysis, have recently demonstrated that Frye's work on generic plots can be applied usefully not only to literary works but also to the kinds of narrative texts that concern me here. Hunt uses Frye's concepts to elucidate the changing rhetorical stances of French revolutionaries as they continually redefined the goals of their quest. White argues that the works of major figures in European historiography (such as Jules Michelet and Leopold Ranke) can be understood as texts that followed one or another type of generic plot.[23]

One possible objection to using Frye's work to look at a Chinese event is that his main concern is with European and American literature, and the scholars such as Hunt and White who have applied his ideas to other kinds of texts have likewise tended to focus upon the work of Western authors. There may indeed be limits to how well some features of Frye's theory translate to the Chinese case; making sense of the Chinese literary tradition may require that his description of specific genres be modified or his schema expanded to include additional genres. For my purposes, however, all that is important is to ask whether his categories can help us make sense of Chinese as well as Western tales of Tiananmen, and I believe there is good reason to think that they can.

My basis for saying this is that accounts of 1989 are usually treated as part of a larger story, that of the Chinese Revolution, and both Chinese and Western metanarratives of this event tend to fit easily into the romantic or tragic categories Frye outlines. He defines romantic quests as myths in which the "essential plot element is adventure" (often the killing of a monster) and the contrasts between heroes (who represent "spring, dawn, order, fertility, vigor, and youth") and villains (who represent "winter, darkness, confusion, sterility, moribund life, and old age") are clear-cut.[24] Chinese Communist historians have taken great pains to create an image of the revolution as just such an epic struggle between good (brave cadres, loyal peasants, valiant soldiers, and patriotic workers) and evil (imperial rulers, warlords, and corrupt

KMT officials), in which the forces of youth and spring win victory after victory over the forces of age and winter.[25]

This image of the revolutionary change resonates with long-standing tendencies in Chinese oral, literary, and historiographic traditions. Popular storytellers in China have always been fond of tales of brave and virtuous men who are forced to step outside of the established order to fight unjust officials and then end up in positions of power. Such romantic tales form the core of some of the most famous Chinese historical novels and operas, such as *The Water Margin* and *The Romance of the Three Kingdoms*. The clear division Communist historians make between heroes and villains is also reminiscent of the dynastic histories of imperial times, with their biographical sections devoted to life stories of models of Confucian rectitude, on the one hand, and wicked officials, on the other. By heroicizing the epic struggles the CCP waged to build a "New China" freed from the hold of old forces (the anciens régimes Young describes in his chapter), Communist historians have created a tale that fits in well with enduring cultural myths. It is also one filled with episodes whose very names (the Long March, the war against Japanese aggression, the Great Leap Forward) are quintessentially romantic.

Many Westerners have been drawn toward similarly romantic narrative stances. Some have subscribed to the CCP's brand of romanticism. Others have created an equally romantic vision of the quest but (following KMT historians) have claimed that since 1949 villains have temporarily prevailed. Still others, finally, have viewed the Chinese Revolution as a more morally ambiguous event, a valiant effort that somehow went astray. This third kind of narrative has all of the qualities that Frye associates with tragic myths. Tragic heroes, he argues, must be capable of great deeds yet in some ways all too human; their quests must be noble but ultimately doomed to failure, either because of flaws within the heroes themselves (the element of tragedy that Aristotle stressed) or natural forces beyond their control (what Frye terms a "conspiracy of fate").[26]

Western authors give varying reasons for the "failure" of this tragic quest. Some cite Soviet conspiracies, ideological shortcomings, tactical mistakes, or individual acts of betrayal, whereas others highlight natural forces (such as the economic backwardness of the Chinese nation) and historical contingencies (such as the Japanese invasion). They also differ on the question whether the leaders of the KMT, the heads of the CCP, or the Chinese people as a whole are the tragic figures most deserving of sympathy. What they share is a view of the Chinese Revolution as the work of heroes who (to borrow phrases Hunt uses to describe the tragic phase of the French Revolution) had "an extraordinary destiny within [their] grasp" only to have it slip away, whose "goal was so right" but whose "quest for it inevitably failed."[27]

Accounts of 1989, like these metanarratives of the Chinese Revolution, have tended to take either romantic or tragic turns. Later in this essay, I delineate eight different standard ways of presenting the story of Tiananmen, half of which treat 1989 as a romance and half of which present it as a tragedy. Individual writers often incorporate elements from several of these versions into their own particular narrative of 1989, and in some cases one finds the same author presenting the events as a romance in one context and as a tragedy in another. I do not intend, therefore, to try to pigeonhole everyone who has written about Tiananmen or to place each narrative neatly in one of eight categories. Nonetheless, I hope to show that looking at how these four romances and four tragedies work as stories can help us to put the mythologizing and fictionalizing into perspective.

Myth and Fiction: Preliminary Definitions

Before beginning this process, I must clarify what I mean by saying that all accounts of 1989 can be treated as "mythic" or "fictional" texts. By claiming that all are "mythic," I do not mean they are equally persuasive or equally truthful. The weight of available evidence leaves me with no doubt, for example, that the Chinese government's story of what happened on June 4 deserves to be called part of a "big lie" campaign and is much less accurate than, say, Robin Munro's account. My assumption is simply that, to borrow once more from Cohen's discussion of the Boxers, myth and history are best viewed not as oppositional black-and-white categories but rather as end points on a continuum, and that most texts fall somewhere in the middle. Even careful works of historical scholarship gain narrative power by resonating with the myths of a culture's oral and literary traditions. Conversely, those whose interest in events of the past is solely to use them to serve their own political purposes generally go to great lengths to ensure that their version of history seems at least plausible and attempt to bathe their myths in an aura of facticity.[28]

Even when it is possible to assess the relative accuracy of two different historical accounts, moreover, this does not always tell us all that is worth knowing about the narratives. The stories concerning George Washington that every U.S. schoolchild learns illustrates this. As adults we come to see that some of these tales are much less factual than others. Just because the story of the cherry tree is probably pure fabrication whereas that of the winter at Valley Forge is based on a genuine event, however, does not mean that the former is any less an important part of our national historical memory than the latter. In addition, because the tales of that famous winter survivors told were probably exaggerated at times and each new generation of popular historians has embellished the story of Valley Forge in its own way, it seems foolish to say that only the cherry tree is shrouded in "myth."

It is also dangerous to ignore issues other than accuracy where Chinese history is concerned, as Cohen's essay on the Boxers and Perry Link's recent discussion of the functions of propaganda in the PRC make clear. Link argues persuasively that CCP slogans, pronouncements, editorials, and histories of political events are all part of an esoteric but crucially important language "game"—in which the veracity of a statement is largely irrelevant to both the party spokespeople and their audiences. When Chinese citizens pay attention to this "official language," Link claims, it is not because they expect to hear accurate information but rather because they seek clues concerning how they are expected to behave. Words are not bearers of truth, in this game, but chess pieces: One is well served both to watch how officials use them (to avoid danger) and to study their properties (so that one can manipulate the language to one's own advantage).[29] In light of Link's insightful discussion, it seems foolish to dismiss official tales of Tiananmen simply because they are based on a "big lie." Just as patently false slogans can still tell Chinese citizens how it is safest to act, these obviously mythic stories help us understand the mentality of the CCP.

Throughout the pages that follow, I do try at times to distinguish between accounts on the basis of accuracy. I use information and arguments presented in earlier chapters, as well as other scholarly works, to highlight the weaknesses (including factual errors and faulty logic) of specific types of romantic and tragic treatments of Tiananmen. I conclude the piece by arguing that it is possible to use the contributions in this volume to create a more satisfying tragic version of the events of 1989. I do not deny, however, that this narrative stance is itself mythic: My only claim is that this myth has greater explanatory power than most prevalent ones. My main interest overall, moreover, is not with demythologizing. It is with seeing what different kinds of myths reveal about the language "games" of which they are part.

My earlier use of the term *fiction* also needs to be clarified. I do not wish to imply that everything written about 1989 thus far has been "untrue." We commonly use the term *fictional* as an antonym for *factual*, but (as James Clifford points out) the main thrust of the Latin root, *fingere*, is to describe "something made or fashioned." Clifford goes on to claim that ethnographies are therefore best approached as "fictions." Historians interested in the way linguistic models and literary theory can sharpen our perception and representation of past events have made similar arguments for historiography. For them, as for Clifford, the main point is that the supposedly clear line between novels and objective recitations of "facts" is in reality fuzzy at best and that it may be better to treat ethnographic and historical writings as aesthetic rather than scientific texts.[30]

Michel Foucault's seminal studies of the history of asylums, prisons, and sexuality provide a starting point for many who take what is now being called a "linguistic turn." Particularly influential are Foucault's arguments that many of the seemingly "natural" categories social scientists routinely claimed to be using as neutral descriptive terms—madness, deviance, gender, ethnicity—are in fact social constructions, the definitions of which have as much to do with relations of dominance as with unambiguous, observable "facts." These arguments provide much of the basis for Said's discussion of the "Orient" as a social construct as opposed to a geographically defined place.[31]

The merits and shortcomings of taking a linguistic turn is currently a subject of intense debate within anthropology, history, and other fields.[32] Many of those who do not want to follow this turn to its logical conclusion have, however, come to accept the idea that the differences between the texts

social scientists and novelists create are not as unambiguous as the former
have often liked to think. When I say that narratives of Tiananmen by scholars,
journalists, Chinese propagandists, and historical novelists (at least one of
whom has already used the events of 1989 as a backdrop for his storytelling)
can all be treated as works of "fiction," I do so simply to highlight this point.[33]
I wish to draw attention to the similar kinds of decisions that all four kinds of
authors have to make concerning which characters, demonstrations, acts of
repression, and locations to emphasize and which to downplay or ignore; in
every case the choices they make concerning plot, theme, and characterization
affect the meaning and plausibility of their texts.

Romantic Myths of Tiananmen

Romantic Version Number 1:
The Students as New May Fourth Heroes

Although the last paragraphs have focused primarily upon the mythic and
fictional properties of scholarly works and official propaganda, the most fitting
place to start a discussion of the narratives of 1989 is with the words of the
protesters themselves. It might seem odd at first to claim that their versions
of what took place between April and June tend to be "romantic" as opposed
to "tragic" in nature. As George Steiner argues, definitions of tragedy "must
start from the fact of catastrophe," and the events of June 4 were clearly
catastrophic for the movement.[34] In addition, the terms (such as *canan, canshi,
canju, xuelei,* and *beiju*) that Chinese authors sympathetic to the demonstrators
routinely use to refer to the events of June Fourth are all commonly translated
into English as "tragic" or "tragedy" and are all associated with catastrophic
occurrences.[35]

This said, the protesters' narratives of Tiananmen were seldom tragic in
the Western sense of the word. As Joseph Esherick and I point out in a note
to Chapter 2, the operatic performances known as *beiju* are often more similar
to what Westerners think of as melodrama than they are to Greek or Shakespearean tragedy, leading some literary scholars to argue that China "lacks"
a tragic tradition. Neither the veracity of this argument (which other literary
specialists have disputed) nor the Orientalist assumptions of some of its
proponents (i.e., that Western traditions represent a norm and that other
cultures are not simply different but inferior in some way) need concern us
here.[36] What is important is that when protesters called the events of June 4
part of a *beiju*, they did not mean that there was anything morally ambiguous
about the events in question. Nor did they mean that the victims were defeated
by either their own tragic flaws or a conspiracy of fate. In the narratives of the
protesters, the villains are not mysterious forces at all but savage despots—
one meaning of the character *can*, which serves as the root for several Chinese
terms for tragedy, is "cruel" or "savage"—and those who died are not noble
sinners but heroic innocents.

This makes the protesters' version of June Fourth romantic as opposed to tragic. In their narratives, as in all true romances, attention is directed to the "conflict between a hero and his enemy" and "all the reader's values are bound up with the hero," who possesses the various qualities related to youth and rebirth discussed earlier. The conflict in romances is always between good and evil, according to Frye, and the "nearer the romance is to myth, the more attributes of divinity will cling to the hero and the more the enemy will take on demonic . . . qualities."[37] A fully developed romantic myth will end with virtue triumphing over wickedness, but individual romantic episodes can end with mourning exercises for a hero or heroine who has died for the good of the cause. This "exaltation of the hero" is less a finale than a call to arms aimed at those who survive, a ceremony that launches a new attempt to carry the original quest through to its intended conclusion.[38]

The themes Frye associates with romance began to appear in the movement's rhetoric early on. As Elizabeth Perry has argued in Chapter 7, students began in mid-April to transform the deceased Hu Yaobang into a more heroic figure than he had ever been in life, simultaneously valorizing their own role as patriotic protesters. The new Hu Yaobang celebrated in protest poems was "a star of hope," one of "the people's most glorious heroes," in short, a martyr to a noble cause. He was also somebody who, like all of the romantic deliverers Frye describes, had by his very death helped to further the quest he led. In the outpouring of grief that accompanied the popular mourning for Hu, one writer claimed, one could "see a hundred million living souls awakening the heroic spirit of China." The new generation of awakened heroes destined to carry on his "behest" and "advance the cause of freedom" would be youths determined to serve as the "vanguard of history." They would "bravely bear high the banner of democracy" and battle "villains" and "devils" so that a "new sun" could rise in the sky.[39]

The romanticism of student imagery reached new heights at the time of the May Fourth anniversary. In our discussion of political theater, Esherick and I describe various attempts protesters made to appropriate the official symbolism associated with the May Fourth Movement, and Schwarcz's essay has shown that in contemporary China simply to invoke the year 1919 was to conjure up a series of images with romantic implications. As these and other chapters have suggested, when students spoke of their actions as part of a "New May Fourth Movement," they instantly located themselves within an ongoing tradition of youthful patriotic engagement and linked themselves to an event that the CCP authorities had helped to turn into a sacred national myth. Communist educators and propagandists have spent the last decades treating May Fourth figures much as Western Sunday school teachers and evangelical ministers handle the characters in Biblical parables, hoping to instill a similar familiarity colored by reverence in their charges. Ironically, these efforts ensured that many Chinese would see the "New May Fourth" students of 1989 in romantic terms: as youths attempting to finish the quest to establish a truly "new" and democratic China that the protesters of 1919 had begun and those of 1935, 1976, and other years had continued.[40]

References to 1919 did more than simply link the protesters to positive images of youth, democracy, new cultural values, and revolutionary progress: Such comments also implied that the current CCP leadership was made up of men who were not only old in chronological terms but the representatives of old ideas and practices as well. To call the 1989 protests a "New May Fourth Movement" was to associate figures such as Deng Xiaoping and Li Peng with the anciens régimes of imperial despots and corrupt warlords. When the students argued that they were also carrying on in the tradition of the April Fifth Movement of 1976, they added a third ancien régime to this list.[41] The official CCP line on the protests of 1976 is that they were a revolutionary event that aided Deng's rise to power. Student references to April Fifth implied that Deng was now acting more like a successor to than a true opponent of the former Gang of Four regime.

Throughout the middle and end of May, students used various techniques to embellish their romantic image of 1989 as a sharply defined battle between progressive youth and oppressive age. The "Statement of the May Thirteenth Hunger Strikers" began by reminding readers that the protesters ready to die for the nation were in "the full bloom of youth." Wall posters in late May castigated Deng Xiaoping as an "invalid" leading a "group of elders" and described him as a "last emperor." Some presented him as a modern-day empress dowager.[42] And on May 23 a coalition of protest groups issued perhaps the most romantically titled of all 1989 manifestos: "The Final Battle Between Light and Darkness." This "statement on the current condition" claimed that the newest social movement had "surpassed" those of 1919 and 1976 and launched a "new historical epoch." Victory would be certain as long as the people persevered in their just fight for freedom, despite the attempts of people like Li Peng to "stop the progress of history."[43]

The image of 1989 as a battle between good and evil took on new meaning in the wake of June Fourth, as Wuer Kaixi's famous videotape broadcast from Hong Kong on June 28 (which presents an almost perfectly romantic vision of events) illustrates. On the one side are the "martyrs" who were "innocent" and hoped for peace but who eventually "gave their lifeblood in an effort to keep the sinking ship of China away from dangerous shoals and lead her toward the bright and open ocean." On the other side are "the reactionary warlords" who "revealed themselves" to be "cruelly bestial fascists."[44] Tragic deaths are important primarily for how they affect our emotions or for the lessons they teach us about what we can do to avoid suffering a similar fate.[45] Wuer implicitly rejects such an approach and demands that the deaths of June Fourth be seen in romantic terms—that is, as violence that in some way ensures the final victory of the forces of virtue. The fight against the "beasts" who rule China now continues, he insists, and those who survive are certain to win, thanks to the strength they will gain (through a vaguely defined process of spiritual communion) from the deaths of their fallen comrades. "Their lives [those of the martyrs] have been melded together with ours," he says, so that his life and those of other survivors "no longer belong to us alone."[46]

Other statements protesters issued in June and July 1989 were often more restrained in their imagery than Wuer's rousing call to arms, but many harped on similar themes. His presentation of the authorities as demons in human form, for example, was far from exceptional. Posters in which hard-liners appeared as beasts, modern-day Hitlers, or other kinds of incarnations of evil had become common as soon as martial law was declared in late May, and a June 4 report by Beijing's leading student organization said that in carrying out the massacre, the "fascist government [had] lifted its hypocritical veil and the dictators [had] revealed their disgusting intentions."[47]

Wuer's vision of the deaths at Tiananmen Square serving to guarantee final victory also has many counterparts. The idea that the blood of martyrs can have regenerative and cleansing (as well as polluting) powers was a common one in 1925 and 1926, when police forces under the control of foreigners and native warlords fired on unarmed crowds of protesters in a series of massacres.[48] This same theme resurfaced in 1989. April and May wall posters bearing sanguinary poems (with titles such as "Bloodstains") and essays (which argued that blood could "wash clean the disgrace of autocracy") were followed by post–June Fourth banners that spoke of the blood of martyrs' enriching China's soil.[49] Even if the occupation of Tiananmen Square had ended in catastrophe, the proponents of the New May Fourth romance maintained, this was not the end of the quest but merely a temporary setback, the prelude to a more lasting future victory for the forces of progress, youth, and freedom.

Romantic Version Number 2: The Students as Anti-Communist Heroes

Protesters have not been the only ones to treat the events of 1989 as an epic battle between heroic students (representing the forces of light) and monstrous hard-liners (symbolizing the powers of darkness). Many scholars, politicians, and journalists in Taiwan, Hong Kong, and the West have also created romances of this sort. Some of these have essentially echoed the students' own New May Fourth story, and these need not concern us here. Of more interest are two variations on the theme, beginning with one I label the "end-of-history myth."

This label is taken from a controversial essay by Francis Fukuyama, which argued that Western liberalism was in the process of winning a well-earned and definitive victory over Communist tyrannies throughout the world, a process he described as ushering in the "end of history" (at least in the Hegelian sense of dialectical change).[50] Critics of this article have argued that almost all of its premises are questionable at best—particularly its assumption that all former Communist regimes will inevitably be replaced by Western liberal democracies.[51] The essay remains important both because of its direct influence and because it is representative of the quasi-millenarian expectations that recent events (such as the fall of the Berlin Wall) have triggered, which often find expression in academic and journalistic discussions of the "new world order."

Chinese events would seem at first to pose a problem for the Fukuyama thesis. If the massacres of June are treated as merely a temporary setback, however, anti-Communists can see the protests of 1989 as a prelude to the "end" of Chinese history. This is clearly the implication of works by some Western sinologists (such as those by Simon Leys and his supporters alluded to above), as well as of anti-Communist Chinese partisans of the KMT.[52] Their story of the events goes roughly as follows. The massive demonstrations of 1989 showed that the Chinese people had finally become aware of the venality of the CCP and the bankruptcy of Marxist and Maoist theory. Inspired by Western democratic ideas and emboldened by decades of chafing under the yoke of Communist oppression, the protesters valiantly struggled to free their country from the hold of a repressive ideology and Party apparatus. The protesters may have lost the battle in 1989, but they are destined to win the war and lead China down the same kind of path toward a market economy and democratic institutions that Eastern Europe has begun to follow. The savagery of the government's actions on June 4 was a temporary setback to the cause of freedom, but by offering unforgettable proof of the monstrousness of even so-called moderate Communists like Deng Xiaoping, it actually made the final victory of anti-Communist forces more certain.

Romantic Version Number 3:
The Students as Maoist Heroes

There is one other kind of romantic tale, which I call the New Cultural Revolution myth, that presents the protesters as messianic figures and the authorities as devils incarnate. This account is in most ways the exact inverse of the end-of-history myth, for instead of treating the students as anti-Communists, it presents them as Marxists trying to carry out the Communist Revolution's original vision. Deng Xiaoping's cardinal sin, in this romance, ceases to be his failure to instigate comprehensive enough economic and political reforms and becomes instead his abandonment of egalitarian socialist ideals. The New Cultural Revolution myth has more in common with the New May Fourth one, which also stresses that students were angered by the regime's failure to live up to long-standing revolutionary goals. The key difference is that instead of interpreting the new struggle as a continuation of that of 1919, the New Cultural Revolution myth argues that the students of 1989 were emulating the positive aspects of the Red Guard Movement of the 1960s.

Accounts of this sort are often overlooked because they have been much less central a part of mainstream discourse than the other two kinds of romances described above. Virtually the only authors outside of China who have celebrated (as opposed to criticized) continuities between the Cultural Revolution and 1989 have been those writing for explicitly Maoist publications such as the *Revolutionary Worker*, an organ of the Revolutionary Communist Party (RCP). Their arguments, furthermore, have often been fairly simplistic— that is, they act at times as if the mere fact that some protesters carried portraits of Mao validates the RCP line.

This said, the New Cultural Revolution myth deserves to be treated as more than just a fringe idea, as at least one careful attempt to argue its merits exists: Mark Hager's "Roots of Repression in Deng's China." Hager views the use of Mao portraits as revealing and presents Deng's flirtation with market economy capitalism as a negative development. He breaks with RCP purists on other points, however, when he criticizes the "romanticism" of Western leftists who insist upon treating Mao as a "pure revolutionary hero," and he argues that the Great Helmsman's mistakes were largely responsible for the Cultural Revolution's having ultimately "yielded incalculable mayhem and suffering." He claims, nonetheless, that the image of Mao simply as a "quintessentially authoritarian dictator" is also deeply flawed, as are treatments of the Cultural Revolution that ignore its roots in an effort to "democratize abusive power structures."

His argument about 1989 then unfolds as follows. If one focuses on the early goals of the Red Guards rather than upon "vicious petty intrigues and wars" and the growth of the Mao cult that followed, the protesters of 1989 seem to have a great deal in common with those of the 1960s. Both were concerned with official corruption and despotic tendencies. The Cultural Revolution left a complex legacy, and the protesters of 1989 were certainly not trying to revive all of its features. Nevertheless, one part of that legacy was the "experience of active democracy and dreams of its restoration in more adequate form, which has persisted as a force in Chinese life." The Democracy Wall Movement of the 1970s (in which many former Red Guards took part) and the protests of the late 1980s (in which many former Red Guards served as advisers or inspirational figures) need to be understood as "manifestations" of this force.[53]

Romantic Version Number 4:
The Soldiers as Revolutionary Martyrs

The last kind of romantic myth that deserves consideration is the official account of the protests as counterrevolutionary riots. The hard-line story draws in one way or another from each of the preceding three versions of events but ultimately reverses the implications of each by inverting the positions of heroes and villains. Like New May Fourth accounts, official propaganda argues that in 1989 China faced the same threat it had faced in 1919. The difference is that, for the officials, the familiar danger was not government corruption but foreign attempts to subjugate China. Like the proponents of the end-of-history myth, official propaganda argues that the protests were inspired by anti-Communist forces seeking to overthrow the CCP and turn China into a capitalist country. But according to the official literature, this would have destroyed rather than saved the nation. Like the New Cultural Revolution myth, finally, official propagandists stress the parallels between the Red Guards and the students of 1989. The key distinction here is that the government literature takes it for granted that every aspect of the Cultural Revolution should be repudiated. Like all three previous romances, the story is presented as a clear-cut battle between light and darkness (or in this case "red" patriots and "black" hands) in which the heroes are almost divine, the villains less than fully human.[54] The casting is, however, radically different from that of any other romance: The monsters whose humanity is called into question are not Deng Xiaoping and Li Peng but "troublemakers" like the dissident Liu Xiaobo and "conspirators" like Zhao Ziyang.[55]

It may seem strange at first to term the government's story a "romantic myth," as Frye stresses that romances always involve battles between noble youth and ignoble age. Given that the students were generations younger than those responsible for the crackdown, it may appear farfetched to claim that government spokespeople present Deng Xiaoping's forces as fighting for progressive values of regeneration and try to link the protesters with backwardness and decay. This is, however, precisely what official propaganda pieces—ranging from English-language pictorial histories of PLA actions to compilations of speeches by key government leaders—attempt to do.[56]

Official narratives use three main techniques to associate their cause with romantic forces representing progress, youth, and order. First, they portray the demonstrations as acts of *luan* or *dongluan*. Young, Anagnost, Watson, and others have already discussed the potency these terms had to conjure up negative memories of the "chaos" and "turmoil" of the warlord and Cultural Revolution eras. These words have a long history within Chinese political discourse: Long before the cataclysmic events that those alive today lived through, the terms for chaos were already enshrined as pejorative descriptions for anything that threatened the stability and security of the community.[57] To say that the protesters were creating *luan*, therefore, was to suggest that anyone who could bring an end to the movement would be saving the nation by restoring order. Moreover, because the Deng regime has continually stressed that the post-1978 reforms can only succeed if the political environment remains stable, to put an end to turmoil also accomplishes the romantic goal of defending progress toward a long-term goal.

Second, official narratives go beyond simply treating the task of pacification as a heroic one to personally valorize the soldiers assigned to carry out this romantic quest. All of these young patriots performed "immortal feats," according to Beijing's mayor, and various government spokespeople have singled out for special praise those soldiers who died in action. Along with describing the bravery of these soldiers (and drawing attention to the youthfulness of these heroes), officials have honored fallen members of the PLA with all of the rituals traditionally accorded other kinds of "revolutionary martyrs" (such as the student protesters who died in the "good" student movements of the pre-1949 era): Young Pioneers (the CCP's equivalent to Boy Scouts) have laid wreaths honoring their memory at Tiananmen Square, top government figures have paid highly publicized visits to their families, and hagiographic memoirs by former comrades in arms have been published.[58]

The third way official authors have romanticized the crackdown has been by insisting that the Deng regime is composed of revolutionaries and that all those who oppose it are by definition counterrevolutionaries. This terminology is crucial, as it implies that no matter how youthful many of the protesters were in chronological terms, the demonstrations were somehow linked to one or more of the revolution's anciens régimes. Young has insightfully analyzed the implications of such a linkage in his chapter, so only the briefest reminder is needed here. When officials continually connected the 1989 protests to such discredited phases of the Chinese past as the Nationalist era (the students would turn China into "a bourgeois republic subordinate to the West"), they not only associated their opponents with old values, but they made the crackdown seem just one more stage in an ongoing revolutionary quest to create a "new" China. This imagery continued into 1991, with CCP leaders presenting their policies as part of a "New Long March," a heroic effort to overcome the obstacles (including the activities of reactionary dissidents) that have prevented China from becoming a socialist paradise.

Tragic Myths of Tiananmen

If most Chinese accounts of 1989 can be classified as romances of one sort or another, foreign narratives have more often presented the events in tragic terms. Writing in July 1989, Orville Schell noted the prevalence of the word *tragic* in early attempts observers made to "articulate their feelings in the [immediate] aftermath of the June Fourth massacre," and this word has continued to appear in virtually all of the scholarly and popular accounts of the events published in Western languages, including the preceding chapters in this volume.[59] Words like *tragedy* and *tragic* are employed so loosely in English that their appearance can be misleading at times. For example, even writers with views similar to those of Leys (who I have argued present essentially romantic narratives of 1989) refer in passing to "tragic" features of specific events. This said, most Western accounts (and a few Chinese ones) contain all of the elements that Frye says must be present in fully realized tragic myths: They have heroes who seem both part divine and all too human. The stories begin with heroes "on the top of the wheel of fortune," with their goals seemingly within their grasp. The tales end with nemesis inexorably overtaking and vanquishing the heroes, proving that the quest (though noble) was doomed from the start to fail, because of either the natures of the heroes, the immutable laws of the environment in which the quest was attempted, or some combination of the two.[60]

Although most foreign narratives share this tragic view of 1989, there is a great deal of variety when it comes to exactly how the plot is shaped. I divide foreign tragic accounts, therefore, into four categories, largely on the basis of which political actors are cast in the roles of heroes and villains. In contrast to the four kinds of romance described above, however, it is not always easy to find specific works that exemplify each tragic variation; most texts in fact combine elements from at least two categories. The categories are thus primarily intended to serve as heuristic devices, and the same is true of the titles I give them—each of which is either the name of a Shakespearean tragedy or a classical Greek myth. As artificial as these categories admittedly are, they are useful in that they give a sense of the main themes that shape tragic accounts of 1989, as well as the issues that differentiate these accounts from each other. I would also argue that there is nothing inappropriate about using Elizabethan and Athenian analogies in a discussion of events that occurred in China, as most of the tragic accounts that concern me here were written by Westerners.

Tragic Version Number 1: 1989 as King Lear

Shakespeare's famous rendition of the story of this legendary British monarch seems at first far removed from the events of Tiananmen Square. Upon reflection, however, it is not so hard to understand why some writers have come to treat Deng Xiaoping as a kind of modern equivalent to Lear: a once proud ruler whose body and mind are suffering the infirmities of age. It is also worth remembering that Shakespeare's tragedy centers on the harm that comes from a father's inability to distinguish between loyal and unworthy children. We are meant to feel some compassion for the father: Lear is certainly to blame for much of his own suffering, but the inexorable force of age and the false words of those he mistakenly trusts also play a role in his fall. Our greatest sympathy is directed elsewhere, however. The primary victim in *King Lear* is Cordelia, the faithful daughter who earns her father's wrath by telling him the truth rather than simply what he wants to hear, much as Zhao Ziyang is seen by some as having lost Deng's patronage by insisting (after May 4, 1989) that the popular movement would aid the cause of reform.[61]

The *Time* magazine publication *Massacre in Beijing*, one of the first book-length narratives of 1989 to appear in print, is perhaps the best example of a work that treats Deng's condemnation of Zhao as comparable to Lear's treatment of Cordelia. Writing of the elderly Chinese ruler's former greatness, the authors state that in "the summer of 1986, Deng Xiaoping appeared to be on the verge of accomplishing a feat unprecedented in modern Chinese history [having] put his country firmly on the path to modernization [and] secured what seemed to be a firm guarantee of political stability." They then describe his rapid descent from the top of the wheel of fortune, attributing his transformation into a petty tyrant to forces at least partially beyond his control (a worsening economy, the aging process) as well as character flaws (his erroneous belief that China could import Western technology without being affected by foreign ideas). The authors of *Massacre in Beijing* admit that Deng should be held accountable for the crackdown of 1989, and they present Zhao as a heroic figure to be pitied. They stress, however, that opposition figures were not the only victims of this tragic event. Just as Cordelia's death broke Lear's spirit, the massacres destroyed Deng's "hopes for the kind of political stability and economic progress that would make China a world power in the next century."[62]

The analogy between Cordelia's death and the massacre goes further in some texts, for the protesters (as well as Zhao Ziyang) can be presented as loyal children whose filiality is misinterpreted. Westerners who thought of the pre-1989 Deng Xiaoping as a courageous ruler working to transform China from a socialist dictatorship into a capitalist democracy held onto the hope through April and May that he would realize in time that the students were anxious to achieve this same goal. That Deng ultimately sided with hard-liners like Li Peng and Yang Shangkun (who fill the roles of Cordelia's two evil sisters) and rejected both Zhao Ziyang and the protesters became for them a tragic error similar to Lear's mistaken favoring of Goneril and Regan instead of his one truly filial child. According to this narrative, Deng's vision was clouded by bad advice (given by a "clutch of elderly and semi-retired leaders . . . suspicious of any sweeping innovations") and the haunting power of old memories (of his own "humiliation and banishment" during the Cultural Revolution). These two factors combined to produce a kind of madness similar to Lear's, under the spell of which Deng failed to recognize the loyal students for what they were ("the model of peaceful idealism") and viewed them instead as traitors ("old enemies in new guises returning to pursue the unfinished anti-Socialist battles of decades past").[63]

Tragic Version Number 2: 1989 as Julius Caesar

This alternative version of the tragedy of 1989 also asks its audience to feel compassion for both Zhao Ziyang and Deng Xiaoping. When people who encountered Shakespeare's *Julius Caesar* in school think back upon the play, the line that most often comes to mind is the stricken ruler's comment that Brutus has betrayed him. As various scholars note, however, a close textual reading of the play reveals that Brutus is far from a villain: Caesar may be a victim, but Brutus is actually the true tragic hero of the drama. It is he whom Shakespeare has Antony refer to as the "noblest Roman of them all," and his decision to side with the evil Cassius against Caesar (although it proves his undoing) is treated less as an act of wickedness than as what one Shakespeare scholar calls a "noble error." Even his stabbing of Caesar is motivated by pure (if misguided) impulses: He is trying to prevent his beloved Rome from falling prey once more to political ills (personal as opposed to oligarchic rule) that plagued it in the past.[64]

There are obvious problems with using this plotline to understand tales of Tiananmen. Most importantly, perhaps, China's supreme leader, Deng Xiaoping, was not killed or even purged in 1989, and popular demonstrations do not figure in Shakespeare's political drama set in ancient Rome. Nonetheless, with a little imagination, it is possible to see some Western accounts of the Chinese crisis as reworkings of the tale of Brutus and Julius Caesar, with Deng Xiaoping cast in the role of the former and Zhao Ziyang cast in that of the latter.

Henry Kissinger's August 1, 1989, *Washington Post* opinion piece, "Caricatures of Deng as Tyrant Unfair," is an important example. Just as literary scholars argue that focusing on Brutus as a simplistic betrayer obscures the nobility and complexity of his character, Kissinger wants us to see Deng Xiaoping not as a villain but as a hero who erred when faced with a difficult choice. The brutality of the crackdown should be condemned, Kissinger claims, but we should remember that most (if not all) regimes in other parts of the world would have used some form of violence if dissidents had occupied and refused to leave their nation's major political center. We should also remember that Deng Xiaoping has long been the noblest of all Chinese, at least when it came to normalizing relations with the United States and introducing capitalist economic reforms. According to Kissinger, he is a flawed figure—he listens to the wrong advice, misinterprets situations, and has failed to see that sweeping political reforms must accompany economic ones—but he is much more than simply a power-hungry tyrant. Even in June 1989, according to Kissinger, Deng saw himself (as Brutus did when stabbing Caesar) as protecting the nation from a familiar danger: in this case a resurgence of the kind of mob action that accompanied the Cultural Revolution.

Tragic Version Number 3: 1989 as Romeo and Juliet

The two kinds of tragedies sketched above have centered on high politics and emphasized the actions of top officials. Other kinds of tragic narratives of Tiananmen focus instead upon the character and behavior of the student protesters. The course of events in Shakespeare's *Romeo and Juliet* provides a useful outline for one such student-centered version of the events. In this play, the quest of the hero and heroine is presented as a noble one that is nonetheless destined to fail. Despite the purity of their love, a variety of factors—some, but by no means all, of which are within their control—conspire to ensure that they will not succeed in marrying and living happily as husband and wife.[65] Similarly, various Chinese and Western authors imply that, as virtuous as the goals of the 1989 protests may have been, the inexperience of the students and the intractability of the obstacles they encountered meant that these goals, too, were unattainable.[66]

There are several more specific parallels between some portrayals of the Chinese students and Shakespeare's treatment of the Italian lovers. In both cases, doubts are raised as to how well the heroes really understood their causes. The protesters of 1989 were certainly passionate about the cause of "democracy," but some authors argue that the youths had at best a limited sense of just what the word entailed and that the students' attitude toward figures such as Hu Yaobang and Zhao Ziyang was fickle to say the least. Similarly, although Romeo is often thought of as true love personified, Shakespeare reminds us that he was just as ardent a suitor of Rosaline before Juliet appeared on the scene. In addition, in both cases, the heroes and heroines are portrayed as being able to realize their dreams temporarily within an artificial environment, but they prove unable to carry this small-scale paradise into the real world: Just as the love that blossoms on the balcony and is nurtured by the light of the moon withers in the city in the cruel light of day, the island of pure democracy that the students create in Tiananmen Square remains an isolated phenomenon.

In at least some variations upon the theme of 1989 as *Romeo and Juliet*, yet another parallel appears: Certain Chinese dissidents and Western analysts suggest that impatience may have played as great a role in the Chinese tragedy as it did in the Shakespearean one. If only the students had been less determined to carry the occupation of Tiananmen Square through to the end, these authors imply, the outcome might have been very different. It is hard to say how Romeo and Juliet would have fared if they had each waited a bit longer to get all of the facts before committing suicide, but their chances for happiness would certainly have been greater. Similarly, had the students exercised more caution, Hu Ping and other veterans of events such as the Democracy Wall Movement have argued, the crackdown might have been avoided or at least have been less severe.[67]

Tragic Version Number 4: 1989 *as* Oedipus

The final kind of tragic presentation that needs to be examined here is Greek rather than Shakespearean. To quote W. H. Auden, who has written insightfully on the main difference between these two distinctive forms of Western tragedy, the former leaves one saying, "What a pity it had to be this way," whereas the latter leaves one saying, "What a pity it was this way when it might have been otherwise."[68] Shakespeare gives more credence to notions of free will than did his Greek predecessors. Even in *Romeo and Juliet* (in which fate is accorded a strong role as nemesis), the audience retains some hope that the young lovers will not commit suicide, and when they do die their own folly as well as forces beyond their control are to blame. The Greeks, by contrast, seldom left any room for hope. The audience knew from the start that if the gods or the furies were intent upon thwarting a hero, there was no way that he would escape a dreadful fate. The heroes of Greek tragedies frequently suffer from delusions of grandeur, a prideful conceit that they will be able to escape their destiny, and this is shown as contributing to their ruin. Neither hubris of this sort nor the other kinds of sins against the gods that Greek heroes commit (often unwittingly), are of much real consequence in determining the outcome when compared to fate itself. In most Greek tragedies, in short, "the fall lurks behind every word" and the coming of a predestined catastrophe is always imminent.[69]

Lucian Pye's recent essay "Tiananmen and Chinese Political Culture" presents June Fourth as just such a foreordained calamity. There "was an inevitability in the escalating confrontation," he writes, that made the events of April through June "a Chinese version of a Greek tragedy."[70] The massacre should not have surprised anyone, he insists, and the only Western China specialists who should have been shocked by it were those who had romanticized the nature of the Deng regime and the CCP.

Pye's vision of Chinese communism as an inherently evil force resistant to any kind of fundamental change links him to Leys and other authors who treat 1989 as an anti-Communist romance. What sets Pye apart is his refusal to see the Party's ideology, institutions, and leaders as the only villains. For him, nemesis takes the form of an intransigent, authoritarian political culture whose roots go back much farther than 1949 or even the founding of the CCP and that he claims has continually frustrated all nineteenth- and twentieth-century attempts to transform China into a freer and more modern nation.

This vision of Chinese political culture, which he spells out in much more detail in the earlier works that Perry discusses in her Introduction, leads him to be anything but sanguine about the future prospects for a democratic China. The bloodshed of June Fourth will neither cleanse the nation nor change the basic rules of Chinese politics, he predicts, but will only lead to more violence "driven by the dictates of revenge."[71]

In a sense, Pye's essay goes beyond tragedy when he tries to place the events at Tiananmen Square into a broader historical framework that fits Frye's definition of ironic myth. According to Frye, such myths frequently take the form of a "parody of romance: the application of romantic mythical forms to a more realistic content that fits them in unexpected ways."[72] This is precisely what Pye does when he shifts his attention away from 1989 to the modern period as a whole and claims that the very notion that China has ever experienced a true "revolution" (a central starting point for most romantic interpretations of 1989) is nonsensical. If one focuses on real transformations in mentality and social life, as opposed to "wishful dreams" and hopeful rhetoric, he claims, little has changed in China in the last century and a half. Each successive effort to create a new China has merely led to the replication of old patterns of authoritarian rule; whereas romance depends upon forward motion, modern China has been stalled in a vicious cycle.

Although his vision of modern Chinese history veers toward irony, Pye treats the protesters much as Greek playwrights treated tragic heroes. The very circumstances of their birth (in this case within a political environment fundamentally inhospitable to the growth of democratic or egalitarian thought and action) plays a role in sealing their doom, as it does for Oedipus. In contrast to the Oedipus trilogy, in 1989 it was the fathers who slew the sons (and daughters) rather than the other way around. Nonetheless, one comes away from Pye's essay with a sense that China's history has left it under the same kind of long-standing curse, with the power to punish the innocent as well as the guilty, that haunted the family of Oedipus. And for Pye, the protesters' main sin (like that of Oedipus) was a kind of hubris. A "blind confidence that virtue should conquer all" led them to believe that they could succeed where "revolutionaries" of the past had failed, and this left them "vulnerable to the realities of Chinese authoritarianism."[73]

A Critique of Eight Straw Men

Earlier I described my four tragic categories as ones created to serve "heuristic purposes," but perhaps a blunter (and fairer) statement would be that in the eight versions of the tale of Tiananmen sketched out above I have created straw men. Even some of the writers whose works I have used to illustrate specific plots make use of more sophisticated lines of argumentation than my bare-bones sketches of their texts would suggest, and it would be impossible to place many other accounts of 1989 into a single category without doing an even greater disservice to their authors. Neither analyses of 1989 that Andrew

Nathan, Lowell Dittmer, and Andrew Walder offered in an early symposium on Tiananmen, for example, nor most of the chapters in works such as *Perspectives on the Chinese People's Movement*, a collection edited by Tony Saich, fit cleanly into any of my eight narrative categories.[74] The same is true of Jonathan Spence's discussions of Tiananmen: These should be easier to classify (because they have taken the fairly straightforward narrative forms of textbook chapters and introductions to sourcebooks), but his nuanced, historically grounded interpretations of the events incorporate both romantic and tragic elements. The Chinese accounts published to date have generally been simpler to categorize, though there are signs that this situation is beginning to change (at least where former protesters and their supporters, if not CCP officials, are concerned). Shen Tong's autobiography, with its mixture of personal and movement history and its ambiguous assessments of various issues, is difficult to place in any of my eight categories.[75] Similarly, conversations with Su Xiaokang have convinced me that if he ever writes an extended narrative of 1989, the work will be hard indeed to pigeonhole.

Although the categories I have offered are best treated as straw men, analyzing their weak spots seems a useful first step toward constructing a more satisfying mythology of 1989. Straw men may be easy to knock down, but we can still learn something from the exercise. In addition, examining texts that readily fit into my categories can indirectly help us see how hybrid narratives (that combine elements from two or more plotlines) work. To take but one example, John Fincher's essay entitled "Zhao's Fall, China's Loss" presents a considerably more complex interpretation of 1989 than *Massacre in Beijing*. Fincher incorporates elements from various kinds of tragic and romantic tales of Tiananmen to create a narrative hard to categorize.[76] He also introduces important new arguments into the debate on the causes and consequences of the crisis, such as a claim that the spread of cities and the growth of a semi-urbanized population have made obsolete our (and the CCP hard-liners') vision of an overwhelmingly "peasant" China (i.e., as a country with 80 percent of its populace living essentially untouched by metropolitan culture). Nonetheless, the title he gives his piece positions Zhao as a central tragic figure in his narrative and thus suggests that a critique of the *King Lear* approach may provide some insight into his line of reasoning as well as that of the authors of *Massacre in Beijing*.

What, then, are the primary weaknesses of the eight plotlines outlined above? It is easiest to begin with the four romances, as most of the preceding chapters have tried (in one way or another) to suggest that any vision of 1989 as an unambiguous struggle between pure good and unadulterated evil is extremely problematic. For example, although sympathetic to the protesters' goals, Elizabeth Perry and Lee Feigon have stressed that the students who occupied Tiananmen Square often replicated features of the ideology and Party structure they opposed. Their chapters argue that, despite the wall posters heralding the students as the creators of a completely "new" and enlightened China, the protesters were influenced by a variety of decidedly "old" ideas relating to social class and gender. Vera Schwarcz has also suggested that student claims to represent the May Fourth legacy, as opposed to that of the Cultural Revolution, need to be balanced against the reemergence during the movement of patterns of crowd politics reminiscent of Red Guardism. In a provocative law review article, William Alford also reminds us that members of the same generation of students who took to the streets in the name of enlightenment in spring 1989 had been involved in anti-African riots six months before. And in a powerful recent essay, Geremie Barmé discusses the extent to which the protesters of 1989 fell prey to the same kind of "movement mentality" that permeates the CCP's official campaigns.[77]

None of the contributors to this volume presents as extensive a critique of the end-of-history myth as the one Dirlik and Prazniak have recently published.[78] Various chapters do, however, point to some of the key problems with the image of students as romantic heroes striving to free their nation from the hold of an evil Communist ideology. Daniel Chirot suggests that the end-of-history concept needs at least to be modified, arguing that anger inspired by governmental corruption and a general sense of "moral rot," as opposed to disgust with the formal ideology of Marxism, played the fundamental role in leading protesters in various countries to challenge ruling Communist parties in 1989. Ernest Young, who stresses that the protesters and their opponents shared many similar viewpoints concerning the anciens régimes plaguing China, goes further by suggesting that the demonstrators may not have been repudiating the CCP's "revolution" as much as they were simply trying to get it back on course. Ann Anagnost directly attacks the idea that all ideologies other than capitalism have become archaic and that the threatened leaders of Communist countries now cynically use Marxist concepts solely to defend their efforts to maintain their power. Perhaps even more damning to anti-Communist myths of Tiananmen than Anagnost's discussion of the continuing importance of ideology in China's countryside, however, is Timothy Cheek's argument that right up to June Fourth intellectual dissidents still tended to see themselves as loyal critics, trying to radically reform rather than overthrow the Communist system.

Joseph Esherick and I criticize efforts to present the students as enlightened May Fourth democrats and committed anti-Communists in our chapter, which also addresses some of the shortcomings of the New Cultural Revolution myth. In this last regard, we stress that treating the use of Mao posters as "proof" that the students identified with the goals of the Cultural Revolution is problematic at best. Mark Hager is right in claiming that the Western media underestimated the continuing influence Marxist ideology has had for Chinese dissidents and that they often overlooked or obscured the tactical and ideological continuities between the Red Guards and the protesters of 1989, including those John Israel mentions in his chapter. Nonetheless, as Israel and other contributors argue, the students took great pains to distance themselves from the legacy of the Cultural Revolution, and many of the similarities with Red Guard activism that emerged were inadvertent, not intentional. There were pragmatic reasons for the students to repudiate all features of the Cultural Revolution to be sure, as memories of the chaos of the "ten bad years" continue to haunt many Chinese. The extant evidence makes it hard to believe, however, that all student repudiations of the Red Guard legacy stemmed from strategic calculations as opposed to genuine convictions.

So much has been said about the inconsistencies and inaccuracies of the Chinese government's interpretation of 1989, both in the preceding chapters and in a wide range of works by eyewitness observers, that it may seem that little comment needs to be made about the shortcomings of the fourth romantic tale of Tiananmen I describe.[79] As obviously unfounded as many of its claims are, however, the hard-line version of events should be taken seriously, if for no other reason than that the CCP has gone to such great lengths to lend what Paul Cohen calls an "aura of facticity" to its myth. Chinese television has shown carefully edited documentaries in which violence against soldiers is highlighted and the lone protester's famous confrontation with a tank is presented as "proof" of the enormous restraint that the military showed under stress. Official publications (including works intended for foreign readers, such as a PLA-sponsored pictorial history of the events that provides English-language captions for each picture) exploit errors made by the Western press, citing tales of rivers of blood flowing in Tiananmen Square as evidence that nothing the capitalist media said should be believed.[80] Propagandists and academics have also published collections of source materials, the "documents" in which range from photographs of crowd violence to reprints of the writings of noted "counterrevolutionaries."[81] No matter what form official narratives take, in sum, close attention is often paid to providing "proof" of one sort or another to back up the government's claims. Even the Beijing mayor's report on the protests (which Young discusses in his chapter) contains fairly precise references to specific foreign newspapers to back up its claim that the protests were manipulated from abroad.[82]

One clear sign of the bankruptcy of the regime's romance, however, is that this very concern with facticity has often undermined the official line. The government has had to ban at least two major official publications because they could too easily be "misinterpreted" as contradicting rather than reinforcing the orthodox version of events. One was a detailed chronology of protest activities in cities throughout China prepared for limited circulation to school officials. Eventually this was deemed too sensitive for even this select audience, apparently because the impression it gave of a truly national (and largely spontaneous) outburst made the government's insistence that a small group of malcontents was behind the "turmoil" harder to believe.[83] The other banned work was a massive two-volume collection of memoirs by close to two hundred soldiers who took part in the crackdown. This fascinating compilation—the chapters of which have titles such as "Knocking Down the 'Goddess' Statue" (vol. 1, pp. 259–262), "The Last Four Hours of Six [Soldier] Martyrs" (vol. 2, pp. 58–63), and "The People's Liberation Army: OK!" (vol. 2, pp. 429–431)—was quickly removed from open circulation, in part because of the frequent references contributors made to being spat at and cursed by ordinary citizens. This was seen as undermining official attempts to present the soldiers as delivering the masses from the threat posed by a few "bad elements" and "enemies of the people."[84]

The tragic myths of Tiananmen stand up better to scrutiny, on the whole, than do their romantic counterparts. Here too, however, earlier chapters point to key weaknesses. The comments that Esherick and I make about the limitations of factional explanations are a case in point. The best discussions of intra-Party struggle certainly help us understand a great deal about how the movement evolved.[85] Nonetheless, treatments of 1989 as contemporary versions of *King Lear* or *Julius Caesar* put too much emphasis upon the actions of high officials and draw our attention away from the primary arenas of action (such as the streets) and the broader forces that precipitated conflict (such as intractable economic difficulties that would have posed dilemmas for any leadership group).[86]

Previous chapters and other scholarly works also suggest that these first two tragic versions of the tale of Tiananmen are based upon a variety of overly simplistic or fallacious assumptions. Did age, bad advisers, and maybe a touch of Lear-like madness really transform a noble leader into a completely new person in 1989, or were there continuities between "Deng the Reformer" (whom foreign opinionmakers of the mid-1980s had valorized as a brave pragmatist intent upon using "Western-style capitalism" to save China) and his tyrannical successor, "Deng the Repressor"? Was the behavior of the latter (and his regime) really based on a determination to maintain power that had nothing to do with a continuing ideological commitment to some vision of socialism and revolution? Was Zhao Ziyang's behavior in 1989 as unambiguously heroic and self-sacrificing as Cordelia's in *King Lear*, or was Zhao too prone to the kinds of vices (greed, nepotism, corruption, an interest in maintaining his own power) usually attributed to his rivals, such as Li Peng? And were the protests the result of frustration triggered by the leadership's failure to introduce political reforms fast enough to keep pace with generally successful economic ones (Deng's great tragic mistake, in Kissinger's view), or rather were the very "successes" of the economic reforms a cause of considerable popular dissatisfaction (as Huang Yasheng argues in a convincing essay on the reforms and 1989)? These are the questions that the contributors to this volume and other scholars have been asking, and the answers they have given raise significant doubts about the explanatory power of the *King Lear* and *Julius Caesar* plotlines.[87] The authors of earlier chapters also tend to agree on one basic failing of these two versions of the tale of Tiananmen: The tragic figures most deserving of our sympathy are not Deng Xiaoping or Zhao Ziyang but the protesters.

What, then, of the tale of Tiananmen that I compare to *Romeo and Juliet*, a version of events that *does* treat the protesters as the central tragic figures in the plot? This narrative looks fairly good in light of the preceding chapters. The main problem with it is that, like the New May Fourth romance, it presents too hagiographic an image of the students. Not only were the protesters fickle in their devotion to leaders like Hu Yaobang and Zhao Ziyang, Perry and others remind us, they were also capable of elitist behavior that cut them off from social forces that might have helped them transform more than just isolated spots such as Tiananmen Square. Youthful naiveté and impetuosity may have contributed to the tragedy of 1989, but authoritarian and elitist follies more frequently associated with age than with youth also played a role.

Some participants in the movement were clearly aware of the dangers these more "mature" vices posed for the protests. For example, the author of an article that appeared in the May 25, 1989, issue of the dissident journal *Democracy Forum* warned that "the outmoded ideas and sentiments of the dying order [were] invading the cradle of our democratic order [i.e., Tiananmen Square] in a new form." If protesters did not take heed of the lingering influence of a "master-slave framework" imbued by centuries of "autocratic rule," the author continued, "the student movement [would] simply become another autocratic and bureaucratic stratum."[88] The "June 2 Hunger Strike Declaration," issued by three prominent intellectuals and artists (including Liu Xiaobo and the rock singer Hou Dejian), is a second important case in point. Its authors begin with a call for the "birth of a new political culture" based on an egalitarian sense of citizenship, in which everyone is "first and foremost a citizen and only second a student, a professor, a cadre, a soldier, and so forth." The declaration harshly criticizes the regime for bringing "shame to the Communist Party" by using martial law to suppress "democratic ways of expressing the popular will." The authors also point out, however, that those who supported the movement still "lacked a sense of themselves as citizens," and that it was time for the protesters to spend less energy on "sloganeering" and "begin turning our talk into democratic practice."[89]

One might have expected that I would save my harshest words for the fourth tragic narrative of Tiananmen, as Perry's Introduction explicitly distances our approach to political culture in this book from that of Pye. Although I agree with her arguments, however, it is worth stressing here that Pye's version of events in fact has a good deal in common with many of those presented in earlier chapters. Like Pye, most contributors to this volume have highlighted the continuities linking the imperial, Nationalist, and Communist periods of Chinese history. Like Pye, many of us have focused our attention on the way in which cultural factors—patterns of interaction, rituals, beliefs inculcated through education, ideas concerning how the world should work and how one finds one's place in it—shape acts of protest and repression. And, like Pye, many of us have emphasized the need to take the symbolism of the movement very seriously.

This said, the contributors to this volume generally break company with Pye on at least two crucially important issues. The first relates to historical change. The differences between pre- and post-1949 are often overstated, but the previous chapters show that the China of 1989 is in fundamental ways quite different from that in which the May Fourth Movement or even the Cultural Revolution took place. Continuities relating to such things as repertoires of collective action and definitions of the role of intellectuals have been stressed throughout the preceding pages. Authors of earlier chapters have also insisted, however, that even when seemingly familiar concepts (such as the village compact system), slogans (such as "Science and Democracy"), or tactics (such as the carrying of Mao posters) have been revived in recent years, these "old" symbols and forms have often been handled in new ways and invested with novel meanings. In short, when taken as a whole, the chapters in this volume contradict Pye's claim that no revolution worthy of the name has taken place in China. They suggest instead that we need to think in terms of not one but several Chinese "revolutions," each of which has tried to present itself as part of an ongoing quest, but each of which has also subtly changed the rules of Chinese politics. Each revolution has transformed the ideological concerns of both the powerful and the powerless and even the relationship between these two groups, leaving rulers and their opponents with new configurations of anciens régimes against which to define their quests.

A second and related way in which most or all of the contributors part company from Pye is that they tend to treat culture as a more fluid and less deterministic force. Although Watson and Perry are the only ones who take time to explicitly state what they mean by the term, most contributors have shared their assumption that culture needs to be treated as something that people create and recreate rather than as an externally imposed set of belief structures and patterns of behavior, that is, as something that creates as well as circumscribes choices. Contributors to this volume have certainly drawn attention to ways in which features of China's cultural inheritance (authoritarian and patriarchal traditions, an orientation toward ritual-based politics, a tendency of intellectuals to think in terms of loyal service to the state, and so forth) helped limit the achievements of the protesters of 1989. They have stopped far short, however, of treating political culture as a curse condemning each new generation to replicate the mistakes of the past, implying instead that though old patterns may be hard to break, they can and in practice continually are being broken.

Toward History: 1989 as a Promethean Myth

It is much easier to use the preceding chapters to highlight the shortcomings of straw men than it is to use them to construct if not a purely "historical" account of 1989, than at least a more satisfying myth of Tiananmen. One essential problem is simply that the contributors, who work in different disciplines and have different orientations, not surprisingly do not agree with each other on a variety of substantive and interpretive issues.

It is possible, however, to use this collection to begin to sketch out the general contours of a tale of Tiananmen that would have greater explanatory power than the eight versions discussed above. The central characters in this narrative would be the protesters themselves, but attention would also be paid to a variety of other actors, beginning with the high officials whose factional struggles affected the growth of the movement, the soldiers who were ordered to suppress the protests, and the journalists who covered the events. It would also have to make room for the contributions made by many who took no direct part in the events and yet fulfilled a crucial role: that of the audience for whom acts of street theater and acts of repression were performed, and to whom competing versions of the story of Tiananmen were told.

This myth would definitely be more tragic than romantic; references to the "tragedy of 1989" appear in many of the preceding chapters, as does an insistence that the students be treated as flawed heroes rather than paragons of virtue. Whether it would be more like a Shakespearean or Greek tragedy is harder to say. The failure of the movement would be attributed in part to factors beyond the control of the protesters. It would, however, stop short of treating June Fourth as a foreordained catastrophe, leaving considerable room for the role of free will. The intractability of forces of repression and traditions of authoritarianism would be seen as helping to seal the fate of the protesters, but so, too, would the behavior of student leaders and the decisions that activists made when creating their own politics and culture within the movement. As far as historical precedents are concerned, the events of 1989 would be seen as related to but also significantly different from earlier PRC struggles.

What kind of implications for China's future does this new mythology have? Given the visions of catastrophe the term *tragedy* conjures up, one might imagine that following this kind of narrative leads only to gloomy predictions. Some of the foregoing essays reinforce this assumption by stressing the enormity of the cultural and political obstacles that future generations of protesters will have to overcome in order to succeed where the demonstrators of 1989 failed. I would like to end this essay, however, by suggesting that adopting this sort of tragic plotline does not necessarily require one to abandon all hope.

The main potential source of optimism lies in the idea that political culture is a fluid rather than static force, and that just as cataclysmic events change individual psyches, they also leave their mark on political cultures. The protesters may not have succeeded in creating the kind of "new political culture" the authors of the "June 2 Hunger Strike Declaration" envisioned, but the demonstrations and the violence that followed certainly did not leave the old political culture unscathed. The China of today, in short, is different in important ways from that of 1989. Its population (at least in the cities) is now more cynical of all claims made in official language. Its young workers and students are more experienced in staging impressive acts of street theater. And its dissidents are much readier to accept the possibility that saving the nation may require overthrowing as opposed to merely reforming the CCP. Differences such as these create room for hope: To leave open the possibility that the events of 1989 may have fundamentally altered Chinese political arrangements, and perhaps even Chinese political culture itself, is to suggest that those who died on June 4 may not have sacrificed their lives in vain.

It may seem that my language has now moved from pure tragedy toward romance. It is worth remembering, however, that historical and mythological traditions are filled with examples of tragic heroes who through their own failure destroyed obstacles that would otherwise have thwarted those who followed. The classic tale of Prometheus is perhaps the best example of this: By giving fire to humans he doomed himself to a bitter fate, but this heroic act changed forever the rules by which mortals and immortals interacted. I would argue that the tragic heroism of people like Wang Dan, Chai Ling, and those who died in the massacres of early June may someday be viewed in a Promethean light. Like Prometheus, their sacrifices may prove to have transformed a power relationship that had hitherto seemed impervious to change: the relationship between China's twentieth-century rulers and those they rule. It is perhaps fitting, therefore, that one slogan of the protesters at Tiananmen Square was: "Seeds of fire cannot be extinguished."

Notes

1. Simon Leys, "The Curse of the Man Who Could See the Little Fish at the Bottom of the Ocean," *New York Review of Books*, July 20, 1989, p. 29.

2. Stephen J. Solarz, "Kissinger's Kowtow," *Washington Post*, August 6, 1989, p. B7; Thomas Oliphant, "A China Lesson Bush Misses," *Boston Globe*, August 13, 1989, p. A30; Miles Kahler, "The Myopic New China Lobby," *New York Times*, August 26, 1989, p. 15; Chalmers Johnson, foreword to George Hicks, ed., *The Broken Mirror: China After Tiananmen* (London: Longman, 1990), pp. vii–xiv.

3. For an insightful sample critique of foreign media coverage of 1989, see William P. Alford, "'Seek Truth from Facts'—Especially When They Are Unpleasant: America's Understanding of China's Efforts at Legal Reform," *UCLA Pacific Basin Law Journal*, 8, 2 (1990), pp. 177–196, esp. pp. 188–189.

4. Student attempts to adapt their communication to appeal to specific audiences are dealt with in detail in Jeffrey N. Wasserstrom, *Student Protests in Twentieth-Century China: The View from Shanghai* (Stanford: Stanford University Press, forthcoming), ch. 8 and epilogue. Perhaps the clearest example in 1989 relates to the role of nationalism. Whereas English-language student propaganda made few references to the "patriotic" side of the protests and instead highlighted almost exclusively their "democratic" aspects, in Chinese-language texts references to *aiguo* (love of country) were almost as frequent as those to *minzhu* (democracy); for examples, see the documents translated in *Chinese Sociology and Anthropology*, 23, 1 (1990), a special issue edited by James Tong and Elaine Chan entitled *Fire and Fury: The Democracy Movement in Beijing, April–June*, esp. pp. 51–52, 83, and 88.

5. Paul Cohen, "The Contested Past: The Boxers as History and Myth" [tentative title], *Journal of Asian Studies* (forthcoming 1992). A perceptive general discussion of the distinction (or lack thereof) between mythical and historical narratives, which takes a more extreme view than Cohen's is Hayden White, *The Content of the Form: Narrative Discourse and Historical Representation* (Baltimore: Johns Hopkins University Press, 1987).

6. Richard Nixon, "Rapproachement and Democracy," *New Perspectives Quarterly*, 6, 2 (1989), pp. 57–58; Henry Kissinger, "The Caricature of Deng as a Tyrant Is Unfair," *Washington Post*, August 1, 1989, p. A21.

7. William Pfaff, "The Myth of China," *Baltimore Sun*, June 8, 1989, p. A17; Johnson, foreword to Hicks, *Broken Mirror*, and William McGurn, "The U.S. and China: Sanctioning Tiananmen Square," in Hicks, *Broken Mirror*, pp. 233–245.

8. Miriam London, "The Romance of *Realpolitik*," in Hicks, *Broken Mirror*, pp. 246–256; see also Leys's own contribution to that volume, "After the Massacres," pp. 155–161.

9. Arif Dirlik and Roxann Prazniak, "Socialism Is Dead, So Why Must We Talk About It?" *Asian Studies Review*, 14, 1 (1990), pp. 3–25. This article is the opening piece to a symposium edited by Nick Knight, *Looking at China After Tiananmen*, which contains other pieces that present similar criticisms of those who champion Simon Leys and his views. See, for example, Michael Dutton, "The Massacre and Method," pp. 30–35. For still another insightful critique of the realpolitik school, see Marie Gottschalk, "The Failure of American Policy," *World Policy Journal*, 6, 4 (1989), pp. 667–684, which argues that the "realism" of Bush's China policy is based on a variety of "unrealistic assumptions."

10. Sarah Lubman, "The Myth of Tiananmen," *Washington Post*, July 30, 1989.

11. Hicks, *Broken Mirror*, p. xviii; Jane Macartney, "The Students: Heroes, Pawns, or Power-Brokers?" in ibid., pp. 3–23.

12. Robin Munro, "Who Died in Beijing, and Why," *Nation*, June 11, 1990, pp. 811–822.

13. Not all of Munro's conclusions have gone unchallenged by Westerners who were in Beijing at the time; see, for example, the comments concerning the events in Tiananmen Square in Michael Duke, *The Iron House* (Salt Lake City: Peregrine Smith Books, 1990).

14. Harold Isaacs, *Scratches on Our Minds* (New York: John Day, 1958); Pearl Buck, *The Good Earth* (New York: Triangle Books, 1931).

15. Bill Brugger, "Do We Need to Reassess the Chinese Regime After the Events of Mid 1989?" in Knight, *Looking at China*, pp. 36–40.

16. None of the contributors to *Looking at China* mentions *Scratches on Our Minds*, but many of its contributors present arguments that complement those Isaacs makes. See also the opening sentences of the important essay by Henry Rosemont, Jr., "China: The Mourning After," *Z Magazine* (March 1990), pp. 85–96.

17. Edward Said, *Orientalism* (New York: Vintage Books, 1979).

18. Edward Graham, "The 'Imaginative Geography' of China," in Warren Cohen, ed., *Reflections on Orientalism* (East Lansing: Michigan State Center for Asian Studies, 1983), pp. 31–44. For other relevant responses to Said's work, see the other contributions to Cohen's *Reflections*; the symposium in *Journal of Asian Studies*, 39, 3 (1980), pp. 481–517; Paul Cohen, *Discovering History in China* (New York: Columbia University Press, 1984), p. 150; and Jonathan Spence, "Western Perceptions of China from the Late Sixteenth Century to the Present," in Paul S. Ropp, ed., *Heritage of China* (Berkeley: University of California Press, 1990), pp. 1–14, which also refers to the enduring relevance of *Scratches on Our Minds*.

19. "Violence in the Other Country: China as Crisis, Spectacle, and Woman," in Chandra Mohanty et al., eds., *Third World Women and the Politics of Feminism* (Bloomington: Indiana University Press, 1991). See also Nick Knight, "Guest Editor's Introduction," in Knight, *Looking at China*, pp. 1–2; and Dutton, "Massacre and Method," p. 32.

20. Dirlik and Prazniak, "Socialism Is Dead," pp. 6–9, 14, and passim.

21. Northrop Frye, *Anatomy of Criticism* (Princeton: Princeton University Press, 1957), pp. 158–238.

22. Scott Simmie and Bob Nixon, *Tiananmen Square* (Seattle: University of Washington Press, 1989).

23. Lynn Hunt, *Politics, Culture, and Class in the French Revolution* (Berkeley: University of California Press, 1984), pp. 34–39; Hayden White, *Metahistory* (Baltimore:

Johns Hopkins University Press, 1973), esp. pp. 1–42. See also, Lynn Hunt, "Introduction: History, Culture, and Text," in Hunt, ed., *The New Cultural History* (Berkeley: University of California Press, 1989), pp. 1–24.

24. Frye, *Anatomy*, pp. 186–206, esp. pp. 187–188.

25. Two of many illustrative works are: Hu Sheng, *Cong yapianzhanzheng dao wusiyundong* (From the Opium War until the May Fourth Movement) (Beijing: Renmin, 1982); and Shandong Province High School Party History Lecture Group, Zhonggong gongchandang lishi jiangyi (Lectures on the history of the Chinese Communist Party) (Jinan: Shandong renmin, 1980). For an example of seasonal imagery of the sort Frye has in mind, see Wang Min et al., eds., *Chuntian de yaolan* (The cradle of spring) (Beijing: Gongqingtuan, 1984), which contains memoirs by student protesters who worked to turn the "winter" of KMT rule into the "spring" of the CCP's "liberation" of the nation.

26. Frye, *Anatomy*, pp. 206–223.

27. Hunt, *Politics, Culture, and Class*, p. 37. A good discussion of the tendency to present the Chinese Revolution in tragic terms can be found in John Fitzgerald, "The Misconceived Revolution," *Journal of Asian Studies*, 49, 2 (1990), pp. 323–343.

28. Cohen, "The Contested Past."

29. Perry Link, "Identity: Language and Ideology," a piece that will appear as a chapter in his *Evening Chats in Beijing: The Agonies of Contemporary Chinese Intellectuals* (tentative title) (New York: Norton, forthcoming). I am grateful to Dr. Link for sharing this important work in progress with me.

30. James Clifford, "Introductions: Partial Truths," in James Clifford and George Marcus, eds., *Writing Culture: The Poetics and Politics of Ethnography* (Berkeley: University of California Press, 1986), p. 6, quoted in Aletta Biersack, "Local Knowledge, Local History: Geertz and Beyond," in Hunt, *New Cultural History*, pp. 72–96; Hayden White, "The Question of Narrative in Contemporary Historical Theory," *History and Theory*, 23, 1 (1984), pp. 1–33; Lynn Hunt, "Introduction," p. 21.

31. Said, *Orientalism*, pp. 3 and 22. A useful introduction to Foucault's thought is Hubert L. Dreyfus and Paul Rabinow, *Michel Foucault: Beyond Structuralism and Hermeneutics* (Chicago: University of Chicago Press, 1982).

32. See Gabrielle Spiegel, "History, Historicism, and the Social Logic of the Text in the Middle Ages," *Speculum*, 64 (1989); and Biersack, "Local Knowledge, Local History."

33. William Bell, *Forbidden City: A Novel of Modern China* (New York: Bantam, 1990).

34. Steiner, *The Death of Tragedy* (New York: Knopf, 1961), p. 8.

35. Chen Ping, "Shinian gaige weihe daozhi zhengzhi beiju?" (Why have ten years of reform led to political tragedy?), *Zhongguo lun?* 30, 5 (1990), pp. 9–13; Ding Chu, *Minzhu yundong de Sunzi bingfa* (Sunzi's military strategy in the democracy movement) (San Francisco: Minzhu Zhongguo shulin chubanshe, 1989), p. 1; Wu Mouren et al., *Bajiu Zhongguo minyun jishi* (Annals of the 1989 Chinese democracy movement) (New York: privately published, 1989), pp. 656, 782, 789, and passim; *Beiping dadusha* (The great slaughter in Beijing) (Taipei, 1979), preface. See also the Hong Kong newspapers *Dagongbao* and *Wenhuibao*, June 4, 1989.

36. For an extended discussion of the idea that China has no tragic tradition, the implications of this claim, and citations to works that argue that one or another particular Chinese drama should indeed be called a "tragedy," see Yun-tong Luk, "The Concept of Tragedy as Genre and Its Applicability to Classical Chinese Drama," in Ying-hsiung Chou, ed., *The Chinese Text: Studies in Comparative Literature* (Hong Kong: Chinese University Press, 1986), pp. 14–27. Two important recent discussions of the lesser importance of tragedy in Chinese as opposed to Western mythic and literary traditions,

which avoid the Orientalist assumption that this difference makes China in any sense inferior to the West, are David N. Keightley, "Early Civilization in China: Reflections on How It Became Chinese," and Paul Ropp, "The Distinctive Art of Chinese Fiction," in Ropp, *Heritage of China*, pp. 13–54 and 309–334, esp. pp. 20–21 and 311–315.

37. Frye, *Anatomy*, pp. 187–188.

38. Frye, *Anatomy*, p. 187.

39. Han Minzhu, ed., *Cries for Democracy* (Princeton: Princeton University Press, 1990), pp. 5–8, 39, 43–45.

40. The first calls for a "New May Fourth Movement" came about a month before the anniversary itself. See "Xinwusi xuanyan" (New May Fourth proclamation), as reprinted in Shiyue Pinglun (October review), ed., *Zhongguo minyun yuanziliao qingxuan* (A critical selection of original materials from the Chinese democracy movement) (hereafter ZMYQ) (Hong Kong: Shiyue Pinglun, 1989), vol. 2, p. 185. For sample later evocations of May Fourth, see ZMYQ, vol. 1, p. 82, and vol. 2, p. 191; Tong and Chan, *Fire and Fury*, pp. 15–17, 76–77, and 82–83; and Han, *Cries*, pp. 134–140.

41. For a detailed comparison of 1976 and 1989 by protesters, see the wall poster in ZMYQ, vol. 1, p. 65, an English-language translation of which appears in Mok Chiu Yu and J. Frank Harrison, eds., *Voices from Tiananmen Square* (New York: Black Rose Books, 1989), pp. 54–55. See also the documents in Han, *Cries*, pp. 121–124 and 321.

42. See Yu and Harrison, *Voices*, pp. 95–97; and Han, *Cries*, pp. 199–201, 310, and 335–337.

43. ZMYQ, vol. 2, p. 27; trans. in Tong and Chan, *Fire and Fury*, pp. 49–51.

44. For Wuer's speech, see Han, *Cries*, pp. 376–377.

45. White, *Metahistory*, p. 9.

46. Wuer in Han, *Cries*, pp. 376–377.

47. Yu and Harrison, *Voices*, p. 191, and see also pp. 176–200; Han, *Cries*, p. 359, and the picture of a wall poster presenting Li Peng as a man-eating monster in Wasserstrom, *Student Protests*, photographic section.

48. For the events themselves, and the "fetishization of blood" that followed, see Vera Schwarcz, *The Chinese Enlightenment* (Berkeley: University of California Press, 1986), pp. 158–163; and Wasserstrom, *Student Protests*, ch. 4.

49. Han, *Cries*, pp. 44–45; Human Rights in China, ed., *Children of the Dragon* (New York: Macmillan, 1990), p. 181; Wu, *Bajiu Zhongguo minyun jishi*, p. 788.

50. Francis Fukuyama, "The End of History," *National Interest* (Summer 1989), pp. 3–18.

51. Stanley Hoffman, "A New World and Its Troubles," *Foreign Affairs* (Fall 1990), pp. 115–122; see also Dirlik and Prazniak, "Socialism Is Dead."

52. Two English-language examples of works by these kinds of Chinese authors are Maria Hsia Chang, "The Meaning of the Tiananmen Incident," and Lin Yu-siang, "China's Reunification and Tiananmen," both of which appear in *Global Affairs* (Fall 1989). For examples of more simplistic versions of the "New Cultural Revolution myth," see *Revolutionary Worker*, May 22 and June 19, 1989.

53. Mark Hager, "Roots of Dissent," *UCLA Pacific Basin Law Journal*, 8, 2 (1990), pp. 197–266; quotes are from pp. 204, 209, and 214.

54. The best example of official color symbolism appears in a work on 1989 entitled *Hong yu Hei de Jishi* (A true account of the red and the black) (Shanghai: Renyaojian, 1989).

55. Two key documents that spell out the hard-line romance appear in Wu, *Bajiu Zhongguo minyun jishi*, pp. 52–53 and 301–305; for translations of these and related works, see the appendixes to Yi Mu and Mark V. Thompson, *Crisis at Tiananmen*, (San Francisco: China Books, 1989), pp. 155–236. At least one entire work devoted to

278 Jeffrey N. Wasserstrom

"proving" Liu's villainy has been issued: Zheng Wangli, ed., *Liu Xiaobo Qiren Qishi* (Liu Xiaobo and his troublemaking) (Beijing: Beijing qingnian chubanshe, 1989).

56. A valuable general introduction to official publications on 1989 (as well as other kinds of materials), can be found in James Tong's introduction in *Chinese Law and Government*, 23, 1 (1990), pp. 3–9. This special issue of the journal is devoted to Tiananmen and contains translations of important speeches by several top government officials defending the hard-line story.

57. I am grateful to Paul Cohen for reminding me (in a personal communication) of the pre–warlord-era roots of concern with and fear of *luan*.

58. For examples, see the newspaper reports reprinted in *Xuechao, dongluan, baoluan* (Student storms, turmoil, disturbances) (Sichuan: Sichuan renmin chubanshe, 1989); see also the PLA pictorial work and memoir collection discussed later in this essay.

59. Orville Schell, introduction to David C. Turnley and Peter Turnley, *Beijing Spring* (New York: Stewart, Tabori, and Chang, 1989), p. 19.

60. Frye, *Anatomy*, pp. 206–223.

61. My interpretation of *King Lear* has been influenced by Harriet Honigmann, "Dramatic Judgement in *King Lear*," in Robert B. Heilman, ed., *Shakespeare: The Tragedies—New Perspectives* (Englewood Cliffs, N.J.: Prentice-Hall, 1984), pp. 163–174; Kenneth Muir, *Shakespeare's Tragic Sequence* (London: Hutchinson, 1972), pp. 117–141; and James C. Bulman, *The Heroic Idiom of Shakespearean Tragedy* (Newark: University of Delaware Press, 1985). My general understanding of this and other Shakespearean tragedies has also been shaped by Northrop Frye, *Fools of Time: Studies in Shakespearean Tragedy* (Toronto: University of Toronto Press, 1967).

62. Donald Morrison, ed., *Massacre in Beijing* (New York: Warner, 1989), pp. 235–250, esp. pp. 235 and 236.

63. Michael Fathers and Andrew Higgins, *Tiananmen: The Rape of Peking* (New York: Independent, 1989), quotes from pp. 1 and 9.

64. My reading of *Julius Caesar* has been most heavily influenced by Nicholas Brooke, "On *Julius Caesar*," in Heilman, *Shakespeare*, pp. 50–63; quotes taken from pp. 61 and 62. See also Bulman, *Heroic Idiom*, pp. 51–55; Muir, *Shakespeare's Tragic Sequence*, pp. 42–54; and H. B. Charlton, *Shakespearean Tragedy* (Cambridge: Cambridge University Press, 1949), pp. 74–78.

65. James L. Calderwood, "*Romeo and Juliet*: A Formal Dwelling," in Heilman, *Shakespeare*, pp. 37–49. See also Charlton, *Shakespearean Tragedy*, pp. 53–56, which addresses the question why Shakespeare gives "fate" a more decisive role in this play than in most of his other tragedies; and Muir, *Shakespeare's Tragic Sequence*, pp. 34–41.

66. This is the sense one gets from many journalistic treatments of the events; one of the best remains Simmie and Nixon, *Tiananmen Square*.

67. See Hu's statement in Human Rights in China, *Children*, pp. 210–211; see also Frank Viviano, "Dissidents Criticize Pre-Tiananmen Protests," *San Francisco Chronicle*, August 21, 1989.

68. W. H. Auden, "The Christian Tragic Hero: Contrasting Captain Ahab's Doom and Its Classic Greek Prototype," in Lionel Abel, ed., *Moderns on Tragedy* (Greenwich, Conn.: Fawcett, 1967), pp. 40–44.

69. Karl J. Reinhardt, "Oedipus Tyrannus," in Abel, *Moderns on Tragedy*, p. 188. See also Albin Lesky, *Greek Tragedy* (New York: Barnes and Noble, 1965), pp. 63–64 and passim; and Charlton, *Shakespearean Tragedy*, p. 10.

70. Lucian Pye, "Tiananmen and Chinese Political Culture," *Asian Survey*, 30, 4 (1990), pp. 331–347, quote from p. 347.

71. Pye, "Tiananmen," p. 345; for his general interpretation of Chinese political culture, see *The Spirit of Chinese Politics* (Cambridge: Cambridge University Press, 1968).

72. Frye, *Anatomy*, p. 223.

73. Pye, "Tiananmen," p. 331.

74. Andrew Nathan, Lowell Dittmer, and Andrew Walder, "Tiananmen 1989: A Symposium," *Problems of Communism* (September-October 1989); Tony Saich, *Perspectives on the Chinese People's Movement: Spring 1989* (Armonk, N.Y.: M. E. Sharpe, 1990). Two chapters in the latter volume do, however, follow what I have called the "New May Fourth Movement" plotline quite closely: Lawrence Sullivan's "The Emergence of Civil Society in China, Spring 1989" (pp. 126–144) and my own essay on "Student Protests and the Chinese Tradition, 1919–1989" (pp. 3–24). The comparatively romantic vision of 1989 I present in that piece, as opposed to the more tragic spin I put on events in the present volume, illustrates a general point: A wide variety of factors (the intended audience, the amount of information available when writing, and so forth) have led individual authors to follow differing plotlines in differing texts dealing with Tiananmen. Because I am aware of this, my goal in this essay is not to associate specific writers with particular generic plots (as White's is in *Metahistory*), but rather to highlight the romantic and tragic elements in designated texts.

75. Jonathan Spence, *The Search for Modern China* (New York: Norton, 1990), and introduction to Han, *Cries*, pp. xi–xvi; Shen Tong and Marriane Ye, *Almost a Revolution* (Boston: Houghton Mifflin, 1990).

76. Fincher, "Zhao's Fall, China's Loss," *Foreign Policy*, 76 (Fall 1989), pp. 3–25.

77. Alford, "'Seek Truth from Facts,'" p. 188 and accompanying note; Geremie Barmé, "Traveling Heavy: The Intellectual Baggage of the Chinese Diaspora," *Problems of Communism* (January-April 1991), pp. 94–112, esp. pp. 104–105. Although the racist behavior Alford cites clearly contradicts the implications of the new May Fourth myth, neither this racism nor the elitism of the 1989 protesters necessarily distances them from their flesh-and-blood counterparts of 1919. As I argue in *Student Protests*, ch. 2 and epilogue, a variety of features of the May Fourth Movement that do not fit in with idealized visions of that event (such as outbursts of anti-Japanese violence and the creation of highly bureaucratic and hierarchical protest organizations) have too often been ignored or downplayed by historians in China and the West.

78. Dirlik and Prazniak, "Socialism Is Dead."

79. Sample refutations of the "big lie" by eyewitness accounts can be found in Fathers and Higgins, *Tiananmen: The Rape of Peking*, pp. 134–145; Simmie and Nixon, *Tiananmen Square*, pp. 197–206; Lee Feigon, *China Rising: The Meaning of Tiananmen* (Chicago: Ivan R. Dee, 1990), pp. 244–258; and Munro, "Who Died in Beijing, and Why." For an important (though brief) scholarly critique of the "big lie," see Helmut Martin, *Origins and Consequences of China's Democracy Movement 1989* (Cologne: Bundesinstitut für Ostwissenschaftliche und Internationale Studien, 1990), pp. 29–31.

80. People's Liberation Army, *Quelling Counter-revolutionary Rebellion in Beijing* (Beijing: PLA, 1989), a copy of which can be found in the New York Public Library's Tiananmen Collection. A work in Chinese that is clearly intended for foreign as well as domestic readers is *Beijing Fengbo 50 Wen* (Fifty questions about the Beijing unrest) (Beijing: Huayi Chubanshe, 1989), a catechism of the official line that uses the old-style (or complex) characters usually eschewed in the PRC but favored in Taiwan and Hong Kong.

81. Along with previously cited works, see Guangming ribao, eds., *Pingbao yingyong pu* (A guide to the heroic quelling of the violent disturbances) (Beijing: Guangming ribao chubanshe, 1989).

82. Translated in Yi and Thompson, *Crisis at Tiananmen*, pp. 194–233. This report is a good deal more carefully documented than were many explicitly scholarly works published in the People's Republic prior to the early 1980s, though the use of evidence is cavalier to say the least.

83. *Jingxin dongpade 56 tian* (A soul-stirring 56 days) (Beijing: Dadi chubanshe, 1989).

84. PLA Zongzheng wenhuabu zhengwen bangongshi (Central Political and Cultural Bureau, Essay Solicitation Department), eds., *Jieyan yiri* (One day of martial law) (Beijing: Jiefangjun wenyi chubanshe, 1989). I am grateful to Eugene Wu for alerting me to the existence (and fate) of this work.

85. See, for example, Tony Saich, "When Worlds Collide: The Beijing People's Movement of 1989," in Saich, *Chinese People's Movement*, pp. 25–49.

86. On this second point, see Kathleen Hartford, "The Political Economy Behind Beijing Spring," in Saich, *Chinese People's Movement*, pp. 50–82.

87. One or more of these issues is dealt with in other contributions to this volume and in works such as the following: Huang Yasheng, "The Origins of China's Prodemocracy Movement: A Tale of Two Reforms," *Fletcher Forum of World Affairs* (Winter 1990), pp. 30–39; London, "Romance," and other contributions to Hicks, *Broken Mirror*; and Dirlik and Prazniak, "Socialism Is Dead."

88. "Reflections Under the Monument to the People's Heroes," trans. in Tong and Chan, *Fire and Fury*, pp. 88–90.

89. Wu, *Bajiu*, vol. 1, pp. 550–553; for a partial translation, see Human Rights in China, *Children*, pp. 122–123. See also Barmé, "Traveling Heavy," for discussion of other dissenting views within the movement, as well as background information on Hou Dejian and Liu Xiaobo.

ABOUT THE BOOK

The 1989 protests in Beijing and other Chinese cities shook the very foundations of Communist Party rule and sent shock waves around the world. The occupation of Tiananmen Square, the confrontation between a lone protester and a row of government tanks, the erection of a goddess of democracy statue, and the June Fourth Massacre in which soldiers of the People's Liberation Army turned their weapons upon unarmed citizens—images such as these appeared instantaneously on television newscasts in countries around the globe, alternately inspiring and horrifying audiences and changing forever their perceptions of China. Defying the predictions of specialists, these events also had a profound impact upon those who study China, forcing the academic world to question many of its most basic premises about contemporary Chinese society and politics. Bringing together works by an interdisciplinary group of leading scholars, this volume is the most comprehensive effort to date to take stock of the changes fueled by the 1989 movement.

Popular Protest and Political Culture in Modern China does not seek to present a unified interpretation of 1989, yet taken as a whole the book provides a compelling case for the need to find new ways of understanding the important role culture plays in shaping political action—with culture broadly defined as a dynamic force that is both rooted in history and constantly changing. Whether critically assessing the way protesters from the intelligentsia treated members of other social groups or analyzing protest actions as exercises in political theater, the contributors share a common concern with the interplay between politics and culture. Until we have a more nuanced understanding of this relationship, they suggest, we will not be able to see why the outcome in Beijing in 1989 differed so radically from that in Budapest, Bucharest, or Berlin.

This volume, an important first step toward such an understanding, will provide thought-provoking reading for anyone who was caught up in the drama and tragedy of Tiananmen Square.

281

ABOUT THE EDITORS & CONTRIBUTORS

Jeffrey N. Wasserstrom, who received his M.A. from Harvard University and his Ph.D. from the University of California at Berkeley, teaches in the history department of Indiana University at Bloomington. A specialist in the social and cultural history of the Chinese Revolution, he is the author of *Student Protests in Twentieth-Century China: The View from Shanghai* (1991). He has also written a variety of articles and chapters on subjects ranging from the historiography of the Boxer Uprising, to China's one-child-per-family policy, to student protest.

Elizabeth J. Perry, professor of political science at the University of California at Berkeley, has focused most of her research on protest movements in modern and contemporary China. She is the author of *Rebels and Revolutionaries in North China, 1845–1945* (1980) and *Shanghai on Strike: The Politics of Chinese Labor* (1992).

Ann Anagnost is assistant professor of anthropology at the University of Washington. Her publications have appeared in *Modern China, Stanford Humanities Review,* and conference volumes such as *Marxism and the Chinese Experience* and have covered a wide range of topics relating to culture, power, and gender in contemporary China. An eyewitness to Janjing protests in spring 1989, she returned to China in 1991 to continue her research on issues related to ideology and rural life.

Timothy Cheek is assistant professor of history at The Colorado College. He is editor of *CCP Research Newsletter.* His research and publications focus on the role of intellectuals in the Chinese Communist Party and on propaganda systems.

Daniel Chirot is professor of international studies and sociology at the University of Washington. He has written several books, including *Social Change in the Modern Age,* and edited *The Crisis of Leninism and the Decline of the Left* and *The Causes of Backwardness in Eastern Europe.* Currently a Guggenheim Fellow, his latest project is a book about modern tyranny.

Joseph W. Esherick is professor of history and Hsiu Professor of Chinese Studies at the University of California at San Diego. Author of *Reform and Revolution: The 1911 Revolution in Hunan and Hubei* and *The Origins of the Boxer Uprising,* he is now writing on the Communist movement of the Shaan-Gan-Ning Border Region in the 1930s and 1940s.

Lee Feigon is chairman of the Department of East Asian Languages and Culture and professor of Chinese history at Colby College. His most recent book is *China Rising;*

he has also written *Chen Duxiu: Founder of the Chinese Communist Party*. His articles have appeared in the *Atlantic*, the *Wall Street Journal*, the *Nation*, *Barron's*, the *Boston Globe*, and the *Chicago Tribune*, as well as in the *Journal of Asian Studies* and the *American Historical Review*. He is presently at work on a book about the way in which Chinese Communist policies in Tibet helped foster the Tibetan resistance movement. Feigon lives in China, Maine.

John Israel is professor of history at the University of Virginia. Author of *Student Nationalism in China, 1927–1937* and many other works, he has just completed the study *Liangda: A Chinese University in War and Revolution*. His current research focuses on the assassination of Wen Yiduo and the December First Movement of 1945. He wishes to thank the Committee on Scholarly Communication with the People's Republic of China for unwittingly placing him in the midst of the student demonstration of September 18, 1985.

Stephen R. MacKinnon is professor of history and director of the Center for Asian Studies at Arizona State University. Recent books include *China Reporting: An Oral History of American Journalism in the 1930s and 1940s* (1987) and *Agnes Smedley: The Life and Times of an American Radical* (1988). He is writing a study of the Chinese press as it interacted with the Western press during the 1930s, with special attention to the free press of Hankou, 1938.

Vera Schwarcz, author of *Long Road Home, The Chinese Enlightenment*, and *Zhang Shenfu—Rebellious Revolutionary* (forthcoming), is at work on a comparative study of the Chinese and Jewish commitment to historical memory. She is also the author of numerous articles on the life of intellectuals in contemporary China. She holds the Freeman Chair in East Asian Studies at Wesleyan University.

James L. Watson is Fairbank Professor of Chinese Society and professor of anthropology at Harvard University. He is a specialist in Southern Chinese ethnography who is currently doing research in the provinces of Guangdong and Jiangsu. He is author of *Emigration and the Chinese Lineage* and coeditor of a number of volumes, including *Death Ritual in Late Imperial and Modern China* (with Evelyn Rawski).

Ernest P. Young is professor of history at the University of Michigan–Ann Arbor. He is currently doing research on late Qing foreign relations and Catholic missions in China. He is the author of *The Presidency of Yuan Shir-k'ai: Liberalism and Dictatorship in Early Republican China* (1977).

INDEX